The Latter Prophets

T. HENSHAW
M.A.

Ruskin House

GEORGE ALLEN & UNWIN LTD
MUSEUM STREET LONDON

*Printed in Great Britain
in* 11–12 *point Ehrhardt Type
by Simson Shand Ltd
London, Hertford and Harlow*

The purpose of the book is to present to the reader the writings of the Latter Prophets, viewed in the light of modern scholarship. A vast amount of work has been done by scholars in this field, and we owe a great debt of gratitude for the new knowledge which they have gained for us by their labours. There is, however, so much that is highly controversial that on many questions it is impossible to speak with absolute certainty. Some conclusions are often purely tentative and are based on a delicate balance of probabilities, while others are little more than conjecture. On disputed points I have in a few cases ventured to express an independent judgement, but in the majority of cases I have been content to state the main theories, leaving the reader to form his own opinion.

In the Bible the prophetic writings are not arranged in their chronological order. In the present book they have been rearranged approximately in the order of their original appearance, in order that the reader may gain a clear conception of the development of prophecy, and of the way in which the prophets directed their messages towards the special conditions and circumstances of their times.

The method of approach to the subject, which I have adopted, is as follows. In Chapter I the term 'Latter Prophet' is defined, and an account is given of the various stages in the growth of the prophetic literature from the time when the prophets first delivered their oracles orally to the time when their utterances were finally fixed in writing. This is followed by a chapter depicting the historical background against which the prophets lived out their lives. Next comes a chapter on the archaeology of the period of the Latter Prophets, which serves to shed light on the historical, cultural and religious background of that period. Then follows a chapter designed to show that the appearance of the Latter Prophets was not an isolated occurrence in the history of Israel, that prophets were not even peculiar to the nation but had a long ancestry going back into the dim and distant past, and that the Latter Prophets attained a truly revolutionary conception of the Deity. Since the works of the Latter Prophets are literature as well as history and the Word of God, and since portions of them are written in poetry, a chapter has been added on the forms and characteristics of Hebrew poetry. These introductory chapters are followed by others on the Latter Prophets themselves, each dealing, whenever possible, with the life and character of an individual prophet, the date of his ministry, the contents, unity and style of his book, and its permanent contribution to the religious heritage of both Jews and Gentiles. In the appendices will be found useful information on The Priesthood, Sacrifice, The Messianic Hope, The Calendar, Feasts and Fasts, and Weights, Measures and Money, together with a series of Chronological Tables. The text has not been burdened with a multitude of footnotes and references, which tends to distract the attention of the interested reader and to damp his ardour.

My indebtedness to a large circle of Old Testament scholars is apparent throughout the book. If I mention the names of W. F. Albright, W. O. E. Oesterley, T. H. Robinson, H. W. Robinson, H. H. Rowley and J. Skinner, I shall be far from enumerating all those from whom I have learnt. I wish to express my deep indebtedness to Professor N. H. Snaith, M.A., D.D., Principal of Wesley College, Headingley, Leeds, for his kindness in reading the typescript, calling my attention to many slips, especially in the chapter on 'The Historical Background', and making numerous valuable suggestions which have been embodied in the text. Finally my grateful thanks are due to my wife for typing the manuscript and for helping in the correction of the proofs.

T. HENSHAW

CONTENTS

CHAPTER I

The Prophetic Literature

PROPHETIC BOOKS IN HEBREW CANON

In the Hebrew Canon the 'Prophets' are divided into the 'Former Prophets' and the 'Latter Prophets'. The 'Former Prophets' consist of the four historical books, namely Joshua, Judges, Samuel and Kings, which may have been included among the 'Prophets' because they were supposed to have been written by a succession of prophets or because some of their utterances were recorded in them. It is, however, not the 'Former Prophets' but the 'Latter Prophets' that are our immediate concern.

The Latter Prophets

The 'Latter Prophets' comprise four volumes, namely, Isaiah, Jeremiah, Ezekiel and The Twelve. The Twelve includes Hosea, Joel, Amos, Obadiah, Jonah, Micah, Nahum, Habakkuk, Zephaniah, Haggai, Zechariah and Malachi. The first three books in the collection are often called 'The Major Prophets' and the last twelve 'The Minor Prophets'. The term 'Minor' is used of the twelve books not because they are in any sense inferior to the others, but because they are smaller than the three which precede them. The book of Amos, for example, marks an epoch not only in the spiritual history of Israel, but also in that of mankind. The books comprising the 'Latter Prophets' range over several centuries and are not in chronological order.

The 'Latter Prophets' are sometimes referred to as the 'Writing Prophets' but the term is entirely inappropriate for two reasons. First, the term implies that none of the earlier prophets ever wrote down or dictated any account of his words and deeds; but there is some evidence for thinking that written records of some of the earlier prophets once existed but have failed to survive. It is probable that the compiler of the books of Kings derived some of his material from lives of Elijah and Elisha, which would doubtless contain some of the oracles of the prophets, together with a certain amount of legendary material. In 2 Chronicles ix. 29, reference is made to the history of Nathan the prophet, the prophecy of Ahijah the Shilonite, and to the visions of Iddo the seer. Second, the term suggests that each of the prophets wrote the whole of the book which contains his oracles; but a critical analysis of the books shows that we are dealing not with literary units, but with compilations. It is quite evident that they are not regular and orderly compositions, each with a main theme, a logical development of thought and a uniform style, which we should expect if it came from the hands of a single author. Instead, we often come across sections containing a series of unrelated subjects loosely joined together, sudden changes of metre and wide differences of style. Above all, the material embodied in these books is of various dates, ranging from about the middle of the eighth century BC to late in the post-exilic age.

Growth of the Books

It would appear that the prophetic books passed through three stages of development before they reached their final form.[1] In the first stage the prophet delivered his oracles which consisted for the most part of short poems. Occasionally the oracles were longer, as for example, the Song of the Vineyard and the Taunt Song in Isaiah v. 1–7 and xiv. 4b–21 respectively. Some of the prophets probably wrote down a portion of their oracles or dictated them to a scribe. We know that Jeremiah dictated his oracles to Baruch and commanded him to read them publicly in the Temple on a fast day (Jer. xxxvi. 4–7). The latter obeyed the command but later the roll was burnt by the king (Jer. xxxvi. 23). 'Then took Jeremiah another roll, and gave it to Baruch the scribe, the son of Neriah, who wrote therein from the mouth of Jeremiah all the words of the book which Jehoiakim king of Judah had burned in the fire: and there were added besides unto them many like words' (Jer. xxxvi. 32). We surmise, however, that it was customary for the oracles of a prophet to be retained in the memory of his immediate disciples, and handed on by word of mouth until they were finally committed to writing by some person interested in prophecy. It is likely that they were first written down on ostraca, that is, pieces of pottery, like the Lachish letters.

[1] T. H. Robinson, *Prophecy and the Prophets in Ancient Israel*, 1923, Revised ed., 1950, pp. 50–59.

In the second stage the detached oracles of the prophet were gathered together to form collections, which would be written not on ostraca but on leather or papyrus. A good example of such a collection is found in the book of Isaiah i. 2–31 which consists of an appeal to heaven and earth against the ingratitude of the people (vv. 2, 3), a lament (vv. 4–9), a denunciation (vv. 10–17), an appeal and a warning (vv. 18–20), an elegy (vv. 21–26), a prediction of the redemption of Jerusalem and the destruction of the wicked (vv. 27, 28), and a fragment on tree worship (vv. 29–31).[1] We notice that the oracles in the collection deal with a variety of subjects and that no attempt has been made to arrange them in logical order. Moreover, on examination we find that the oracles are not all in the same metre. An oracle in a collection is often introduced with the words, 'Thus saith the Lord', or words of similar meaning (Am. ii. 4; Is. viii. 5; Jer. ii. 1). Such words are intended to authenticate the oracle which follows, as proceeding not from the prophet himself or from any false prophet but from Yahweh. Sometimes the words, 'saith the Lord', or words of similar meaning, are added to the end of an oracle as a kind of signature (Am. ii. 16; Is. xlv. 13; Ezek. xiv. 11).

The principles which governed the selection of the oracles in these collections are not clear. In some cases the oracles seem to have been brought together in a haphazard manner, and in other cases the grounds of connection seem to be quite inadequate. Sometimes we find a series of oracles against foreign nations (e.g. Am. i. 1–15; Is. xiii–xxiii; Jer. xlvi–li). Obadiah appears to be solely a collection of utterances against Edom. In some cases the oracles have been arranged on the catchword principle; the occurrence of a particular word in one oracle has recalled another containing the same word, which immediately follows (Is. i. 9, 10). In other cases oracles of perhaps widely different dates have apparently been brought together because each begins with the same initial word (Is. v. 8, 11, 18, 20, 21, 22). It is often difficult to tell when one oracle ends and another begins. The compilers have not worried overmuch about arranging the oracles in chronological order, with the result that we are often not certain to what part of the prophet's ministry an oracle belongs.

From time to time the owner of a collection of oracles would add other material, which did not really come from the prophet but which he thought was worthy of him. This accounts for the fact that we sometimes find the same oracle assigned to two different prophets,

---

[1] Verses 27, 28 and 29–31 are probably later insertions.

though it may not have belonged to either. In such cases there are usually slight differences between the two and one may be shorter than the other (Is. ii. 2–4=Mic. iv. 1–4; Obad. 1–4=Jer. xlix. 14–16; and Obad. 5, 6=Jer. xlix. 9, 10a).

While the poetic utterances of the prophet were in process of collection two other kinds of material were also being gathered together. The first kind consisted of prose narratives containing accounts in the first person of the prophet's experiences. Examples of this kind can be found in Amos (vii. 1–9), Hosea (iii), Isaiah (vi), Jeremiah (xviii) and Ezekiel (x). Zechariah i–viii and xi. 4–16 are entirely in this form. Most of this material is undoubtedly the work of the prophet, but why should he deliver his oracles partly in poetry and partly in prose? Some critics think that in moments of ecstasy he cast his words in poetic form, but that when the exalted mood had passed and he began to write down his words or to dictate them to a scribe, he turned to prose.

The second kind of material consisted of prose narratives in which events in the life of the prophet were recorded in the third person. Examples of this kind can be found in Amos (vii. 10–17), Hosea (i), Isaiah (vii. 1–9), Jeremiah (xxvi) and Zechariah (xii–xiv). Haggai in its present form and Jonah, with the exception of the psalm in ch. ii. 2–9, are in this form throughout.

At the end of the second stage in the growth of the prophetic books there existed for each prophet one or more collections of these three kinds of material, namely, oracular poetry, prose narratives in the first person, and prose narratives in the third person. But not all this material was genuine. Part of the oracular poetry consisted of the utterances of unknown minor prophets, which had been wrongfully ascribed, while the autobiographical and biographical narratives contained fictitious elements: in other words these collections contained both authentic and unauthentic material.

In the third stage the small collections ascribed to the prophets were worked up into books, the three kinds of material being combined by the compilers in different ways. When it became clear that prophecy had ceased the books themselves were collected and arranged in four volumes. It was at this stage that large anonymous collections were added. To the book of Isaiah were added the collections which we now know as Deutero-Isaiah (Is. xl–lv) and Trito-Isaiah (Is. lvi–lxvi): two collections were added to Zechariah i–viii, namely, chs. ix–xi and xii–xiv, and another collection became the last book of 'The Twelve', namely, Malachi. This final collection was probably made about 200 BC since it contains material dating from the third century BC and the book of Daniel (*c*. 164 BC) was omitted. The prophetic writings were recognized, though not officially, as authoritative Scripture shortly after their publication (*c*. 180 BC).

The Place of Oral Tradition in the Growth of the Prophetic Books

Oral tradition played a great part in the growth of the prophetic books, but not to the extent that some critics in recent times would have us believe. Birkeland, for example, maintains that the prophetic sayings were transmitted exclusively in oral form, that in the process of transmission they were constantly adapted to the needs of the times by circles of writers, and that they were not committed to writing until the post-exilic period by which time the oral form had become petrified.[1] 'The view,' says Eissfeldt, 'that right down into post-exilic times only oral tradition need seriously be considered is certainly to be rejected, as also that our prophetic books were only then written down, after the hitherto exclusively oral tradition had petrified.'[2]

[1] H. Birkeland, *Zum hebräischen Traditionswesen: die Komposition der prophetischen Bücher des Alten Testaments*, 1938, p. 25.

[2] O. Eissfeldt. Article on the Prophetic Literature in *The Old Testament and Modern Study* (Ed. Rowley), 1951, pp. 159 ff.

CHAPTER II

The Historical Background

ISRAEL AND JUDAH, 800–722 BC

Israel

For about a hundred years before the time of Amos, Israel had been at the mercy of Syria, but towards the end of the ninth century BC Syrian domination began to be menaced by the rise of Assyria, and with the weakening of Syrian pressure Israel was able to make a temporary recovery. Under Jehoash (801–786 BC) Israel recovered from the Syrians the cities east of the Jordan which had been lost in the previous reign. Jeroboam II (786–746 BC) continued the success of Jehoash. He recovered Gilead to the east of the Jordan and 'restored the border of Israel from the entering in of Hamath (on the Orontes in Syria) unto the sea of the Arabah' (2 Kgs. xiv. 25). Israel now found herself in control of the caravan routes. This success was facilitated by the weakness of three contemporary Assyrian kings, namely, Shalmaneser IV (782–772 BC), Ashur-dan III (772–754 BC) and Ashur-nirari V (754–745 BC). With the death of Jeroboam II kings followed one another rapidly. His son Zechariah (746–745 BC) after a short reign was murdered by Shallum (745 BC) and he in turn by Menahem (745–738 BC).

Under Tiglath-pileser III (745–727 BC) the weakness displayed by Assyria in the three previous reigns was arrested. A vigorous ruler, he at once embarked upon a career of conquest. In 743 BC, after campaigns in Northern Babylonia and in the hill-country to the north-east of the Tigris, he advanced to the Euphrates with the intention of conquering Syria. In alarm the Syrian kings combined and summoned to their aid Sarduris III, ruler of the Armenian kingdom of Urarti. Tiglath-pileser completely defeated Sarduris and captured Arpad about 743 BC. After two more years of campaigning he became master of Northern Syria, including Damascus, and marched against Samaria, but withdrew when Menahem agreed to pay tribute (2 Kgs. xv. 17–20). Menahem was succeeded by his son Pekahiah (738–737 BC) who was murdered by Pekah (737–732 BC). During Tiglath-pileser's absence in Media and Urarti, Rezin of Damascus organized a coalition against Assyria. Pekah now joined with Rezin and both demanded that Ahaz, king of Judah, should support their contemplated revolt. Ahaz refused, and in consequence they invaded Judah with the intention of deposing him and placing 'the son of Tabeel' on the throne (Is. vii. 6), whereupon Ahaz took the fateful step of appealing to Assyria for help (2 Kgs. xvi. 7, 8). This appeal was immediately granted and the confederates suffered a terrible fate. In 734 BC Tiglath-pileser attacked Israel, devastated Galilee, annexed all of Israel except Ephraim and Western Manasseh, and deported part of the population to Assyria (2 Kgs. xv. 29). The turn of Rezin followed. Damascus was captured in 732 BC, its king executed and its territory annexed, while its people were deported to Kir (2 Kgs. xvi. 9). Pekah did not long survive his confederate, being assassinated by Hoshea, who submitted to Assyria and was allowed to occupy the throne (732–724 BC).

Tiglath-pileser died in 727 BC and was succeeded by Shalmaneser V (727–722 BC). In 724 BC Hoshea, probably relying on promises of support from So, king of Egypt, with whom he had treasonable correspondence, refused to pay his yearly tribute. His hopes of Egyptian aid, however, proved delusive. Shalmaneser marched into Palestine and captured and imprisoned him (2 Kgs. xvii. 4), afterwards laying siege to Samaria, which held out for nearly three years, during which time Shalmaneser died and was succeeded by Sargon (722–705 BC) by whom the city was eventually captured in 722 BC. Many thousands of the inhabitants were deported to Assyria (2 Kgs. xvii. 6) and the kingdom of Israel became an Assyrian province. It was, however, no part of the Assyrian policy to leave the country desolate. Sargon brought in people from other parts of the empire and settled them on the land (2 Kgs. xvii. 24). These newcomers intermarried with the original inhabitants and the mixed race thus produced came to be called the Samaritans.

Judah
Recovery in Israel was accompanied by a similar recovery in Judah. Amaziah (800–783 BC) defeated the Edomites with great loss and captured the city of Sela (2 Kgs. xiv. 7). Encouraged by this success, he attacked Israel but met with disaster. In the battle of Bethshemish

he was defeated and captured; part of the wall of Jerusalem was dismantled to render its defences useless, and a heavy indemnity and a
certain number of hostages were exacted (2 Kgs. xiv. 8–14). Amaziah
was released and re-established upon the throne, but he never recovered the prestige which he had lost in his war with Israel. Some
years later a conspiracy was formed against him and he sought refuge
in Lachish, but was pursued by his enemies and slain (2 Kgs. xiv.
19). He was succeeded by his son Azariah (or Uzziah).

During the long reign of Azariah (783–742 BC) Judah reached the
summit of her power. He recovered Elath, on the north-eastern arm
of the Red Sea, from the Edomites, and fortified it, evidently with
the object of consolidating his position on the caravan route to
Arabia (2 Kgs. xiv. 22). According to 2 Chronicles xxvi. 6–15 he
fought with success against the Philistines and built cities in their
land, thus gaining control of the important caravan route in the
coastal plain, subdued the Arabians and the Ammonites, and re-
organized his army. It is said of him that 'his name spread abroad
even to the entering in of Egypt; for he waxed exceeding strong'
(2 Chron. xxvi. 8). In his later years he was afflicted with leprosy,
and the duties of government were discharged by his son Jotham
who afterwards succeeded him as king.

Jotham (742–735 BC) found himself threatened with attack from
the allied forces of Pekah of Samaria and Rezin of Damascus, but
hostilities did not break out until the accession of his son Ahaz.

Ahaz (735–715 BC) appealed to Assyria for help and sent an
embassy with a rich gift to the court of Tiglath-pileser to procure
his support (2 Kgs. xvi. 7, 8), which was promptly forthcoming. The
defeat of the two confederates, Pekah and Rezin, has already been
related. Ahaz paid dearly for Assyrian aid, for the price paid was
more than the treasures of the Temple and of his palace. As a result
of his compact with Tiglath-pileser Judah became a tributary state
of Assyria.

Conditions in Israel and Judah

The economic, social, moral and religious conditions in Israel and
Judah during this period were much the same. In both kingdoms
great prosperity was followed by moral and spiritual decline, though
it would appear that the inhabitants of Judah did not sink to the
same depths of degradation as those of Israel. The conquests made
by the two kingdoms led to the acquisition of a large quantity of

plunder from the captured cities, while the recovery of the caravan routes brought about the development of trade and commerce and a great increase in wealth. The royal houses no longer held a monopoly of trade. With the increase of wealth there arose a wealthy class of merchants who lived in luxury and led dissolute lives (Am. iii. 12, 15, vi. 3–6; Is. ii. 7, iii. 16–23, v. 11, 12, xxviii. 1–4). According to Amos and Isaiah the women were just as bad as the men (Am. iv. 1; Is. iii. 16–23, xxxii. 9–14). The increase of wealth at one end of the social scale was accompanied by grinding poverty at the other. The wealthy merchants used their power unscrupulously, oppressing the poor generally and bribing the judges in the law courts in order to gain possession of the land of the small peasant land-owner (Am. ii. 6, iii. 10, v. 7, 10–12, viii. 4–6; Is. i. 23, iii. 14, 15, v. 23). By about the middle of the eighth century BC the small peasant proprietor had almost disappeared, and the land was in the hands of the wealthy capitalists, who let it to tenant farmers at enormous rents or cultivated it themselves by means of slave labour.

The connection between religion and morality, which had been characteristic of Yahwism, was ignored or forgotten. Men were most assiduous in performing their duties at the various sanctuaries, but unjust and merciless in their dealings with their fellow men (Am. iv. 4, 5, v. 21–24; Hos. iv. 1, 2, vi. 8; Mic. vi. 6–8; Is. i. 11–17). To add still further to the corruption, the religion of Yahweh was contaminated by the introduction of the beliefs and practices of the Canaanite cults. Yahweh was conceived as a Baal, that is, a fertility god, and His worship was accompanied by gross immorality (Am. ii. 7, 8; Hos. ii. 5, 8, 16, iv. 12–14, 17, 18, x. 5, 6, xiii. 2). Moreover contact with Assyria had led to the introduction of heathen gods (Am. v. 26, viii. 14) and heathen superstitions (Is. ii. 6–11, 18–22).

We happen to know a little about the worship which went on in the two kingdoms. We are told that Jeroboam I (922–901 BC), king of Israel, set up gold bulls at Bethel and Dan, saying to the people, 'Behold thy gods, O Israel, which brought thee up out of the land of Egypt' (1 Kgs. xii. 28, 29). Of the later kings of Israel, Jeroboam II, Zechariah, Menahem, Pekahiah and Pekah, we read that they did not abandon the sins by which Jeroboam, the son of Nebat, had led Israel into sin (2 Kgs. xiv. 24, xv. 9, 18, 24, 28). Of Ahaz, king of Judah, it is stated that 'he walked in the way of the kings of Israel, yea, and made his son to pass through the fire, according to the abominations of the heathen, whom the Lord cast out from before the children of Israel. And he sacrificed and burnt incense in the high places, and on the hills, and under every green tree' (2 Kgs. xvi. 3, 4). On his visit to Tiglath-pileser at Damascus he saw there an altar of a pattern which was unknown to the Israelites, and resolved to make it the model of a new altar to take the place of the altar of Solomon in the Temple. Accordingly he sent a copy of the altar to Urijah, the priest at Jerusalem, with instructions to build one like it (2 Kgs. xvi. 10–16). The altar was probably Assyrian rather than Syrian, and we may surmise that Ahaz, as a vassal king, was compelled to introduce the worship of Assyrian deities into Judah.

It is clear that the morale of the people had been undermined by prosperity, moral laxity and the degradation of religion. In their corrupt state they could not stand the attacks of a determined and vigorous foe; nothing short of a moral and religious reformation could save them from destruction. 'Seek the Lord,' said Amos, 'and ye shall live' (Am. v. 6).

JUDAH, 722–587 BC

Judah survived the downfall of her more powerful rival, Israel, by nearly 150 years, probably owing to the submissive policy of Ahaz and her geographical position, lying as she did off the main road that ran from the north down the coastal plain to Egypt, and along which marched the contending armies of the greater eastern powers. Soon after the fall of Samaria revolts broke out at Hamath and Damascus in Syria, at Gaza in Philistia, and at Samaria, with the support of Egypt. In 720 BC Sargon, the king of Assyria, marched west and suppressed the revolts, making the land of Hamath 'a heap of ruins', and defeating the Egyptians and Philistines at Raphia on the Egyptian border. In these rebellions Judah apparently took no part.

Ahaz was succeeded on the throne by his son Hezekiah (715–687 BC), who followed his father's example and acknowledged the overlordship of Assyria. In 711 BC the Philistines, Edomites and Moabites, probably inspired by Egyptian intrigues, attempted to throw off the Assyrian yoke but failed. With the capture of Ashdod and the deportation of its inhabitants the revolt ended. Hezekiah seems to have been implicated in this revolt, but he must have promptly submitted for Sargon called himself the 'subjugator of the land of Judah whose situation is far away'. It was perhaps about this time that Merodach-baladan, a Chaldean chieftain and a man of real ability, who had usurped the throne of Babylon in 721 BC, sent an embassy to Hezekiah, ostensibly to congratulate him on his recovery from an illness but actually to persuade him to join in a general revolt against Assyria. Some critics, however, place it at the beginning of Sennacherib's reign. The biblical account of Hezekiah's illness and the embassy appears at the close of his history; but the fact that Hezekiah was still in possession of his treasures shows clearly that they must have occurred before Sennacherib invaded Judah and compelled him to pay a heavy fine of three hundred talents of silver and thirty talents of gold, which left his treasury empty.

In 705 BC Sargon died and was succeeded by Sennacherib (705–681 BC). With the accession of a new sovereign it seemed as though the Assyrian empire would collapse. Merodach-baladan made himself master of Babylon from which he had been driven out by Sargon in 710 BC, and organized a revolt in the west. The Phoenicians, Philistines, Edomites, Moabites and Ammonites revolted, and Hezekiah, probably encouraged by promises of support from the Egyptian king, Shabaka, threw in his lot with the rebels, refused to pay the customary tribute to Assyria and co-operated with the anti-Assyrian party of Philistia (2 Kgs. xviii. 7, 8). In view of the attack which he knew would follow, he strengthened the fortifications of Jerusalem (2 Chron. xxxii. 5) and excavated the Siloam tunnel through the solid rock in order to supply the city with water in time of siege (2 Kgs. xx. 20; cf. 2 Chron. xxxii. 30). Sennacherib dealt with the rebellion piecemeal. First he marched against Merodach-baladan, deposed him and placed a Babylonian of the royal house, named Belibni, on the throne as a tributary king (702 BC). He was now free to turn his attention to the west. Marching down the coast he first captured Zidon, whereupon, alarmed by his spectacular success, the Edomites, Moabites and Ammonites hastened to submit and pay tribute. Then he subdued Philistia, and at Eltekeh near Ekron, routed the Egyptians who had come to the assistance of the rebels. Next he devastated Judah, capturing forty-six towns, and besieged Jerusalem. The biblical account of the events connected with the siege are somewhat confused and does not agree with the Assyrian account, but two facts are clear, namely, that the city was not captured and that Hezekiah submitted and paid a heavy fine. Whether Hezekiah's attempts at negotiation with Sennacherib's officers, recorded in 2 Kings xviii. 17–xix. 36, took place before or after the payment of the fine, we do not know. News of an invasion of Babylonia by Merodach-baladan probably caused Sennacherib to raise the siege and to retire to Nineveh. He made no further attack on Jerusalem. After the subjugation of Palestine he spent his time in the building of his walls and palaces at Nineveh and in warlike expeditions. For several years he was engaged in war with the Elamites, and a great battle was fought at Khaluli on the Tigris (691 BC) in which he claimed the victory; but it is probable that the battle went against him, for he was compelled to retreat leaving the Elamites in possession of the field. In 690 BC he swooped down upon Babylon and laid it in ruins. On his assassination in 681 BC he was succeeded by his son Esarhaddon.

Hezekiah was devoted to the worship of Yahweh and sometime during his reign—in his first year according to 2 Chronicles xxix. 3 initiated a religious reformation. He removed the high-places (i.e. hill shrines), which lent themselves readily to abuse and to contamination by heathen cults, cut down the sacred poles and demolished the bronze serpent, called Nehushtan, made by Moses (2 Kgs. xviii. 4).[1] His attempts at a religious reformation, however, were only partially successful, for in the next reign there was a violent reaction in favour of heathenism.

Hezekiah reigned for some years after his unsuccessful rebellion but nothing further is related about him. On his death he was succeeded on the throne by his son Manasseh.

Esarhaddon (681–669 BC) was a wise and prudent ruler who adopted a policy of pacification and conciliation in his dominions. He rebuilt Babylon, destroyed in the previous reign, so that when the Elamites invaded Babylonia they found no support among the inhabitants and were compelled to retreat. Instead of wreaking vengeance on the invaders of his territory he treated them leniently. The great ambition of his life was the conquest of Egypt. His army met with a check in its first campaign in 675 BC, but in 671 BC Memphis was captured and Taharka (Tirhakah) was forced to flee into Ethiopia. Esarhaddon was now master of Lower Egypt. Assyrian officers or Egyptian nobles, among whom was Necho, ruler of the

---

[1] It is highly improbable that the bronze serpent dated back to the time of Moses. All we know is that it was an ancient symbol in Jerusalem in the days of Hezekiah. But archaeologists have found many traces of serpent worship in ancient Palestine. According to Rowley (*The Rediscovery of the Old Testament*, 1945, pp. 81 ff.) serpent worship was practised in Jerusalem in the Jebusite shrine there, before the capture of the city by David. It is probable that Zadok was priest of the shrine.

feudatory kingdom of Sais, were appointed governors of the nomes or districts, supported by Assyrian garrisons. No sooner, however, had Esarhaddon left, than Taharka revolted, seized Memphis and massacred the Assyrian garrison. Esarhaddon hastened to crush the revolt but died on the way.

His younger son, Ashurbanipal, known to the Greeks as Sardana-palus (669–626 BC), succeeded to the throne, while his elder son became vassal king of Babylonia. He continued the campaign against Egypt and finally in 663 BC captured and destroyed Thebes, making Psammetichus viceroy of the country. But about ten years later Psammetichus threw off the Assyrian supremacy which was never again asserted.

The great triumph of Ashurbanipal was his conquest of Elam. On his return from the west he invaded the country, defeated and slew the king, and installed another king as a vassal of Assyria with diminished territory (c. 658 BC). In 652 BC his brother and vassal, Shamash-shum-ukin, king of Babylon, revolted and was joined by the Elamites. During the war which ensued an Assyrian force blockaded Babylon, and Shamash-shum-ukin set fire to his own palace and perished in the flames (648 BC). The Assyrians then advanced into Elam and destroyed Susa, its capital (646 BC), and the country was annexed to the Assyrian empire.

Assyria was now at the height of her power, but towards the close of his reign decline set in. Barbarians from the steppes of Russia and from Central Asia, known to the Greeks as Cimmerians and Scythians, burst into the Assyrian empire. About 626 BC a horde of Scythians penetrated to the borders of Egypt but they were induced to retire by the Egyptian king on payment of a heavy bribe. They seem to have left Jerusalem untouched both on their way to Egypt and on their return. The excitement and terror which their invasion aroused are probably reflected in the prophecies of Zephaniah and Jeremiah. Our knowledge of these invaders is vague, but there is no doubt that they were instrumental in destroying the Assyrian power in the west. Ashurbanipal died in 626 BC leaving a weak and exhausted empire to his successors. Constant wars over a long period of time had depleted the ranks of the Assyrian forces and impoverished the state. During the latter part of Ashurbanipal's reign his forces, which contained recruits from his subject peoples, were inferior in quality and were no match for the western warriors. Assyria never realized that she had duties to the peoples whom she had conquered; their lands were plundered and exploited for her own benefit and no attempt was made to unite them in common allegiance to the throne. The empire was built upon force and kept together by force: when the might of the Assyrian army was destroyed the doom of the empire was sealed.

During the reigns of Esarhaddon and Ashurbanipal, Judah apparently remained quiet, though the people doubtless waited for a favourable opportunity to assert their independence. According to 2 Chronicles xxxiii. 10-13, Manasseh was captured and taken prisoner to Babylon, but was allowed to return to Jerusalem. There is, however, no confirmation of his capture and imprisonment in the Assyrian records, though it is possible that he may have joined in the revolt of 652 BC and that on its failure he was compelled to pay homage to Ashurbanipal.

In the sphere of religion Manasseh's reign (687–642 BC) witnessed the most serious threat to the continuation of a distinctive Israelite worship that ever existed either before or after. He is said to have restored the local sanctuaries which Hezekiah had destroyed, and to have given official recognition to the worship of Baal and to the practice of divination and magic; sun-worship and star-worship were also approved. Like Ahaz he made his son to pass through the fire (2 Kgs. xxi. 1–9). He is said to have 'shed innocent blood very much, till he had filled Jerusalem from one end to another' (2 Kgs. xxi. 16). This statement probably refers to the persecution of the disciples of the great prophets who were ardent supporters of Yahweh and refused to accept his syncretistic religion.

Manasseh died in 642 BC and was succeeded by his son Amon who followed in the ways of his father. After a brief reign of two years (642–640 BC) he was murdered by his courtiers, who were in turn murdered by 'the people of the land' (2 Kgs. xxi. 24).

Amon was succeeded on the throne by his son Josiah (640–609 BC) who was only eight years old (2 Kgs. xxii. 1), so that the government of the country for a time must have been in the hands of a regent. By the death of his father at an early age he escaped the corrupting and degrading influences which would otherwise have been brought to bear upon him in his childhood and youth. He must have come under the influence of the reform party in Judah, for we read of him that 'he did that which was right in the eyes of the Lord, and walked in all the way of David his father, and turned not aside to the right hand or to the left' (2 Kgs. xxii. 2). The destruction of the Assyrian power in the west left him free to undertake a complete religious reformation. His religious reforms were based on the central part of Deuteronomy, which was discovered during the repair of the Temple in 622 BC (2 Kgs. xxii. 3–8). This part was read publicly and the king and the people entered into a solemn covenant to obey its teaching. The local shrines, which were all seats of Canaanite worship, and which the ordinary Judaean followed rather than the worship of Yahweh, were destroyed, the Temple and Jerusalem were cleansed of foreign cults and the worship was centralized at Jerusalem. The work of reform was concluded by the celebration of the Passover with a splendour which surpassed all previous celebrations of the feast. Ephraim as well as Judah was compelled to accept the reforms (2 Kgs. xxiii. 2–23). After Josiah's death there seems to have been a return to the old heathen practices. Ezekiel describes how in the sixth year of Jehoiachin's exile (692 BC) he was carried in a trance to the Temple at Jerusalem, where he saw a statue of an idol which provoked Yahweh to resentment, a secret chamber in which all kinds of reptiles and animals were worshipped, women wailing for Tammuz and a group of men worshipping the rising sun (Ezek. viii).

After the death of Ashurbanipal, Nabopolassar established himself as king in Babylon and formed an alliance with the Medes, who inhabited the region between the Zagros Mountains and the Caspian Sea, with the object of destroying Nineveh. In 616 BC Nabopolassar attacked the Assyrians, but in the campaigns both of this and the following year he was unsuccessful. In 614 BC he concluded an alliance with the Medes for the destruction of Assyria as their common object, and two years later Nineveh fell before their combined forces. A new seat of government was set up at Harran but this was also captured by the allies in 610 BC. The Assyrians still continued to fight on and Necho, king of Egypt (609–593 BC), sent an expedition to help them. In 609 BC his forces were met at Megiddo by Josiah, king of Judah, who was now free from the control of Assyria and had no wish to become the vassal of Egypt. According to 2 Chronicles xxxv. 23, 24 Josiah fell in battle, but the language of 2 Kings xxiii. 29 suggests that he was seized at an interview and slain, possibly as a traitor. Judah now passed under the control of Egypt. In 605 BC an Egyptian army under Necho was utterly defeated by Nabopolassars's son, Nebuchadrezzar, at Carchemish on the Euphrates. The result of the destruction of Assyria and the defeat of Egypt was not the independence of Judah but the substitution of Babylon for Assyria as her enemy. Carchemish is one of the decisive battles of the world, for it marked the end of the Assyrian empire and of the Egyptian hopes of world dominion.

On the death of Josiah 'the people of the land' anointed his son Jehoahaz, who was also called Shallum (Jer. xxii. 11; 1 Chron. iii. 15) as their king (2 Kgs. xxiii. 30; Jer. xxii. 10–12). Jehoahaz (609 BC) had little opportunity of showing what his intentions were, for three months after his accession to the throne, Necho deposed him and made his elder brother, Eliakim, king of Judah, changing his name to Jehoiakim, probably as a mark of servitude, and laying upon him a heavy tribute (2 Kgs. xxiii. 33–35).

Jehoiakim (609–598 BC) was a selfish, cruel, luxurious ruler, desirous of emulating Solomon in the splendour of his court and the magnificence of his buildings. Jeremiah charges him with employing forced labour in the construction of his palaces, with having neither eyes nor heart for anything but selfish gain, the shedding of innocent blood, outrage and oppression, and contrasts his conduct with that of his father Josiah, who ruled justly and maintained the cause of the poor and the needy (Jer. xxii. 13–19). Under him there was a reaction against the religious reforms of Josiah. The people once more resorted to the high places (Jer. xiii. 27) and revived the worship of the Queen of heaven (Jer. vii. 18, viii. 2).

After the battle of Carchemish (605 BC) it is probable that he submitted to Nebuchadrezzar; but in 598 BC he refused to pay his customary tribute, probably owing to Egyptian intrigues. Bands of Chaldeans, in combination with bands of Syrians, Moabites and Ammonites began to ravage his territory (2 Kgs. xxiv. 2), but in the course of these attacks Jehoiakim died, possibly in battle (2 Kgs. xxiv. 6; Jer. xxii. 19, xxxvi. 30). Jehoiakim was succeeded by his son Jehoiachin, also called Jeconiah and Coniah, who was eighteen years of age and reigned only three months (598 BC). Jerusalem was invested, and when Nebuchadrezzar himself took the direction of the siege Jehoiachin promptly capitulated. He and his family, together with many of the best people in the land, were carried into captivity to Babylon (2 Kgs. xxiv. 14, 16). Another son of Josiah, namely Mattaniah, was placed on the throne of Judah and his name changed to Zedekiah.

Zedekiah (598–587 BC) was a weak character, quite unfit to deal with the difficult situation which confronted him. There were two parties in the state, one advocating an alliance with Egypt and the other counselling submission to Babylon. It was not long before he fell completely under the influence of the pro-Egyptian party. Egypt was constantly stirring up trouble among the nations of the west. In 594 BC Zedekiah opened negotiations with Edom, Moab, Ammon, Tyre and Zidon, with the object of planning a general revolt (Jer. xxvii) but the negotiations came to nothing; it is possible that Zedekiah was summoned to Babylon to clear himself of suspicions raised against him (Jer. li. 59). In 588 BC, in spite of protests by Jeremiah, he took the fatal step and raised the standard of revolt (2 Kgs. xxiv. 20; 2 Chron. xxxvi. 13), apparently with the support of Egypt and in conjunction with the Ammonites (Ezek. xvii. 15, xxi. 18–20). Jerusalem was once more besieged, the siege lasting a year and a half. In the course of it an Egyptian army advanced to its relief and the investing army for a time retired (Jer. xxxvii. 5). But the Egyptian forces either withdrew without fighting or were defeated by the Babylonians, for the siege was soon resumed. The city suffered terrible hardships but in the end a breach was made in the walls and the king and his army fled. But the fugitives were pursued, and the king was captured in the plains of Jericho and taken to Riblah to appear before Nebuchadrezzar. There his sons were put to death in his presence, and he himself was blinded before he was taken in chains to Babylon where he ended his days as a prisoner (2 Kgs. xxv. 1–7; Jer. xxxix. 1–7, lii. 1–11). After a month the walls of Jerusalem were dismantled, the Temple, the palace and the principal houses were destroyed, and the sacred vessels and ornaments of the Temple were either broken in pieces or carried away. All the inhabitants, except the poorest, who were left to cultivate the land, were transferred to Babylon (2 Kgs. xxv. 8–21; Jer. lii. 12–20).

The desolation of Judah was practically complete but the poor peasants still remained. Nebuchadrezzar appointed Gedaliah, a member of the older nobility, as governor (2 Kgs. xxv. 22). Gedaliah, who was a brave, wise and kindly man, made his headquarters at Mizpah and set about restoring the national life. He gathered round him a band of the best men in the land, including Johanan, the son of Kareah, and the prophet Jeremiah. But he roused the enmity of his neighbours, and a certain Ishmael, of the royal house of Judah, with the support of the Ammonites, slew him and all his attendants, both Jews and Babylonians, and taking some prisoners with him departed for Ammon. Johanan with an armed force pursued the murderer and recovered the prisoners; but fearing the wrath of Nebuchadrezzar because they had failed to maintain order, he and all those with him fled to Egypt taking the reluctant prophet, Jeremiah, with them (2 Kgs. xxv. 23–26; Jer. xl–xliii. 7). Judah had suffered the same fate as Israel, and so the Jewish state at last came to an end. It is true that from 142–63 BC she was practically independent, but even then the country was nominally a part of the Seleucid empire.

DECLINE AND FALL OF THE BABYLONIAN EMPIRE, 587–539 BC

After the fall of Jerusalem Nebuchadrezzar besieged Tyre for thirteen years, but, according to Josephus, he failed to capture it. The prevalent idea that he made a temporary conquest of Egypt rests upon insufficient and doubtful evidence. His death in 562 BC proved to be the beginning of the break-up of the Babylonian empire. His successors, Amel-Marduk (Evil-merodach), who released Jehoiachin (2 Kgs. xxv. 27–30), Neriglissar and Labashi-Marduk, were undistinguished and short-lived. With the death of the last in 556 BC the dynasty of Nabopolassar came to an end, and the priests placed on the throne Nabonidus, a scholar and an archaeologist, who was probably a wealthy merchant. He was absorbed in the study of architecture and archaeology and left the administration of affairs to his son Belshazzar. It was not long before he caused offence by collecting in Babylon the images of the various local deities in the empire, thereby rousing the anger not only of the people, whose gods had been removed, but also of the priests who felt that their god Marduk was being grossly insulted by the introduction of foreign deities.

About 550 BC Cyrus, the Persian king of Anshan in Elam, seized the crown of Media from Astyages and united the two kindred peoples, the Medes and the Persians. Deutero-Isaiah, the great prophet of this time, declared that he had been raised to power by Yahweh in order that he might be the instrument of His divine purpose (Is. xliv. 28, xlv. 1; cf. xli. 2, 25, xlv. 13, xlvi. 11, xlviii. 14, 15). Alarmed by this sudden menace, Croesus, king of Lydia, formed an anti-Persian alliance with Egypt, Babylonia and Sparta. But Cyrus struck at Croesus before his allies could come to his aid, captured Sardis, the Lydian capital, took Croesus prisoner and turned his kingdom into a Persian province (546 BC). In the same year he commenced operations against Babylon, but they were not completed till 539 BC when Gobryas, the Persian governor of Assyria and Gutium, completely defeated the Babylonians, at Opis, slew Belshazzar, who in the book of Daniel vii. 1 is called 'king of Babylon', and entered Babylon apparently without resistance. Cyrus himself entered the city in triumph amid the jubilation of priests and people, and the Babylonian empire ceased to exist.

The Exile, 587–538 BC

The Jewish exiles in Babylon were not reduced to slavery; they seem to have enjoyed almost complete freedom though they were not allowed to leave the country or take part in public affairs. That they were able to move about freely may be inferred from the letter which Jeremiah addressed to them, urging them to make homes for themselves and to take an interest in the welfare of their new land (Jer. xxix. 4–7). They were allowed to live in communities or settlements: there was, for example, such a settlement at Tel-abib by the River Chebar, a canal south-east of Babylon (Ezek. i. 1, iii. 15, 23). In these settlements they were allowed to retain their traditional organization (Ezek. xiv). They were thus able to retain their national identity which might have been lost had they been scattered among the Babylonians. They were allowed to have their own houses (Jer. xxix. 5; Ezek. viii. 1, xii. 1–7), to marry (Jer. xxix. 6; Ezek. iii. 24, xxiv. 18), to follow their own pursuits and to enjoy the fruits of their labour. At first they would doubtless follow the pursuit of agriculture, as the names of some of their settlements seem to indicate. Thus Tel-abib means 'the hill of the ears of corn', Tel-melah (Ezra ii. 59) perhaps 'the barren hill', and Tel-harsha (Ezra ii. 59) 'the hill of the plough'. In the course of time some of the more enterprising among them would move into the cities and engage in trade. There is evidence for thinking that they were so successful in business that in the process of time they acquired considerable wealth. Those who returned to their native land in 538 BC contributed liberally to the fund for the rebuilding of the temple (Ezra ii. 69) while some twenty years later contributions were sent from Babylon to Jerusalem (Zech. vi. 9). The Murashu tablets (see p. 56) indicate that in the fifth century BC the descendants of the Jewish exiles were allowed to engage in trade and accumulated wealth. It is said that it was in Babylon that the Jews acquired that aptitude for trade which has distinguished them for centuries in Europe.

Towards the end of the Babylonian empire the exiles, for some unknown reason, seem to have been subjected to persecution (Is. xlvii. 6). There is a striking contrast between the tone of Jeremiah and Ezekiel and that of Deutero-Isaiah.

The importance of the Exile in the religious history of the Jews cannot be over-estimated. It is a mistake to suppose that all the exiles were sincere worshippers of Yahweh. By the time of the destruction of Jerusalem religion had sunk to a low level in Judah, and exile did not result in a sudden transformation. We are told that in pre-exilic days they 'mingled themselves with the nations, and learned their works' (Ps. cvi. 35). In Babylon with its magnificent temples and its huge idols this temptation was strong. Many Jews must have witnessed the imposing procession on New Year's Day, when the god Marduk was taken from his temple in Babylon to a sanctuary outside the city and brought back again the next day (Is. xlv. 20). It is not surprising that some succumbed to the temptation (Ezek. xiv. 3–9, xx. 30–42, xxxvi. 25). Others again lost faith and hope, believing that Yahweh had abandoned them and that they would never see their native land again (Ezek. xii. 22, xxxvii. 11). There were some, however, who were ardent patriots and devoted followers of Yahweh, who were determined to preserve both their national identity and their religion at all costs. During the exile there was a spiritual reformation, which wrought a change for the better in the religion of even the most pious of them. Amid the idolatries of Babylon the superstitious rites and immoral practices of the Canaanites and the worship of foreign deities ceased to exercise their malign influence over them. Various causes contributed to this —the stern teaching of the prophets, the study of the Law, the reaction against the monstrous idolatry of the Babylonians, the absence of a court and an aristocracy to set the fashion in the worship of foreign cults, and escape from the fascination of the Canaanite high places. Closer contact with other peoples led them to realize that Yahweh must have some relation with other nations besides their own; hence it dawned upon them that Yahweh was not merely the greatest of the gods but the God of the whole earth. Deutero-Isaiah, who wrote towards the close of the Exile, pours scorn upon idols (xl. 19, 20, xli. 6, 7, xliv. 9–20) and teaches a pure monotheism (Is. xliv. 6).

The destruction of the state and the Temple led to the development of personal religion, which had been first stressed by Jeremiah. There was an increasing tendency to regard religion as a personal relationship between God and man rather than as primarily a relationship between God and nation. Deprived of their native land and of their Temple, they learnt that neither was essential to true religion. Taught by the prophet Jeremiah (xxix. 12–14), they made the great discovery that they had not left Yahweh behind them, and that He could be worshipped in a private house in Babylon just as well as in the magnificent Temple at Jerusalem. Hence the tendency was for religion to become less formal and more spiritual. They could no longer offer sacrifices since their Temple and altar had gone, and since the land in which they dwelt was unclean (Ezek. iv. 13); but they had other practices connected with their religion which were independent of local conditions and which they now stressed. Of these the chief were circumcision and Sabbath-observance (Ezek. xx. 12–21, xxii. 8–16, xxiii. 38) which became the hallmarks of Judaism wherever it existed.

It is in the Exile that we find the beginnings of Synagogue worship. Since the captives could no longer worship in the Temple at Jerusalem they had to find some other place of meeting. We are told that the elders were accustomed to assemble in the house of Ezekiel for help and counsel (Ezek. viii. 1, xiv. 1, xx. 1–3). On their return to their native land the Temple was rebuilt and its ritual restored, but the meetings which they had been accustomed to hold in exile were not discontinued. In the course of time buildings, or synagogues as they were called, were erected for public worship in every town and village and a regular order of service was established, consisting of prayers and psalms, the reading of the Scriptures and preaching. What originally had been a temporary expedient for the preservation of the nation's religion, eventually became the chief institution of Judaism.

There is reason to believe that the Exile was a time of considerable literary activity. What documents the exiles took with them into exile we do not know, but it is clear that parts of the Pentateuch, Joshua, Judges and 1 and 2 Kings, as we have them today, are older than the Exile. The two books of Kings in their present form must have been written during the Exile, for they bring the narrative down to the release of Jehoiachin from prison in Babylon (562 BC), and make no reference to a return. The two prophetic books Ezekiel and Deutero-Isaiah are also generally assigned to the period.

THE PERSIAN EMPIRE, 539–331 BC

Cyrus' conquest of Babylon added all the component parts of that empire to his own, so that he now ruled from the Aegean Sea in the west to the Caspian Sea in the east, and from Armenia in the north to the deserts of Arabia in the south.

He was a wise and tolerant ruler and his regime was not only accepted but also welcomed. The peoples deported by the Assyrians and Babylonians were as far as practicable restored to their homes, and the images of the gods, whom previous conquerors had carried off, were returned to the old shrines and the ancient rites were permitted. In accordance with his conciliatory policy the exiled Jews were allowed to return to their native land. After the conquest of Babylon he spent the remaining years of his life in the organization of his empire. On his death in 539 BC the crown passed to his son Cambyses.

The chief event of the reign of Cambyses (530–522 BC) was the conquest of Egypt in 525 BC, which was necessary if the Empire was to be safe on its western border. While he was away in Egypt a revolt broke out in Asia under a certain Gaumata who impersonated Cambyses' brother Bardiya (Smerdis) whom Cambyses had secretly put to death. Cambyses died suddenly on his way to quell the revolt, but it was successfully suppressed by his kinsman Darius, the son of Hystaspes, and the pretender slain. Then Darius in virtue of his royal descent was made king.

Darius I (522–486 BC) was not generally acknowledged by his subjects and revolts broke out in various parts of the empire, but by 518 BC he had made his position as king secure. In 514 BC he led an expedition against the Scythians in Europe in revenge, it is said, for the great Scythian invasion a century before, but his forces met with disaster and were compelled to retire. The revolt of the Greek cities of Asia Minor led him to undertake the conquest of Greece, but his forces were defeated at Marathon (490 BC) and were compelled to withdraw with great loss. Further action against Greece was delayed by a revolt in Egypt, which he was preparing to crush when he died in 486 BC and was succeeded by his son Xerxes I, who is called in the book of Esther, Ahasuerus.

The greatness of Darius I lay in his genius for organization. The empire was divided into twenty provinces, each under a governor, called a satrap, and hence called a satrapy. He was purely a civil governor, the military organization being entirely separate. His power was checked by the presence of a royal secretary whose duty it was to report to the king on the administration of the province. The royal authority was further safeguarded by periodic inspections by travelling commissioners, called the 'king's ears' or the 'king's eyes'. Each satrapy was independent as regards internal affairs but paid an annual fixed tribute into the royal treasury. In the east it was paid in produce, but in the west, chiefly in Asia Minor, in coined money—the gold 'daric', which bore the king's name and was one of the purest coins that were ever struck. The organization which Darius established survived with minor changes until the conquest of Persia by Alexander the Great.

Xerxes I (486–465 BC) crushed the revolt in Egypt and then attacked Greece, but his forces were defeated at Salamis in 480 BC and at Plataea in 479 BC. The defeat of the Persians was so complete that the attempt to conquer Greece was never renewed. Xerxes I was murdered in 465 BC and after a short usurpation by his murderer Artabanus, his son Artaxerxes (Longimanus) succeeded in obtaining the throne, and in restoring order. Artaxerxes I (465–424 BC) favoured the Jews and under Nehemiah the walls of Jerusalem were built. Of the succeeding Persian kings—Xerxes II (424–423 BC), Darius II (423–404 BC), Artaxerxes II (Mnemon, 404–358 BC), Artaxerxes III (Ochus, 358–338 BC) and Arses (338–336 BC)—little is known. Darius III (Codomannus, 336–331 BC) spent his reign in a vain struggle with Alexander the Great who defeated him at Granicus (334 BC), Issus (332 BC) and Gaugamela (331 BC), thereby gaining undisputed possession of the whole Persian empire.

The Return and the Second Temple

The history of the return of the Jewish exiles from Babylon to Palestine is somewhat obscure. The sources from which our information is derived are the book of Ezra, compiled by the Chronicler about two hundred years after the events, and the two prophetic books of Haggai and Zechariah i–viii (the remainder of the book is of later date) which are contemporary documents. According to the book of Ezra, Cyrus issued an edict permitting the exiles to return to their native land in order that they might rebuild their ruined Temple (Ezra i. 2–4). The sacred vessels were restored and about 50,000 people returned to Jerusalem under the leadership of

Sheshbazzar (Ezra i. 7–11), erected an altar and laid the foundation of the Temple. 'And they offered burnt offerings thereon unto the Lord, even burnt offerings morning and evening' (Ezra iii. 3). But the work of building was interrupted by the people of the land and was not resumed until the second year of the reign of Darius I, king of Persia, that is, 520 BC. But in the contemporary documents, namely, the books of Haggai and Zechariah i–viii, there is no mention of a return on a large scale or of an early attempt at rebuilding the Temple. It was not until eighteen years after the return of the first exiles, that is, 520 BC, that the proposal to rebuild the Temple was first made (Hag. i. 1, 2, 12). Haggai represents the Temple as being still in ruins, and urges its restoration on the grounds that failure to build was the cause of bad harvests, poverty and other calamities which had befallen them, and that the Temple should be ready for the Messianic Age which was about to dawn (Hag. ii. 6, 7; cf. Zech. vi. 9–15). Haggai gives no hint of any hostility between the returned exiles and 'the people of the land', but actually represents the two classes as co-operating in the work.

It is now possible to reconstruct the history of the return of the Jewish exiles in Babylon and of the rebuilding of the Temple. A decree permitting the return was made by Cyrus. The substantial historicity of this decree has been confirmed by modern archaeological discoveries, its Jewish colouring being doubtless due to the Chronicler whose aim was to demonstrate that the return was in accordance with the will of Yahweh. Probably in its original form it contained nothing more than a simple permission for the exiles to return. Cyrus restored the sacred vessels, which had been carried away by Nebuchadrezzar, to Sheshbazzar who headed a small band of returning exiles. On their arrival at Jerusalem they found the reality quite different from their expectations. The city was still in ruins, but the Temple was still standing, though dilapidated, and the altar in position. The territory which they could call their own was very small, covering an area about twenty-five miles long from Ai in the north to Beth-zur in the south, and thirty miles wide from Zanuah in the west to the Jordan in the east. They settled down and resumed their national life, joining in the sacrifices with 'the people of the land'. Between 538 BC and the death of the Persian king Cambyses in 522 BC many Jews had undoubtedly returned to Palestine, among whom were Zerubbabel, the son of Shealtiel and grandson of Jehoiachin, the legitimate heir of the Davidic house, and the High Priest Joshua (Jeshua). The death of Cambyses was followed by widespread revolts, and it looked as if the empire would collapse. Haggai and Zechariah believed that the Messianic Age was about to dawn and that the rule of the heathen was ended. Spurred on by the two prophets, the Jews began to rebuild the Temple and held a ceremony which was virtually a coronation of Zerubbabel. Unfortunately for them the new Persian king, Darius, who was an outstanding personality, defeated all his rivals and reunited the empire, and presumably Zerubbabel was put to death. Henceforth we hear of no representative of the Davidic house, and when, long afterwards, the Jews gained their independence under the Macca-bees, leadership passed to the priestly tribe of Levi. The foundations of the Temple were laid in the second year of the reign of Darius, that is, 520 BC (Hag. i. 15), and the work was completed in the sixth year, that is, 516 BC (Ezra vi. 15).

From the Second Temple to Nehemiah, 516–445 BC

From the completion of the Temple to the coming of Nehemiah (445 BC) there is a gap of about seventy years in the historical re-cords, but some information may be gleaned from the books of Trito-Isaiah (Is. lvi–lxvi) and Malachi, which are usually assigned to that period. The high hopes raised by the optimistic predictions of the Prophets had not been realized; the Messianic Age which the people had confidently expected had not dawned. Instead of enter-ing upon a time of unprecedented prosperity they found it difficult to obtain the bare necessities of life; instead of becoming the greatest nation on earth they were still under the yoke of the Persian con-querors and beset by enemies. Their native rulers were unworthy of their high calling and spent their lives in drunken idleness (Is. lvi. 9–12). Religion and morals were at a low ebb. A section of the com-munity was guilty of superstitious and idolatrous rites (Is. lvii. 3–13, lxv. 3, 4, lxvi. 17). The Temple was standing and public services were being held in it (Is. lvi. 7, lx. 7, lxii. 9, lxv. 11, lxvi. 6; Mal. i. 10, iii. 1, 10), though the walls of Jerusalem were still in ruins (Is. lviii. 12, lx. 10). The priests were wearied with the whole routine of the Temple services and accepted inferior or blemished animals for sacrifice (Mal. i. 6–13), while the people neglected to pay their tithes and offerings (Mal. iii. 8, 9). Many were so perplexed by the turn of events that they began to doubt the justice of Yahweh and the wisdom of trying to serve Him (Mal. i. 2, ii. 17, iii. 14, 15).

Morality was divorced from religion. Men divorced their Jewish wives in order to contract marriages with foreign women (Mal. ii. 10–16), while perjury, adultery and oppression prevailed (Mal. iii. 5). It was probably towards the end of this period that an attempt was made to rebuild Jerusalem (Ezra iv. 12). But certain opponents of the Jews, interpreting this as an act of disloyalty, informed Artaxerxes I who ordered the work to cease 'until a decree shall be made by me' (Ezra iv. 21).

The Work of Nehemiah, 445–433 BC

Nehemiah was a Jew who held the office of cup-bearer to Artaxerxes I at Shushan, the winter residence of the Persian kings. From his brother Hanani and other Jews, who had come from Jerusalem, he learnt of the ruined state of the city and the miserable condition of the people who had escaped the second deportation. It seems that there had been some attempt to rebuild the walls and gates of the city and that they had been broken down and burnt (Neh. i. 1–3). Nehemiah was greatly distressed by the wretched state of the Jews in Judah, and asked the king for permission to return for the purpose of rebuilding the walls. Artaxerxes complied with his request, and granted him leave of absence for a set period, passports for the journey, a letter to Asaph, the keeper of the king's forest, to provide him with the timber necessary for the projected work, and an armed escort (Neh. ii. 6–9).

On his arrival at Jerusalem he surveyed the ruined walls by night, called the leaders of the people together and urged them to begin the work of restoration at once. They took up the project with alacrity, saying, 'Let us rise up and build' (Neh. ii. 11–18). The opposition was led by Sanballat, the Horonite, with the support of Tobiah the Ammonite and Geshem the Arabian, and took the form of mockery and of representing the work as rebellion against the king (Neh. ii. 19–20). However, obstacles were overcome and the walls were built in fifty-two days (Neh. vi. 15), but according to Josephus the work took two years and four months. Nehemiah entrusted the government of Jerusalem to his brother, Hanani, and Hananiah, the governor of the castle (Neh. vii. 1–3), and initiated a scheme for increasing the population of the city (vii. 4, 5; xi. 1, 2).

Nehemiah was governor of Judah for twelve years, that is, from 445–433 BC (Neh. v. 14). At the end of the period he returned to Persia and 'after certain days' paid a second visit to Jerusalem

(Neh. xiii. 6).[1] During his absence a number of abuses had developed. Eliashib the High Priest had allowed Tobiah the use of a room in the courts of the Temple; the Levites did not receive tithes and dues according to the Law, and were compelled to seek their livelihood in the fields; and the laws relating to the Sabbath were broken. Jews had married foreign wives, one of the sons of Joiada, the son of Eliashib, even marrying the daughter of Sanballat; many of the children of such marriages could not speak the language of their fathers. Nehemiah ejected Tobiah and his 'household stuff' and had the room cleansed ceremoniously (Neh. xiii. 4–9), insisted upon the payment of the lawful tithes and dues to the Levites (Neh. xiii. 10–14), vindicated the sanctity of the Sabbath by putting an end to trading on that day (Neh. xiii. 15–22) and banned foreign marriages for the future (Neh. xiii. 23–29).

In two directions Nehemiah's work had far-reaching results. It was through his insistence upon the payment of tithes and dues that the priests became the wealthiest class in the community and in time secured the political power in the state. His prohibition of mixed marriages not only helped to preserve the identity of the nation and the purity of the true religion, but also contributed to the growth of the narrow and exclusive spirit which characterized the Jews, although the nobler view also found expression as may be seen in the book of Jonah.

The Work of Ezra, 397 BC

It has been generally assumed that Ezra preceded Nehemiah, on the ground that the date of Ezra's coming to Jerusalem is given as the seventh year of Artaxerxes (Ezra vii. 7, 8), and that of Nehemiah as the twentieth year of Artaxerxes (Neh. ii. 1). The traditional order depends upon the assumption that in both cases the reference is to Artaxerxes I. But there are good reasons for believing that Ezra followed Nehemiah, that the latter came to Jerusalem in the twentieth year of Artaxerxes I (465–424 BC), that is, in 445 BC, and the former in the seventh year of Artaxerxes II (404–358 BC), that is, in 397 BC. The reasons for holding this view are as follows: (1) It would be extremely unlikely that there would be two leaders in such

---

[1] Some critics maintain that Nehemiah returned to Persia immediately after the completion of the walls. This theory gives an interval of twelve years between the visits of Nehemiah and affords ample time for the development of the abuses existing at his second visit. But Nehemiah states that he was governor from the twentieth to the thirty-second year of Artaxerxes.

a small community. (2) In Ezra ix. 9 reference is made to a wall protecting Jerusalem, which must be that which was constructed by Nehemiah. (3) Though Ezra and Nehemiah are represented as co-operating with each other, they took independent action in the matter of mixed marriages. Nehemiah only prohibited intermarriage with heathen women in the future (Neh. xiii. 23–29), whereas Ezra insisted upon the dissolution of those marriages which had already been contracted (Ezra x. 3). It is probable that the harsher policy is the later. (4) From Ezra x. 6 we learn that Jehohanan, 'the son of Eliashib' ('son' here means 'grandson' as in Gen. xxix. 5) was a contemporary of Ezra. But this Jehohanan is identical with Jonathan, the grandson of Eliashib (Neh. xii. 22, 23), who was a contemporary of Nehemiah (Neh. xiii. 4, 7, 28). According to the Elephantine Papyri (see p. 56) Jehohanan was High Priest in 408 BC.

Ezra was a Jewish priest who lived in Babylon, probably in the days of Artaxerxes II.[1] He is described as 'a ready scribe in the law of Moses' (Ezra vii. 6) and as one who had set his heart upon studying the Law, obeying it and teaching it in Israel (Ezra vii. 10). In the seventh year of the reign of Artaxerxes he was sent on a mission to Jerusalem to inquire into the condition of the community in regard to its religious affairs (Ezra vii. 14), and to appoint magistrates and judges to all the people west of the Euphrates (Ezra vii. 25). According to the biblical records the king issued a decree which gave Ezra an immense treasure, and almost unlimited powers over the royal exchequer and the political administration of the country west of the Euphrates (Ezra vii. 12–26). This decree is suspect because of its Jewish colouring; it is extremely unlikely that a Persian king should confer such wide powers upon a Jewish exile. A decree was doubtless issued to provide for the better government of Judah, but in its present form it reflects the attitude of the author of the book. Ezra makes no use of these wide powers and appears as purely a social and religious reformer.

On his arrival at Jerusalem, Ezra was distressed to learn of the marriage of many Jews with foreign women, and made public confession of the sin in the name of the people (Ezra viii. 32–ix. 15). It was agreed that a commission should be appointed to investigate the

---

[1] Some modern critics, notably Torrey (1910), Hölscher (1923) and Loisy (1933), maintain that Ezra is the creation of the Chronicler. It is, however, practically certain that he is a real historical character for Jewish traditions always had a core of truth in them.

actual condition of affairs and to see that all foreign wives were expelled (Ezra x). His great work, however, was the promulgation of the Law which he read and expounded at a great assembly of the people (Neh. viii. 1-12). This law is usually identified with the Priestly Code, or rather that part of it which had been formulated in Babylon. Later a covenant was made with Yahweh which was sealed by Nehemiah and other representatives of the people (Neh. ix. 38). By the terms of this covenant the people undertook not to contract mixed marriages, to observe the Sabbath, to remit debts in the seventh year, to pay annually a third of a shekel for the service of the Temple, to supply wood for the altar and to pay first fruits and tithes (Neh. x. 29-39). With this deliberate acceptance of the Law by the citizens of Jerusalem a new era was begun among the Jewish people. 'Henceforth they were to be the people of a Book, and not men attending upon the spoken word of the prophet. The prophet must decrease, while the scribe, the lawyer, the interpreter of a written law must increase.'[1]

Little is known of the history of the Jewish people from the time of Ezra until the advent of Alexander the Great. There seems to have been a revolt against Artaxerxes III, in which the Jews joined and which resulted in the deportation of a large number of them. It was probably during this period that the Samaritans built their temple on Mount Gerizim.[2] Archaeology has shown that in the fourth century BC the High Priests of Judah had the right to levy their own taxes for the maintenance of the Temple and to strike their own silver coins. Already they were strongly influenced by Greek culture 'which was soon to engulf the world and to usher in a new era, fraught with both evil and good'.[3]

THE JEWS IN THE GREEK PERIOD (331-63 BC)

The Struggle for Palestine

In 334 BC Alexander the Great invaded the Persian Empire. Crossing into Asia Minor, he met and routed the Persians on the River Granicus and eventually conquered the whole of Asia Minor. Con-

---

[1] E. R. Bevan, *Jerusalem under the High-Priests*, 1904, p. 9.
[2] John Hyrcanus destroyed the Samaritan temple on Mount Gerizim in 128 BC. According to Josephus it had been in existence for 200 years; and if this is correct we have a date which takes us back to about the middle of the fourth century BC.
[3] W. F. Albright, *The Biblical Period*, 1952, p. 55.

tinuing the struggle he defeated the army of Darius III at Issus (332 BC) and by 331 BC had conquered Syria, Phoenicia, Palestine and Egypt, where he founded Alexandria. He was now free to strike at the heart of the Persian Empire. Passing through Syria he crossed the Euphrates, defeated Darius at Gaugamela, near Nineveh, and marched on Babylon which opened its gates to him (331 BC). The conquest of the Persian Empire was now complete. With its overthrow Palestine came under Greek rule.

On the death of Alexander the Great in 323 BC, his vast empire collapsed. Three kingdoms gradually emerged, two of which are connected with the Jews, namely, the Ptolemaic kingdom, founded by Ptolemy Soter (323–283 BC), which included Egypt and Palestine, and the Seleucid kingdom, founded by Seleucus Nicator (312–280 BC), which embraced Asia Minor, Syria and Babylon. The founders of these two kingdoms and their successors were missionaries of Greek culture. The Ptolemaic kings all bore the name of Ptolemy while the Seleucid kings were named either Seleucus or Antiochus. There was constant strife between the two royal houses, the chief bone of contention being Palestine, or Coele-Syria, as the Persians called it. The final struggle for its possession took place in the reign of Antiochus III (223–187 BC). Shortly after his accession to the throne he invaded Palestine but achieved little success; in 217 BC he met with a crushing defeat near Raphia in Southern Palestine and was compelled to give up the idea of conquest. For several years he was engaged elsewhere, but the death of Ptolemy IV (221–203 BC) and the accession of his son Ptolemy V (203–181 BC), who was a minor, presented him with an opportunity which he was quick to seize. He routed the Egyptians at Panion (198 BC) and the whole of Palestine fell into his hands. In passing through his newly conquered territories, he entered Jerusalem where he was received with open arms, for the Jews had found the Ptolemaic rule burdensome and fondly imagined that the rule of the Seleucids would be more bearable.

Internal Strife in the Jewish State

At the close of the second century BC the Jewish state was torn by dissensions. One cause of trouble was the High Priesthood. It would appear that in the Persian period the High Priest had been responsible for the payment of the imperial taxes. But according to Josephus, the High Priest, Onias II, who held office in the reign of Ptolemy IV, refused to pay the taxes, whereupon a certain Joseph of the house of Tobias contrived to get himself appointed to the position of tax-farmer for the whole of Palestine. This naturally caused great bitterness between the two rival houses. Moreover there were two parties in the state. One party was that of the 'Hasidim' or 'pious ones' who were devoted to the Law and were opposed to all foreign influences. The other party was that of the 'Hellenizers' who welcomed and fostered Greek culture; they were men of wealth and position, the majority of them belonging to the priestly aristocracy. The house of Onias II was supported by the 'Hasidim' and that of Tobias by the 'Hellenizers'.

Antiochus III fell in battle in 187 BC and was succeeded by his son Seleucus IV (187–175 BC), who, at the instigation of a hellenistic Jew, ordered his chief minister, Heliodorus, to seize the Temple treasure. His failure to carry out the order is said to have been due to an apparition which checked him. Seleucus IV was murdered by Heliodorus in 175 BC and was eventually succeeded by his brother Antiochus IV (Epiphanes, 175–163 BC).

The Maccabaean Period

By this time there was great unrest among the Jews. Trouble arose over the appointment of the High Priest. To Antiochus the High Priest was merely a local governor whose appointment was in his hands as head of the state; but to the Jews he was the direct representative of Yahweh and could not be appointed by any ruler. While the High Priest Onias III was absent from Jerusalem, his brother Jason secured the position by offering Antiochus a bribe. Three years later the king deposed him and appointed in his place Menelaus, who offered a still larger bribe. Passions were roused when Lysimachus, the brother of Menelaus, stole the holy vessels of the Temple; and when Menelaus contrived to murder Onias, Jason, who had fled to Ammonite territory, returned to Jerusalem and drove him out. Antiochus regarded the expulsion of Menelaus as an act of rebellion and at once took action. He plundered the Temple, slaughtered the people and reinstated Menelaus in the High Priesthood.

The Jews continued to refuse to acknowledge Menelaus and Antiochus determined to stamp out Judaism. The observance of the Sabbath, the practice of the rite of circumcision, the offering of sacrifices, the keeping of the feasts, and the possession of the

Scriptures were forbidden on pain of death. Heathen altars were commanded to be set up throughout the land on which swine's flesh was to be offered; an idol of Zeus was placed in the Temple and a Syrian garrison established in the city (167 BC).

Rebellion broke out at Modein, a village near Lydda, where a priest named Mattathias not only refused to obey the command, but also slew an apostate Jew, who was in the act of offering a heathen sacrifice, together with the King's officer who was in charge. Raising the standard of revolt, he fled to the hills and called upon all loyal Jews to join him. On the death of Mattathias his place as leader of the rebels was taken by his third son Judas, who defeated the royal forces, took Jerusalem, with the exception of the citadel, and cleansed and rededicated the Temple to the service of Yahweh, amid the frantic joy of the people (164 BC). The object of the revolt, namely, religious freedom, had thus been obtained, but Judas desired political freedom as well. Accordingly he continued the struggle, defeated the Syrian forces at Adasa, but was himself defeated and killed at Elasa (160 BC).

The leadership of the Jewish people was now assumed by Judas's brother Jonathan, who was allowed to establish himself at Michmash (158 BC). In 152 BC Jerusalem, with the exception of the citadel, was placed in his hands and he was allowed to assume the High Priesthood. He extended his territory, secured the abolition of the payment of tribute to the Syrian court, but failed to eject the Syrian garrison from the citadel of Jerusalem. In 142 BC he was trapped and murdered by Tryphon, a Syrian general.

Jonathan's brother, Simon, now succeeded to the leadership and to the High Priesthood. He consolidated his position by strengthening the strongholds in Judaea and by capturing the citadel of Jerusalem. In a great assembly of the nation he was proclaimed High Priest and civil and military governor for ever, 'until there should arise a faithful prophet' (1 Macc. xiv. 41). Under him the political independence of the Jews was practically achieved.

Simon was succeeded by his son John Hyrcanus (134–104 BC) who embarked upon a career of conquest. He occupied territory east of the Jordan, overran Samaria and destroyed the Samaritan temple on Mount Gerizim; but his most notable achievement was his conquest of the Idumaeans (the Edomites) whom he compelled to adopt the Jewish faith and become members of the Jewish community. It was during his reign that the two main sections of the Jewish people crystallized into the parties of the Pharisees and the Sadducees. It is probable that Hyrcanus was the first to assume the title of 'King'.[1]

John Hyrcanus was succeeded by his son Aristobulus (104–103 BC), who in his short reign of one year conquered Galilee and compelled the inhabitants to accept Judaism. He was so much the lover of Hellenism that he was given the title of 'Philhelline', lover of all things Greek. On his death he was succeeded by his brother, Alexander Jannaeus (103–76 BC), who continued the policy of his predecessors, so that he eventually ruled over almost the whole of the country from Dan to Beersheba. He was not, however, destined to enjoy peace, for his ambitions and his character roused opposition, especially among the Pharisees, and civil war broke out. In their extremity the Pharisees called in the help of their ancestral enemies, the Syrians, and Alexander was forced to take refuge in the hills. The sight of their own king in flight before their ancestral enemies caused a revulsion of feeling among the people and they rallied to his support. The Syrians were expelled and Alexander returned in triumph. When he died he left behind his widow, Alexandra, and two sons, Hyrcanus and Aristobulus. Alexandra herself became Queen (76–67 BC) and Hyrcanus High Priest. She made peace with the Pharisees and gave them the dominant place in the counsels of the nation, but they used their power to persecute their Sadducaean opponents. Upon her death she should have been succeeded by Hyrcanus as elder son, but his brother Aristobulus forced him to give up both the kingship and the High Priesthood. Antipater, governor of Idumaea, now persuaded Hyrcanus to make a bid for power and to call in the help of the Nabataean Arabs. They invaded Judaea and Aristobulus was shut up in Jerusalem. The civil war led to the intervention of Rome. The two brothers appealed to Pompey, who had established the province of Syria, to arbitrate between them. Pompey delayed in giving his decision and Aristobulus, growing restless, prepared to act on his own, whereupon the former marched against Jerusalem and captured the city in 63 BC. The kingship was abolished, and Judaea was incorporated in the province

[1] Josephus probably concealed the fact that Hyrcanus was the first Hasmonaean king, ascribing this assumption to Hyrcanus' son and successor, Aristobulus. There are traces that Josephus was concealing the true fact, probably because he had painted Hyrcanus in glowing colours and wished to avoid what would have been a reflection on his hero. The Pharisees would resist his assumption of the kingship on the ground that he was not of the lineage of David.

of Syria. Hyrcanus, who was a harmless creature, was maintained in the High Priesthood. With this settlement a new period in Jewish history begins.[1]

---

[1] It has been thought advisable to complete the history of the Greek period, though there is probably nothing in the prophetic books later than about the middle of the second century BC.

Archaeology and the Prophetic Period

INTRODUCTION

Archaeology as a distinct science with a special technique of its own has been in existence just over a hundred years, but during that time it has made rapid progress and achieved remarkable results. In its relation to that part of the Old Testament, known as the 'Latter Prophets', it deals chiefly with the remains of buildings, sculptures, inscriptions, pottery, papyri and domestic furniture in Mesopotamia and Palestine. The first difficulty to be overcome was the decipherment of the cuneiform writing of Mesopotamia. In 1835 Henry C. Rawlinson (afterwards knighted), having heard of an inscription on the face of a high rock overlooking a main road at Behistun in Western Persia, succeeded with extreme difficulty in taking a copy of it. It is carved in three languages—Persian, Elamite and Babylonian—and records the victories of Darius I (522–486 BC) over his rebellious satraps. The decipherment of the inscription by Rawlinson in 1847 enabled modern historians to recover the lost language and history of Babylonia and Assyria. It provided the key to all the cuneiform tablets subsequently discovered, thus doing for Babylonia and Assyria what the Rosetta Stone did for Egypt.[1]

[1] The Rosetta Stone was discovered in 1799 by a Frenchman while he was engaged in improving a fort at Rosetta near Alexandria. On the capitulation of Egypt to the British in 1801 it was brought to England and deposited in the British Museum. It is a mutilated slab of black basalt bearing inscriptions in three different scripts—Greek, Egyptian hieroglyphics and demotic, that is, the Egyptian cursive writing used for ordinary purposes. It was at once inferred that the three inscriptions were different forms of the same text. The Greek text was easily deciphered and proved to be a decree drawn up by the priests of Memphis in honour of Ptolemy V (196 BC). A Frenchman, Jean François Champollion, succeeded in deciphering the whole of the inscription by 1822, thus providing the key to the translation of the Egyptian hieroglyphics. The discovery of the Rosetta Stone was an epoch-making event in archaeological research, since it meant that for the first time the ancient Egyptian language could be understood. We now have an extensive knowledge of the political and economic conditions of ancient Egypt and of its art, literature and religion.

ISRAEL AND JUDAH, 800–722 BC

Excavations carried out at Samaria in 1908–11 unearthed a large number of potsherds inscribed in ink in Hebrew characters and belonging, it is thought, to the early years of the eighth century BC. They consist of consignment notes, recording the quantities of wine and oil dispatched from different districts, presumably to the royal steward, and provide some useful information concerning the economic and religious conditions of the kingdom of Israel. Apparently for taxation purposes the old tribal divisions were ignored and taxes were paid in wine and oil. Some of the potsherds bear names compounded with 'Baal', such as Ahibaal, and names compounded with Yahweh, such as Abedyah and Gaddiyah. These names reflect the struggles of the times between Baalism and Yahwism. The potsherds are also important, because they give us an exact idea of the script employed by the Israelites in the early eighth century BC.

In 1932 many ivories were discovered at Samaria belonging to the ninth and eighth centuries BC. Many of these ivories are of good workmanship, being embellished with gold-leaf and enamel or with lapis lazuli and coloured glass. Most of them show a strong Egyptian influence and were manufactured in Phoenicia, while others are more akin to North Syrian work and were manufactured in the region of Damascus. Some of these ivories were used as inlay to decorate expensive furniture. The prophet Amos denounced those who lived in 'houses of ivory' (Am. iii. 15) and lay upon 'beds of ivory' (Am. vi. 4). Obviously houses could not have been made of ivory; hence the term 'ivory houses' and 'ivory beds' indicate houses and beds decorated with ivory inlay.

Excavations on the site of Megiddo in 1907–9 revealed many interesting objects, including the seal of Shema, 'the servant of Jeroboam', probably Jeroboam II.

The prophets Amos and Hosea both bear witness to the prosperity of Israel in the reign of Jeroboam II (786–746 BC). Amos describes the luxurious life of the wealthy classes and their unscrupulous oppression of the poor. They lay upon beds of ivory, stretched themselves on their couches, ate lambs out of the flock and stall-fed calves, sang idle songs to the sound of the viol, drank wine and anointed themselves with unguents (Am. vi. 1–6). There is nothing in the biblical account of Jeroboam II's reign to account for the sudden and unexampled prosperity, but a study of the Assyrian annals shows that it was due to the exhaustion of Israel's old enemy Syria and to the decline of Assyria. Jeroboam was able to take advantage of the weakness of both countries to extend his dominions, foster trade and commerce and accumulate wealth.

In his description of the 'day of Yahweh' Amos declared, 'And it shall come to pass in that day, saith the Lord God, that I will cause the sun to go down at noon, and I will darken the earth in the clear day' (Am. viii. 9). The prophet may have been using figurative language, but it is thought by many critics that he had in mind an eclipse of the sun, which according to the Assyrian annals occurred in June 763 BC.

In 2 Kings xv. 19 it is stated that 'there came against the land Pul the king of Assyria; and Menahem gave Pul a thousand talents of silver, that his hand might be with him to confirm the kingdom in his hand'. The campaign referred to in this verse is evidently that described in the Assyrian annals of the year 738 BC in which we are told that in the course of his campaign Tiglath-pileser overthrew a Syrian confederacy which had been formed against him, and that among those who were compelled to pay tribute were 'Azariah of Yaudi' and Menahem of Samaria. Azariah has been identified by some critics with Azariah of Judah. If, however, our chronology is correct, Azariah had died about 742 BC and therefore the identification is impossible; but in any case it is unlikely that he could have gained the ascendancy over the Syrian states. It is more likely, as many critics have suggested, that 'Yaudi' denotes a state in Syria which has nothing to do with Judah.

Brief references are made in the biblical narratives to Tiglath-pileser's campaign against Israel and Syria in the Syro-Ephraimitic War (734 BC). In the biblical account of his campaign against Israel we read that he took Ijon, Abel-beth-maacah, Janoah, Kedesh, Hazor, Gilead, Galilee and Naphtali, and deported the inhabitants to Assyria (2 Kgs. xv. 29). Excavations carried out at Hazor in 1955 provided sufficient evidence to prove that the city was destroyed towards the close of the eighth century BC, presumably by Tiglath-pileser. A thick layer of ash covered all the rooms, and several things suggested that the city was abandoned in a hurry. Much of the pottery was still intact and one cooking pot was still on an oven. In the biblical account of his campaign against Syria we are told that he captured Damascus, deported its inhabitants, and slew Rezin, its king (2 Kgs. xvi. 9). An account of these two campaigns also appears in the Assyrian annals but additional information is supplied. We are told that Tiglath-pileser deported all the inhabitants of 'the land of Omri' (evidently an exaggeration), established Hoshea as king over them and compelled him to pay tribute, hanged the nobles of Rezin, king of Damascus, cut down his gardens and plantations, not one escaping, and destroyed sixteen districts of Syria so that they looked like 'mounds left by a flood'.

In 724 BC Hoshea revolted, probably relying upon promises of support from So, king of Egypt (2 Kgs. xvii. 4). This King So is generally identified with 'Sibe' or 'Sibu', who appears in the Assyrian inscriptions as the 'tartan' or commander-in-chief of the Egyptian forces who were defeated at Raphia in 720 BC. Many critics, however, reject the further identification with the Pharaoh Shabaka, on the ground that since he was commander-in-chief in 720 BC he could not have been king at the time of Hoshea's revolt. Still, it is probable that he is to be identified with Shabaka, and that for several years he was regent and commander-in-chief in Lower Egypt before he eventually succeeded his father Piankhi on the throne.

Shalmaneser V, who had succeeded Tiglath-pileser in 727 BC, deposed Hoshea and besieged Samaria. The biblical narrative suggests that Shalmaneser carried the siege to a successful conclusion (2 Kgs. xvii. 1–6), but the Assyrian record of the event makes it clear that the city was finally captured by his successor Sargon II (722–705 BC). According to the biblical account 'Israel was carried away out of their own land to Assyria' (2 Kgs. xvii. 23); but later history shows that all the inhabitants of the kingdom could not have been deported (cf. 2 Chron. xxx. 1–6). This is confirmed by Sargon, who in his annals says that he besieged Samaria and carried away 27,290 of its inhabitants. This number no doubt included the majority of the people of the city, but the people of the country districts would be left to cultivate the land.

JUDAH, 722–587 BC

An Assyrian inscription records that in 720 BC a revolt broke out in which Hamath and Damascus, under a certain Yaubidi, Hanno of Gaza, together with the Philistines, and Samaria took part, with the support of Egypt. The revolt was suppressed, Yaubidi being defeated at Karkar, and the Philistines and Egyptians under the leadership of Hanno and the tartan Sibe (or Sibu) respectively at Raphia. No mention is made of the fate which befell Samaria. There is no reference to this revolt in the biblical records.

The Assyrian annals relating to the year 711 BC tell of a revolt of Azuri, king of Ashdod, and of his efforts to obtain the aid of the kings of Philistia, Judah, Edom and Moab. 'To Pharaoh king of Egypt, a prince who could not save them, they sent presents . . . to gain him as an ally.' Sargon deposed Azuri and appointed Ahimaty his brother to be king in his stead. But the people rose against him and placed a certain Yavani on the throne, whereupon Sargon dispatched an expedition under his tartan or commander-in-chief. Ashdod was captured and Philistia became an Assyrian province. Hezekiah seems to have been involved in the revolt, for Sargon in one inscription claims to have subdued Judah. An allusion to the Assyrian punitive expedition against Ashdod is found in Isaiah xx. 1.

In the biblical record references are made to Shebna, the palace-governor of Hezekiah, who was denounced by Isaiah for building a splendid tomb (Is. xxii. 15, 16). He was apparently superseded by Eliakim before Sennacherib's invasion and given the lower office of scribe or secretary (Is. xxxvi. 3, xxxvii. 2). An inscription discovered at Siloam in 1870 has recently been deciphered as that of a royal steward. It has been suggested that the tomb from which the inscription was removed may be that of Shebna.

On the death of Sargon in 705 BC his successor, Sennacherib, was faced with widespread revolt. Among the rebels in the west was Hezekiah, who, probably relying upon the support of Egypt, prepared to throw off the Assyrian yoke. In order to withstand the Assyrian attack, which he realized would follow his refusal to pay tribute (2 Kgs. xviii. 7), he strengthened the fortifications of Jerusalem (2 Chron. xxxii. 5) and secured its water supply by bringing the waters of the Virgin's Spring in the Kidron valley through an underground tunnel, into the Pool of Siloam (2 Kgs. xx. 20; cf. 2 Chron. xxxii. 30). In 1880 an inscription in Phoenician or early Hebrew characters was accidentally discovered on a wall of a rock-hewn tunnel which runs a winding course of 586 yards from the Virgin's Spring to the Pool of Siloam. No names are mentioned on the inscription, but it records how the tunnel was cut from both ends until the workers met, 'and the waters flowed from the spring to the pool for a distance of 1,200 cubits, and 100 cubits was the height of the rock over the heads of the excavators'. It is reasonable to suppose that the inscription and the biblical account refer to the same operation.

The famous Taylor Prism or hexagonal cylinder, discovered at Nineveh, and now in the British Museum, gives a vivid account of Sennacherib's campaign against Judah in 701 BC supplementing the biblical narrative found in 2 Kings xviii. 13–xix. 37. Luli (Elulaios) of Zidon had apparently gained control over the whole of Phoenicia, the people of Ashkelon had deposed Sharruludari, son of Rukipti, and made Sidka king in his place, and in Ekron the king, Padi, had been similarly deposed and sent to Jerusalem in chains. Sennacherib drove out Luli, forcing him to take refuge in Cyprus, and made Ethbaal king of Zidon in his place, took Ashkelon, sent the new king Sidka a prisoner to Babylon and restored his predecessor, routed an Egyptian and Ethiopian force at Eltekeh, captured Ekron, and restored to the throne Padi who seems to have been handed over by Hezekiah. Then he devastated Judah, captured forty-six walled cities and 200,150 persons, and shut up Hezekiah 'like a caged bird' in Jerusalem, his royal city. One of the last cities to be captured was Lachish. The siege was specially commemorated in bas-reliefs (now in the British Museum) on the walls of Sennacherib's palace at Nineveh. One bas-relief shows Sennacherib seated on a hill outside the town, with officers, attendants and soldiers about him, and captives from the town brought before him. The text attached to the scene reads, 'Sennacherib, king of hosts, king of Assyria, sat upon his throne of state, and the spoil of the city of Lachish passed before him.' Recognizing the futility of continuing the struggle Hezekiah submitted and was compelled to pay a heavy fine, though no mention is made of the capture of the city.

The biblical narrative tells us that Sennacherib returned to Nineveh where he was slain by Adrammelech and Sharezer as he was worshipping 'in the house of Nisroch his god' (2 Kgs. xix. 37). A chronicle tablet records the fact that Sennacherib was assassinated by his son on a certain day in the twenty-third year of his reign, but no name is given. According to an inscription of Esarhaddon, discovered at Nineveh in 1927–8, the brothers of Esarhaddon plotted against him after his father had chosen him as his successor and he went into hiding. After a time he marched against 'those scoundrels', compelled them to flee 'to an unknown land' and established himself on the throne. Thompson, however, suggests that Esarhaddon instigated the murder of Sennacherib and that he was compelled to withdraw from public life because popular opinion was against him.[1] The Rassam cylinder of Ashurbanipal records that after a revolt Ashurbanipal cut down the people who had cut down Sennacherib, 'the father of my father, my begetter', as an offering.

There is no confirmation in the Assyrian inscriptions of Manasseh's capture and imprisonment in Babylon as recorded in the book of 2 Chronicles xxxiii. 10–13, though not in that of 2 Kings. An Assyrian inscription, however, mentions the fact that he was among the kings whom Esarhaddon summoned to Nineveh. It is possible, therefore, that he had been engaged in some rebellion against Assyria. Hall, however, suggests that his captivity took place in the reign of Ashurbanipal. He has little doubt that the account in the book of 2 Chronicles is a piece of genuine history, 'and that in his old age Manasseh was moved in chains to Babylon, no doubt to answer for a real or suspected participation in the schemes of Shamash-shum-ukin'.[2] (See p. 23.)

Until recently it was generally supposed that the fall of Nineveh took place in 606 BC. But in 1923 Gadd deciphered a tablet, covering events which occurred between the years 616 and 609 BC and affording first-hand information concerning the fall of Nineveh and the Assyrian empire. It showed that Nineveh fell to the Medes and Babylonians not in 606 BC, as previously believed, but in 612 BC, though the empire continued the struggle for existence some years longer. After the fall of the capital the remnant of the Assyrian forces fled to Harran where a certain 'tartan', Ashur-uballit, assumed the crown, but they were driven out of the city by the Medes and the Babylonians in 610 BC. The following year the Assyrians, supported by an Egyptian, force, tried to recover Harran. The tablet breaks off at the point where Nabopolassar is marching to the relief of the beleaguered garrison. It would appear that he defeated the combined Assyrian and Egyptian forces and drove them back across the Euphrates. Now according to 2 Kings xxiii. 29, 'Pharaoh-necoh king of Egypt went up against the king of Assyria to the river Euphrates: and king Josiah went against him; and he slew him at Megiddo, when he had seen him'; Until the publication of the tablet by Gadd it was generally assumed that the Egyptian king was taking advantage of the weakness of Assyria to gain territory. It is clear, however, that he was going to the assistance of the king of Assyria,

[1] R. C. Thompson, *The Prisms of Esarhaddon and of Ashurbanipal*, 1931, pp. 7 ff.

[2] H. R. Hall, *The Ancient History of the Near East*, 9th edition, 1936, p. 508.

doubtless because he feared the growing power of the Medes and the Babylonians. Josiah, who by this time was practically independent, had no desire to come once more under the control of Assyria, tried to stop the Egyptians joining forces with the Assyrians and lost his life in the attempt. It is significant that Josephus tells us that Pharaoh-necho went 'to fight against the Medes and the Babylonians' (Antiquities x. 5.1). In the biblical record the ambiguous Hebrew preposition has been mistranslated and we should read that Pharaoh-necho was marching 'to the help of' Assyria.

The Lachish Letters discovered in 1935 and 1938 by J. L. Starkey in the ruined guard-room of Lachish (Tell-ed-Duweir) in the course of his excavations there, shed some light upon the closing years of the kingdom of Judah. The letters consist of twenty-one inscribed potsherds, a few giving lists of names or business records, and the remainder messages addressed to the governor of the city by a commander of a neighbouring fort a short time before the capture of Jerusalem by Nebuchadrezzar in 587 BC. The biblical narrative tells us how 'the king of Babylon's army fought against Jerusalem, and against all the cities of Judah that were left, against Lachish and against Azekah; for these alone remained of the cities of Judah as fenced cities' (Jer. xxxiv. 7). In one of the letters the writer is watching for the fire-signals from Lachish while those from Azekah have apparently ceased. Several names mentioned in the letters appear in the book of Jeremiah, namely, those of Gemariah (xxix. 3, xxxvi. 10), Jaazaniah (xxxv. 3), Neriah (li, 59) and Elnathan xxxvi. 12). Nedabiah, a son of Jehoiachin (1 Chron. iii. 18) is also mentioned. In one letter references are made to a prophet, but only the last three letters of the name have survived. This prophet has been identified with Uriah, who was slain by Jehoiakim (Jer. xxvi. 20–23), and with Jeremiah, but these identifications are not generally accepted.[1]

The letters are important as being the first Hebrew literary remains of any length which have survived from the pre-exilic period, and as showing the nature of the Hebrew script and language at the beginning of the sixth century BC. Historically they give us a glimpse of life in a guard-room in the last days of the Judaean monarchy and thus help to fill in the background of the biblical narrative.

In the biblical account of the fall of Jerusalem it is stated that a breach was made in the walls, 'and all the men of war fled by night

[1] H. Torczyner, *The Lachish Letters*, 1938.

by way of the gate between the two walls, which was by the king's garden' (2 Kgs. xxv. 4). Excavations show that there were two walls, an inner and an outer, about thirty feet apart. Duncan suggests that the soldiers escaped down the passage between the two walls, and out by the fountain gate beside the Pool of Siloam which opened on to the king's garden.[1]

It has often been assumed that after the destruction of Jerusalem in 587 BC only a comparatively few of the inhabitants were deported to Babylon, and that the natives soon emerged from their hiding places and rebuilt their ruined homes. Archaeology, however, provides an overwhelming mass of evidence for the total devastation of Judah in the Babylonian invasion. 'The results,' says Albright, 'are uniform and conclusive; many towns were destroyed at the beginning of the sixth century BC and never again occupied; others were destroyed at that time and partly reoccupied at some later date; still others were destroyed and reoccupied after a long period of abandonment. . . . There is not a single known case where a town of Judah proper was continuously occupied through the exilic period.'[2]

THE EXILE AND RETURN, 587–538 BC

Archaeology sheds some light upon the exile and return of those who were deported to Babylon after the fall of Jerusalem in 587 BC. The biblical narratives tell us that Evil-merodach, the successor of Nebuchadrezzar, released Jehoiachin king of Judah and gave him a fixed allowance as long as he lived (2 Kgs. xxv. 27–30). In some of the Babylonian tablets containing the names of persons to whom fixed allowances of grain and oil were made by the court, occurs the name of 'Yaukin, king of the land of Yahud'.[3]

The Babylonian exile came to an end with the conquest of Babylon by Cyrus king of Persia in 539 BC. According to 2 Chronicles xxxvi. 23 and Ezra i. 2, 3, Cyrus in the first year of his reign issued a decree in which he claimed that Yahweh, 'the God of heaven' had given him all the kingdoms of the earth and had commanded him to

---

[1] J. G. Duncan, *Digging Up Biblical History*, 1931, Vol. 1, pp. 206 ff.

[2] W. F. Albright, *The Archaeology of Palestine*, 1949, pp. 141 ff.

[3] After the fall of Jerusalem in 587 BC a few Jews, including Jeremiah, sought refuge in Egypt, settling at Tahpanhes, a fortified town on the north-east border of Egypt where the road crosses the frontier. Here in 1908 Petrie discovered the remains of Pharaoh's house, mentioned in the book of Jeremiah (Jer. xliii. 8, 9).

rebuild the Temple at Jerusalem. This claim is strange when we remember that Cyrus was not a worshipper of Yahweh, and that the Jews were not the only people who had been deported to Babylonia. But archaeology provides us with a clue to the solution of the problem.

Cyrus in his famous cylinder, discovered by Rassam, gives an account of the events leading up to and culminating in the capture of Babylon, and of his general policy towards the people whom he had conquered.

'He (the god Marduk) sought out a righteous prince, a man after his own heart, whom he might take by the hand; and he called his name Cyrus, king of Anshan, and he proclaimed his name for sovereignty over the whole world. . . . He commanded him to go to Babylon, and he caused him to set out on the road to that city, and like a friend and ally he marched by his side; and his troops, with their weapons girt about them, marched with him in countless numbers, like the waters of a flood. Without battle and without fighting Marduk made him enter into his city of Babylon; he spared Babylonian tribulation, and Nabonidus, who feared him not, he delivered into his hand.'[1]

Now Nabonidus, the last king of Babylonia and father of Belshazaar, gathered into Babylon the images of the gods of all the cities of his empire, thus causing offence not only to the peoples who had been deprived of their gods, but also to the priests of Babylon who felt that their god Marduk was being insulted by the introduction of the inferior local deities. The discontent roused by the policy of Nabonidus contributed in no small degree to the success of Cyrus's campaign against Babylon. After his capture of the city Cyrus at once reversed the policy of his predecessor. He describes on his cylinder how he returned the gods to their places, collected and restored the deported peoples to their homes, and made the gods of Sumer and Akkad, whom Nabonidus 'to the anger of the lord of the gods had brought into Babylon', dwell in peace in their own shrines, 'in habitations dear to their heart'. He expresses the wish that all the gods whom he restored may pray daily before Bel and Nebo for a long life for him and that they may speak a gracious word for him. Among the gods restored to their shrines was the moon-god of Ur On a broken cylinder found there Cyrus says, 'Sin (the moon-god) the illuminator of heaven and earth, with his favourable sign deli-

[1] *Guide to the Babylonian and Assyrian Antiquities*, British Museum, 1922, p. 144.

vered into my hands the four quarters of the world, and I returned the gods to their shrines.'

It is obvious that Cyrus's concession to the Jews was not a mark of special favour, but part of his policy of conciliation towards subject peoples. The Jewish colouring of the edict of Cyrus, found in 2 Chronicles xxxvi. 23 and Ezra i. 2, 3, is doubtless due to the compiler of the books who wished to show that Yahweh used Cyrus to bring about the return of the Jewish exiles to their native land.

THE PERSIAN PERIOD, 539–331 BC

The Jews in Egypt

In the early years of the present century a number of Aramaic papyri were discovered at Elephantine or Yeb, an island in the Nile, near the first cataract, about 400 miles south of Cairo. These papyri cover the whole of the fifth century BC and are mostly dated both by the Jewish month and the Egyptian month, allowing us to arrive at the year in which each was written with a certain degree of assurance. They are mostly domestic, business and legal documents, belonging to members of a Jewish colony in Elephantine, but among them are copies of letters despatched to the authorities in Palestine.

These documents shed considerable light upon the social and religious life of the small Jewish community. From them it is clear that the frontier fortress of Elephantine had been occupied by Jewish mercenary troops 'since the days of the kings of Egypt' (i.e. the native kings before the Persian conquest). They had their own temple with its priesthood and ritual, which was in existence when Cambyses invaded Egypt in 525 BC, but they were not monotheists in the strict sense of the term since along with Yahweh they worshipped at least three subordinate deities, Anath-bethel, Asham-bethel and Haram-bethel. Apparently they knew nothing of the Deuteronomic Code which centralized all sacrificial worship in one place (Deut. xii. 1–14). Snaith calls their worship 'stark polytheism'[1] while Albright maintains that what appear to be separate deities are 'hypostatized aspects of Yahweh'.[2]

In 410 BC their temple was destroyed by an Egyptian mob organized by a certain Waidrang, who took advantage of the temporary absence of the Persian governor Arsames, whereupon the priest

[1] Article on 'The Religion of Israel' in *Record and Revelation*, 1938, p. 257.
[2] W. F. Albright, *Archaeology and the Religion of Israel*, 1942, pp. 168–74.

Jedoniah and his colleagues wrote to Bagoas, known to us from Josephus (Ant. xi. 7, 8) and to the High Priest Johanan, whom we meet in the book of Nehemiah (xii. 22), asking for permission to rebuild it, but they received no answer to their letter. Two years later they wrote again to Bagoas, at the same time informing him that they had reported the whole matter to Delaiah and Shelemiah, the sons of Sanballat, the governor of Samaria. In the biblical narrative Sanballat was the opponent of Nehemiah, but we are not told that he was the governor of Samaria. The authorities of Judah and Samaria gave their consent verbally to an envoy, who apparently drew up a memorandum of the interview, which has survived. It reads, 'They said to me, Let it be an instruction to you in Egypt to say to Arsames about the altar-house of the God of Heaven, which was built in the fortress of Yeb formerly before Cambyses, which Waidrang, that reprobate, destroyed in the fourteenth year of Darius the king, to rebuild it on its place as it was before, and they may offer the meal offering and incense upon that altar as formerly was done.'

An earlier papyrus (419 BC) contains a Persian order for the observance of the Feast of Unleavened Bread. It is unlikely that the Persian kings took much interest in the details of Jewish ritual; no doubt they merely published a decree embodying the wishes of the Jewish leaders.

The Jews in Babylon

At the beginning of the present century several hundreds of tablets were unearthed at Nippur, which proved to be the records of the banking firm of Murashu and Sons which flourished in the reigns of Artaxerxes I (465–424 BC) and Darius II (423–404 BC). Among the clients of the firm were many with Jewish names, showing that in the fifth century BC the descendants of the Jewish exiles were allowed to engage in trade and to acquire wealth.

The Jews in Palestine

A few buildings of the Persian period have been excavated, but the only one of any importance is the villa on the mound of Lachish which dates from the late fifth or early fourth century BC. Many silver coins, struck in imitation of Attic coins, with the head and the owl of Athene, but with the Hebrew or Aramaic inscription 'Yehud' (Judah), and belonging to the fourth and perhaps the early third century, have been discovered. They prove that the Jews enjoyed a measure of self-government under the Persians, since the High-Priest had the right to levy taxes and strike silver coins for the up-keep of the Temple. The discovery of these coins, together with large quantities of Ionian and Attic black-figured pottery show that the Greek influence in Palestine was strong in the Persian period.

THE GREEK PERIOD, 331–63 BC

Archaeology has supplied us with little information concerning the life and religion of the Jews in the Greek period. Of the remains which have been unearthed the most important are the houses and painted tombs of Marisa, the tombs of Arag-el-Emir one of which bears the name of 'Tobiah', the descendant of Nehemiah's foe (Neh. ii. 10, 19, vi. 12, xiii. 4, 8), and the fortifications of Samaria, Beth-zur and Gezer. Numerous coins and Greek jar-handles have also been discovered at Samaria, Beth-zur and other places, showing the Greek influence in Palestine.

Until 1947 no Hebrew manuscript of the Old Testament (apart from a few fragments found in Egypt) existed earlier than the ninth century AD, nor was it thought possible that they could ever have survived in the moist climate of Palestine. But in 1947 some Bedouins, wandering near Ain Feshka at the northern end of the Dead Sea, accidentally discovered a cave in which they found a number of jars containing scrolls of leather and parchment. These scrolls were recovered and sold, four to the Syrian Orthodox Convent of St Mark in Jerusalem and the rest to the Hebrew University there. The date of the manuscripts is still in dispute. When first they became known they were assigned to the last two centuries BC, but now the majority of scholars prefer a date in the first century BC or AD. The most important of these documents are the following:

(1) a complete scroll (A) of Isaiah.

(2) a scroll (B) containing a portion of Isaiah. These two scrolls give us a text of Isaiah which is several centuries earlier than the Massoretic text, which was fixed by the Jewish Rabbis about the seventh century AD.

(3) the commentary on Habakkuk. This interprets the prophecies of Habakkuk in the light of contemporary events, and supports the critics who maintain that the third chapter of the book is a later addition.

(4) the 'Sectarian Manual of Discipline', describing the oath of initiation and the ritual of a sect called the 'Community of the New Covenant'.

(5) a collection of psalms called 'Songs of Praise' or 'Thanksgiving', written in a style closely resembling that of the Psalms and other poetic writings of the Old Testament.

(6) the book of the 'Wars of the Sons of Light against the Sons of Darkness', so called from the chief characters in it and the action in which they are engaged. The Sons of Light are defined as the tribes of Levi, Judah and Benjamin, and the Sons of Darkness as the Edomites, Moabites, Ammonites, Philistines and the Kittim of Asshur.

(7) fragments of Genesis, Leviticus, Deuteronomy, Judges, Daniel, Jubilees, etc., besides hitherto unknown works.

The discovery of these scrolls has led to further excavations. Many fragments of biblical and non-biblical texts have been found in the caves at Qumran, a little to the south of the caves at Ain Feshka. In one of the caves two rolled-up copper rolls have been brought to light. These have been successfully opened by cutting them into strips and their contents deciphered. They indicate the whereabouts of a good deal of hypothetical treasure. Discoveries have also been made at the Wadi Muraba'at, about twelve miles south of Qumran. There are letters written by Simon Bar Cochba, the leader of the revolt against the Romans in AD 135, and some Greek and Aramaic documents, and a few biblical texts, including the beginning of a third scroll of the book of Isaiah, belonging to the second century AD. None of the Muraba'at fragments seems to have any connection with the sect of the Qumran scrolls. From Khirbet Mird, about half-way between Qumran and the Muraba'at caves, have come some Old Testament fragments, a number of New Testament fragments in Greek, and some non-biblical fragments also in Greek. An unknown site has yielded some biblical fragments, including fragments of a Greek version of the Minor Prophets.

When all these newly-found fragments have been deciphered, they will exercise considerable influence upon the textual criticism of the Old Testament and shed light upon the background of Christianity.

CHAPTER IV

The Prophets

Meaning of 'Prophet'

The English word 'prophet' is derived from the Greek 'prophetes' which means, 'one who speaks for another', 'spokesman', 'interpreter'. It denotes one who reveals or interprets the will of a god. Ancient Hebrew had three words for prophet, namely, 'hōzeh', 'rō'eh', and 'nābī'. 'Hōzeh' and 'rō'eh' are probably synonymous terms and may be translated 'seer' or 'gazer'.

The seer was a man endowed with second sight, that is, he could become conscious of sights and sounds beyond the reach of ordinary people. Such a person was Samuel who assisted Saul to recover his lost asses and apparently took a small fee for his services (1 Sam. ix. 5–8). The origin of the term 'nābī'. which is that most frequently used for 'prophet', is obscure, but it is generally considered to be derived from an Akkadian root, meaning 'to call', 'to speak'. A prophet or 'nābī', therefore, is one who speaks in the name and with the authority of God (cf. Exod. iv. 15, 16, vii. 1). Albright, however, rejects this interpretation on the ground that the etymological meaning of the word is, 'one who is called', and that a 'nābī' is, therefore, 'one who is called by God to communicate the divine will'.[1]

The Difference Between Seer and Prophet

It is commonly supposed that the seer was originally distinct from the prophet. The seer, it is said, lived in isolation and was not subject to ecstatic experiences, gaining his supernatural knowledge by his skill in interpreting omens or by dreams and second sight. He waited to be consulted and gave his oracles calmly and with dignity. The prophet, on the other hand, was gregarious and subject to fits of ecstasy, claiming to deliver his oracles by divine revelation. It is

[1] W. F. Albright, *From the Stone Age to Christianity*, 1940, pp. 231 ff.

probable, however, that no hard and fast line can be drawn between the two. In 1 Samuel ix. 9, we find the statement, 'For he that is now called a Prophet was before time called a Seer'. This is generally taken to mean that in the course of time 'seer', whether 'hōzeh' or 'rō'eh', and 'nābī' became interchangeable. Rowley, however, suggests that the seer continued to be distinct from the prophet (nābī), but that 'a less precise age failed to distinguish them by name'.[1]

The Prophet's Call

The prophet, or rather the true prophet, did not become a prophet by his own volition, but felt that the call of Yahweh was irresistible. 'The lion hath roared, who will not fear? the Lord God hath spoken, who can but prophesy?' (Am. iii. 8). 'And if I say, I will not make mention of him, nor speak any more in his name, then there is in mine heart as it were a burning fire shut up in my bones' (Jer. xx. 9). Some wished to evade the call, feeling their own inadequacy for the task and knowing the opposition they would be likely to meet. Isaiah trembled before the vision in the Temple because he was a man of unclean lips and dwelt in the midst of a people of unclean lips (Is. vi. 5). Jeremiah shrank from the task entrusted to him, pleading his youth and inexperience. 'Ah, Lord God! Behold, I cannot speak; for I am a child' (Jer. i. 6). But when the call came to the prophet it could not be denied, for at the same time he felt the pressure of Yahweh's hand upon him (Jer. xv. 17; Ezek. i. 3, iii. 4, viii. 1, 3). Absolutely convinced of his call, he prefaced his message with the words, 'Thus saith the Lord', or 'The word of the Lord came', or words of similar import.

The Prophet's Function

The common assumption that the prophet was a man whose chief function was to prophesy is incorrect. Prediction was undoubtedly one of his functions (cf. Deut. xiii. 1–3, xviii. 22; Is. xli. 21–23) but it was incidental and not fundamental to his mission. Nor would it be accurate to assert that he was primarily a social reformer or a statesman. It is certainly true that he was interested in contemporary history, holding strong views on the pressing problems of the day, and expressing them in public fearlessly, often in the face of opposition and persecution. Amos and Micah, for example, denounced the

---

[1] Article on the 'Nature of Prophecy in Recent Study' in *HTR*, 1945, vol. xxxviii, p. 10.

oppression of the poor (Am. ii. 6, iv. 1, viii. 5; Mic. ii. 2, 9) and the corruption of the courts (Am. v. 12; Mic. iii. 11). Jeremiah administered a stern rebuke to Jehoiakim for employing forced labour and defrauding the workmen of their wages (Jer. xxii. 13–19). Hosea opposed those who sought an alliance with Egypt and Assyria (Hos. vii. 11, viii. 9, xi. 5, xii. 1). Isaiah warned Ahaz against appealing to Assyria for help against Syria (Is. vii. 20; cf. 2 Kgs. xvi. 7–9), and in the reign of Hezekiah disapproved of any military alliance with Egypt (Is. xxx. 1–5, xxxi. 3). Jeremiah opposed any alliance with Egypt or Assyria (Jer. ii. 18, 36), and Ezekiel condemned those who sought help from Egypt against Babylonia (Ezek. xvii. 15). Haggai and Zechariah welcomed Zerubbabel as the civil head of the restored community (Hag. ii. 4; Zech. iv. 6–10). When, however, the prophet dealt with social and political problems he did so not as a social reformer or as a statesman, but as the spokesman of Yahweh. To him social and political problems were moral and religious problems. They denounced social injustice because they believed in a God of righteousness who demanded obedience to his moral demands. Alliances with foreign powers showed disloyalty towards Yahweh or rebellion against his rule (Is. xxxi. 1; Jer. ii. 18, 19). Military power could not give a guarantee of security (Hos. xiv. 3; Is. viii. 6, 7); strength came from faith in Yahweh (Is. vii. 9). He was not primarily a predictor of future events or a social reformer or a statesman. He was first and foremost the spokesman of Yahweh, called to declare His mind and purpose. Micah defined the prophetic function in the words, 'But I truly am full of power by the spirit of the Lord, and of judgement, and of might, to declare unto Jacob his transgression and to Israel his sin' (Mic. iii. 8). The prophet was called by Yahweh to denounce and expose sin wherever he found it and to endeavour to redeem men from the error of their ways. As the spokesman of Yahweh he came forth as a preacher of righteousness, his words being charged with a passionate intensity and a terrible sense of urgency. 'The prophet,' says Albright, 'was a man who felt himself called by God for a special mission, in which his will was subordinated to the will of God which was communicated to him by direct inspiration. The prophet was thus a charismatic spiritual leader, directly commissioned by Yahweh to warn people of the perils of sin and to preach reform and revival of true religion and morality.'[1]

[1] W. F. Albright, *From the Stone Age to Christianity*, 1940, p. 232.

The Earliest Prophets

The prophets of Israel had a long history behind them. There are indications that in her desert wanderings and in the troubled times of the Judges there were outstanding personalities to whom the name of prophet (or prophetess) was applied. Both Abraham (Gen. xx. 7) and Moses (Deut. xviii. 15; Hos. xii. 13; Jer. xv. 1) were called prophets. Miriam, the sister of Moses, was a prophetess (Exod. xv. 20), while Deborah was both a judge and a prophetess (Jud. iv. 4). An unknown prophet was sent to Israel in the days of the Midianite oppression (Jud. vi. 8). These early prophets, with the exception of Moses, are somewhat shadowy figures and little is known of them. They were succeeded by a long line of prophets in unbroken succession, culminating in the canonical prophets whose activity extended from about the middle of the eighth century BC to about the middle of the fourth century BC.

The Early Ecstatic Prophets

It was not until the time of Saul and the establishment of the monarchy that the prophets really became prominent. In 1 Samuel x. 5, 6, 10–13, we read of a band of prophets coming down from the high place to the accompaniment of psaltery, timbrel, pipe and harp, and prophesying. When Saul met them he caught the contagion, becoming 'another man', and prophesied also, so that the on-lookers exclaimed, 'Is Saul also among the prophets?' Later we learn that when Saul sent messengers to Naioth to take David, they found Samuel at the head of a company of prophets, prophesying, and that they yielded to the prophetic impulse and prophesied also. When Saul himself joined them he, too, caught the contagion, lying down naked all that day and night (1 Sam. xix. 18–24). These bands of prophets had all the appearance of the modern Dervish. They worked themselves up into a frenzy by means of music and dancing, during which they uttered their so-called prophecies, which, however, were not expressed in intelligible speech, but resembled the 'speaking with tongues' or incoherent speech mentioned in Acts (Acts ii. 4, x. 46, xix. 6) of which Paul said he would rather speak five words with his understanding than ten thousand words in a tongue (1 Cor. xiv. 19). The association of Saul with these 'sons of the prophets' immediately after Yahweh had anointed him 'prince over his inheritance' (1 Sam. x. 1), suggests that Samuel had organized them into bands for the purpose of going round the countryside, singing the old national songs and preparing the people for the establishment of the monarchy.

Prophets became a regular feature of Israelite society. Some two hundred years after the death of Samuel we find bands of them at such places as Bethel (2 Kgs. ii. 3), Jericho (2 Kgs. ii. 5, 7, 13) and Gilgal (2 Kgs. iv. 38). It would appear that bands of prophets were sometimes attached to the court, as in the case of the four hundred prophets whom Ahab summoned for consultation before his attack on Ramoth-gilead (1 Kgs. xxii. 6). They generally delivered their oracles with one voice (1 Kgs. xxii. 11, 12). By the middle of the eighth century BC they had become discredited, as being men who earned their living by predicting the future and telling people and rulers what they wished to know. Amaziah, the priest at Bethel, was only reflecting public opinion when he took for granted that Amos was prophesying for money. 'O thou seer, go, flee thee away into the land of Judah, and there eat bread, and prophesy there' (Am. vii. 12). Amos repudiated any connection with them. 'I was no prophet, neither was I a prophet's son but I was an herdman, and a dresser of sycomore trees: and the Lord took me from following the flock, and the Lord said unto me, Go, prophesy unto my people Israel' (Am. vii. 14, 15). Micah charged them with prophesying falsely for the sake of material gain (Mic. iii. 5, 11). Isaiah denounced them for their drunkenness, for giving wrong guidance and for speaking smooth things (Is. xxviii. 7, xxx. 10). Jeremiah declared that they were as bad as the people of Sodom and Gomorrah. They were guilty of prophesying by Baal, of immorality, of lying and abetting evil-doers, of telling those who scorned the words of Yahweh that all was well, of stealing Yahweh's words from one another and of passing off their own lying dreams as divine revelations (Jer. xxiii. 13-32). Zephaniah describes them as light and treacherous persons (Zeph. iii. 4), and Ezekiel denounces them for prophesying only what they feel without a real vision (Ezek. xiii. 3, 6).

Pagan Ecstatic Prophets

Ecstatic prophets were not confined to Israel. An Egyptian record relates that an Egyptian envoy, visiting Byblos, a seaport on the Phoenician coast (*c.* 1100 BC), was unable to obtain his request until a young nobleman in a frenzy declared that its Baal had granted the desire of Amon, the Egyptian God. There are references to the same phenomenon in classical literature. We read of the ravings of Cassan-

dra in the Agamemnon and those of the Cumaean Sibyl in Aeneid
vi., while Plato in Timaeus 71b asserts that only those are to be
called prophets who speak in ecstasy. In the centre of the Temple of
Apollo at Delphi there was a small opening in the ground from which
from time to time intoxicating vapours rose. Over the opening stood
a tripod on which the priestess, called Pythia, sat whenever the
oracle was to be consulted. The guardians of the shrine, called
prophets, interpreted her frenzied utterances after she had inhaled
the vapour, and communicated them to the persons who had come
to consult the oracle. The Canaanites also had their prophets. We
read that Ahab summoned 450 prophets of Baal and 400 prophets of
the Asherah, which ate at Jezebel's table, to the contest with Elijah
on Mount Carmel (1 Kgs. xviii. 19), and that they cried aloud, and
cut themselves with knives and lances, as was their practice, 'till the
blood gushed out upon them' (1 Kgs. xviii. 26–29). It is thought that
the ecstatic prophets originated in Asia Minor and spread to Greece,
Syria and Canaan. All the evidence suggests that ecstatic prophecy
formed no part of Israel's desert life, but it was adopted from the
Canaanites and gradually transformed.

Early Individual Prophets

In addition to the bands of ecstatic prophets there were individual
prophets, like Nathan, Ahijah, Elijah and Elisha. Their origin is uncertain, but it is commonly supposed that they originated in the
organized bands of ecstatics, that they were men who were superior
to their fellows in moral character and spiritual insight, and that they
acted independently. 'A certain definite stage in the evolution of the
prophet, as we understand the term today, was reached when one of
the individuals in the band separated himself and delivered a message
out of harmony with that of the rest.'[1] These early independent
prophets were a power in Israel. Nathan was David's confidential
adviser and took a prominent part in the political manoeuvre which
placed Solomon on the throne instead of his elder brother (1 Kgs. i.
1–40); but he also regarded himself as guardian of the King's morals
(2 Sam. xii. 7). It was Ahijah, a prophet of Shiloh, who incited
Jeroboam to revolt against Solomon (1 Kgs. xi. 26–29). Elijah became a political force of the highest importance, defending the
rights of oppressed individuals (1 Kgs. xxi. 1–24) and opposing the
introduction of foreign cults into the Israelite religion (1 Kgs. xviii.

[1] T. H. Robinson, *Prophecy and the Prophets of Ancient Israel*, Revised ed. 1950, p. 39.

1–41). With these early individual prophets the emphasis tended to shift from the ecstatic experience to the moral and spiritual requirements of Yahweh. Their words and deeds were preserved either orally or in writing, and have been incorporated in the biblical books of 1 and 2 Samuel and 1 and 2 Kings. Indeed, the memory of them exceeded even that of Thomas Becket in Medieval England, but it was a memory of deeds rather than of words.

Influence of Early Prophets
These early prophets played an important part in the history of Israel. They were ardent nationalists and helped to keep alive the spirit of patriotism among the people. It is probable that the communities of prophets became centres for the preservation of Israelite traditions and that they were an important source for the compilation of Israelite history.

The Canonical Prophets
The early independent prophets were the forerunners of the canonical prophets who form perhaps the most remarkable group of religious teachers the world has ever known. They attained a conception of Yahweh, which today may be considered a truism but which to their contemporaries was new and revolutionary.

There are certain elements in their teaching which are common to all of them. According to Oesterley and Robinson the most important of these are the following:

1. Yahweh rules the world according to Law. He is not a capricious being but is consistent in all His actions.

2. Yahweh is Lord of Nature and of History.

3. Yahweh is the Lord of the end of things. He will bring the present world order to an end; but His purpose will be, not as is generally supposed, to destroy the enemies of Israel and to exalt her, but to vindicate on her His own moral principles by punishing her for her faithlessness. She will receive the due reward of her sins at the hands of a perfectly righteous God.

4. Yahweh is the Lord of universal morality. His laws are valid for all nations and their violation will meet with punishment.

5. Yahweh is in a special sense the God of Israel. As His chosen people they have not only special privileges but also special responsi-

bilities. If they fail to shoulder their responsibilities they will incur special punishment.

6. Yahweh's supreme demand is for righteousness, not for ritual. Sacrifice can never be a substitute for moral conduct.

In addition to these common elements in the teaching of the prophets, each has his own marked individuality and stresses some particular aspect or aspects of the general teaching. For example Amos stresses the justice of Yahweh, Hosea His love and Isaiah His holiness and majesty.

Place of Ecstasy in the Prophetic Experience

Some modern critics maintain that the canonical prophets, unlike the early prophets, were not subject to ecstatic experiences; but the evidence to the contrary is too strong to be rejected. Amos had his dreams or visions of which he said, 'The Lord showed me' (Am. vii. 1, 4, 7); the call to the prophetic ministry came to Isaiah in a vision (Is. vi. 1–8); Micah tells us that he was 'full of power by the spirit of the Lord and of judgement, and of might, to declare unto Jacob his transgression, and to Israel his sin' (Mic. iii. 8). Jeremiah felt himself controlled by an external power (Jer. iv. 23–26), and on one occasion had to wait ten days before the word of Yahweh came to him (Jer. xlii. 7). Ezekiel was undoubtedly subject to trance and catalepsy (Ezek. iii. 23–27, iv. 4–8, viii. 1, 2). He felt himself, like a psychic medium, lifted into the air and transported to distant places (Ezek. viii. 3, xi. 1, xxxvii. 1, xl. 1, 2). 'The fact that the great prophets so far surpassed their predecessors in their apprehension of spiritual truth is no reason for denying the reality of the ecstatic element in their experience, or for explaining it away as a mere rhetorical accommodation to traditional modes of expression.'[1]

True and False Prophets

It is clear that there was a deep cleavage in the ranks of the prophets. Each side declared that the prophets on the other side were false prophets. We have already shown that the great canonical prophets despised the professional bearers of the same name. The former 'feel themselves to be altogether a new kind of prophet, channels of a new religious impulse and a revolutionary message'.[2] The first sign

---

[1] J. Skinner, *Prophecy and Religion*, 1922, pp. 4 ff.
[2] C. H. Dodd, *The Authority of the Bible*, 1928, pp. 58 ff.

of a distinction between the 'false prophets' and the 'true' is seen in the case of Micaiah, whose prediction was opposed to that of the 400 prophets whom Ahab had gathered for consultation on the eve of his attack on Ramoth-gilead (1 Kgs. xxii. 6). The question came into prominence in the course of the conflict of Jeremiah with the professional prophets of his time (Jer. xxiii. 9–32, xxviii, xxix). It is interesting to note that the question is raised in the book of Deuteronomy, the nucleus of which, according to the general consensus of opinion, belongs to the reign of Josiah, during the early period of Jeremiah's activity. Deuteronomy xviii. 22 lays down the rule that the genuineness of the prophet is to be judged by the fulfilment or otherwise of his predictions: the true prophet's predictions are fulfilled and those of the false prophet are not. It would appear that this was not considered satisfactory, for in ch. xiii. 1–5, we are told that the test of the genuineness of the prophet is the moral and spiritual content of his message. No prophet who invites the people to serve other gods is to be listened to under any circumstances. The prediction of such a prophet may be fulfilled but Yahweh has allowed his prediction to come to pass to test the loyalty of the people. Although the greater canonical prophets despised the professional prophets as being 'false prophets', we need not assume that all the latter were imposters. Micaiah did not charge the 400 prophets with insincerity; he believed that Yahweh Himself had inspired them to utter in good faith a lie in order to destroy Ahab (1 Kgs. xxii. 19–23). According to Jeremiah the distinguishing mark of the true prophet was the prediction of doom. A prophecy of success needed confirmation as a prophecy of doom did not (Jer. xxix. 8, 9). This solution of the problem, however, cannot be considered satisfactory. It is true that the greater prophets were usually prophets of doom, but by this test Deutero-Isaiah with his vision of restoration and message of hope would be considered a false prophet. How then was the true prophet to be distinguished from the false? Outwardly there was no difference between them. Both claimed to speak in the name of Yahweh, but spoke from a deep personal conviction, and both would appeal to ecstatic experience as proof of the genuineness of their predictions. But both could not be the true interpreters of the mind and purpose of Yahweh. The solution of the problem is to be sought in the realm of the spirit. The true prophet had an overwhelming sense of being in direct contact with Yahweh and of being dominated by Him. The false prophet had no such overwhelming experience. He had never stood in the council of Yahweh; his predictions came not by divine inspiration, but issued from his own heart, that is, they were the product of wishful thinking.

The Relation of the Prophets to the Cult

There is evidence that the prophets were closely connected with the sanctuary. Samuel, who was trained for the priesthood (1 Sam. i. 24–28) but identified himself with the prophets (1 Sam. iii. 20), presided at the sacrificial meal at Ramah (1 Sam. ix. 13, 22, 23). The bands or guilds of prophets are chiefly mentioned in places where there were sanctuaries (1 Sam. x. 5; 2 Kgs. ii. 3, iv. 38). There are many passages in the Old Testament in which priests and prophets are coupled together (Jer. xxiii. 11, xxvi. 7; Lam ii. 20). In what way the prophets were connected with the sanctuary is uncertain. According to Johnson they were cult officials, who presumably had special quarters in the sanctuary but were not necessarily permanent residents there. As spokesmen of Yahweh they gave oracles, and as representatives of the people were specialists in prayer. In the post-exilic period the priests succeeded in reducing them to the rank of Temple singers.[1] Rowley agrees that they were cult officials, but suggests that their functions—whatever they were—were different from those of the priests, and that they were recruited quite differently. He is not convinced that they were resident officials attached to particular shrines.[2] Meek holds that the earlier prophets were definitely cult officials, but doubts if many of the canonical prophets had any connection with the sanctuary.[3]

The End of the Prophets

In the Exile prophets arose and continued the work of their predecessors. With Ezekiel and the nameless prophet whose words are preserved in Isaiah xl-lv, the golden age of prophecy came to an end. Prophets, such as Haggai, Zechariah and Malachi, arose in the post-exilic period, but they were intellectually and spiritually inferior to their predecessors. Moreover, the conditions of the times were not favourable to the prophetic gift.

---

[1] A. R. Johnson, *The Cultic Prophet in Ancient Israel*, 1944, p. 63.

[2] H. H. Rowley, *The Rediscovery of the Old Testament*, 1945, p. 98. See also his article in *HTR*, vol. xxxviii, 1945, pp. 13–16.

[3] T. Meek, *Hebrew Origins*, 1936, Revised ed., 1950, pp. 178–80.

With the fall of Jerusalem in 587 BC the Jews lost their national independence and henceforth were, except for a brief period, under the domination of foreign conquerors until the destruction of Jerusalem by the Romans in AD 70 when they were dispersed. The exiles in Babylon developed an intense hatred of idolatry and abandoned it before their return to their native land. It would appear, however, that some of the returned exiles, influenced either by the Samaritans who were of mixed race and religion, or by the inhabitants in and around Jerusalem, who had not been deported to Babylon, reverted to the practice of combining the worship of Yahweh with that of alien cults, for idolatry is denounced in Isaiah lvii. 3–13, lxv. 2–5, lxvi. 3, 17, and in Zechariah xiii. 2. But the majority of the returned exiles remained loyal to Yahweh, and in the course of time what little idolatry there was died out. So great was their hatred of it, that when in the second century BC Antiochus Epiphanes tried to eradicate their religion and turn the sanctuary of Yahweh into a heathen temple they rose in rebellion against him.

In the Exile the conviction grew that the religion of Yahweh could be preserved only by strict adherence to legal precepts. Under the influence of Ezekiel and the priestly class the Priestly Code was compiled, containing the bulk of the regulations for the ritual of the sanctuary and for the ordering of the priesthood. It was probably this code, or excerpts from it, which was promulgated by Ezra on his return to Palestine in 397 BC. Its acceptance by the people marks the beginning of a new era in the history of Judaism, for from henceforth they became the people of a Book, depending upon a written Law rather than on the spoken word. The Law was held in increasing reverence as the complete and final revelation of the mind and will of God. The influential leaders now were not the prophets, who delivered their message orally as the representative of Yahweh, but the priests whose chief concern was the Temple and its ritual which they believed were essential to true religion, and the scribes who devoted the whole of their lives to the interpretation and development of the Law.

The loss of national independence, the abandonment of idolatry, and the imposition of a legal code upon the people narrowed the field of the prophets' activity, with the result that in the life of their day they found little to interest or inspire them. Of those who belonged to the prophetic order a few either carried on the work of their great predecessors but on a much reduced scale, or spent their days lost in dreams of the future and producing a type of literature known as Apocalyptic. The remainder—and they formed the majority—became mere fortune-tellers trading upon the credulity of the people. They fell into such disrepute that in Zechariah xiii. 2–5 we are told that any man posing as a prophet must either be put to death or discard his hairy mantle, repudiate his professional status, and claim to be a simple peasant. The prophets gradually decreased in number and in the Greek period finally disappeared.

Influence of the Prophets

It is difficult to assess the influence of the Prophets in their own age. Isaiah felt that his message would harden and not soften the people (Is. vi. 9). Ezekiel complained that those who came to listen to his oracles did not mean to obey them. 'And lo, thou art unto them as a very lovely song of one that hath a pleasant voice, and can play well on an instrument: for they hear thy words, but they do them not' (Ezek. xxxiii. 32). Amos was ordered to leave Bethel (Am. vii. 12, 13) and Jeremiah was imprisoned (Jer. xxxvii. 16–21, xxxviii. 6) and finally taken forcibly to Egypt (Jer. xliii. 6). It was their sense of failure that induced them, or at least some of them, to commit their messages to writing. They wrote them 'for the time to come for ever and ever' (Is. xxx. 8; Jer. xxxvi. 32). But they appear to have had a certain measure of success. Amos and Jeremiah would not have been persecuted had there been no danger that they might influence the people. Their denunciations of the ruling classes must have met with considerable popular approval. The fact that attempts at a religious reformation on prophetic lines were made by Hezekiah (2 Kgs. xviii. 3–6) and Josiah (2 Kgs. xxii–xxiii. 25) shows that the prophets of the eighth century BC—Amos, Hosea, Micah and Isaiah—had not laboured in vain. Haggai and Zechariah inspired the people to undertake the task of rebuilding the Temple.

If, however, they made no great impact upon their own age, they have exercised a profound influence upon succeeding generations. Their words were not forgotten; they were treasured by their disciples and regarded with ever increasing veneration until we find that by about the beginning of the second century BC they were recognized as divinely inspired. The prophets contributed to Judaism, and ultimately to Christianity, the great doctrine of ethical-monotheism, by which is meant that there is one God who is perfect in righteousness and demands from His worshippers obedience to

His moral demands, the belief that human history is under the sovereignty of God who will one day bring men and nations to judgement, a new conception of religion, according to which religion became a matter of the heart and of righteous living rather than of ritualistic practices, the discovery of the immeasurable worth of the individual, and the belief in a Golden Age of righteousness and peace, which led to the emergence of the idea of the Kingdom of God. In addition to the contribution which they made to Judaism and Christianity, they helped to preserve the identity of the nation during and after the Exile.

CHAPTER V

The Forms and Characteristics
of Hebrew Poetry

Origin of Poetry

Strange as it may appear, the literature of a people begins in poetry not in prose which is a later development. The earliest examples of Babylonian and Egyptian literature are poetical in form, while in ancient Greece the songs of the bard appeared before the prose works of the historian and philosopher. The same is also true of our own literature. Among the Hebrews, as among the peoples of many other nations, literature doubtless began in poetry. The reasons why early man was accustomed to express his thoughts in poetic form are not difficult to discover. He was strongly imaginative and naturally responsive to rhythm; imagination and rhythm are two of the essential characteristics of poetry. His love of rhythm was stimulated by the rhythmic movements which were constantly before his eyes in the world of Nature—the swaying of the trees, the alternation of day and night, the regularity and orderly progression of the seasons, the rise and fall of the waves, and the ebb and flow of the tide. Moreover, poetry has to do with the emotions as well as with the intellect, and it is a well-known fact that when the emotions are roused speech tends to become rhythmical. Hence any incident in the life of early man which fired the imagination and roused the emotions might result in a song.

Origin of Hebrew Poetry

The origin of Hebrew poetry is to be found in tribal lays sung round the camp fire. An event, such as a heroic deed, a victory over an enemy, the ingathering of the harvest, a burial, or a wedding, would be made the occasion of a song. Ideas and emotions connected with the worship of the deity would be expressed in psalms, and oracular utterances of the patriarchs would also be given in poetic form.

These early songs, both secular and sacred, would naturally be crude in expression and would be transmitted orally from one generation to another until they were finally fixed in writing. Thus, in the course of time, the nation would possess collections of triumphal odes, harvest songs, elegies, love lyrics, wedding songs, psalms and oracles.

It was evidently customary for rich families to employ minstrels in their houses from early times. When Jacob stole away from Lanan the latter declared, 'Wherefore didst thou flee secretly, and steal away from me; and didst not tell me, that I might have sent thee away with mirth and with songs, with tabret and with harp' (Gen. xxxi. 27). Barzillai, the Gileadite, would not go to the court at Jerusalem as David desired, because in his extreme old age he could no longer take food and drink, or hear the voices of singing men and women (2 Sam. xix. 35). Koheleth tells us that in his search for happiness, he built himself a pleasure house, amassed silver and gold and secured singers, both men and women (Eccles. ii. 8). It is clear that secular and sacred songs were a feature of Hebrew life in all ages.

Poetry in the Old Testament
The Old Testament contains a good deal of poetry. Certain books are entirely poetical in form; these are The Psalms, The Proverbs, the dialogue of Job, The Song of Songs and Lamentations. In addition, songs and fragments of songs are embedded in the historical books, while the prophets in their exalted moods frequently burst forth into poetry. The author of Ecclesiastes sometimes cast his thoughts into the form of gnomic poetry. Most of the Hebrew poetry which has been preserved in the Old Testament is of a religious type, but there are poems included in it of a purely secular character, such as the Song of Lamech (Gen. iv. 23, 24), David's lament over Saul and Jonathan (2 Sam. i. 19–27) and his lament over Abner (2 Sam. iii. 33, 34). The whole output of ancient Hebrew poetry is not included in the Old Testament. References are made to three collections of poems which are no longer extant; these are the Book of the Wars of the Lord (Num. xxi. 14, 15), probably a collection of songs celebrating great events in the history of the nation, the Book of Jashar (Josh. x. 12, 13; 2 Sam. i. 18), probably a collection of songs, celebrating the achievements of national heroes, and a collection of lamentations, which is said to have contained Jeremiah's lament for Josiah (2 Chron. xxxv. 25).

Parallelism

There are two fundamental principles of Hebrew poetry. The first is that every line (technically called a verse) must consist of at least two parts, each of which is commonly called a 'stichos' (plural, 'stichoi'). The two members of the line together form a distich or couplet. The second is that there must be a balance of thought between the two parts. This device is known as 'parallelism' because the two parts of the line are parallel expressions of the same thought. For this reason parallelism has been called 'a rhyme of thought'. Bishop Lowth in his famous lectures 'On the Sacred Poetry of the Hebrews' (1753) was the first to discover the principle of parallelism. He and other scholars have distinguished six kinds of parallelism.

Synonymous Parallelism. The second part of the line repeats the thought of the first part in slightly different form.

e.g. He hath cast me into the mire,
　　　and I am become like dust and ashes (Job xxx. 19).
　　The Lord hath his way in the whirlwind and in the storm,
　　　and the clouds are the dust of his feet (Nah. i. 3).

Antithetic Parallelism. The second part of the line completes the first part by the introduction of a contrast.

e.g. For the Lord knoweth the way of the righteous:
　　　but the way of the wicked shall perish (Ps. i. 6).
　　Then shall they cry unto the Lord,
　　　but he will not answer them (Mic. iii. 4).

Synthetic or Constructive Parallelism. The second part of the line completes the thought of the first.

e.g. I have refrained my feet from every evil way,
　　　that I might observe thy word (Ps. cxix. 101).
　　O Israel, return unto the Lord thy God;
　　　for thou hast fallen by thine iniquity (Hos. xiv. 1).

Emblematic Parallelism. A truth is stated in the first part of the line and is reproduced in the second part of the line by means of a simile or metaphor.

e.g. For riches certainly make themselves wings,
　　　like an eagle that flieth toward heaven (Prov. xxiii. 5).

Sometimes the emblem may come first.

e.g. As a cage is full of birds,
　　　so are their houses full of deceit (Jer. v. 27).

Climactic or Ascending Parallelism. The thought is built up to a climax by the repetition of a key word or phrase.

e.g. Give unto the Lord, O ye sons of the mighty,
    give unto the Lord glory and strength (Ps. xxix. 1).

   That day is a day of wrath,
      a day of trouble and distress,
    a day of wasteness and desolation,
      a day of darkness and gloominess,
      a day of clouds and thick darkness,
    a day of the trumpet and alarm
      against the fenced cities,
      and against the high battlements (Zeph. i, 15, 16).

Introverted Parallelism. This kind involves two complete lines in which the four members are so arranged that the first is parallel to the fourth and the second to the third, that is, it is the complete lines which are parallel, not the members within the line.

e.g. The way of peace they know not;
      and there is no judgement in their goings,
    they have made them crooked paths,
      whosoever goeth therein doth not know peace (Is. lix. 8).

A cursory reading of the poetical portions of the Old Testament will show that parallelism is very common and that much of their charm is due to it, but its frequent use without any variation in its form would soon produce monotony. Hence instead of the couplet we find, though rarely, the monostich or single line (Ps. xviii. 1, lxxxvii. 1), but more commonly combinations of three and four lines, known as tristichs and tetrastichs. The tristichs may be arranged in many different ways. For example the three lines may be all parallel (Ps. i. 1), or the first two may be synonymous and the two form an antithetic parallelism with the third (Jer. xv. 20). Similarly tetrastichs may exhibit various kinds of construction. For example, the first line may be parallel to the third and the second to the fourth (Jon. ii. 2), or the first line may be parallel to the fourth and the second to the third (Ps. li. 1).

There are other less common and more intricate forms of parallelism but these cannot be discussed owing to exigences of space. Sufficient matter, however, has been given to enable the reader to understand the main aspects of a difficult subject, which is not entirely clear to scholars themselves.

Since Lowth's day G. B. Gray has carried the study of parallelism a step further. He distinguished two kinds, namely, (1) complete parallelism and (2) incomplete parallelism. Complete parallelism exists when every term in the first member of the line is parallel to a term in the second. Incomplete parallelism exists when the terms of the second member do not correspond exactly to those of the first. Incomplete parallelism falls again into two classes, namely, (1) incomplete parallelism with compensation and (2) incomplete parallelism without compensation. Incomplete parallelism with compensation exists when the two members of the line contain the same number of terms, but only some of the terms in the two members are parallel. Incomplete parallelism without compensation exists when one member of the line (usually the second) contains a smaller number of terms than the other. For examples of all these forms of parallelism the reader should consult his work on 'The Forms of Hebrew Poetry', 1915.

Rhythm or Metre

Hebrew poetry is characterized by a correspondence, not only of thought, but also of sound or rhythm. In English poetry the line is divided into a number of feet, each foot containing a definite number of syllables with one accented syllable. In Hebrew poetry, on the other hand, there are no feet; the line has a definite number of accented syllables and the unaccented syllables are not counted. The line is divided into two parts (sometimes three) by a strong pause, and there is also a definite pause at the end so that the sense does not run on from one line to the next. The following are the chief rhythms or metres:

2 : 2. Each member of the line has two accented syllables.

e.g. The nations raged, the kingdoms were moved:
      he uttered his voice, the earth melted (Ps. xlvi. 6).

This is rarely used. Its staccato notes are used to indicate a state of emotional tension due to fear or joy.

3 : 2. The first member of the line has three accented syllables and the second two.

e.g. Can a maid forget her ornaments,
      or a bride her attire?
  Yet my people have forgotten me
      days without number (Jer. ii. 32).

This metre is called the 'Elegiac' or 'Quinah' metre and is often employed in laments for the dead. But it is also employed in other kinds of poems, especially by the prophets. It is used by Jeremiah in his warnings and appeals to the nation and by Deutero-Isaiah and many Psalmists to express praise and thanksgiving.

3 : 3. Each member of the line has three accented syllables.

e.g. Shall mortal man be more just then God?
   Shall a man be more pure than his Maker? (Job. iv. 17).

This metre is well adapted for the brief, forceful expression of ideas. The whole of the Book of Job and most of the Psalter are written in it.

4 : 3. The first member of the line has four accented syllables and the second three. It may be sub-divided and described as 2 : 2 : 3.

e.g. I beheld the earth, and, lo, it was waste and void;
   and the heavens, and they had no light.
  I beheld the mountains, and, lo, they trembled,
   and all the hills moved to and fro.
  I beheld, and, lo, there was no man,
   and all the birds of the heavens were fled (Jer. iv. 23–25).

Rhyme

Rhyme plays but a small part in Hebrew poetry. The riddle propounded by Samson at his wedding feast (Jud. xiv. 14) and his reply to the Philistines when they discovered the answer to it (Jud. xiv. 18) are in rhyme. The song attributed to Samson's foes (Jud. xvi. 24), the closing words of Psalm vi. and Job x. 9–18 are also in rhyme. Apparently Hebrew poets did not regard it as an essential element of poetry.

Strophes or Stanzas

Hebrew poetry has no strophes or stanzas in the strict sense of the term. We think of a strophe as a group of lines combined according to some definite plan whereby it can be easily recognized. But Hebrew poets apparently did not consider the strophe a fundamental characteristic of poetry, being more concerned with the forceful expression of their thoughts than with rules of versification. It has long been recognized that the lines of many poems can be grouped into larger units to which the term 'strophes' or 'stanzas' has been applied. These so-called strophes, however, are not constructed on any definite plan such as we find in the Greek choral odes. Often it is found that the strophes of a poem do not have the same number of lines, while the corresponding lines in the different strophes vary in length. While most scholars have accepted a strophic theory, the attempt to divide all Hebrew poems into strophes with an equal number of lines in each has led to extensive alterations in the text, many sentences and words being omitted to suit a strophic theory.

In some poems the strophic form can be readily detected. A refrain repeated at regular intervals is decisive evidence of the strophic form (Is. ix. 8–21). Most alphabetic acrostics have a strophic structure (Ps. cxix.). The presence of the word Selah (Ps. xlvi.) at the end of a line is said to indicate the end of a strophe; but since the meaning of the term is obscure, we cannot say with certainty that it was used for this purpose.

Literary Characteristics

Simplicity. The charm of Hebrew poetry is found not in its poetic forms, but in its literary characteristics. The first thing that strikes the reader is its simplicity, both of construction and style. Hebrew poets used the complex sentence sparingly, preferring the simple sentence, or the compound sentence.

e.g. I will walk before the Lord
> in the land of the living (Ps. cxvi. 9).

He rebuketh the sea, and maketh it dry,
> and drieth up all the rivers:
Bashan languisheth and Carmel,
> and the flower of Lebanon languisheth (Nah. i. 4).

The Hebrews were an emotional and imaginative people and were not given to abstract thought. There are few abstract terms in ancient Hebrew, preference being given to concrete nouns which have a pictorial value. The adjective also is rare; poets had their favourite descriptive terms, such as 'goodly' and 'pleasant' which they used again and again.

e.g. The lines are fallen unto me in pleasant places;
> yea, I have a goodly heritage (Ps. xvi. 6).

And wolves shall cry in their castles,
> and jackals in the pleasant palaces (Is. xiii. 22).

There is no elaboration of detail, much being left to the imagination of the reader. Instead of the detailed account of the defeat and death of Saul and Jonathan we have the simple statement:

Thy glory, O Israel, is slain upon thy high places!
How are the mighty fallen! (2 Sam. i. 19).

The transitoriness of human life is described in a few brief words.
e.g. My days are swifter than a weaver's shuttle (Job vii. 6).

All flesh is grass,
  and all the goodliness thereof is as the
  flower of the field (Is. xl. 6).

Use of *Similes* and *Metaphors*. A striking characteristic of Hebrew poetry is its use of similes and metaphors. These are taken for the most part from the familiar landscape, or from the details of everyday life in the home and in the open air.

e.g. Simile.

  But let judgement roll down as waters,
    and righteousness as a mighty stream (Am. v. 24).

  For your goodness is as a morning cloud,
    and as the dew that goeth early away (Hos. vi. 4).

Similes are generally short but occasionally we find a series of them.

e.g. It is he that sitteth upon the circle of the earth,
  and the inhabitants thereof are as grasshoppers;
that stretcheth out the heavens as a curtain,
  and spreads them out as a tent to dwell in:
that bringeth princes to nothing;
  he maketh the judges of the earth as vanity (Is. xl. 22, 23).

e.g. Metaphor.

  The Lord is my shepherd;
    I shall not want (Ps. xxiii. 1).

  Her princes in the midst of her are roaring lions;
    her judges are evening wolves (Zeph. iii. 3).

Literary Devices. Various literary devices, such as repetition, the rhetorical question, the exclamation, the imperative, and contrast are often used for the sake of effect and to secure variety and vividness in the style.

e.g. Repetition.

  Awake, awake, put on thy strength, O Zion;
  put on thy beautiful garments,
    O Jerusalem, the holy city (Is. lii. 1).

  Lo, I will bring a nation upon you from far,
    O house of Israel, saith the Lord:
  It is a mighty nation,
    it is an ancient nation,
  a nation whose language thou knowest not,
    neither understandest what they say (Jer. v. 15).

e.g. Rhetorical question.

  The lion hath roared, who will not fear?
  The Lord God hath spoken, who can but prophesy? (Am. iii. 8).

For the Lord of hosts hath purposed,
　　and who shall disannul it?
And his hand is stretched out,
　　and who shall turn it back? (Is. xiv. 27).

e.g. The exclamation.

Say unto the cities of Judah,
　　Behold, your God! (Is. xl. 9).

Woe unto him that striveth with his Maker!
　　a potsherd among the potsherds of the earth! (Is. xlv. 9).

e.g. The imperative.

Come to Bethel, and transgress;
　　to Gilgal, and multiply transgression;
and bring your sacrifices every morning,
　　and your tithes every three days (Am. iv. 4).

O Israel, return unto the Lord thy God,
　　for thou hast fallen by thine iniquity (Hos. xiv. 1).

e.g. Contrast.

Though they dig into hell,
　　thence shall mine hand take them;
and though they climb up to heaven,
　　thence will I bring them down (Am. ix. 2).

Woe unto them that call evil good,
　　and good evil;
that put darkness for light,
　　and light for darkness;
that put bitter for sweet
　　and sweet for bitter! (Is. v. 20).

Attitude to Nature

Another characteristic of Hebrew poetry is the prominence given to
Nature in it. This is not surprising for the Hebrews were a pastoral
and agricultural people living their lives in garden, vineyard and
field. Palestine was a small country, about the size of Wales, so that
they would have no difficulty in becoming acquainted with its
physical features—the rugged mountains and dark valleys, the
desolate places and fertile plains, and the rivers and water-brooks.
To the east and south the wilderness stretched away into the distance
while in the west was the sea 'great and wide'. Moreover, the country
was subject to heat, droughts and famine. At times the heat was so
great that they longed to shelter beneath the shadow of a great

rock; rivers and wells dried up, grass withered and crops perished, and then they experienced the pangs of hunger and thirst. They knew that Nature could be benign and cruel, friendly and terrifying. Their eyes seem always to have been open to its sights and their ears to its sounds. They are aware of the mountains and valleys, wilderness and fertile plains, rivers and water-brooks, green pastures and still waters, the dew on the mountain and the rain upon the mown grass, the ascending vapours and the dark clouds in the sky, the flash of lightning and the roll of the thunder, the tree planted by the streams of water and the boughs of the goodly cedars, the fading flower and the withering leaves, the sheep in the field and the cattle on the hills, the wild-asses roaming the desert and the horse rejoicing in his strength, the owl in the waste places and the sparrow on the housetop, the nests of the sparrow and swallow in the Temple and that of the stork in the fir-tree. They had listened to the voice of the thunder, to the sound of waters in tumult and to the roar of the lion in search of its prey.

The Hebrew poets always see Nature in relation to Yahweh. His infinite power and majesty are seen in creation.

> The heavens declare the glory of God,
>> and the firmament showeth his handywork (Ps. xix. 1).

> The Lord hath his way in the whirlwind and in the storm,
>> and the clouds are the dust of his feet.
> He rebuketh the sea, and maketh it dry,
>> and drieth up all the rivers;
> Bashan languisheth, and Carmel,
>> and the flower of Lebanon languisheth.
> The mountains quake at him,
>> and the hills melt,
> And the earth is upheaved at his presence,
>> yea, the world, and all that dwell therein (Nah. i. 3–5).

Yahweh prepares rain for the earth, makes grass grow upon the mountains (Ps. cxlvii. 8), gives snow like wool and scatters the hoar frost like ashes (Ps. cxlvii. 16). All creatures look to Him for their food in due season (Ps. cxlv. 15). Natural objects are sometimes personified and made to rejoice in His eternal purposes. When Israel escaped from Egypt and crossed the Red Sea and the river Jordan, 'the mountains skipped like rams, the little hills like young sheep' (Ps. cxiv. 4). When Deutero-Isaiah thought about Yahweh's redemption of His people he burst forth into a paean of praise, calling upon the heavens to sing, the earth to shout, and the mountains, forests and trees to break forth into singing (Is. xliv. 23).

It is sometimes said that although the Hebrew poets were keenly observant of Nature, they did not love it for its own sake. If we possessed all their literature we should be in a position to speak with certainty on the subject, but unfortunately most of it has been lost. There is one passage in the Song of Songs, describing the approach of spring, which proves that the author was sensitive to the beauty and charm of Nature.

> For, lo, the winter is past,
>   the rain is over and gone;
> The flowers appear on the earth;
>   the time of the singing of birds is come,
> and the voice of the turtle is heard in our land;
> The fig tree ripeneth her green figs,
>   and the vines are in blossom,
>   they give forth their fragrance (Songs of Songs ii. 11-13).

CHAPTER VI

Amos

LIFE AND CHARACTER OF AMOS

Amos was a native of Tekoa, a small town about six miles south of Bethlehem, and followed the occupations of a shepherd and a tender of sycomore trees (i. 1, vii. 14). His occupations would take him to the market towns of the Northern Kingdom where he would have the opportunity of studying the social, moral and religious conditions of the people. In those markets, too, he would meet with travellers from whom he would gain information concerning the people of other lands. He was acquainted with the history of the surrounding nations (i. 3–ii. 3) and knew what were the original homes of the Philistines and the Aramaeans (ix. 7). He had heard of the activities of the Philistine slave-traders (i. 6), the prevalence of plagues in Egypt (iv. 10) and the frequent inundations of the River Nile (viii. 8, ix. 5). Though a native of Judah he delivered his message to Israel, probably because it was the more powerful of the two kingdoms, and because Bethel, Gilgal and Beersheba rather than Jerusalem were the religious centres. The place which he chose to deliver his message was Bethel on the occasion of a popular festival. His denunciation of the people, more especially of their leaders, and his warnings that the expected 'day of Yahweh' would not be a day of victory but of defeat (v. 18) doubtless displeased the king, the priests and the people. Amaziah, the priest of Bethel, taking him to be a professional prophet belonging to one of the prophetic guilds, bade him begone to Judah and prophesy there for hire. Amos withdrew from Bethel, after declaring that he was neither a prophet nor a prophet's son, but a man whom Yahweh had taken from following the flock to prophesy to Israel (vii. 10–15). His prophetic activity must have been very brief: according to the prefatory title of the book the relevations were all made to him 'two years before the earthquake' (i. 1). After his withdrawal from Bethel nothing further is heard of him. He probably returned to Tekoa and resumed his occupation as a shepherd and tender of sycomore trees.

Amos is revealed in his book as an austere character, outspoken, courageous and tenacious. His character was moulded to a large extent by his environment and early training. Living in the country he grew up to be a keen observer of nature. He had watched the corn being threshed with instruments of iron (i. 3), and wagons packed with sheaves leaving the fields at harvest-time (ii. 13). He had seen birds caught in snares (iii. 5), gardens and vineyards devastated by blasting and mildew (iv. 9), fig trees, olive trees and the grass of the fields devoured by locusts (iv. 9, vii. 2), and snakes coiled up among the stones of ancient walls (v. 19). He knew all about the tall cedars and the strong oaks (ii. 9), the dangers which men had to face from wild beasts (iii. 8, v. 19), and the havoc caused by lions among the flocks (iii. 12). His training as a shepherd gave him a high conception of the duties of those who held positions of responsibility, and made him fearless in defence of the needy and the oppressed. Accustomed to the simple, strenuous life of the country, he despised the luxurious habits and vices of the wealthy classes in the cities of the Northern Kingdom (ii. 6–8, iv. 1, vi. 4–6). Living in the country away from the local sanctuaries, he would be in close touch with the purer faith of the Israelites before it was contaminated by the introduction of the beliefs and practices of the Canaanite cults, and before men deliberately ignored the moral demands of their religion. 'In the wilder hills,' says Robinson, 'where Israel had first established herself, in the great desert spaces which nurtured that hardier type to which Amos himself belonged, there were still those who clung to the earlier and more truly Mosaic form of religion. This double tradition of Israelite faith is not always obvious, but there are indications which point surely to its existence. It was not an accident that Elijah himself, the forerunner of the great ethical prophets, came also out of the wild.'[1] It is not surprising, therefore, that his wrath should be roused by the debased Yahwism which he found at Bethel and Gilgal, and that he should declare ironically, 'Come to Bethel, and transgress; to Gilgal, and multiply transgression' (iv. 4).

In the clear air of the desert he learnt the lesson that nothing happened without a cause. If two men travelled together they must have agreed to do so; if a lion roared in the jungle he had killed his prey; if a young lion growled in his lair he had made a capture; if a

[1] T. H. Robinson, *Prophecy and the Prophets in Ancient Israel*, Revised ed. 1950, p. 66.

bird dropped into a trap someone must have baited it; if a trap sprang up from the ground it had caught something; if a trumpet was blown in a city there must have been some cause for alarm; if a calamity befell a city, Yahweh must have been the cause of it. Hence, when he sought the reason for the disaster which was about to fall upon the Northern Kingdom, he found it in the sins of the people and the consequent wrath of Yahweh. As he meditated upon the situation, he felt absolutely convinced that Yahweh was calling him to pronounce judgement upon the Northern Kingdom. 'The lion hath roared, who will not fear? The Lord God hath spoken, who can but prophesy?' (iii. 8).

In spite of the strength and nobility of his character he was not a lovable personality, for he lacked humanity. In his judgement of men he was harsh and intolerant, making no allowance for human frailty. To him Yahweh was a God of justice rather than of mercy—a God who demanded righteousness from his servants and punished all evil-doers. He was convinced that nothing but destruction awaited Israel in the immediate future. Fire would destroy the surrounding nations because of their inhuman and ruthless conduct (i. 3–ii. 3). This conviction, he was convinced, was based upon direct revelation. 'Surely the Lord God will do nothing, but he revealeth His secret unto his servants the prophets' (iii. 7). As for Israel, Yahweh would call in a foreign foe that would devastate the whole land (vi. 14). The palaces of the rich, the dwellings of the poor, the sanctuary at Bethel, and the pleasant vineyards would all be involved in a common ruin (iii. 15, v. 11, vi. 11). The women of Samaria would be cast upon the refuse heaps (iv. 3), the worshippers at Bethel would try in vain to escape (ix. 1–4) and those who escaped death would go into captivity (v. 27, vi. 7–14). The land would be filled with the sound of mourning and lamentation (v. 16, 17). He probably found no difficulty in believing in the sudden destruction of nations, for Tekoa was on the edge of the wilderness of Judaea, and the nearness 'gave the ancient nations of Judaea, as it gives the visitor to-day, the sense of living next-door to doom: the sense of how narrow is the border between life and death. . . . The desert is always in face of the prophets, and its howling beasts and dry sand blow mournfully across their pages, foreboding of doom'.[1] In spite of his harshness and intolerance there was in his heart a touch of pity. He pleaded with the people to hate the evil and to love the good; then perhaps a

[1] G. A. Smith, *Historical Geography of the Holy Land*, 25th ed., 1931, pp. 313 f.

faithful few might survive the impending destruction to enjoy Yahweh's blessings and favour. In the vision of the plague of locusts a swarm of locusts swept over the land, devouring all the grass. Recognizing that the calamity was sent as a judgement he besought Yahweh to pardon Israel and his petition was granted. 'The Lord repented concerning this: It shall not be, saith the Lord' (vii. 3). In the vision of the fire, fire dried up the great deep and threatened to burn up the tilled land. Again he pleaded with Yahweh to spare Israel and Yahweh relented. When, however, in the vision of the plumb-line, Yahweh showed him that He could no longer pardon Israel but that He would bring upon her corrupt sanctuaries and ruling house the fire and sword of the conqueror, he made no further intercession, but went forth to proclaim the message of impending destruction. It is not surprising that he is sometimes called the 'prophet of doom'.

According to the title, which is a later editorial addition, Amos delivered his message 'in the days of Uzziah King of Judah, and in the days of Jeroboam the son of Joash King of Israel, two years before the earthquake'. There is no need to doubt the accuracy of this date, since it is confirmed by the internal evidence of the book itself as to the general historical background. We learn that under Jeroboam II (786–746 BC) the Northern Kingdom reached the height of its prosperity and power (iv. 4, 5, v. 21–23, vi. 1, 13), and that the wealthy classes became morally and spiritually corrupt (ii. 6, iv. 4, v. 21–23, viii. 5, 6). Some years must have elapsed before their degradation became so pronounced as to rouse the wrath of Amos. He must have been active before the end of Jeroboam II's reign, otherwise he would not have predicted the fall of his dynasty (vii. 9). His ministry, therefore, must be fixed in the latter part of that king's reign. In ch. viii. 9 he says, 'And it shall come to pass in that day, saith the Lord God, that I will cause the sun to go down at noon, and I will darken the earth in the clear day'. These words suggest that he had seen the eclipse of the sun, which, it has been calculated, was almost total at Nineveh in 763 BC. The reference in the title to the earthquake (also mentioned in Zech. xiv. 5) may be ignored since the date of that event is unknown. We shall probably be correct if we fix the date of the prophet's ministry in the period 760–750 BC.[1]

[1] R. S. Cripps in *The Book of Amos*, 1929, suggests 743 BC or 741 BC as the date for the commencement of Amos' prophetic activity, on the ground that Assyria did not

CONTENTS

The book of Amos falls naturally into three parts:

(1) Chs. i–ii. Prophecies against the surrounding nations, all introduced by a common formula 'For three transgressions of . . . ,
yea, for four, I will not turn away the punishment thereof',
followed by a prophecy against Israel.

(2) Chs. iii–vi. Several short discourses denouncing Israel. Three
begin with the words, 'Hear this word' (iii. 1, iv. 1, v. 1). Probably the word 'woe' should be added to ch. v. 7.

(3) Chs. vii–ix. A series of five visions of judgement, with some
biographical matter and a promise of the restoration and prosperity of Judah.

These three parts may be summarized thus:

Chapters i–ii
Chs. i–ii. 5. Title and motto (i. 1, 2). Amos denounces the sins of
Israel's neighbours, namely, Damascus (i. 3–5), Philistia (i. 6–8),
Phoenicia (i. 9, 10), Edom (i. 11, 12), Ammon (i. 13–15), Moab
(ii. 1–3) and Judah (ii. 4, 5).
Ch. ii. 6–16. The prophet denounces Israel in even stronger terms.
The Israelites sell as slaves innocent men who refuse to bribe their
judges, and poor men for such a trifling debt as a pair of sandals.
They trample down the poor like dust, practise immorality in the
name of religion (vv. 6, 7), lie down on clothes taken in pledge, and
in the house of Yahweh drink wine purchased with unjust fines (v. 8).
Yahweh has led the Israelites through the wilderness, destroyed the
Canaanites and raised up inspired men to lead them; but they have
corrupted the Nazarites and silenced the prophets. Destruction and
exile await them (vv. 9–16).

Chapters iii–vi
Ch. iii. 1–8. Israel (here includes Judah) has forgotten that her
privileges as Yahweh's chosen people involve special responsibilities. Her privileged position, far from securing her against punishment, requires it. Nothing happens without a cause; therefore, when
the prophets speak it is because Yahweh has revealed His secrets to

---

constitute a serious threat to Israel until the accession of Tiglath-pileser in 745 BC and
his attack on northern Syria two years later.

them, and when Yahweh is angry it means that judgement is at hand.

Ch. iii. 9–15. The heathen of Philistia and Egypt are summoned to look on the disorder and oppression of Samaria. The ruling classes have no proper sense of what is right and store their palaces with goods taken by robbery and violence. For their sins a foreign foe shall destroy their city so completely that nothing worth saving shall be left. Bethel itself shall be razed to the ground together with all the palaces of the wealthy.

Ch. iv. 1–3. The prophet denounces the women of Samaria, who oppress the poor and demand of their husbands wine to drink. They shall be dragged through breaches in the walls and flung on refuse heaps.

Ch. iv. 4–13. With bitter irony he attacks their worthless worship. They love to sacrifice every morning, to pay their tithes every three days, to burn cakes of leavened bread as a thank-offering; but Yahweh has shown them that such empty worship is a sin against Himself by sending calamities upon them—famine, drought, blight, locusts, pestilence, slaughter and destruction of cities. Since they have persisted in their evil ways, they must prepare to meet their God.

Ch. v. 1–17. The prophet now has a vision of Israel destroyed in battle, laments her fall, and appeals to the people to forsake Bethel, Gilgal and Beersheba and return to Yahweh and live (vv. 1–9). He charges them with perverting justice, silencing honest criticism, and oppressing the poor. Those who crush the poor shall never enjoy the luxurious houses they build for themselves or enjoy the wine of the vineyards they plant for themselves, but if they seek good and not evil Yahweh will be generous to them (vv. 10–15). On all sides shall be heard the sounds of wailing and lamentation for the dead (vv. 16, 17).

Ch. v. 18–27. The prophet warns them of the approaching 'day of Yahweh', which shall be not a day of victory as they confidently expect, but a day of defeat. Yahweh has no pleasure in their feasts, solemn assemblies, offerings, hymns and melodies. He demands not sacrifice, but justice and righteousness. In the wilderness sacrifice was not offered to Him. Because of their idolatry they shall go into captivity beyond Damascus.

Ch. vi. The prophet denounces the leaders of Samaria who feel secure in their mountains. They imagine themselves to be the world's most notable people, but in reality they are no better than the Syrians and Philistines. They put off the evil day; they lounge upon couches, feed upon delicacies, sing idle songs, drink wine and anoint themselves with costly ointments, but they are indifferent to the sufferings of their fellow men. Their revelry shall cease and they shall go into captivity; a foreign foe shall harry them from the pass of Hamath to the wady of the Arabah.

Chapters vii–ix

Chs. vii–ix. 8a. This section consists of a series of visions sounding the doom of Israel, interrupted by the account of Amaziah's attempt to intimidate Amos. First comes the visions of the devouring locusts (vii. 1–3), the consuming fire (vii. 4–6), and the plumb-line (vii. 7–9). The last vision rouses the hostility of Amaziah, the priest of Bethel, who bids the prophet begone to Judah and earn his living there by prophesying. The prophet retorts that he is not a professional prophet and warns him that he and the people of Israel shall be led into captivity (vii. 10–17). Next comes the vision of the summer fruits (viii. 1–3), which is followed by a number of loosely connected fragments in which the prophet denounces the wealthy merchants who oppress the poor, resent the observance of the Sabbath because it interferes with their business, falsify their weights and measures, traffic in the lives of the poor, and sell the very refuse of their wheat. Yahweh shall convulse the earth, the sun shall be darkened, joy shall be turned into lamentation, and the end shall be utter misery and despair (viii. 4–14). The last vision is that of the smitten sanctuary and the destruction of the worshippers (ix. 1–8a).

Ch. ix. 8b–15. The prophet predicts that Israel shall not be utterly destroyed. A faithful remnant shall escape, the house of David shall be restored, and the nation shall enjoy lasting happiness and prosperity.

UNITY

The greater part of the book is generally recognized as being the work of Amos. Doubts have been cast upon the originality of several passages, but the only ones which are rejected by most critics are Chs. ii. 4, 5 and ix. 8b–15. In Ch. ii. 4, 5, no specific crime is brought against Judah, but only a general charge of failure to observe the law of Yahweh: this is unlike Amos who elsewhere gives concrete examples of the sins he denounces. The style, too, is Deuteronomic in character. The passage is thought to be of post-exilic origin. In ch. ix. 8b–15 the people are promised a new age, not of justice and righteousness as we should naturally expect from Amos, but of material prosperity. 'And they shall plant vineyards, and drink the wine thereof; they shall also make gardens and eat the fruit of them' (ix. 14). Moreover, although Amos addresses Israel, the passage deals with Judah, and presupposes the fall of the dynasty (ix. 11) and the Exile (ix. 14, 15).

PERMANENT INFLUENCE

The book of Amos is our chief authority for the social, moral and religious conditions of the Northern Kingdom in the reign of Jeroboam 11. We learn that with the increase of wealth there arose a new wealthy class of merchants, who, forgetting the old simple way of life to which their fathers had been accustomed, lived in luxury and idleness and succumbed to the temptations of drunkenness and gluttony (iv. 1, vi. 4–6). They oppressed the poor, selling honest folk for money and the needy for a pair of shoes (ii, 6, iv. 1): in their greed for gain they falsified weights and measures, 'making the ephah small, and the shekel great and dealing falsely with balances of deceit' (viii. 5). Judges were corrupt browbeating honest men, accepting bribes and denying justice to the poor (v. 12). To such oppression they added the sin of immorality (ii. 7). The connection between religion and morality, which had been characteristic of Yahwism, was either ignored or forgotten. They were zealous in their attendance at the solemn assemblies, in the offering of sacrifices, in the payment of tithes and freewill offerings, and in the keeping of the feasts, but in their dealings with their fellow men they forgot justice and mercy (iv. 4, 5, v. 21–24).

In the book Amos stands out primarily as a social and moral reformer, but his social and moral ideas sprang out of his exalted conception of the deity. His mind was filled with the thought of the incomparable greatness of God. Yahweh was a living God and the Creator of the Universe. 'For, lo, he that formeth the mountains, and createth the wind, and declareth unto man what is his thought, that maketh the morning darkness, and treadeth upon the high places of the earth; the Lord, the God of hosts, is his name' (iv. 13; cf. v. 8, ix. 5, 6). He was also the Ruler of all nations, moving them as He willed and using them as the instruments of His purpose (vi. 14). He had chosen the children of Israel above all the families of the earth to be the medium of His purpose and will. He had delivered them from bondage in Egypt, led them through the wilderness to the Promised Land (ii. 10; cf. iii. 1, 2) and raised up from among them prophets and Nazarites (ii. 11, 12). But he had also guided other nations. 'Have not I brought up Israel out of the land of Egypt, and the Philistines from Caphtor, and the Syrians from Kir?' (ix. 7). He was not only the Creator of the Universe and the Ruler of all nations, but a God of absolute righteousness who demanded from His worshippers right conduct and loving devotion to Himself (iv. 4, 5, v. 21–24). It is obvious that he had given up the popular idea that there existed many gods, each having his own chosen people. In his view Yahweh was the only true God, the Creator of the Universe, the Lord of history, and a God of absolute righteousness. He was therefore a monotheist, though he did not state categorically that there was only one God. His monotheism was not the result of philosophical speculation on the nature of God; it was based on faith in a living, righteous God who was active in history.

Amos has sometimes been called the first monotheist. The title, however, has been ascribed by some scholars to the Egyptian king Akhnaton (1377–1360 BC) who established the worship of the 'Aten' or 'Aton', and by others, to Moses, the founder of Yahwism. It is doubtful, however, if either of them was a monotheist in the strict meaning of the term. It is probable that Akhnaton aimed at establishing monotheism and approximated to it more closely than any other person in the ancient East, but he died before he had accomplished his purpose and his religion was swept away. As regards Moses, Israelite tradition nowhere says or indicates that he was a monotheist. He made Yahweh the God of the Israelites, but it would appear that he did not claim that other nations were also under His control, nor did he deny the existence of other gods. His worship, therefore, was probably not monotheistic but monolatrous, that is, he worshipped one God but at the same time recognized the existence of others. 'It may be said with considerable assurance that Moses sowed the seeds of monotheism, but the real fruitage did not come until centuries later because it could not. An idea cannot be born in a day, it comes only in the fullness of time.'[1] Monotheism was first explicitly taught by Deutero-Isaiah. 'And there is no God

[1] T. J. Meek, *Hebrew Origins*, Revised ed. 1950, p. 215.

else beside me; a just God and a Saviour; there is none beside me.
Look unto me, and be ye saved, all the ends of the earth: for I am
God, and there is none else. By myself have I sworn, the word is gone
forth from my mouth in righteousness, and shall not return, that unto me every knee shall bow, every tongue shall swear.' (Is. xlv. 21–23.)

Amos gave to his countrymen a new conception of religion. According to the popular view religion meant no more than the performance of certain prescribed rites and ceremonies: provided these
were duly performed Yahweh was satisfied. He was indifferent to the
character of the worshipper and to his attitude towards Himself.
Such a view meant that there was no connection between religion
and morality, and that there was no intimate relationship between
the worshipper and his God. Amos proclaimed that Yahweh was a
God of absolute righteousness who demanded righteousness of life
from His worshippers. Because He was righteous it was His will that
man, who was made in His own image, should reflect His own righteousness. The performance of rites and ceremonies without right
conduct was a mockery and of no value in the sight of Yahweh, who
demanded not frequent attendance at the sanctuaries, or abundant
offerings or punctual tithes, or an elaborate and impressive ritual, or
vocal and instrumental music, but right conduct, justice and fair
dealings as between man and man. 'I hate, I despise your feasts, and
I will take no delight in your solemn assemblies. Yea, though ye
offer me your burnt offerings and meal offerings, I will not accept
them: neither will I regard the peace offerings of your fat beasts.
Take thou away from me the noise of thy songs; for I will not hear
the melody of thy viols. But let judgement roll down as waters, and
righteousness as a mighty stream' (v. 21–24). To emphasize the truth
that ceremonial worship was of no value in the sight of Yahweh,
Amos reminded the people that in their wilderness wanderings
there were no sacrifices. He asked the question, 'Did ye bring unto
me sacrifices and offerings in the wilderness forty years, O house of
Israel?' (v. 25). Clearly expecting the answer 'No'.[1] With Amos
religion and morality were inextricably interwoven.

[1] There are differences of opinion regarding the attitude of the pre-exilic prophets
towards sacrifice. The relevant passages are: Am. v. 21–25; Hos. vi. 6; Is. i. 11–15;
Mic. vi. 6–8; and Jer. vii. 21–23. Some critics hold that they absolutely condemned
sacrifice, and others that they did not reject it as such but only as offered by wicked
men. For a discussion of the subject see J. Skinner, *Prophecy and Religion*, 1922, pp. 165–
184; H. H. Rowley, *The Rediscovery of the Old Testament*, 1945, pp. 109–113; and N.
Snaith, *Mercy and Sacrifice*, 1953, pp. 88–101.

Amos, however, was not the first to proclaim the truth that Yahweh demanded right conduct from those who professed to serve Him. There was an ethical strain in Israelite religion from the days of its foundation by Moses. Nathan had rebuked David for his adultery with Bathsheba (2 Sam. xii. 1–15) and Elijah had rebuked Ahab for the murder of Naboth (1 Kgs. xxi. 17–24). But in the historical books it is so mixed up with their other material that it does not stand out as in the book of Amos, which deals with this and this only. His message to the people is summed up in the words, 'Seek the Lord, and ye shall live' (v. 6) and, 'Seek good, and not evil, that ye may live: and so the Lord, the God of hosts, shall be with you, as ye say' (v. 14). Henceforth it became the standard teaching of all true prophets. When, after many years during which no prophet appeared, John the Baptist was recognized by thousands of Jews as a prophet, in his ethical teaching recorded by Luke (iii. 17) we have this same message. It is only one of the truths about God. Hosea was to supply another of equal importance. Until men recognized God's justice they could hardly recognize His mercy.

Amos taught that privilege implied responsibility. The current belief among the people of Israel was that since they were Yahweh's chosen people He would continue to protect them and bestow His favours upon them irrespective of their manner of life. They looked forward with eager expectation to a coming day of Yahweh when, it was confidently believed, He would triumph over all their enemies and give them great glory. Amos agreed that a day of Yahweh was approaching, but he saw it in quite a different light. He declared that because they had known better, their punishment would be more severe than that inflicted upon other nations that had not had the same opportunities. The day of Yahweh would be not a day of triumph but one of catastrophe. 'Woe unto you that desire the day of the Lord! wherefore would ye have the day of the Lord? It is darkness and not light' (v. 18). Because of the lack of justice and righteousness in the land, Yahweh would cause them to go into captivity beyond Damascus (v. 27).

Amos made an important contribution to religious thought by his emphasis upon the inexorableness of the moral law. Neither men nor nations could violate it and hope to escape punishment. It was as though a man fled from a lion and a bear met him, or went into the house and rested his hand on the wall and a serpent bit him (v. 19). For Israel to imagine that she could escape punishment was just as foolish as men who would attempt to drive horses over crags or to plough the sea with oxen (vi. 12). The people might try to save themselves from destruction by digging down to Sheol, or by climbing up to heaven, or by hiding on Mount Carmel or in the depth of the sea, or by going into exile. But all their efforts would be of no avail: no matter where they fled the arm of Yahweh would reach them, for He had set His eyes upon them for evil and not for good (ix. 4). To Amos the moral law was not the Decalogue, which had been revealed to his people, but an integral part of the law of God which had been in the world from the beginning and had been revealed by Him to His servants, the prophets. It had been made known to Amos, as part of that revelation, that the world was under the control of a just and righteous God who required of men that they should take Him as the moral pattern of their lives. Hence he concluded that the world was a moral order, and that those whose lives were not in harmony with it were doomed to destruction.

STYLE

For many years it was customary to accept the view of Jerome that Amos was a rustic and unskilled in speech. This view, which seems to have been based upon the fact that the prophet was only a wool-grower and dresser of sycomore trees, can no longer be accepted. He was far from being an ignorant man without the ability to express his thoughts. As we have already shown, he had some knowledge of the surrounding heathen nations and was a keen observer of the social, moral and religious conditions of Israel. It was not unusual in the East for a countryman to be an accomplished writer.

The style of Amos is clear, vigorous and often impassioned. A great variety of picturesque images is employed, most of them being drawn from pastoral and country life (ii. 9, 13, iii. 4–6, v. 8, 19, 24, ix. 2–4). In his use of these images he reveals great poetic skill and originality. Like most Hebrew writers he makes frequent use of apt figures of speech, especially simile and metaphor, and knows how to employ the literary devices of contrast (v. 19, viii. 9, 10, ix. 2) and repetition (ii. 11, v. 4–8, vii. 3–6) with fine effect. There are many memorable passages scattered through the book (iii. 1, 2, iv. 4, 5, 12, 13, v. 8, 9, 14, 15, 18–20, 21–24, vi. 14, ix. 2–4). Far from being homely and rustic, his style is on a level with the best models in classical Hebrew literature.

CHAPTER VII

Hosea

LIFE AND CHARACTER OF HOSEA

Hosea, the son of Beeri, appears to have come from the Northern Kingdom, perhaps from the land of Benjamin (v. 8, 9), for he addressed his message in the main to Ephraim or Israel, that is, the Northern Kingdom, referred to its king as 'our king' (vii. 5), and showed himself familiar with localities within its border (i. 4, iv. 15, v. 1, vi. 8, 9, xii. 11). His knowledge of the intrigues going on in the land suggests that he belonged to the upper classes, perhaps to the circle of priests.

There is no mention in his book of any inaugural vision in which he heard the call to the prophetic ministry: instead we have an account of his experience with Gomer, 'a wife of whoredom', whom he had married at Yahweh's command, as a result of which he became a prophet, for he regarded his relations with her as symbolic of Yahweh's union and experience with His people. Just as Gomer had proved unfaithful to him, so Israel had been unfaithful to Yahweh (i. 2). He called his three children by symbolic names, signifying the indignation of Yahweh against His people. To his eldest son he gave the name of Jezreel, signifying that the dynasty of Jehu would perish at Jezreel (i. 4). His second child, a daughter, he called Lo-ruhamah ('no mercy'), for Yahweh would no longer have mercy upon the house of Israel (i. 6). The third child, another son, he called Lo-ammi ('not my people'), for Israel was no longer the people of Yahweh (i. 9). Nothing more is known about either his private or his public life.

He was an educated man, tender-hearted and sensitive, craving for love and fellowship and with a poetic disposition. Like all true poets he was endowed with imagination and acute powers of observation. He had noted the morning cloud and the dew upon the grass (vi. 4, xiii. 3), the thorns spreading over the paths (ii. 6), the springs and fountains (xiii. 15), the standing corn (viii. 7), the hemlock in the furrows of the field (x. 4), the shimmering heat of the oven (vii. 4, 7) and the smoke ascending from the chimney (xiii. 3). He had watched the stubborn heifer at work and the lamb feeding in a broad pasture (iv. 16), the kindly driver easing the yoke of his tired oxen (xi. 4), the fowler spreading his net (vii. 12), the farmer ploughing, harrowing, sowing, and reaping (x. 11, 12), the wild ass standing alone (viii. 9) and the bird in flight (ix. 11). Such images as these he had stored in his memory, and when the time came, used them to illustrate his teaching.

According to the title of his book (i. 1) Hosea must have begun his prophetic activity in the prosperous days of Jeroboam 11. Some of his prophecies point to the period of anarchy which followed Jeroboam's death in 746 BC; the court was corrupt, conspiracy rife, and kings were assassinated (vii. 3, 5, 7, viii. 4). In chs. v. 13, viii. 9, and x. 5, 6 there are probably allusions to the tribute paid by Menahem to Tiglath-pileser. It is generally thought that he ceased to prophesy before the Syro-Ephraimitic War (734 BC), since he apparently knows nothing of the alliance between Syria and Egypt against Ahaz, or of the fall of Damascus. There are, however, some scholars who conclude from chs. xi. 11 and xiii. 16 that he continued to prophesy until after the fall of Samaria (722 BC) and predicted the return from captivity.

CONTENTS

The book falls naturally into two parts:

(1) Chs. i–iii. Two accounts of the prophet's unhappy marriage, one in the third person and the other in the first. The unfaithfulness of his wife and his own love for her in spite of her sin are symbolic of Israel's unfaithfulness to Yahweh and of Yahweh's never-failing love for His people.

(2) Chs. iv–xiv. A series of discourses denouncing Israel's sin, threatening punishment, calling her to repentance and promising forgiveness and restoration.

These two parts may be summarized thus:

Chapters i–iii
Chs. i–ii. 9. The title (i. 1). Hosea is commanded to take a harlot for

his wife and have 'children of harlotry'. He marries Gomer, who subsequently bears three children to whom he gives the symbolic names of Jezreel, Lo-ruhamah and Lo-ammi, in order that he may make them the texts for his prophetic message to Israel (i. 2–9).

Chs. i. 10–ii. 1. The children of Israel are to increase and are to be called 'the sons of the living God', while Judah and Israel are to be united under a single ruler and to go forth to a great victory at Jezreel.

Ch. ii. 2–13. Israel has been unfaithful to her divine husband in going after the local Baalim for gifts of bread, water, wool, flax, oil and drink. She shall learn by bitter experience that these material gifts belong to Yahweh, who shall withdraw His gifts and reduce her to poverty and misery.

Ch. ii. 14–23. Yahweh shall bring her into the wilderness, where, as in the days of the Exodus, she will respond to His love. The very names of the Baalim shall be forgotten. In that day she shall be betrothed to Yahweh for ever in a bond of righteousness, justice, kindness and love: strife shall be banished from the land and she shall enjoy abounding prosperity.

Ch. iii. Hosea is commanded to marry an unnamed woman who is loved by a paramour and is an adulteress. He obeys by purchasing her and setting her apart for what seems a probationary period. Yahweh shall deal with Israel in the same way. She shall remain for a time without king or chief, without sacrifice or sacred stone, and without ephod or teraphim: afterwards she shall return to Yahweh and His goodness.

Chapters iv–xiv

Ch. iv. The whole nation is morally corrupt, for there is no truth, nor mercy, nor knowledge of God in the land—nothing but perjury, lying, murder, stealing, debauchery and bloodshed on bloodshed (vv. 1–2). No one protests for the people are no better than the priests. The latter reject the instruction of their God and batten on the sins of the people, encouraging them to believe that by multiplying offerings they are pleasing Him. Both the people and the priests shall be punished for their sins (vv. 3–11). The prophet denounces the people for their idolatry and debauchery and warns Judah not to follow Israel's evil example (vv. 12–15). Israel is like a stubborn heifer and Yahweh cannot feed her 'as a lamb in a large place'. Because of the idolatry and debauchery of the

D

people, the tempest (i.e. the Assyrians) shall sweep them away (vv. 16–19).

Ch. v. 1–15a. Judgement is declared against the priests and the ruling classes because they are responsible for the false worship at the sanctuaries. When Ephraim (i.e. Israel) and Judah fall, they will seek in vain to propitiate Yahweh with their flocks and herds; but their doom and desolation are certain. Appeals to Assyria for help are futile. Yahweh shall rend them as a lion and there shall be none to deliver them. He will wait until they repent and seek His face.

Chs. v. 15b–vii. 2. In their distress Ephraim and Judah will turn to Yahweh but they will regard their sins too lightly. They will come offering sacrifices; but Yahweh requires love, not sacrifice, 'and the knowledge of God more than burnt offerings' (v. 15b–vi. 6). Evidence of Israel's crimes can be found at the sanctuaries—Adam-town, Gilead, Shechem and Bethel. Israel defiles herself, and Judah, too, conspires against Yahweh. Yahweh's efforts to heal His people only serve to reveal their guilt more clearly (vi. 7–vii. 2).

Ch. vii. 3–16. Kings and princes gladly share in the prevailing wickedness—drunkenness and immorality—and the court itself is a scene of treachery, conspiracy and assassination (vv. 3–7). Israel has mingled with foreign nations who have devoured her strength. She cries to Egypt for help and flies to Assyria, but Yahweh shall punish her for her misdeeds. The people have not prayed to Him with sincerity but have howled for corn and wine beside their altars; therefore their princes shall fall by the sword and their overthrow shall provoke the scorn of the Egyptians (vv. 8–16).

Ch. viii. A foe is coming against Israel to execute divine judgement upon her. The people have set up kings and princes without Yahweh's consent and have wasted their silver and gold in the making of images. But Yahweh detests the calf at Samaria; it is no God and shall be smashed. The sources of the national life are withered and the people count for nothing among the nations (vv. 1–8). They have wilfully turned to Assyria and sent love-offerings to Egypt. They have multiplied altars which have become places of sin. Yahweh does not accept their sacrifices and shall visit their sins upon them. They shall return to Egypt and the citadels of Judah shall be destroyed by fire (vv. 9–14).

Ch. ix. The joy of Israel in her false worship shall turn into the sorrow of exile. The people shall return to Egypt and eat unclean food in Assyria. In a strange land they shall have no opportunity of sacrificing to Yahweh. Egypt shall be their grave and all their wealth shall be destroyed in the day of visitation. The prophet is God's watchman and yet men are hostile to him in the temple of his God (vv. 1–9). In the wilderness Israel found favour with Yahweh, but when the people came to Baal-peor, they gave themselves up to impure worship and became abominable like that which they worshipped. Because of their doings at Gilgal Yahweh shall drive them from His land; because they are deaf to His voice they shall become wanderers among the nations (vv. 10–17).

Ch. x. Israel's many altars shall be destroyed, the king shall be powerless to help her, and the bull of Beth-aven (Bethel) shall be carried off to Assyria. The high places of Aven, the source of Israel's sin, shall be destroyed (vv. 1–8). Ever since the days of Gibeah Israel has sinned. Yahweh is about to gather the nations against her. She is like a heifer that desires only the light task of treading out the corn, but she must learn the harder tasks (drawing, ploughing, and harrowing). She has sown wickedness and reaped disaster. The tumult of war shall rise in her midst; all her fortresses shall be ruined and her king swept away (vv. 9–15).

Ch. xi. 1–11. Yahweh brought Israel out of Egypt, but the people proved disloyal, sacrificing to the Baalim and burning incense to the graven images. He protected them as a father, healed them in sickness, and treated them as a kindly driver who eases the yoke of his tired oxen; but it was all in vain. They must go back to Egypt or Assyria must be their king: because of their idolatry their cities shall be given up to the sword. Yet so great is Yahweh's love for them that He cannot let them go. He is God not man, kinder than the kindest father and gentler than the gentlest driver. The exiles shall return from Egypt and Assyria.

Chs. xi. 12–xii. 14. Israel surrounds Yahweh with lies and deceit (nor has Judah been faithful). She piles up fraud and falsehood and enters into relations with Assyria and Egypt. She has the faults of her ancestor Jacob, who from the beginning was a supplanter and in manhood had power with (or strove with) God. She cheats in order to become rich. She shall again dwell in tents and Gilead shall be overthrown. Because she has provoked Yahweh most bitterly, He shall execute judgement upon her.

Ch. xiii. Israel has persistently lapsed into idolatry; therefore she shall be swept away. Yahweh brought her out of Egypt, cared for her in the wilderness and gave her plenty, but she forgot Him. He is about to turn against her like a wild animal and destroy her (vv. 1–8). She is responsible for her own ruin and her kings are powerless to save her. Her sin is stored up and she will not escape the coming judgement. Yahweh cannot redeem her from death, for Samaria has rebelled against Him and must suffer all the horrors of war (vv. 9–16). Ch. xiv. Israel is urged to return to Yahweh. She promises that she will no longer trust in foreign alliances and idols, and Yahweh assures her of forgiveness and promises the restoration of her old fruitfulness. The final exhortation urges the study of the teaching of the book.

THE PROBLEM OF HOSEA'S MARRIAGE

The problem of Hosea's marriage has been much discussed in recent years. There are two accounts of his marriage, one in ch. i. and one in ch. iii. What is the relation between the two? Some critics maintain that the whole story is an allegory without any historical foundation, others that they may refer to two different women, others that they may record two different stages in the prophet's relations with the same woman, and others that they may be two different accounts of the same events, though in ch. iii. no children are mentioned. The generally accepted view in this country is that these two accounts refer to two different stages in the prophet's relations with the same woman, Gomer. It is assumed that he knew nothing against this woman when he was originally told to marry her, and that he afterwards discovered her infidelity to him and named the children accordingly. Then it is held that she left him—perhaps seduced at one of the festivals of Baal-worship at which promiscuity prevailed —and became a temple prostitute, and Hosea had literally to buy her from the temple authorities. It strikes us that the critics have derived a more connected account than is admissible from the book. The double infidelity is unlikely. All that seems certain to us is that it was well known that Hosea's oracles were the product of his unfortunate marriage experience but that the tradition was preserved in different forms. Actually this is quite enough to know, since it explains how it came about that he interpreted Yahweh's relations to Israel as a marriage, and any worship of other gods as adultery, and how this analogy became stereotyped in Jewish literature, and was carried over by Paul into Christianity.

UNITY

Some critics maintain that all the passages in the book in which reference is made to Judah are emendations or additions by Judaean editors who adapted the book to later Jewish needs, basing their argument on the fact that Hosea's message is directed to the Northern Kingdom. These passages are as follows:

(a) Emendations: v. 10, 12, 13, 14, vi. 4, xii. 2.

(b) Additions: i. 7, i. 10–ii. 1, iii. 5 (David 'the king'), iv. 15a, v. 5b, vi. 11, viii. 14, x. 11, xi. 12b.

Several of these passages are doubtless unauthentic, but it is not unlikely, however, that Hosea would occasionally refer to Judah.

All the hopeful passages in the book have been assigned by some critics to a later date, on the ground that they are inconsistent with the teaching of Hosea who proclaims the doom of Israel. These passages are, i. 7, i. 10–ii. 1, ii. 14–23, iii. 5, v. 15, vi. 1–3, vi. 11b–vii. 1a, xi. 10, 11, xiv. 1–9. But this judgement is far too sweeping. There is no reason to doubt the genuineness of the passages which envisage a new beginning for the Northern Kingdom. These are ii. 14–23, v. 15, vi. 1–3, xi. 10, 11, xiv. 1–9. The suspected passages are comparatively few and do not affect the substantial unity of the book.

PERMANENT INFLUENCE

To the book of Hosea we are indebted for the light it sheds upon the state of the Northern Kingdom in the author's own day. He saw clearly that the nation was decadent and that it was hastening to its fall. The people were guilty of idolatrous worship and immoral practices at the local sanctuaries (ii. 5, 8, 16, iii. 1, iv. 12–14, 17, 18, x. 5, 6, xiii. 2). There was no truth or mercy or knowledge of God in the land—nothing but perjury, lying, murder, stealing, debauchery and bloodshed on bloodshed (iv. 1, 2; cf. v. 1, 4, vi. 8, vii. 1, 5, 13, x. 4, xii. 7, 8). They had set up kings who had been powerless to heal the wounds of the nation, and who, relying on military power, had forgotten Yahweh who alone could save them (viii. 4, xiii. 4). In foreign politics they had sought alliances with Assyria and Egypt, which had sapped the strength of the nation (vii. 11, viii. 9, xi. 5, xii. 1).

Hosea is important for his conception of the character of God and of the relationship which existed between Him and Israel. Like Amos he believed that Yahweh was a just God who punished evil-doing. The moral and spiritual decay of Israel was due to her disloyalty to Yahweh. He could not be represented by images (viii. 4–6, xiii. 2). He was absolute righteousness and required of His worshippers not sacrifice or ritual offerings, but loving-kindness towards one's neighbours and faithfulness to Himself (vi. 6, x. 12, xii. 6). Israel must pay the penalty of her sin; she had sown the wind and must reap the whirlwind (viii. 7). She would be carried away into Egypt or Assyria and eat unclean food, while nettles would cover her silver idols and thorns spring up in her shrines (ix. 1–7). Her cities would be given up to the sword (xi. 6) and Yahweh would tear her like a wild beast (xiii. 7, 8). She could not avert disaster merely by a light-hearted confession of sin: the goodness of the nation was as transitory 'as a morning cloud, and as the dew that goeth early away' (vi. 4; cf. xiii. 3).

To the truth that God was just he added the greater truth, that He was also loving and merciful. The prophet's experience of the faithlessness of his wife, whom he still loved, led him to a deeper realization of the nature of the bond between Yahweh and Israel. The bond uniting them was that of love. The love of Yahweh for Israel was like that of a husband for his wife, even for an unfaithful wife, and of a father, for his child. He was Israel's God (ix. 1) and called her out of Egypt. 'When Israel was a child, then I loved him, and called my son out of Egypt' (xi. 1; cf. xii. 13). In the wilderness she was specially dear to Him. 'I found Israel like grapes in the wilderness; I saw your fathers as the firstripe in the fig-tree at her first season' (ix. 10). He gave her a land in which to dwell (ix. 3, 15), blessed her with 'the corn, and the wine and the oil and multiplied unto her silver and gold' (ii. 8). He gave the priests the Law (iv. 6). Though she forsook Him for the local Baalim, He behaved towards her as a father teaching his child to walk. 'Yet I taught Ephraim to go; I took them on my arms; but they knew not that I healed them' (xi. 3). Israel had played the harlot, but if she repented He was ready to take her back. 'And I will betroth thee unto me for ever; yea, I will betroth thee unto me in righteousness, and in judgement, and in loving-kindness, and in mercies. I will even betroth thee unto me in faithfulness: and thou shalt know the Lord' (ii. 19, 20). He could not cast off one whom He had loved so dearly. A man in his anger might disown an erring son, but Yahweh was God and not man. He was long-suffering and of great mercy. 'How shall I give thee up

Ephraim? . . . I will not execute the fierceness of mine anger, I will not return to destroy Ephraim; for I am God, and not man; the Holy One in the midst of thee' (xi. 8, 9). Hosea hoped that in the furnace of affliction the soul of Israel would be purified. When that happened Yahweh would forgive and restore them. 'I will heal their back-sliding, I will love them freely: for mine anger is turned away from him. . . . They that dwell under his shadow shall return; they shall revive as the corn, and blossom as the vine: the scent thereof shall be as the vine of Lebanon' (xiv. 4, 7). Because of the prophet's emphasis upon the love and mercy of God, He has been called the 'St. John of the Old Testament'.

It is interesting to note that Hosea taught that there were not two standards of morality, a higher one for women and a lower for men. 'I will not punish your daughters when they commit whoredom, nor your brides when they commit adultery; for they themselves (the men) go apart with whores, and they sacrifice with the harlots' (iv. 14). The principle which he laid down over two thousand years ago was not recognized in this country until recent times.

STYLE

Hosea's prophecies are the work of a poet whose heart is torn by conflicting emotions. On the one hand he is fired by a deep love of his fellow countrymen, and on the other he sees clearly and with sorrow that their moral and spiritual decay must inevitably bring disaster upon them. His style, therefore, is the expression of intense emotion. Its chief characteristics are abruptness, force, pathos and tenderness. Frequently the thought is so condensed that it becomes ambiguous or obscure. Some of his passages possess a lyrical quality which entitles him to a high place among the poets in Hebrew litera-ture. His work is rich in sayings which have been taken up into Christian literature. Of these we may mention the following: 'Like people, like priest' (iv. 9); 'Ephraim is joined to idols; let him alone' (iv. 17); 'Come, and let us return unto the Lord; for he hath torn, and he will heal us; he hath smitten, and he will bind us up' (vi. 1); 'For I desire mercy, and not sacrifice; and the knowledge of God more than burnt offerings' (iv. 6); and, 'Sow to yourselves in right-eousness, reap according to mercy; break up your fallow ground; for it is time to seek the Lord, till He come and rain righteousness upon you' (x. 12).

CHAPTER VIII

Micah

LIFE AND CHARACTER OF MICAH

Micah was a younger contemporary of Isaiah. Whereas, however, the latter was apparently a man of noble birth, a native of Jerusalem, a frequenter of the court and the associate of persons of high rank, Micah was a poor peasant of Moresheth-gath (i. 14), a village situated in the Shephelah, a range of low hills between the central highlands of Judah and the coastal plain. As he grew up to manhood he learnt to sympathize with the peasants, who, he saw clearly were being exploited and oppressed by the wealthy landowners and those in authority. We know nothing of his call to the prophetic ministry, but he was conscious that Yahweh had laid upon him the duty of declaring 'unto Jacob his transgression, and to Israel his sin' (iii. 8). His message was in the main addressed to Judah, that to Samaria apparently being merely introductory. He seems to have taken no great interest in politics, being primarily an ethical and religious reformer, with an intense faith in the righteousness of Yahweh, a passion for right conduct, a burning hatred of injustice and a deep sympathy with the poor.

The precise date of Micah's prophetic activity cannot be determined. According to the title of the book he prophesied 'in the days of Jotham, Ahaz, and Hezekiah, kings of Judah'; but too much reliance must not be placed upon this statement as it is a later editorial addition. There is, however, no need to doubt the accuracy of the statement of the elders, found in Jeremiah xxvi. 18, that he prophesied 'in the days of Hezekiah king of Judah', since it was written little more than a century later than the prophet himself. Further, his denunciation of Samaria shows that he had begun to prophesy before the fall of the city in 722 BC. How far into the reign of Hezekiah his career extended we do not know.

CONTENTS

The book of Micah falls into three clearly marked sections.

(1) Chs. i–iii. Denunciation of the sins of Israel and Judah and the pronouncement of doom upon them.

(2) Chs. iv–v. Prophecies of restoration.

(3) Chs. vi–vii. Exhortations to repentance, threats of punishment, and the penitent attitude of the people towards Yahweh with promises of future restoration.

These three sections may be summarized thus:

Chapters i–iii

Ch. i. 1–9. The title (i. 1). The earth and all that dwell upon it are warned that Yahweh is about to execute judgement upon Israel and Judah because of their sins, which are concentrated in their respective capitals, Samaria and Jerusalem. Samaria shall become a ruin and its idols shall be destroyed. At the thought of the impending ruin the prophet breaks out into violent lamentation, for he sees the same fate advancing upon Judah (vv. 2–9).

Ch. i. 10–16. After warning the people against proclaiming their sorrows among the Philistines, he makes a series of puns on the names of various towns in the Shephelah which are doomed.

Ch. ii. 1–11. The prophet denounces those who 'devise iniquity and work evil' because it is in their power to do so. They eject the poor from their lands and homes, but Yahweh, too, has His plan, which is to give the lands of the oppressors to the heathen (vv. 1–5). He tells those who sneer at his message believing that Yahweh is not impatient and would not wreak His vengeance upon them, that Yahweh is with the upright not with the oppressors of the innocent. They strip the robes from the peaceful wayfarers, evict women from their happy homes, and rob the children of their share in Yahweh's land and worship. They themselves shall leave the land which they have polluted (vv. 6–10). It is the false prophet who promises wine and strong drink, who is now popular (v. 11).

Ch. ii. 12, 13. Yahweh shall gather the survivors of Israel, and shall shepherd them into the fold (i.e. Palestine), with the stir and noise of numbers. He shall break through the barrier of their captivity like the leading ram that opens the way for the flock, and shall lead them through the gate as their king.

Ch. iii. 1–4. The prophet warns the rulers of Judah, who should be the guardians of justice but who cruelly oppress those whom they govern. A day of darkness is coming upon them when they will turn to Yahweh in vain.

Ch. iii. 5–8. False prophets give incorrect predictions for the sake of material gain but they shall be deprived of all divine illumination. A day of darkness shall come upon them, when they will long for divine guidance but shall receive no answer and shall go mourning. Micah is conscious that he is inspired by Yahweh 'to declare unto Jacob his transgression, and to Israel his sin'.

Ch. iii. 9–12. He again warns the rulers who have founded the prosperity of Jerusalem upon violence and injustice. Judges, priests and prophets are animated by love of money. Jerusalem shall be destroyed.

Chapters iv, v

Ch. iv. 1–4. In after days Jerusalem shall tower over every hill and become the religious centre of the world. Pilgrims from all nations shall flock to it to be instructed in Yahweh's ways. Nations shall learn the art of war no more and every man shall dwell in safety.

Ch. iv. 5. Israel will be true to Yahweh no matter what idols other nations may worship.

Ch. iv. 6–8. In that day Yahweh shall restore those whom He has driven out and afflicted and shall reign over them in Zion for ever. Jerusalem shall be restored to her former dominion.

Ch. iv. 9, 10. There is no king-counsellor in Zion. The daughter of Zion shall go into captivity to Babylon, but Yahweh shall rescue her from captivity.

Ch. iv. 11–13. Many nations muster against Zion, eagerly expecting to desecrate her; but Yahweh has gathered them together to destroy them. They shall be threshed as sheaves and their possessions consecrated to Yahweh.

Ch. v. 1. Zion is cutting herself grievously in the intensity of her mourning, for she is besieged and her judge (i.e. king) is insulted.

Ch. v. 2–4. The ruler who is to deliver Israel shall arise from the insignificant town of Bethlehem. After his birth the fortunes of Israel shall change; the exiles shall return and He shall rule over them in the strength of Yahweh and His strength shall extend to the ends of the earth.

Ch. v. 5–6. When the Assyrian attempts to invade the land, the people shall raise up ample leaders ('seven shepherds and eight principal men') who shall drive them out.

Ch. v. 7–9. The remnant of Jacob shall be like the dew to those nations who submit to it, and like a raging lion to those who resist it.

Ch. v. 10–15. In that day Yahweh shall destroy all the horses and chariots, fortresses and strongholds, and all sorcery and idolatry, and shall inflict drastic punishment upon the disobedient nations.

Chapters vi, vii

Ch. vi. 1–8. Israel is summoned to enter into a legal controversy with Yahweh in the presence of the mountains. Yahweh demands to know in what way He has deserved the ingratitude and neglect of the nation. Acknowledging her sins the nation inquires how Yahweh is to be approached. Will He be satisfied with the multiplication of sacrifices or even with the sacrifice of a man's first born son? The prophet declares that Yahweh demands justice, mercy and the humble walk with God.

Ch. vi. 9–16. Yahweh denounces the inhabitants of Jerusalem for their dishonesty, violence and falsehood, and threatens punishment in the shape of invasion, famine, plunder and slaughter. Jerusalem shall become a desolation and its inhabitants objects of derision among the heathen. Their punishment will be well-deserved because they have followed the cruel policy of the dynasty of Omri.

Ch. vii. 1–6. The prophet laments the utter degradation of the national life—violence, the corruption of justice and the destruction of social and family ties.

Ch. vii. 7–13. The predicted blow has fallen, and the penitent people wait patiently for the intervention of Yahweh who will vindicate His people. The foe that mocked Israel's God shall be confounded, the walls of Zion shall be rebuilt and her exiled inhabitants shall return from all quarters.

Ch. vii. 14–17. Yahweh is invoked to shepherd them with His staff and to restore them to the lost pastures in Bashan and Gilead. He promises them that He will show them marvellous things as in the days of the Exodus. The heathen shall be struck deaf and dumb and prostrate themselves in terror before him.

Ch. vii. 18–20. There is no God like Yahweh who forgives iniquity and delights in mercy. He shall cast all their sins into the depths of the sea, and show them the loyalty and love which He showed to their fathers from the days of old.

AUTHORSHIP

The book of Micah is not a literary unit but a compilation, the only part which can confidently be assigned to the prophet being chs. i–iii (omitting ii. 12, 13). The rest of the book is generally denied to him. Ch. ii. 12, 13 presupposes the Exile and is probably a post-exilic addition. Chapters iv and v consist of a series of short prophecies or fragments of prophecies, namely, iv. 1–4, 5, 6–8, 9, 10, 11–13, v. 1, 2–4, 5, 6, 7–9, 10–15. The general character of ch. iv. 1–4, which describes the coming reign of universal peace, shows that it is later than Micah's time. Moreover the first three verses are almost identical with Isaiah ii. 2–4; their double appearance in almost identical form prevents their acceptance as being the work either of Isaiah or Micah. All the rest of the prophecies seem to be of post-exilic origin. Some critics, however, taking 'Assyrian' in its literal sense, ascribe ch. v. 5, 6 to Micah, but no argument can be based upon this interpretation as the term 'Assyrian' was applied to many late oppressors of Israel (cf. Lam. v. 6; Ezra vi. 22; Zech. x. 11). Others regard ch. v. 10–15 as the work of Micah, but the ideas in the passage—the abolition of warfare and idolatry, and the execution of judgement upon the nations—suggest a post-exilic date.

Chapters vi.–vii. 6 are assigned by many critics to an anonymous prophet writing in the reign of Manasseh (687–642 BC) for the following reasons. There is a considerable difference in tone between this passage and the undoubted work of Micah. The hope and buoyancy of chs. i–iii (omitting ii. 12, 13) have given place to despair and sadness. In chs. i–iii Micah denounces the leaders of the people only, whereas in chs. vi.–vii. 6 his denunciation extends to the whole nation. The reference to the oppressive rule of Omri (876–869 BC) and his son Ahab (869–850 BC) in ch. vi. 16 points directly to the ruthless persecution in the reign of Manasseh. There is a connection between the reference to the sacrifice of the first-born in ch. vi. 7 and Moloch-worship practised in Manasseh's reign. Against these arguments it may be said that even if the passage does belong to Manasseh's reign, it may still be the work of Micah, since it is quite possible that his prophetic ministry extended beyond the reign of Hezekiah, though the fact is not supported by the title (i. 1). Moreover, the teaching of the passage with its emphasis upon the moral demands of Yahweh, resembles that of Micah. Chapter vii. 7–20 is clearly post-exilic in date. The punishment has fallen upon the nation and the exiles are scattered throughout the world, but the walls of Jerusalem are to be rebuilt and the exiles are to return to her. The passage, too, has affinities with many of the Psalms.

PERMANENT INFLUENCE

In estimating the permanent importance of the book of Micah we shall consider only chs. i–iii (omitting ii. 12, 13).[1] Micah stands out in the pages of the Old Testament as the champion of the poor peasants of Judah, his anger blazing forth at the injustice and suffering which he saw on every side. With a bitterness which is unsurpassed in the history of prophecy he denounced the greed of the wealthy landowners, who deprived the peasants of their lands and homes (ii. 2, 9), the corruption of the rulers, whom he likened to cannibals (iii. 3), and the avarice of the judges, priests and prophets (iii. 11). Jerusalem would be destroyed because its rulers had founded its prosperity upon violence and injustice (iii. 10–12).

Like Amos, Hosea and Isaiah he has exalted religious and ethical conceptions. Yahweh was a God of absolute righteousness who made moral demands upon all nations, including Israel. So long as men acted righteously they would enjoy the divine favour (ii. 7), but if they devised iniquity and worked evil they would be surely punished (ii. 1–3). Micah, in fact, taught that religion and morality were inseparable.

The prophecies of Micah are few in number, but his exalted conception of the Deity, his passion for righteousness and his championship of the poor and the oppressed entitle him to a place among the goodly fellowship of the prophets.

---

[1] Chapters iv–vii summarize the teaching of Amos, Hosea and Isaiah, and follow in general the line of thought pursued by Deutero-Isaiah and other later prophets of hope. If, however, they are not marked by originality they do enshrine some of the finest passages to be found in the Old Testament. True religion has never been better defined than in the immortal words, 'He hath shewed thee, O man, what is good; and what doth the Lord require of theee, but to do justly, and to love mercy, and to walk humbly with thy God?' (vi. 8). Our imagination is stirred by the passage describing a world at peace. 'But they shall sit every man under his vine and under his fig tree; and none shall make them afraid' (iv. 4). The section closes with a fine passage extolling the pardoning mercy of God. 'Who is a God like unto thee, that pardoneth iniquity, and passeth by the transgression of the remnant of his heritage? He retaineth not his anger for ever, because he delighteth in mercy. He will turn again and have compassion upon us; he will tread our iniquities under foot; and thou wilt cast all their sins into the depths of the sea' (vii. 18, 19).

STYLE

Micah's style is characterized by vigour, intensity of feeling and vivid imagery. He makes frequent use of rhetorical questions (i. 5, ii. 7, iii. 11), imperatives (i. 10, 13, 16, iii. 1), apt similes (i. 4, 6, 8, iii. 12) and metaphors (iii. 2, 3, 10). In ch. i. 10–15 he also employs the pun, that is, he plays upon the names of towns and villages doomed to destruction. Among the Hebrews punning was not considered humorous and was quite consistent with expression of intense feeling.

CHAPTER IX

Isaiah i–xxxix

INTRODUCTION

For centuries it was believed that our book of Isaiah (i–lxvi) was written by the prophet Isaiah who lived in the latter part of the eighth century BC. In Ecclesiasticus xlviii. 23–25 (c. 180 BC), Ben Sirach, commemorating the great heroes of the past, says of Isaiah, 'In his time the sun went backward, and he lengthened the king's life. He saw by an excellent spirit what should come to pass at the last, and he comforted them that mourned in Zion. He showed what should come to pass for ever and secret things or ever they came.' It is clear that Ben Sirach took for granted that the whole of the book (including xl–lxvi) was written by the prophet whose name it bears. In the New Testament frequent quotations are cited as the words of the prophet Esaias (e.g. Mt. iv. 15, 16; Jn. xii. 40; Rom. x. 20). The view that the book is the work of a single writer was held until relatively modern times. Recent scholarship, however, has proved beyond reasonable doubt that the book is not a literary unit but a compilation.

The book falls into two main divisions, namely chs. i–xxxix and chs. xl–lxvi. Most critics are agreed that all the Isaianic prophecies are to be found in the first division, though it also contains material belonging to a much later period than that of Isaiah. Since 1892 most critics, following Duhm, have divided the second division into two, chs. xl–lv with their Babylonian background being known as Deutero-Isaiah, and chs. lvi–lxvi with their Palestinian background being known as Trito-Isaiah. These three divisions (i–xxxix, xl–lv, lvi–lxvi) will be discussed separately.

LIFE AND CHARACTER OF ISAIAH

Isaiah, the son of Amoz, who must not be confused with the prophet Amos, was apparently born in Jerusalem between 770 and 760 BC.

It is significant that in his writings he shows familiarity with the city and its vicinity rather than with the country. He is well acquainted with the Temple and its ritual (i. 11–15, vi. 1–7), the potter and his clay (xxix. 16; cf. xxx. 14), the orchards and vineyards outside the city walls (i. 8, v. 1–6), the waters of Shiloah 'that go softly' (viii. 6), the fashionable women (iii. 16–23) and the drunken revellers (v. 11, 12). It is generally thought that he was a man of noble birth, since he seems to have had easy access to kings and to have been on intimate terms with persons of high rank. He must have been married shortly before or after 742 BC, because he had a young son who was old enough to go with his father to meet Ahaz 'at the end of the conduit of the upper pool' in Jerusalem (vii. 3). Nothing is known of his wife except that she is termed a prophetess (viii. 3). He had at least two sons to whom he gave the names Shear-jashub (vii. 3) and Maher-shalal-hash-baz (viii. 1–3), which, like his own name Isaiah ('Yahweh saves' or 'Yahweh is salvation'), signify certain characteristic elements in his teaching. His call to the prophetic ministry came 'in the year that king Uzziah died', that is, about 742 BC, and he prophesied in the reigns of the three successive kings, Jotham, Ahaz and Hezekiah. His message was addressed mainly to Judah, though some of his prophecies were directed against Israel. During his long ministry he was not only a prophet but also the most prominent statesman in the kingdom. Soon after the invasion of Sennacherib he disappears from history. Whether he outlived Hezekiah is not known for certain, but a later tradition asserts that he was sawn asunder in the reign of Manasseh.

The name of Isaiah is more familiar to most readers than that of any other Hebrew prophet. His claim to fame rests chiefly upon his deep religious faith, the nobility of his thought, the beauty of his language, and his fervent patriotism, statesmanship, courage and tenacity of purpose. He was in many ways the noblest among the prophets. Even before his call to the prophetic ministry he was evidently concerned about the alarming conditions in the nation and felt the need of patriots to work for its reformation (vi. 1–13). When as a young man he heard in the Temple the call of Yahweh for someone to carry His message to the people, he answered the challenge, 'Whom shall I send, and who will go for us?' with the words, 'Here am I, send me,' even though he was informed that his mission would prove a failure and that judgement would fall upon the nation (vi. 8–13). His ready response was in striking contrast to the hesitation and fears of Jeremiah (Jer. i. 6–8), and the passivity of Ezekiel (Ezek. iii. 12–15). Before the holiness and majesty of Yahweh he became conscious of his own limitations, but was so moved that from henceforth all his life must be lived in the light of that vision. Unlike Amos, whose prophetic activity was apparently confined to a brief visit to Bethel (Am. vii. 10–16), he laboured for some forty years as the devoted servant of Yahweh.

It would appear that Isaiah was subject to fits of ecstasy when he felt that the hand of Yahweh was upon him (viii. 11). He had visions (vi.), heard Yahweh speaking to him in his ears (v. 9, xxii. 14), sometimes acted in a strange manner (xx. 1, 2), sang and lamented in public (v. 1–6), and was convinced that he was divinely inspired (vi. 6–10). Though he was subject to fits of ecstasy, he, unlike the earlier ecstatic prophets, was fully aware of what he was doing and saying. 'In action as in speech,' says Skinner, 'he ever proves himself the sanest of men. His political vision is clear and untroubled, his judgement unerring, his maxims invariably reasonable and wise.'[1]

He was a man who had the courage of his convictions and the determination to proclaim them no matter at what cost to himself. Believing that Yahweh was an omnipotent and absolutely righteous God, Lord of history, demanding from His worshippers not ritual observance but righteousness of life, and preserving those who put their trust in Him, he strove unceasingly during his long career to bring about a moral and spiritual reformation among the people, and to persuade them to put their trust not in military strength or in foreign alliances, but in Yahweh. 'No rank,' says Driver, 'escapes his censure. The soothsayers, and other professors of occult arts, who found in Judah an only too ready welcome; the men of wealth and influence, who ignored the responsibilities of office or position; the leaders of opinion, who possessed weight in the government, or gave a tone to society; the irreligious, short-sighted politicians who nevertheless knew how to put forward their views in an attractive and plausible guide; a powerful minister, whose policy he saw was calculated to jeopardize the state; the women whose frivolity and thoughtlessness on two distinct occasions suggested to him his darkest apprehensions for the future; the masses whom he saw sunk in indifference or formalism; the king himself, whether it were Ahaz, in his wilfulness and insincerity, or Hezekiah listening incautiously to the overtures

[1] J. Skinner, *Isaiah, i–xxxix*, Revised ed. 1915, p. lxxi.

of a foreign potentate—all in turn receive his bold and fearless rebuke.'[1]

In spite of opposition he never gave way to despair, for he was convinced that though disaster would fall upon the nation a remnant would be saved (vi. 13, xvii. 6). He looked forward to the day when an ideal king of the Davidic line would rule in Zion as Yahweh's representative in righteousness and peace (iv. 2–6, vii. 14–17, ix. 2–7, xi. 1–9, xxxii. 1–5, xxxiii. 17–22). He was a statesman and a prophet, a social reformer and a poet. With the possible exception of Jeremiah he was the most many-sided and influential among the Hebrew prophets.

CONTENTS

The first part of the book of Isaiah falls naturally into six main sections.[2]

(1) Chs. i–xii. Prophecies concerning mainly Judah and Jerusalem.

(2) Chs. xiii–xxiii. Prophecies concerning mainly foreign nations. Of the passages in this division ten bear the title of 'burden' (Authorized Version, 'Oracle') which is the translation of the Hebrew word 'massa'='lifting up', and is applied to the lifting up of the voice. These 'burdens' or 'oracles' are directed against Babylon (xiii–xiv. 23), Philistia (xiv. 28–32), Moab (xv, xvi), Damascus and Northern Israel (xvii. 1–11), Egypt (xix), 'the wilderness of the sea', that is, Babylon (xxi. 1–10), Dumah, that is, Edom (xxi. 11, 12), Arabia (xxi. 13–17), 'the valley of the vision', that is Jerusalem (xxii. 1–14) and Tyre (xxiii. 1–14).

---

[1] S. R. Driver, *Isaiah: His Life and Times*, 1888, p. 108.

[2] Some of the sections seem to have been formed by the union of several smaller collections. There are, for example, indications that the first section (i–xii) is not a unity but a collection of collections. Chapter i opens with a title dating the visions, that is, the prophetic oracles, 'in the days of Uzziah, Jotham, Ahaz and Hezekiah', and limiting them to Judah and Jerusalem. This title is appropriate for this section only, for from chapter xiii onward there are many prophecies relating to foreign nations. Chapter ii also has a title, limiting the visions to Judah and Jerusalem but making no mention of any dates. The presence of this second title and absence of any dating suggest that chapter ii marks the beginning of a second collection, probably earlier than the first, which seems to have been used by the main compiler as a general introduction. Chapter vi opens with the call of Isaiah, which we should expect to come first as do the calls of Jeremiah and Ezekiel in the books which bear their names. This chapter, therefore, would appear to mark the beginning of a third collection which extends to the end of chapter xii. Some critics find other collections in the section but there is little or no evidence for them.

The oracles in this section which do not bear the title of 'burden' are, ch. xiv. 24–27 (destruction of Assyria), ch. xvii. 12–14 (destruction of the Assyrian army), ch. xviii (the impending overthrow of Ethiopia), ch. xx (the Assyrian conquest of Egypt and Ethiopia), ch. xxii. 15–25 (denunciation of Shebna), and ch. xxiii 15–18 (the rebuilding of Tyre).

(3) Chs. xxiv–xxvii. A prophecy of a world judgement and the future blessedness of Israel.

(4) Chs. xxviii–xxxiii. A collection of prophecies dealing mainly with the relations of Judah to Assyria and Egypt. The prophecies are arranged in six groups, each headed by the word 'Woe' (xxviii. 1, xxix. 1, 15, xxx. 1, xxxi. 1, xxxiii. 1).

(5) Chs. xxxiv–xxxv. A prophecy of vengeance on Edom and the future blessedness of Israel.

(6) Chs. xxxvi–xxxix. A historical narrative reproduced with slight alterations from the book of 2 Kings xviii. 13–xx. 19.

The six sections may be summarized thus:

Chapters i–xii
Ch. i. The title (v. 1). Yahweh denounces the infidelity and ingratitude of His people (vv. 2, 3). The prophet, in his own name, remonstrates with them for their rebellion and points out the serious condition to which their sin has brought the country (vv. 4–9). Yahweh declares that He will not accept their elaborate and costly sacrifices, which are no substitute for righteousness of life, and the practice of justice and mercy (vv. 10–17). He gives them the choice of obedience and prosperity or disobedience and destruction (vv. 18–20), and laments over the moral decline of Jerusalem, declaring that He will restore her to righteousness (vv. 21–26), deliver her from her troubles and destroy the idolaters (vv. 27–31).

The dates of these prophecies cannot be determined with certainty. They may all date from Isaiah's early ministry; but some critics assign vv. 2–17 to the time of Sennacherib's invasion of Judah in 701 BC and vv. 27–31, which probably consist of two fragments, vv. 27, 28 and vv. 29–31 to the post-exilic period.

Ch. ii. 1–4. New title (v. 1). In time to come all nations shall resort to Jerusalem to learn Yahweh's ways. The acceptance of Yahweh as arbitrator in all international disputes shall put an end to war and usher in a reign of universal peace.

The date and authorship of this passage are uncertain, since it occurs with slight variation in Mic. iv. 1–4. We do not know whether Isaiah borrowed from Micah or vice versa, or whether both are indebted to an earlier writer. There is also the possibility that it comes originally from a later prophet and that it was inserted here and in Micah by the editor of these books.

Ch. ii. 5–22. The prophet denounces the people for their adoption of foreign superstitions, their display of wealth, their confidence in their military resources and their idolatry, and foretells the coming of the 'day of Yahweh'.

This passage belongs to the early period of Isaiah's ministry. It contains a number of verses of a poem which have probably been misplaced. Verse 5 is a pious exhortation based on the preceding oracle and is an editorial addition. Verse 22, which is the reflection of a reader, must be a very late addition, since it is absent from the Septuagint.

Chs. iii–iv. 1. The prophet predicts a period of anarchy (iii. 1–7). The impending ruin of Jerusalem and Judah is due to the guilt of the court and the nobles (iii. 8–12). Yahweh appears and calls them to account for their oppression of the poor (iii. 13–15). In the approaching ruin so many of the male population will perish that the women will outnumber the men by seven to one (iii. 16–iv. 1).

The dates of these passages are uncertain, though the passages fit in well with the early days of Isaiah's ministry. Ch. iii. 25, 26 breaks the connection between ch. iii. 24 and ch. iv. 1 and are probably an editorial addition.

Ch. iv. 2–6. The prophet sees in a vision the land glorious with vegetation, and the people cleansed and holy, and over-shadowed by the protecting presence of Yahweh.

By some critics this passage is assigned to the post-exilic period on grounds of style, ideas and imagery, but the main ideas—the salvation of a remnant, purification through judgement and the transformation of Nature—can be found in Isaiah.

Ch. v. The prophet relates the parable of the vineyard, setting forth Yahweh's care for Judah and the people's unworthiness (vv. 1–7). In a series of woes he denounces the rapacious landowners, the drunkards, the sceptics, the enemies of the moral order, the self-confident and the dissolute, and the corrupt judges (vv. 8–24). Yahweh will summon an invincible army from the end of the earth which shall carry them away (vv. 25–30).

The prophecies probably belong to the period of the Syro-Ephraimitic

War (734 BC). Verses 15, 16 interrupt the connection between vv. 14 and 17 and are probably a marginal quotation of ch. ii. 9, 11, 17 made from memory but with significant modifications. Verses 25–30 may be reckoned as a continuation of vv. 1–24, but many critics think they should follow ch. x. 4.

Ch. vi. Isaiah has a vision of Yahweh on His throne and is called to the prophetic office.

It is dated 'in the year that king Uzziah died' (that is, about 742 BC). The last clause, 'so the holy seed is the stock thereof' (v. 13), does not appears in the Septuagint and most critics regard it as a later addition.

Ch. vii. 1–17. Accompanied by his son, Shear-jashub (a remnant only shall return), Isaiah meets Ahaz and assures him that Syria and Ephraim are doomed to fall (vv. 1–9). In order to strengthen the king's faith the prophet challenges him to ask Yahweh for a sign which will prove that He is not forgetful of His people. The king refuses to do this, whereupon the prophet declares that Yahweh Himself will give him a sign. A Jewish damsel shall have a son who shall be called Immanuel (i.e. 'God is with us'); and before he is old enough to distinguish between good and evil, Syria and Ephraim shall have been overrun by the Assyrians (vv. 10–17).

This passage belongs to the period of the Syro-Ephraimitic War (734 BC).

Ch. vii. 18–25. Yahweh shall summon the Assyrians who will devastate the land.

This passage consists of a series of short utterances probably compiled from several of Isaiah's prophecies concerning the Assyrian invasion.

Ch. viii. 1–4. The prophet is bidden to set up a great tablet bearing the inscription 'Maher-shalal-hash-baz', that is, 'Swift (is) spoil, speedy (is) prey', and to take responsible witnesses, so that when the prediction is fulfilled, they may be able to assure the people that by this inscription the prophet had foretold the speedy downfall of Damascus and Samaria. He is commanded to call his son, born some time later, by the name on the tablet, for before the child shall be able to cry, 'My father, and, My mother', Damascus and Samaria shall be despoiled.

The date of the incidents described in this passage is some time before the fall of Damascus in 732 BC.

Chs. viii. 5–ix. 1. The prophet declares that since Judah has rejected Yahweh's gentle government He shall bring upon her the might of

Assyria (viii. 5–8). All coalitions of foreign nations directed against Judah shall fail for Yahweh is with her (viii. 9, 10). Yahweh alone is to be feared and no coalition of foreign nations directed against her need cause alarm (viii. 11–15). The prophet trusts his message to his disciples; and in the meantime his children with their symbolical names will remain as warnings (viii. 16–18). He warns those who resort to necromancers (viii. 19–22) and predicts a glorious future for Zebulon and Naphtali (ix. 1).

The prophecies contained in ch. viii. 5–18 belong to the period of the Syro-Ephraimitic War. Ch. viii. 19–22 seems to consist of a number of detached fragments of uncertain dates and authorship. Ch. ix. 1 probably comes from a post-exilic editor.

Ch. ix. 2–7. The prophet depicts the future glory of the people of Judah as if it has already come. Yahweh has multiplied the nation and broken the oppressor's yoke. A child has been born, who shall wear the insignia of royalty on his shoulder and shall be called 'Wonderful Counsellor, God-like Hero, Father for ever, Prince of Peace'. He shall sit on the throne of David and shall rule over a wide domain in justice and righteousness. The zeal of Yahweh shall secure the fulfilment of the prophecy.

The date of this prophecy has been much discussed. Some critics assign it to the time of Sennacherib's invasion of Judah in 701 BC and others to the post-exilic period. Skinner dates it about 734 or 733 BC.

Chs. ix. 8–x. 4+v. 25–30. This passage consists of a poem divided into five strophes, each ending with the refrain, 'For all this his anger is not turned away, but his hand is stretched out still' (ix. 12, 17, 21, x. 4, v. 25). Ephraim (i.e. the Northern Kingdom), because of her self-confidence, has been punished by attacks from the Syrians and Philistines (ix. 8–12). Her continued impenitence has been avenged by a sudden disaster embracing all classes (ix. 13–17). Wickedness has spread among the people like a forest fire. The land is in a state of anarchy, and the people in their distress behave like cannibals (ix. 18–21). The prophet denounces the unjust law-givers who deny justice to the poor and the friendless. Nothing shall save them in the day of the divine judgement (x. 1–4). For the meaning of ch. v. 25–30 see p. 116.

The prophecy must be assigned to the period before the Ephraimitic War, for Syria is opposed to Ephraim and there is no mention of an alliance between them.

Ch. x. 5–34. Assyria is represented as Yahweh's rod to punish nations that have roused His anger. But regardless of her mission she plans to exterminate nations far and wide, and boasts that Yahweh will not be able to protect Jerusalem against her attacks. Yahweh shall punish her for ascribing her conquests to her own power and deprive her of her martial strength (vv. 5–19). A remnant of Israel shall put its trust not in earthly power, but in Yahweh (vv. 20–23). Yahweh encourages the inhabitants of Zion to lay aside their fears of Assyria, for very soon He shall destroy her and free them from the oppressor's burden (vv. 24–27). The Assyrian army will march against Jerusalem but shall meet with sudden annihilation (vv. 28–34).

The prophecies, so far as they are Isaiah's, appear to belong to the period between the capture of Carchemish by Sargon in 717 BC and Sennacherib's invasion of Judah in 701 BC. Doubts have been cast upon large portions of this section.

Ch. xi. 1–9. An ideal king shall spring from the family of David. The spirit of Yahweh in its sixfold manifestation shall rest upon him, and with this equipment he shall inaugurate a new age of justice and peace, the blessings of which shall extend even to the animal world.

This passage is closely connected with ch. ix. 2–7, and is probably to be assigned to the same date. Some critics, however, deny the Isaianic authorship of the passage, on the ground that the reference to the 'stump' of a felled tree in v. 1 implies that the monarchy has been overthrown. But the word may be used to indicate the decadent condition of the monarchy in the pre-exilic period.

Ch. xi. 10–16. The prophet predicts the return of the exiles of Judah and Ephraim and the triumph of the reunited monarchy over all its neighbours.

We can feel sure that this passage is not the work of Isaiah, for the dispersion of the people over a wide area suggests the exilic period. Before that time the only wholesale deportations, which had taken place, had been those from the Northern Kingdom to the Assyrian empire (2 Kgs. xv. 29, xvii. 6).

Ch. xii. When the exiles are restored and reunited, they shall sing two hymns of praise to Yahweh (vv. 1, 2, and vv. 3–6). The two hymns have literary affinities with the Song of Moses (Exod. xv.), Psalm cv. and parts of Isaiah xxiv–xxvii. Their imitative character show that they were not written by Isaiah.

Chapters xiii–xxiii

Ch. xiii. 1–22. Yahweh announces His purpose to destroy Babylon through the agency of the Medes. She shall be like Sodom and Gomorrah, desolate for ever.

In the prophecy Babylon is described as 'the glory of kingdoms, the beauty of Chaldean's pride' (xiii. 19); but in the time of Isaiah she was a province of Assyria, not an independent and oppressive power. The Medes did not begin to threaten her until the middle of the sixth century BC. It is clear, therefore, that the prophecy must have been written towards the close of the Exile.

Ch. xiv. 1–4a. Yahweh shall restore Israel to her own land and her oppressors shall serve her. When He has rescued her she shall sing 'this parable' ('taunt-song') against the king of Babylon.

These verses serve as an editorial link between the preceding prophecy and the taunt-song which begins at v. 4b.

Ch. xiv. 4b–21. The tyrant has been overthrown and the earth is at peace. He who thought to become superior to the celestial powers and to sit among the gods, is now in the furthest recesses of Sheol.

This taunt-song was probably composed towards the close of the Exile. Some critics maintain that it was written on the occasion of the death of the Assyrian king Sargon or Sennacherib and that it was adapted by a later editor to the fall of Babylon. There is, however, little evidence for this theory.

Ch. xiv. 22, 23. Yahweh again announces His purpose to destroy Babylon.

These two verses differ both in form and in subject-matter from the preceding taunt-song. They were probably added in post-exilic times as a further prediction of destruction, since Babylon had not been destroyed on the scale expected.

Ch. xiv. 24–27. Yahweh has sworn to destroy the Assyrians in Palestine.

The prophecy probably belongs to the period of Sennacherib's invasion of Judah in 701 BC.

Ch. xiv. 28–32. The Philistines, who are rejoicing in the fall of their oppressor, are warned that his successor will smite them with greater severity. Their envoys (who were probably negotiating an alliance with Judah) must take back the message that Judah has in Zion, founded by Yahweh, an assured defence.

There is no reason to doubt the Isaianic origin of the passage, but its precise date cannot be determined. It may belong to about the time of

Tiglath-pileser's death in 727 BC, or Shalmaneser's in 722 BC, or Sargon's in 705 BC.

Chs. xv–xvi. Maob has been devastated by an enemy and her inhabitants have been put to flight (xv. 1–9). The fugitives send for help to the people of Judah but their appeal is rejected because of their arrogance. The prophet laments over the desolate state of the Moabite vineyards (xvi. 1–12). The utter destruction of Moab shall take place within three years (xvi. 13, 14).

The prophecy is generally regarded as the work of an older prophet, which Isaiah republished, adding an appendix (xvi. 13, 14), foretelling the destruction of Moab which had apparently recovered her former prosperity in the meantime. The occasion of the original prophecy was probably the conquest of Moab by Jeroboam II. Some critics think that the occasion of the prophecy was the Nabataean conquest of Moab in the fifth century BC.

Ch. xvii. 1–11. The prophet announces the impending fall of Damascus and Ephraim. Only a remnant of Ephraim shall escape (vv. 1–6). The survivors will abandon their idols and recognize Yahweh as the sole source of their strength (vv. 7, 8). Ephraim shall become a desolation because of her forgetfulness of Yahweh and her adoption of heathen cults (vv. 9, 10).

The close connection between Damascus and Ephraim suggests that they have formed an alliance. The date of the prophecy must be earlier than the fall of Damascus in 732 BC. Since reference is made to the invasion of Judah by the allied forces, we may fix the date about 734 BC. Verses 7, 8 are probably a late addition since they break the connection between vv. 6 and 9.

Ch. xvii. 12–14. The prophet hears the ocean-like roar of the advancing foe (the Assyrians), but Yahweh shall scatter them.

The date of the prophecy is uncertain, but it is probably about 701 BC when Sennacherib threatened Jerusalem.

Ch. xviii. The Ethiopian monarch has sent ambassadors to Jerusalem, apparently to induce Hezekiah to throw off the Assyrian yoke. Isaiah sends them back with the assurance that when the time is ripe Yahweh shall destroy the Assyrians without the arms of Ethiopia (vv. 1–6). Ethiopia shall then pay homage to Yahweh at Mount Zion (v. 7).

The prophecy probably belongs to the period 705–701 BC. Verse 7 is usually regarded as a post-exilic addition.

Ch. xix. 1–15. Yahweh shall execute judgement upon Egypt, stirring up civil war and delivering the country into the hands of a 'cruel lord'. Physical and social calamities shall ensue, rivers drying up, vegetation withering, industries collapsing and the traditional wisdom of Egypt failing.

There is no adequate reason to doubt Isaianic authorship for the prophecy. The date of the prophecy is uncertain. It may be about 720 BC when Sargon defeated the Egyptian forces at Raphia, or about 711 BC when Egypt sowed revolt in Philistia but with little success, or about 702 BC when Judah was planning an alliance with Egypt. Some critics reject Isaianic authorship and assign the prophecy to the post-exilic period.

Ch. xix. 16–25. Egypt shall fear Yahweh and Judah. Five cities shall speak Hebrew and a sacred stone pillar shall be erected to Yahweh at the border of Egypt. Through the experiences of punishment and deliverance Egypt shall recognize Yahweh as the one true God. A great highway shall connect Egypt and Assyria, and the two states with Israel shall form a triple alliance.

The prophecy is generally assigned to the post-exilic period for the following reasons. Its tone is much more sympathetic towards Egypt than that of the first part. The style is different from that of Isaiah. In Isaiah's day there could not have been five Hebrew-speaking cities in Egypt. Such a reference, however, would suit the post-exilic period when there were extensive Jewish colonies in Egypt. If the prophecy is of post-exilic origin, 'Assyria' in v. 23 stands for 'Syria'.

Ch. xx. For three years before the fall of Ashdod Isaiah had walked naked and barefoot like a captive, to call attention to his message that Egypt and Ethiopia would be conquered by the Assyrians, and that it was futile to look to them for help.

The date of the prophecy is 711 BC when Ashdod was captured by the Assyrians after a short resistance.

Ch. xxi. 1–10. The prophet in a vision sees Babylon besieged by the Elamites and Medes and is appalled by the sights and sounds of war. For a time the issue is uncertain, but in the end a watchman recognizes the victorious army returning from the overthrow of the city.

Most critics hold that the prophecy was written shortly before the capture of Babylon by Cyrus in 539 BC.

Ch. xxi. 11, 12. The prophet hears a voice from Edom, inquiring whether the period of distress is nearly over. The prophet replies that brighter days may dawn for Edom, but they will be quickly followed by further calamities. He invites the inquirer to consult him again, when the purpose of Yahweh may be more clearly revealed.

The date of the prophecy is unknown, but it may be the work of the author of ch. xxi. 1–10.

Ch. xxi. 13–17. The prophet, addressing the Dedanites, a tribe of Arabian caravan traders, declares that they will be driven by the pressure of war to take refuge in the bush of the desert. He calls upon the people of Tema to supply their necessities. He predicts that within a year Kedar will be so reduced in numbers that only an insignificant remnant will survive.

The date of the prophecy is unknown. Some critics fix it in the time of Isaiah when some of the desert tribes were attacked by the Assyrians, others about 590 BC when Jeremiah predicted evil for Dedan (xxv. 23; cf. xlix. 7, 8), and others towards the close of the exilic period when the Dedanites were in danger from the Persians. Verses 16, 17 are probably a fragment which has been added by an editor to the original prophecy.

Ch. xxii. 1–14. The prophet denounces the inhabitants of Jerusalem for indulging in revelry at a time of crisis. He laments over the dead warriors and refuses to be comforted, for a day of disaster is at hand (vv. 1–4). He sees in a vision the city surrounded by enemies and the valleys filled with archers, chariots and horsemen (vv. 5–7). Reverting to the past, he describes the hasty measures taken to put the city in a state of defence (vv. 8–11). Yahweh called the people to mourn, but they continued to feast. For this untimely revelry they shall surely die.

The prophecy probably belongs to the time of Sennacherib's invasion of Judah in 701 BC.

Ch. xxii. 15–25. The prophet announces the coming deposition of Shebna, the steward of the royal house, and the appointment of Eliakim in his place. Eliakim's nepotism shall bring about his downfall.

The prophecy may be dated some time before Sennacherib's invasion of Judah in 701 BC. Verses 24, 25 may be an editorial addition.

Ch. xxiii. 1–14. The Phoenician traders are warned of the approaching fall of Tyre and Zidon and the dispersal of their inhabitants to their colonies, where calamity shall again overtake them.

The date of the prophecy is very doubtful. We know of no attempt to besiege Tyre in the time of Isaiah, except from a somewhat obscure source referring it to Shalmaneser V (727–722 BC). Sennacherib fought in Phoenicia (701 BC) but he did not besiege Tyre. It is certain that the city was not destroyed on either occasion. According to Josephus, Nebuchadrezzar invested the city for thirteen years (585–572 BC) but failed to capture it. It was destroyed by Alexander the Great in 332 BC after a siege of seven months.

Ch. xxiii. 15–18. After seventy years Tyre shall recover and resume her former occupation, but the profits of her merchandise shall be consecrated to the service of Yahweh.

The prophecy is probably a post-exilic addition. The 'seventy years' of v. 15 has the ring of being taken from Jeremiah's forecast of the length of the captivity of Judah (Jer. xxv. 11, 12; xxix. 10).

Chapters xxiv–xxvii

Ch. xxiv. A great catastrophe is about to overwhelm the world, obliterating every distinction of class and spreading desolation far and wide. A city (unnamed) shall be destroyed and the whole human race, with the exception of a small remnant, shall perish (vv. 1–13). The destruction will be greeted with songs of praise by the remnant (vv. 14–16) but such rejoicings are premature, for further calamities shall come upon mankind (vv. 17–20). In that day Yahweh shall punish the hostile heavenly powers together with the earthly kings and reign in glory in Zion (vv. 21–23).

Ch. xxv. Yahweh is praised because He has overthrown a hostile city (vv. 1–5). He shall prepare a great feast in Zion for all nations and there shall be no more death, or sorrow or shame (vv. 6–8). He shall save His people, but Moab shall be trampled under foot (vv. 9–12).

Ch. xxvi. The nation praises Yahweh for the strength of Jerusalem and for the overthrow of a proud hostile city (vv. 1–6). The people have waited for the manifestation of Yahweh's judgements; for the inhabitants of the world will learn righteousness only through the discipline of his judgements (vv. 7–10). Yahweh has destroyed their foreign masters, increased their numbers and extended their territory (vv. 11–15). The faithful dead shall awake and sing (vv. 16–19). The people are urged to hide until Yahweh has punished the inhabitants of the world for their sins (vv. 20, 21).

Ch. xxvii. Yahweh shall overthrow the hostile powers (v. 1), but Israel shall be to Him as a pleasant vineyard, filling the world with fruit (vv. 2–6). Israel shall be pardoned provided she abandons her idolatry. The hostile city (its identity is unknown) shall become a desolation (vv. 7–11). Yahweh shall gather the Jews from the heathen world and they shall worship him at Jerusalem (vv. 12, 13).

These chapters (xxiv–xxvii) are wholly eschatological in character and have more points of contact with Apocalyptic than with Prophecy. They are certainly not the work of Isaiah, for the ideas embodied in them are far in advance of those of his day. Among the novel ideas may be noted the vastness of the convulsions which are to afflict the world (xxiv. 1–3), the existence of the celestial enemies and their punishment (xxiv. 21, 22), the banquet of all nations in Zion (xxv. 6), the resurrection from the dead (xxvi. 19), and the representation of world empires under the figures of great monsters (xxvii. 1). The style, too, is quite different from that of Isaiah. It is laboured and artificial, and shows a fondness for alliteration, unusual terms of expression and obscure images. The chapters are assigned by some critics to the latter half of the fourth century BC and by others to the close of the second century BC.

Chapters xxviii–xxxiii

Ch. xxviii. 1–4. The prophet denounces the drunkards of Israel and depicts the fall of Samaria.

The prophecy is undoubtedly of Isaianic origin and must be dated shortly before the fall of Samaria in 722 BC.

Ch. xxviii. 5–6. Yahweh will be a crown to the remnant of His people and the inspirer of both judge and warrior.

These two verses are perhaps a later addition, written concerning Judah.

Ch. xxviii. 7–22. The prophet denounces the leaders of Jerusalem for their drunken excesses. They imagine that they have made a covenant with death whereby they have secured immunity from disaster; but in the day of judgement it will prove a vain delusion. Only those who put their trust in Yahweh will escape. Yahweh will again intervene as he did in the time of David.

The prophecy was probably written shortly before Sennacherib's invasion of Judah in 701 BC.

Ch. xxviii. 23–29. Just as the farmer adapts his methods to suit the particular work which he has to do, so Yahweh in dealing with His people adapts His methods to suit their requirements.

There is no need to doubt the Isaianic origin of these verses. They may well be a continuation of the preceding prophecy.

Ch. xxix. The prophet predicts that Ariel, that is, Jerusalem, shall be encompassed by her foes but that Yahweh shall rescue her by a sudden display of His power (vv. 1–8). The leaders of the people are blind and in consequence none can understand the prophetic vision (vv. 9–12). Because of the formalism and insincerity of their religion, Yahweh shall adopt startling measures against them (vv. 13, 14). The prophet denounces those who seek to hide their plans from Yahweh (the reference is probably to those who were intriguing with Egypt) and predicts a glorious transformation of Nature and a Golden Age for the poor and the oppressed (vv. 15–24).

All the prophecies in this chapter seem to belong to the same period of Isaiah's ministry, probably 701 BC. Some critics regard vv. 5–8 and vv. 15–24 as later additions.

Ch. xxx. 1–5. The prophet denounces those who are negotiating an alliance with Egypt.

The prophecy probably belongs to the period of the revolt against Sennacherib (705–701 BC). Some, however, maintain that it is to be dated by v. 4 which says, 'For his princes are at Zoan and his ambassadors are come to Hanes.' The two places mentioned are supposed to mark the limits of Lower Egypt, north and south, which was all that the nominal Pharaoh could claim just before the conquest of all Egypt by the Ethiopian Shabaka. Hence, it is alleged, that the prophecy must belong to the period of the revolt under Sargon (714–711 BC).

Ch. xxx. 6–17. The prophet denounces the futile negotiations with Egypt and predicts an overwhelming disaster for Israel, because the people despise the message of Yahweh and trust in oppression and duplicity.

The prophecy presumably belongs to the same period as the preceding one.

Ch. xxx. 18–26. The prophet predicts a glorious future for the nation.

The authorship and date of the prophecy are uncertain. It contains some of the ideas and phrases of Isaiah, but its authenticity has been rejected by some critics on the ground that in v. 20 (according to some MSS.) Yahweh is represented as the Teacher of His people. Such a conception indicates the post-exilic period.

Ch. xxx. 27–33. Yahweh suddenly appears to execute judgement upon the Assyrians. The Jews greet the destruction of their enemies with songs of rejoicing while a vast pyre has been prepared to consume the Assyrian dead.

Some critics reject the Isaianic authorship of this passage because of its colourful description of the destruction of the Assyrians. If it is the work of Isaiah, it belongs to the same period as ch. xxx. 1–17.

Ch. xxxi. The prophet denounces those who trust in the horses and chariots of Egypt. The Egyptians are only human and shall meet with disaster. Yahweh shall protect Jerusalem and destroy the Assyrians.

The chapter belongs to the same period as ch. xxx. 1–17. Verses 6, 7 break the connection between vv. 5 and 8 and are probably a later addition.

Ch. xxxii. 1–8. An ideal commonwealth is depicted. Kings and nobles shall govern in righteousness and shall grant protection to all who need it. Public opinion shall be purified and in judging a man character alone shall count.

The Isaianic authorship of this passage has been denied by some critics, chiefly on the ground of the unusual vocabulary and the colourless description of the future king as compared with ch. ix. 6, 7 and ch. xi. 1–9. But vv. 1–5, in spite of some peculiarities of language, are probably to be assigned to Isaiah. The date of their composition cannot be determined but they probably belong to the close of the prophet's ministry. Verses 6–8, however, resemble Proverbs in contents and manner (cf. xxi. 24) and are probably a later addition.

Ch. xxxii. 9–20. The prophet invited the luxurious women of Jerusalem to mourn over the impending devastation of the country and its capital; the desolation shall not be permanent. The life-giving energy of the spirit shall be poured out and Nature and human society shall be transformed (vv. 15–20).

Some critics reject the Isaianic authorship of vv. 9–14 on the ground that the theme—the luxurious women of Jerusalem—is treated quite differently in chs. iii. 16–iv. 1. If the verses are Isaianic, they must be assigned to the early period of his ministry, when he looked forward to the ruin of the capital. As regards vv. 15–20 there is no reason to doubt that they are Isaianic, although v. 19 strikes a discordant note and is generally regarded as a later addition.

Ch. xxxiii. The prophet predicts that Yahweh shall destroy the cruel and treacherous foe, deliver Israel and reign triumphantly in Zion.

The date of this prophecy cannot be determined. There is much in it which suggests that the oppressor is Assyria and that it belongs to the period immediately before Sennacherib's invasion of Judah in 701 BC. But some of the ideas embodied in it would hardly fit Isaiah's time. The language, too, resembles that of the late Psalms, and there is a considerable number of non-Isaianic words. Some critics assign it to the post-exilic period.

Chapters xxxiv–xxxv

Ch. xxxiv. In the day of judgement Yahweh's wrath shall fall upon all nations, especially Edom. Her land shall be bathed in blood and shall be desolate from generation to generation.

The deep hatred of the Edomites revealed in this chapter was due to their cruelty on the occasion of the destruction of Jerusalem in 587 BC (Lam. iv. 21, 22; Ps. cxxxvii. 7; Jer. xlix. 7–22)—cruelty which the Jews never forgot for centuries. This deep hatred points to the post-exilic period as the probable date for the composition of the chapter.

Ch. xxxv. The prophet describes the triumphant return of the Jewish exiles to Zion.

The chapter is obviously designed to afford a striking contrast to the preceding chapter. It presupposes the Exile and shows dependence upon Deutero-Isaiah (xl–lv). Hence it must be assigned to the post-exilic period.

Chapters xxxvi–xxxix

It is plain that the Isaianic prophecies, real or assumed, ended with chapter xxxv. Chapters xxxvi–xxxix form a historical appendix reproduced with slight alteration from 2 Kings xviii. 13–xx. 19. They contain narratives of three historical events, namely, (1) the unsuccessful attempts of Sennacherib to capture Jerusalem (xxxvi–xxxvii), (2) Hezekiah's sickness and recovery (xxxviii), (3) Merodach-baladin's congratulatory embassy to Hezekiah (xxxix). The statement that Hezekiah paid a heavy tribute to the king of Assyria (2 Kgs. xviii. 14–16) is omitted from these chapters, while the Psalm of Hezekiah is added (xxxviii. 9–20). This Psalm consists of two parts, namely, (1) a lament of a man sick unto death (xxxviii. 10–14), and (2) a song of thanksgiving for recovery (xxxviii. 15–20). The linguistic evidence suggests that it is of post-exilic origin.

PERMANENT INFLUENCE

The book of Isaiah is important for the light it sheds upon the history of the Kingdoms of Israel and Judah, more especially the latter, during the last forty years of the eighth century BC. Isaiah is pre-eminently the statesman-prophet. He saw more clearly than any other man in Judah the evils of his time and the destruction that faced his country. Recognizing that it is righteousness that exalts a nation he demanded of the people moral purity, justice and humanity, and denounced the national sins—the drunkenness of the men (v. 11, 12, 22, xxviii. 7, 8), the wanton vanity of the women (iii. 16, 17), the perversion of justice (i. 23, v. 23, x. 1–4, xxix. 21), the greed of the landowners (v. 8), the oppression of the poor (iii. 14, 15, x. 2), and the prevalence of open violence (i. 15, 21). In foreign policy he was opposed to all entangling political alliances, preferring to trust in the power of Yahweh to defend His people. When Israel allied herself with Syria and wished to force Judah to join their league against Assyria, he tried to reassure Ahaz (vii. 4). At the same time he warned the king—but in vain—of the evil which would follow an appeal to Assyria for help against them. It is well to consider the two policies from a political as distinct from a religious point of view. If, as Isaiah recommended, Ahaz adopted a policy of neutrality, what would Assyria do? Tiglath-pileser was bound to suppress the attempted rebellion against him whatever Ahaz did. Jerusalem would presumably count for nothing in his calculations; it was a mere out-of-the-way hill-top town. Northern invaders invariably followed the coast to Philistia, the really fertile part of Canaan, and to Egypt, the potential enemy which might try to upset their work in Palestine. Isaiah, therefore, was right in thinking that Damascus and Ephraim, the two enemies, would disappear and with them the plot. It may be added, too, that Assyria would have enough on her hands to let Jerusalem alone. Most modern writers think that, considered purely from a political point of view, Isaiah's recommendations were sound.

In the reign of Hezekiah he strongly disapproved of any military alliance with Egypt, and warned the king of the folly of expecting a speedy deliverance from the Assyrian tyranny through Egyptian help (e.g. xxx. 1–5, xxxi. 1–3). As in the days of Ahaz he advocated a policy of non-resistance towards Assyria; but when Sennacherib invaded Palestine he counselled stern opposition. At first sight there seems to have been a contradiction in his attitude. This apparent contradiction, however, can be explained. His political views were all based on the character of Yahweh, who, he believed, controlled all the nations of the world, and would never forsake His people provided they were faithful to Him. Yahweh was a holy God and therefore His people must be holy, too. If they were to remain holy they must separate themselves completely from foreign nations. On

E

this ground he advocated a policy of non-resistance. But when Sennacherib actually invaded Palestine the situation was radically altered. Yahweh, as a holy God, needed a holy city and a holy people for His self-expression, and hence Jerusalem must not be allowed to fall.

The book of Isaiah occupies an important place in the history of the development of religious thought. While there is much in the book which is common to Isaiah and to others of the pre-exilic prophets, there are certain elements which are peculiar to himself. His fundamental conception of God was that of His holiness and majesty (vi. 3). In his vision in the Temple he heard the seraphim crying to one another, 'Holy, holy, holy, is the Lord of hosts' (vi. 3). The name by which he frequently spoke of Yahweh was 'the Holy One of Israel' (i. 4, v. 24, xxx. 11, 12, 15). The people must regard Him as holy and treat Him with reverence and awe (viii. 13, xxix. 23). The attribute of majesty found expression in the picture of Yahweh 'sitting upon a throne, high and lifted up', surrounded by seraphim who veiled their faces before His ineffable glory, and in that of the day of Yahweh, when everything, whether in Nature or civilization that lifted its head against the majesty of Yahweh, would be brought low (ii. 12–17), in the manifestation of His divine power (xiv. 24, 26, 27, xxviii. 2, 21, 22, xxix. 6, xxxiii. 10), and in the representation of idols as mere 'nonentities', who would be flung by man to the moles and to the bats as he fled into the caves of the rocks and the crevices of the cliffs to hide 'from before the terror of the Lord, and from the glory of His majesty' (ii. 18–20).

What exactly did Isaiah mean by 'holiness'? Among the Semitic peoples the word was commonly used to denote the quality which distinguished gods in general from mankind, and did not necessarily have any moral content. Some of the heathen gods were immoral and were recognized as such by their worshippers. Isaiah, however, gave the word a new moral significance. His ascription of 'holiness' to Yahweh implied that He was exalted above all human weaknesses and was absolute moral purity. As such He was opposed to all that was unclean. In the presence of His holiness the prophet was overwhelmed with the sense of his own and the nation's uncleanness. 'Woe is me! for I am undone; because I am a man of unclean lips, and I dwell in the midst of a people of unclean lips: for mine eyes have seen the king, the Lord of hosts' (vi. 5). Since Yahweh was 'the Holy One of Israel' His people must be holy, too, that is, they must be morally pure, just and merciful. It was folly to imagine that sacrifices could be a substitute for justice and mercy. 'To what purpose is the multitude of your sacrifices unto me? saith the Lord: I am full of the burnt offerings of rams and the fat of fed beasts: and I delight not in the blood of bullocks, or of lambs, or of he-goats. When ye come to appear before me, who hath required this at your hand, to trample my courts? Bring no more vain oblations, incense is an abomination unto me; new moon and sabbath, the calling of assemblies, I cannot away with iniquity and the solemn meeting. Your new moons and your appointed feasts my soul hateth; they are a trouble unto me; I am weary to bear them. And when ye spread forth your hands, I will hide mine eyes from you; yea, when ye make many prayers, I will not hear: your hands are full of blood. Wash you, make you clean; put away the evil of your doings from before mine eyes; cease to do evil; learn to do well; seek judgement, relieve the oppressed, judge the fatherless, plead for the widow' (i. 11–17).

Though Yahweh was a righteous God who punished sin He was ever ready to show mercy. No sooner had Isaiah confessed his sin than he was forgiven and counted worthy to be the divine messenger to the nation (vi. 9–13). Yahweh would forgive His erring people if only they would repent. 'Come now, and let us reason together, saith the Lord: though your sins be as scarlet, they shall be as white as snow; though they be red like crimson, they shall be as wool' (i. 18).

Isaiah taught that Yahweh was the God of history, using nations in the fulfilment of His purposes. He declared that Yahweh would whistle for Egypt and Assyria, and would stir up the Syrians and the Philistines that they might ravage the territory of Judah (vii. 18, 19, ix. 11, 12). Assyria was Yahweh's instrument to punish those who incurred His anger. 'Ho Assyrian, the rod of mine anger, the staff in whose hand is mine indignation! I will send him against a profane nation, and against the people of my wrath will I give him a charge, to take the spoil, and to take the prey, and to tread them down like the mire of the streets' (x. 5, 6). The most striking passage which represents Yahweh as the God of history is ch. xiv. 24–26. 'The Lord of hosts hath sworn, saying, Surely as I have thought, so shall it come to pass; and as I have purposed, so shall it stand: that I will break the Assyrian in my land, and upon my mountains tread him underfoot: then shall his yoke depart from off them, and his burden depart from off their shoulder. This is the purpose that is purposed upon the whole earth: and this is the hand that is stretched out upon all the nations.'

Isaiah was pre-eminently the prophet of faith. Throughout his long ministry he taught that the strength and stability of the nation depended upon trust in Yahweh. In predicting the downfall of Ephraim he declared, 'If ye will not believe, surely ye shall not be established' (vii. 9). He warned the leaders of Jerusalem, who believed that they were immune from every kind of danger or evil, that in the divine judgement that was about to overtake them, those alone would escape who put their trust in Yahweh. 'He that believeth shall not make haste', that is, 'shall not be ashamed' or 'shall not give way' (xxviii. 16). He denounced those who were seeking an alliance with Egypt, warning them that their policy would end in the destruction of the state, and reminding them that their strength lay not in foreign alliances, but in tranquil reliance upon the protection of Yahweh. 'For thus, saith the Lord God, the Holy One of Israel, in returning and rest shall ye be saved: in quietness and in confidence shall be your strength' (xxx. 15). Though he predicted the doom of both Israel and Judah, he was firmly convinced that Yahweh would ultimately redeem His people. This quiet confidence in Yahweh's power to protect and to save has been a source of inspiration to both Jews and Christians throughout the centuries.

To Isaiah we owe the doctrine of the Remnant which came to dominate prophetic thought until it was taken over by Christianity. The idea of a Remnant was not new. In 1 Kings xix. 18, we read that after the slaughter of Hazael, Jehu and Elisha, a faithful remnant of 7,000 souls would be left. Amos declared that if the people repented Yahweh would be 'gracious unto the remnant of Joseph' (v. 15). In each case the Remnant consisted of the survivors of the impending catastrophe: there was no conception of the survivors being used by Yahweh to establish a new ideal community. The idea was prominent in the religious thought of Isaiah but with him it acquired a new significance. He was so convinced that a faithful Remnant would survive, that he embodied his conviction in the name of his eldest son, Shear-jashub (vii. 3), which means 'a remnant shall return', that is, 'return to Yahweh', not 'shall return from exile', since at that date there had been no general exile. It is unlikely that he found the Remnant in the Northern Kingdom, for he thought that the state was doomed to almost utter destruction. 'Yet there shall be left therein gleanings, as the shaking of an olive tree, two or three berries in the top of the uppermost bough, four or five in the outmost branches of a fruitful tree, saith the Lord, the God of Israel' (xvii. 6). The gleanings were not the gleanings of the harvest-field—full ears to be used for food or seed corn—they were the poor berries of the olive tree, left hanging on the boughs because they were not worth picking. It is possible that he thought that the entire kingdom of Judah would become the remnant, provided the king adopted the policy of non-resistance which he advocated. If he did think so, he must soon have found cause to change his opinion, for when Ahaz refused to refrain from invoking the aid of Assyria and to trust in Yahweh, he recognized that disaster would inevitably overtake Judah. Finally he seems to have found the Remnant in a portion of the inhabitants of Jerusalem. 'Bind thou up the testimony, seal the law among my disciples. And I will wait for the Lord that hideth his face from the house of Jacob, and I will look for him' (viii. 16, 17). Evidently there were men in Jerusalem who had imbibed the teaching of Isaiah, and were prepared to put their trust in Yahweh rather than in foreign alliances or military strength. In Isaiah's thought the Remnant consisted of those who would not only survive the impending judgement but would also become the nucleus of a new ideal community. 'In his view,' said Skinner, 'the doctrine of the Remnant might be more fitly spoken of as the doctrine of the "kernel"; for it was the conviction that within the actual Israel of the present there is an indestructible germ of true godliness that gave to Isaiah the assurance that in spite of public failure his word had yet an abiding value for the perfect religion of the future.'[1]

Isaiah left behind him the belief that Jerusalem could never be taken. The Assyrians were advancing from the north, their path marked by the smoke of blazing towns, but Yahweh had founded Zion 'and in her shall the afflicted of his people take refuge' (xiv. 32). The leaders of Jerusalem, who had made a covenant with death and hell, hoping thereby to secure immunity from disaster, would find that their refuge of lies would be swept away but that Zion would be safe (xxviii. 16). In the hour of their triumph the enemies of Zion would vanish 'as a dream, a vision of the night' (xxix. 7, 8). Yahweh would come down upon Mount Zion to fight against the Assyrians. 'As birds flying, so will the Lord of hosts protect Jerusalem; he will protect and deliver it, he will pass over and preserve it' (xxxi. 4, 5).

[1] J. Skinner, *Isaiah, i–xxxix*, Revised ed. 1915, p. lxiv.

In answer to Hezekiah's prayer Yahweh would defend Jerusalem against the forces of Sennacherib, 'for mine own sake, and for my servant David's sake' (xxxvii. 33–35).

The belief in the inviolability of Jerasulem was quite natural at a time when it appeared that Yahweh and His Temple were inseparable. The destruction of the Temple would mean the conquest of Yahweh by the god of the conqueror and the end of the religion of Yahweh. That belief was the heritage which Jeremiah sought to destroy. It was for him to recount how the first sanctuary at Shiloh had been utterly destroyed, yet Yahweh Himself had not been conquered, and Jerusalem might well be another Shiloh (Jer. vii. 12–15).

There are several passages in Isaiah which are termed 'Messianic' because they describe the advent of an ideal king of the house of David. They are chs. ix. 2–7, xi. 1–9, xxxii. 1–8. Doubts have been cast upon their Isaianic authorship by many critics but, we think, with no sufficient reasons. To these passages some critics would add ch. vii. 14–17, but with little justification.[1] To understand the Messianic passages it is necessary to distinguish between the author's point of view and that of later writers, notably Christian and Rabbinic.

In ch. ix. 2–7, it is stated that the darkness of oppression has been dispelled by the shining of a great light, causing great rejoicing among men. Yahweh has broken the yoke of the oppressor 'as in the day of Midian' and the soldier's blood-stained war-attire shall be burnt, 'as fuel in the fire'. For a child has been born who shall wear the royal dignity upon his shoulders and shall bear the fourfold title of Wonderful Counsellor, God-like Hero, Father for ever, Prince of Peace. He shall sit upon the throne of David and shall rule over a wide domain in justice and righteousness, thanks to the jealous care of Yahweh.

[1] There is no reference in it to the advent of an ideal king. Isaiah warns Ahaz of the folly of seeking the aid of Assyria instead of trusting in Yahweh, and offers him a sign that Yahweh will protect him. Ahaz says he will not tempt Yahweh by accepting the offer, whereupon the prophet, angered by his refusal, gives him a sign, namely that a young woman will bear a son to whom she will give the name Immanuel (God is with us). Before he is old enough to distinguish between good and bad food, Syria and Ephraim will have been overthrown. The Hebrew word 'almah', translated 'virgin', means no more than a young woman of marriageable age. The 'almah' is any young woman who may give birth to a child at the time of Judah's deliverance from Syria and Ephraim. The sign is one of rebuke and assurance. Ahaz will learn that the faith, which he lacks, is found in one of the common people, and will realize from the fulfilment of the sign that Yahweh's word stands fast. (For other interpretations of the sign see J. Skinner, *Isaiah, i–xxxix*, Revised ed. 1915, pp. 61–68.)

In ch. xi. 1–9 we are told that the Messianic king shall spring from the stock of the almost ruined Davidic family. He shall be filled with the divine spirit and shall be endowed with the spirit of wisdom and understanding, the spirit of counsel and might, and the spirit that fears and reverences Yahweh. Endowed with keen discernment, he shall not judge by appearances nor decide by hearsay; he shall judge with righteousness, smite the ruthless, and slay the wicked. Righteousness and faithfulness shall be the strength of his government. Then shall begin an era of peace which shall extend even to the animal creation, and the earth 'shall be full of the knowledge of the Lord, as the waters cover the sea'.

Chapter xxxii. 1–8 tells us that in the Messianic age king and princes shall reign in righteousness, and protection shall be extended to all who need it. Public opinion shall be enlightened and purified. The true character of each man shall be recognized. No more shall the fool be called noble or the crafty be ranked as a nobleman. The truly noble man devises noble plans and persists in their execution.

These passages have been interpreted by many Christians as referring to the coming of Christ and to the establishment of His kingdom. To hold such a view is to misunderstand the meaning of prophecy, which is the proclamation of profound truths made clear to the prophet by his insight into God's dealings with men in past and contemporary history, rather than the prediction of events in the far distant future. The ideal ruler, promised by Isaiah, was to appear in his own day or perhaps a little later, but not in the far-distant future. The prophecies were never fulfilled: no ideal ruler appeared to overthrow the enemies of Judah and to usher in a Golden Age of prosperity, righteousness and peace. But the conception lived on to haunt the minds of both Jews and Christians, and ultimately led to the proclamation of the more spiritual conception of the kingdom of God which we find in the Gospels. 'Now after that John was delivered up, Jesus came into Galilee, preaching the Gospel of God, and saying, The time is fulfilled, and the kingdom of God is at hand: repent ye, and believe in the Gospel.' (Mk. i, 15).

STYLE

It is difficult to give a just appreciation of Isaiah's writings owing to the corruption of the text, the fragmentary nature of many of the prophecies and the large number of later additions. Of the portions which are generally considered to be his, some are in poetry and some in prose; but it is often difficult to distinguish clearly between the two kinds of writing, because the rhythm of the prose is so distinct and the language so poetical that it is to all intents and purposes poetry. It might aptly be called poetical prose. These uncontested portions, whether in prose or poetry, are undoubtedly the work of a great literary artist. He has all the qualities which are generally supposed to be characteristic of a great poet—nobility of thought, wealth of imagination, the observant eye, the power of graphic description, deep feeling and sincerity.

His style is not uniform throughout for he has the ability to adopt it to suit his theme. It can be majestic as in his account of his vision in the Temple (vi. 1–8), which reaches the level of the sublime, or vigorous as in his denunciations of the national sins (i. 10–17, iii. 16–26, v. 8–24, x. 1–4), or smooth as in his call to repentance (i. 18–20), or lyrical as in the parable of the vineyard (v. 1–7). But whatever style he adopts, it is always clear and concise and is never obscure or prolix. Among the prophets he is pre-eminent for his picturesque and impressive imagery (v. 6, 24, vi. 13, vii. 18, 19, xvii. 5, 6, xxxii. 13–15). He frequently employs apt figures of speech, such as simile i. 8, vii. 2), and metaphor (x. 5, xvii. 10), and the literary devices of repetition (i. 7, 8, xxviii. 7, 10), the rhetorical question (viii. 19, x. 3, 8, 9), exclamation (i. 21, x. 5) and contrast (v. 20, xvii. 13). 'No prophet,' says Driver, 'has Isaiah's power either of conception or of expression; none has the same command of noble thoughts, or can present them in the same noble and attractive language.'[1]

[1] S. R. Driver, *An Introduction to the Literature of the Old Testament*, 9th ed., 1913, p. 229.

CHAPTER X

Zephaniah

LIFE AND CHARACTER OF ZEPHANIAH

Of Zephaniah personally we know nothing beyond what we can gather from his book. According to its title (i. 1), he was the great great-grandson of Hezekiah by whom is probably intended Hezekiah, the king of Judah. We infer that he was a native of Jerusalem, or at any rate delivered his message there, from the fact that he shows knowledge of the religious and moral conditions of the city (i. 4–6, 8, 9, 12, iii. 1–7) and is familiar with its suburbs and surroundings (i. 10, 11), and refers to it as 'this place' (i. 4). It would appear that he occupied an influential position, since he is acquainted with the manner of life of the royal household and of the upper classes (ii. 8, 9). Moreover, though his denunciations are directed almost entirely against the upper classes, he does not speak as one who belongs to the poorer classes and has experienced their sufferings.

Zephaniah stands out in the pages of his book as a strong but not an attractive personality, reminding us of Amos rather than Hosea. Convinced that he had received a revelation from Yahweh he delivered his message fearlessly, though he must have known that it would be likely to rouse hostility against himself. He was a champion of the pure religion of Yahweh, with a deep hatred of idolatry, a stern moralist pronouncing doom upon those who refused to obey the moral demands of Yahweh, and an ardent patriot, opposed to all foreign influences and eager to promote the social, moral and spiritual conditions of his countrymen. But he was lacking in tenderness and compassion. He emphasized not the mercy of Yahweh, but His justice. Yahweh is depicted as searching Jerusalem with a candle for sinners that He might destroy them together with their habitations (ii. 12, 13). He expresses no sorrow for the countless numbers of people who are doomed to destruction nor does he appeal to Yahweh to spare them in His mercy. Everything is to be burnt in the universal conflagration that is to take place 'in the day of the Lord's wrath'. Throughout the book we can almost hear the crackle of the flames. 'No hotter book,' says G. A. Smith, 'lies in all the Old Testament. Neither dew nor grass nor tree nor any blossom lives in it, but it is everywhere fire, smoke and darkness, drifting chaff, ruins, nettles, saltpits, and owls and ravens looking from the windows of desolate palaces.'[1] Medieval art portrayed him as the man with the lantern of the Lord, searching out sinners for destruction.

CONTENTS

The book of Zephaniah may be divided into three parts.

(1) Ch. i. The doom coming upon the nations of the earth, especially upon Judah and Jerusalem.

(2) Ch. ii. An exhortation to Judah to repent, and threats of destruction upon Philistia, Moab, Ammon, Ethiopia and Assyria.

(3) Ch. iii. Denunciation of the sins of Jerusalem, promises of the restoration and salvation of a remnant of Judah, and a hymn of praise to Yahweh for deliverance.

The book may be summarized thus:

Chapter i

Ch. i. 1–13. Title (v. 1). Zephaniah predicts the destruction of every living thing on the earth, especially the idolaters and apostates of Jerusalem (vv. 2–6). The day of Yahweh will be a day of sacrifice to which Yahweh has already invited and consecrated His guests (i.e. the foes, probably the Scythians). His victims will be the officials and the members of the royal house who are guilty of violence and fraud, together with all those who wear foreign apparel or practise foreign customs and superstitions (vv. 7–9). On that fatal day the merchants of Jerusalem shall be wiped out and their treasures seized. Yahweh will search Jerusalem thoroughly and punish those who live at ease in the assurance that He will do nothing (vv. 10–12). They shall be despoiled of their goods and their houses laid in ruins. They shall not enjoy the fruits of their labour (v. 13).

Ch. i. 14–18. The great day of Yahweh is speedily approaching—a day of bitterness and wrath, of trouble and distress, of waste and

---

[1] G. A. Smith, *The Book of the Twelve Prophets*, Revised ed. 1928, p. 48.

desolation, of darkness and gloom, of cloud and thunder, of trumpet-blast and battle-cry. The blood of the people shall be poured out like dust, and their flesh like dung. No silver or gold shall be able to save them from the fire of Yahweh's jealousy.

Chapter ii

Ch. ii. 1–3. Judah is exhorted to seek Yahweh before it is too late, and to strive earnestly to excel in righteousness and meekness that she may be secure in that fearful day.

Ch. ii. 4–15. Doom is pronounced upon Philistia, Moab, Ammon, Ethiopia and Assyria. Gaza, Ashkelon, Ashdod and Ekron shall become a desolation and the sea-coast a pasture ground for flocks (vv. 4–7). Moab and Ammon shall be destroyed as completely as Sodom and Gomorrah. Yahweh shall disable all the gods of the earth and all men shall worship Him in their own countries (vv. 8–11). The Ethiopians shall be slain by the sword (v. 12) and Nineveh shall become a desolation and the haunt of all the beasts of the field (vv. 13–15).

Chapter iii

Ch. iii. 1–7. Zephaniah again denounces Jerusalem for her sins. She is defiant and polluted and filled with oppression; she is disobedient, refuses instruction and has no faith in Yahweh. Her officials and judges are rapacious; her prophets are reckless and faithless, and her priests profane that which is holy and wrest the Law. She cannot escape the judgement of Yahweh, for He is a righteous God and never fails to mete out justice (vv. 1–5). She has not taken warning from the destruction which has fallen upon other nations, but has become more corrupt than ever (vv. 6, 7).

Ch. iii. 8–13. Zephaniah bids the faithful in Jerusalem wait patiently until the fatal day comes, for it is His purpose to assemble all the nations to vent His wrath upon them, for the fire of His fury shall consume the whole earth. Then will He grant the peoples a clean speech that they may call upon His name and worship Him with one consent. His worshippers shall come with offerings even from far-distant Ethiopia (vv. 8–10). In that day Yahweh will remove from her midst all the proud and haughty ones, leaving a few people, humble and poor, who shall trust in His name and dwell in security and peace (vv. 11–13).

Ch. iii. 14–20. Jerusalem is exhorted to rejoice, for her foes have been driven out and Yahweh, her King, is in her midst. He is mighty to deliver her out of all her troubles. He will rejoice over her and renew His love (vv. 14–17). He will deal with all those who afflict her, gather together all her disabled and exiled people, and lift them out of their shame to world-wide praise and fame (vv. 18–20).

DATE

The title tells us that Zephaniah prophesied 'in the days of Josiah the son of Amon, king of Judah' (i. 1), and with this a large portion of the contents seems to agree. The denunciation of the mingling of the worship of Yahweh with that of the Canaanite Baalim, the heavenly bodies, and the Ammonite god Milcom, of the aping of foreign fashions, the practice of alien superstitions and the general infidelity, suggests that the prophecy was delivered before the religious reformation of 622 BC, when the idolatrous worship which had grown apace in the reigns of Manasseh and Ammon was abolished. The prophecy seems to have been inspired by the invasion of a foreign army, which the prophet conceives as being the instrument of Yahweh for the punishment of Judah and Jerusalem. The event which best suits the requirements of the situation is the Scythian invasion of Palestine about 626 BC.

INTEGRITY

It is generally agreed that the book contains a number of editorial additions, though they cannot be indicated with absolute certainty. Chapter ii. 8, 9, announcing the doom of Moab and Ammon, is probably of exilic or post-exilic origin, since it seems to refer to the hostility displayed by these two peoples towards the inhabitants of Judah at the time of the destruction of Jerusalem in 587 BC (cf. Jer. xlviii. 27, 29; Ezek. xxv. 1–7, 8–11). The passage has been expanded by the addition of vv. 10, 11, for v. 10 repeats the thought of v. 8 and v. 11 passes from the consideration of Moab and Ammon to a prediction of the universal judgement of Yahweh. Ch. ii. 15 suggests that the fall of Nineveh is already an accomplished fact. It is based on Isaiah xlvii. 8 and cannot be earlier than the close of the Exile. Some scholars deny the whole of ch. iii to Zephaniah. There is, however, no sufficient reason to doubt the genuineness of vv. 1–7 and vv. 8, 11–13. The first of these two passages contains an attack on Jerusalem parallel to that in ch. i. 1–18, while the second, which predicts a universal judgement and the survival of a faithful remnant of Judah, is the necessary complement to the denunciations levelled against the city. Chapter iii. 9, 10 interrupts the continuity of thought between vv. 8 and 11 and predicts the conversion of the heathen. Since the idea of the universal worship of Yahweh is hardly earlier than the time of Deutero-Isaiah, the passage probably belongs to the late-exilic or post-exilic period. Chapter iii. 14–20 presupposes the Exile and is probably of exilic or post-exilic origin.

PERMANENT INFLUENCE

The book sheds light upon the moral and spiritual conditions of the times. It is clear that Judah is suffering from moral and spiritual corruption. The rulers are likened to wild beasts that prowl by night, catching and devouring their prey, both flesh and bone (iii. 3). The prophets are reckless and faithless, while the priests blur the distinction between the holy and the profane and pervert the Law for their own gain (iii. 4). Many of the people are guilty of idolatrous practices and of disloyalty to Yahweh (i. 4–6).

The prophet makes no real contribution to the development of religious ideas, rather stressing the truths which had already been taught by his predecessors. He is a true successor of Amos, Hosea, Micah and Isaiah in his denunciation of idolatrous practices, foreign superstitions, social injustice, false prophets and priests, and in his view that Yahweh punishes nations for their sins. We are not certain that he was a monotheist. It is true that he denounces those who couple the worship of Yahweh with that of the Canaanite Baalim, the heavenly bodies and the Ammonite god Milcom, but nowhere does he deny the existence of the heathen deities. Considering, however, that he thinks of Yahweh as the supreme Controller of the universe, we shall probably be safe in saying that he was practically a monotheist.

Like his predecessors he stresses the ethical character of Yahweh. He is a righteous God who morning by morning brings forth justice as unfailingly as the light (iii. 5). Because the inhabitants of Judah have sinned against Him they shall be punished. 'Neither their silver nor their gold shall be able to deliver them in the day of the Lord's wrath; but the whole land shall be devoured by the fire of his jealousy' (i. 18). It is noteworthy that he does not think of other

nations as being punished by Yahweh for their sins: they are destroyed as the enemies of Judah. Here he reveals his narrow nationalism, which leads him to suppose that Yahweh must surely punish
the enemies of His chosen people.

The central teaching of the book is that of the speedy coming of
the 'day of Yahweh'. In the eighth century BC the popular notion
of the 'day of Yahweh' as one of triumph for Israel and disaster for
her enemies, was rejected by Amos, who declared that it would be
a day of darkness and not of light (Amos v. 18–20). Zephaniah took
over the idea and developed it. He proclaimed that destruction would
fall not only upon Israel, but upon all nations (iii. 8). On that dread
day Yahweh would make a clean sweep of the earth, destroying both
man and beast, bird and fish (i. 2, 3). His vengeance would fall
especially upon the sinful people of Judah and Jerusalem, who would
be destroyed like animals slaughtered at a sacrificial feast to which
Yahweh had invited His guests, that is, the hostile forces whom He
had chosen as the instruments of His vengeance (i. 7). From Judah
and Jerusalem His vengeance would pass westwards to Philistia
(ii. 4–7), southwards to Egypt and Ethiopia (ii. 12), and northwards
to Assyria (ii. 13, 14). The terrors of the 'day of Yahweh' are
graphically portrayed. 'The great day of the Lord is near, it is near
and hasteth greatly, even the voice of the day of the Lord; the mighty
man crieth there bitterly. That day is a day of wrath, a day of
trouble and distress, a day of wasteness and desolation, a day of
darkness and gloominess, a day of clouds and thick darkness, a day
of trumpet and alarm, against the fenced cities, and against the high
battlements. And I will bring distress upon men, that they shall
walk like blind men, because they have sinned against the Lord:
and their blood shall be poured out as dust, and their flesh as dung.
Neither their silver nor their gold shall be able to deliver them in the
day of the Lord's wrath; but the whole land shall be devoured by the
fire of his jealousy; for he shall make an end, yea a terrible end, of all
them that dwell in the land' (i. 14–18). It is interesting to note that
the famous medieval Latin hymn, 'Dies Irae', is based upon this
terrible description of the 'day of Yahweh'.

The picture, however, is not entirely one of unrelieved darkness.
There was the possibility that the 'meek of the earth' might escape
the coming judgement if they turned to Yahweh before it was too late.
'Seek ye the Lord, all ye meek of the earth, which have wrought his
judgement; seek righteousness, seek meekness: it may be ye shall be

hid in the day of the Lord's anger' (ii. 3). As for Judah, a small company of humble people, who trusted in the name of Yahweh, would survive the judgement (iii. 11–13).

Zephaniah is the first of the canonical prophets whose mind is dominated by the idea of the 'day of Yahweh'. He, therefore, occupies an important position in the development of eschatology.

STYLE

As a writer Zephaniah occupies a minor place in the history of Hebrew literature. He is pre-eminently the prophet of doom whose mind is filled with thoughts of destruction and death. In his description of the approaching 'day of Yahweh' he writes clearly and forcibly, and succeeds in creating an atmosphere of gloom and terror, chiefly by the use of repetition (i. 2, 3, 15, 16, 18), imperatives (i. 7, iii. 8). contrast (i. 13), similes (i. 17, ii. 9, 14) and metaphors (i. 12, iii. 3). Through the gloom only a faint glimmer of light can be seen (cf. ii. 3, iii. 11–13). He lacks, however, the qualities which we generally associate with the true poet, for he has no exalted vision to disclose, no real gift of imagination, no eye for the beauty of Nature, and no tenderness or compassion. Apart from its impressive description of the 'day of Yahweh' his book, judged as literature, has little to commend it.

CHAPTER XI

Nahum

LIFE AND CHARACTER OF NAHUM

Nothing is known of Nahum except that he is described in the title as the 'Elkoshite', that is, a native of Elkosh (i. 1). Elkosh has been identified with Alkosh, a village about twenty-five miles north of Nineveh, with another Galilean village, Elkese, with Capernaum ('village of Nahum'), and with a site near Beit-Jibrin (the ancient Eleutheropolis) about twenty miles south-west of Jerusalem. We cannot be sure of the exact site, but it is probable that, like Micah, he was a native of Judah. In confirmation of this Budde points out that all similar names of places, such as Eltekeh, Eltekon, and Elto-lad, indicate the kingdom of Judah. From his book we gather that Nahum was an ardent patriot and a gifted poet, who longed for the independence of his country and hated the Assyrians for their oppression with his whole soul.

The original prophecy of Nahum (ii. 3–iii. 19) deals exclusively with the approaching overthrow of Nineveh. As the city fell in 612 BC and the prophet alludes in ch. iii. 8–10 to the sack of No-amon (Thebes) in 663 BC the date of the prophecy must fall within the period 663–612 BC. The patriotic fervour, animosity, and confident assurance in the destruction of Nineveh shown by the prophet are hardly conceivable before the death of Ashurbanipal in 626 BC when Jewish nationalism flared up and Josiah, the king of Judah, taking advantage of the weakness of Assyria, succeeded in establishing his independence. According to the prophet the fall of Nineveh is imminent (iii. 12, 13); but the city was not seriously threatened till about 614 BC and was not captured and destroyed till 612 BC. It is probable, therefore, that the prophecy was written shortly before 612 BC. Humbert sees in the whole book a liturgy composed in celebration of the fall of Nineveh for the autumn festival of 612 BC,[1]

[1] P. Humbert, *R.H.P.R.*, 1932, pp. 1–15.

while Halder rejects the theory, maintaining that the book was written about 614 BC by a cultic prophet who foretold the imminent destruction of Nineveh by Yahweh, and that it was a piece of political propaganda against the Assyrians, modelled on the cultic myth of Yahweh's victory over his foes.[1] These two theories, however, have gained little support.

UNITY

The question of the unity of the book is a matter of dispute. The prophecy embodied in chs. ii. 3–iii. 19 is undoubtedly authentic, for the style is uniform throughout and is without parallel in the Old Testament; but doubts have been cast upon the genuineness of the introduction (i. 2–ii. 2). The latter is really an imperfect acrostic poem, the acrostic form of which can be traced at least down to the tenth verse. Attempts have been made to restore the supposed original alphabetic arrangement but without much success. Such a literary form is said to point to a late origin. Moreover, it is out of keeping with the vigorous and vivid style of the undoubted work of Nahum. The poem is didactic in tone, illustrating the general truth that Yahweh takes vengeance on the guilty and protects those who put their trust in Him. It is the product of an age of reflection rather than of prophecy. The prophecy on the other hand is concerned not with theological abstractions but with a definite historical situation. The language of the poem is vague and no reference is made to Nineveh, the assault and sack of which constitute the main theme of the prophecy and are described in great detail. For these reasons, therefore, the poem is generally held to have been composed in the post-exilic period and prefixed as an appropriate introduction to the prophecies.

CONTENTS

The book may be divided into three parts:

(1) Chs. i–ii. 2. Yahweh's vengeance on His adversaries and the deliverance of His people.

(2) Ch. ii. 3–13. The siege, capture and sack of Nineveh, and the end of her brutal tyranny.

(3) Ch. iii. The attack of Nineveh, her humiliation and dishonour,

---

[1] A. Halder, *Studies in the Book of Nahum*, 1947.

a taunt at her inescapable destruction and a dirge over her downfall.

These three parts may be summarized as follows:

Chapters i–ii. 2

Ch. i. 1–10. Title (v. 1). Yahweh is an avenging and a jealous God. He is slow to anger, but great in power and will never absolve guilt. He takes His way through storm and tempest to take vengeance upon His enemies. Neither Nature nor man can endure the heat of His anger. His fury is poured out like fire and the rocks are shattered before Him (vv. 2–6). He protects those who put their trust in Him, but overwhelms those who are rebellious and drives His enemies into the darkness. He does not take vengeance twice upon His foes but makes an end of them. They shall be devoured as fire consumes dry stubble (vv. 7–10).

Ch. i. 11–ii. 2. Out of Nineveh one (i.e. Sennacherib) came forth long ago who devised evil against Yahweh, but though His foes be strong and many, they shall be cut off and pass away. He will humble His people no more, but will burst their bonds asunder (i. 11–13). The name of him who devised evil against Yahweh shall be blotted out, his grave dishonoured, and his temple robbed of its idols. The messenger is hastening with the glad tidings of peace. Judah may hold festival and pay her vows for never again will the villain invade her. His end has come (i. 14, 15). The shatterer is in sight. Nineveh should guard her ramparts and summon up her strength, for Yahweh shall exhalt the dignity and strength of Judah to the standard of that of Isreal in her best days (ii. 1, 2).

Chapter ii. 3–13

Ch. ii. 3–10. The prophet describes the invading army. The soldiers carry crimson shields and are clad in scarlet; their armoured chariots gleam like fire and their horses prance at the muster; their chariots tear through the open country and across the broad spaces, flashing like torches and darting like lightning (vv. 3, 4). They rush to the wall and set up the mantelet; the water-gates are forced and the queen is carried away captive. Nineveh looks like a pool of water with her people flowing from her. No one obeys the command to stand fast (vv. 5–8). The looting begins and there is no end to the plunder. Nineveh is desolate, hearts are fainting and faces grow pale with fear (vv. 9, 10).

Ch. ii. 11–13. What has become of the den whither the old lion (i.e. Nineveh) used to retreat with his lionesses and cubs, filling it with prey (i.e. the plunder of the nations)? Yahweh is against that haunt of cruelty; He will burn it with fire and destroy the lionesses and the cubs.

Chapter iii

Ch. iii. 1–7. The city is soaked with blood and crammed with lies and plunder. Nothing shall be heard in her but the swish of the whip, the rumbling of wheels, the gallop of horses, and the rush of chariots bounding along, while the cavalry charge with swords flashing and spears glinting, and the slain are piled in heaps over which the victors stumble (vv. 1–3). All this is a fitting punishment for one who, like a well-favoured harlot, has fascinated other nations with her charms and brought evil upon them. Yahweh will deal with her as she deserves. She will be exposed to the nations and made an object of derision, and no one will lament her downfall (vv. 4–7).

Ch. iii. 8–17. Nineveh boasts of her strength, but she will fare no better than No-Amon (Thebes) with the Nile round her for a rampart, with the strength of Ethiopia and Egypt as her defence, and Put and the Libyans as allies. Yet she was taken away captive; her children were slain, lots were cast for her leaders and all her nobles were put in chains (vv. 8–10). Nineveh, too, will stagger and swoon, and seek in vain for a refuge from her enemy. Her fortresses shall fall like the first ripe figs which fall at the mere shaking of the fig tree. Her defenders shall prove as weak as women; the gates to her land shall fly open. She may prepare for the siege and strengthen her defences, but it will be of no avail. She shall be destroyed by fire and sword. However many her numbers, however numerous her traders, they shall vanish away. Her princes and officers, too, shall seek shelter at the first opportunity (vv. 11–17).

Ch. iii. 18, 19. Her leaders slumber in death and her inhabitants are scattered upon the mountains. Her wound is fatal, her ruin irretrievable. All who have suffered from her unceasing brutality shall clap their hands over her downfall.

PERMANENT INFLUENCE

Of recent years the book of Nahum has met with severe criticism on account of the spirit of hatred and of vengeance that breathes through it. Some critics assert that the author is not a prophet but a poet fit to be ranked with the authors of the 'Song of Deborah' and the 'Lament of David for Saul and Jonathan'. His poem is a paean of victory over the approaching fall of Nineveh and is devoid of any religious content. Further, it is alleged that the book gained its position in the Hebrew Canon through the title, 'The book of the vision of Nahum the Elkoshite' (i. 1), the prophetic word 'vision' securing its recognition as inspired Scripture. Others again acknowledge him to be a prophet, but they do not class him with the canonical prophets but with the so-called 'false prophets', like Hananiah (Jer. xxviii) who believed that Yahweh might in His anger deliver His chosen people into the hands of their enemies but would never abandon them, and that anyone who taught otherwise was a traitor.

It is difficult to see how Nahum can be denied a place among the canonical prophets. It is true that he has not their spirituality, religious enthusiasm and passion for righteousness. We find in his prophecy no new thought about Yahweh, no denunciation of Judah for her sins, no threats of punishment, no announcement of a final judgement and no promise of a future Golden Age of righteousness and peace. Still his prophecy is not without religious significance. Like Amos and his successors, he believes that Yahweh is in control of the nations: this is not explicitly stated but it is assumed as an axiomatic truth. It is Yahweh who calls up an overwhelming force to destroy Nineveh. 'Behold, I am against thee, saith the Lord of hosts, and I will burn her chariots in the smoke, and the sword shall devour thy young lions: and I will cut off thy prey from the earth, and the voice of thy messenger shall no more be heard' (ii. 13; cf. iii. 5). Yahweh is not only the Controller of the nations, but also a righteous God who hates and punishes evil. He is against Nineveh because she is a city soaked with blood and crammed with lies and plunder, because like a well-favoured harlot she has lured nations with her charms and bewitched them. She shall be exposed like a harlot to the nations and no one shall lament her fall (iii. 1–7).

Nahum is the least attractive of all the prophets. His book is a striking contrast to that of Jonah with its proclamation of the love and care of Yahweh for all mankind. It is easy, however, to condemn him, but after two world wars in which we have suffered at the hands of brutal aggressors, we can understand his attitude towards Assyria and judge him more kindly. A quotation in Luckenbill's

'Ancient Records of Assyria', vol. ii, 1927, p. 311, brings home to us what Assyrian conquest meant. 'For a distance of a month of twenty-five days' journey I devastated the provinces of Elam. Salt and silhu (some prickly plant) I scattered over them. . . . The noise of people, the tread of cattle and sheep, the glad shouts of rejoicing, I banished from its fields. Wild asses, gazelles and all kinds of beasts of the plain I caused to lie down among them, as if at home.' It is not surprising that Assyria fell amid the curses of the nations she had oppressed.

STYLE

The book of Nahum is a work of great literary merit. Nahum is probably the greatest poet among all the prophets. He excels in pictorial and vivid description, bringing before the mind's eye the chariots, like flaming torches, coursing through the streets and broadways (ii. 3, 4), the horsemen with their bright swords and glittering spears (ii. 3), the captured queen, surrounded by her maidens mourning like doves (ii. 7), the spoiling of the vast treasures (ii. 9), the innumerable corpses piled in the streets (iii. 3), and the desolation of the ruined city (ii. 10, iii. 7). With his word-pictures and the speed of his lines he has succeeded in suggesting the excitement and alarm among the defenders of the city (ii. 6, 10, iii. 14), the irresistible onslaught of the ruthless foe (ii. 3–5, iii. 2, 3), the noise and tumult of battle (ii. 4, iii. 2, 3), and the desolation of the ruined city (ii. 10, iii. 15). The imagery, which is drawn from Nature, is brilliant. Nineveh is a den of lions, where the lion tore to pieces for his whelps and strangled for his lionesses, filling his caves with prey and his lair with plunder (ii. 11, 12). The fortresses of Nineveh shall be like fig-trees, the fruit of which falls into the hungry mouth when they are shaken (iii. 12). Fire and sword shall devour the city though the inhabitants be as numerous as the locusts (iii. 15). Her princes and captains shall vanish like the swarms of locusts which camp in the hedges in the cold day but flee away when the sun rises (iii. 17). Her leaders sleep the sleep of death and her inhabitants are scattered upon the mountains like sheep without a shepherd. Events are described with the minimum of detail and in language which is clear and forcible. Effective use is made of repetition (ii. 8, 9, iii. 15), the rhetorical question (ii. 11, iii. 7, 8) and the imperative (ii. 8, 9. iii. 14, 15). The prophecy is really a song of triumph over the approaching downfall of a ruthless power which has brought suffering to the peoples of south-western Asia, and is charged with the spirit of hatred. The siege, capture and complete destruction of Nineveh are depicted so realistically and with such passion, that some readers have assumed, though wrongly, that Nahum must have been an eyewitness of the events which he described.

CHAPTER XII

Habakkuk

LIFE AND CHARACTER OF HABAKKUK

Nothing is known of Habakkuk outside the book which bears his name. Legends have gathered round his name, but they are of doubtful historical value. He was apparently a native of Judah, and assuming that he was prophesying in the reign of Jehoiakim, must have been a contemporary of Jeremiah. From the book we gather that he was a patriot and a faithful follower of Yahweh, and that he had been deeply influenced by the teaching of the eighth century prophets. He was roused to anger at the sight of the suffering of his fellow countrymen, and longed to see the day when Yahweh would execute judgement upon their oppressors. He breathes the spirit of hatred and revenge, and appears to have no conception of Yahweh as a God who is long suffering and of great mercy. As a prophet his visions came to him, not while he was in a state of ecstasy or in a trance, but while he was meditating in isolation upon the ways of Yahweh (ii. 1). Though he doubted the popular view of human suffering his faith finally triumphed over his doubts, and he was content to wait patiently in the belief that Yahweh would in His own good time carry out His eternal purpose and that right would ultimately triumph (ii. 3–5).

CONTENTS

The book may be divided into two parts:

(1) Chs. i–ii. Denunciation of oppressors and thoughts on the persecution of the righteous by the wicked.

(2) Ch. iii. A psalm expressing joyous confidence in Yahweh.

The two parts may be summarized thus:

Chapters i–ii

Ch. i. 1–4. Habakkuk asks Yahweh how long must he complain of violence in the land and gaze on misery and oppression. Before his eyes outrage and injury go on, the law is paralysed, and wicked men hamper the righteous until justice is perverted. Yet He remains silent refusing to listen to his cries for help.

Ch. i. 5–11. He receives the answer that Yahweh is about to in-augurate a new epoch, undreamt of in human history. He is raising up against the evil-doers the fierce and fiery Chaldeans who are already launched on their career of destruction. Like fierce beasts of prey their cavalry are sweeping all before them: they scoff at kings and princes, capture fortresses with a rush, and go forward like the wind, making their own strength their god.

Ch. i. 12–17. He recognizes that Yahweh, the Holy God, who does not die, has appointed them as His instruments of judgement, but cannot understand why He, the altogether Righteous, should remain silent when the impious conquerors destroy the righteous. Men have become like fish of the sea that have no ruler and are easily swept up into the net of the Chaldeans who, happy in their success, offer sacrifices to their nets for yielding so rich a catch and food so plentiful. Are they to go on murdering their victims without pity?

Ch. ii. 1–4. Unable to explain the mystery, he places himself in imagination upon his watch-tower and waits expectantly for a revelation from Yahweh touching the righteous government of the world. Soon the message comes, and he is told to inscribe it upon tablets and make it so plain that it can be read at a glance. The vision will surely be fulfilled at the appointed time. The message is that the powers of the impious man shall fail, but the righteous shall live by his faithfulness.

Ch. ii. 5–20. The proud, treacherous, restless conqueror is as rapacious as the grave and as insatiable as Death; but the time is coming when his victims shall sing songs of mockery over his down-fall (vv. 5, 6a). The prophet now utters a series of woes against the conqueror. He has heaped up plunder, but all those whom he has spoiled shall turn and spoil him (vv. 6b–8). He has built his house with his ill-gotten gains, setting it on high out of the reach of calamity: he has brought shame upon his house and forfeited his own life. The very stones and beams will cry out for vengeance for the blood that has been shed (vv. 9–11). He has built his cities upon blood and crime, but Yahweh has not ordained that the nations

should toil for what must soon be destroyed, or spend their energies
for naught. It is His will that the knowledge of Himself shall be the
treasured possession of all men (vv. 12–14). He causes the peoples
to reel like one who has drunk a poisonous drug that he may exult in
their disgrace. He, in turn, shall drink the cup of Yahweh's wrath,
and his glory shall be turned to shame. The devastation he has
wrought in Canaan shall crush him (vv. 15–17). He trusts in gods of
wood and stone, made by the hands of men and incapable of giving
guidance. But Yahweh is in His holy temple and before Him all
nations stand in silent awe (vv. 18–20).

Chapter iii
Ch. iii. 1–16. The poet has heard of and seen Yahweh's work, and
prays that He will manifest His saving power to His people, and that,
in His wrath, He will remember to be merciful (vv. 1, 2). In answer
to His prayer Yahweh comes from Sinai, approaching from the
direction of Edom and filling heaven and earth with His glory.
Before Him strides Pestilence and behind Him the burning Plague.
As He passes on His way, riding in His chariots of salvation, the
mountains sink low, the floods roar, and sun and moon forget to
shine. He crushes the heathen in His fury for the salvation of His
people, His anointed. He shatters the house of the wicked, laying
bare the foundation to the rock. Over the sea He strides with His
steeds while the mighty waters surge. So awful is the sight that the
poet trembles, but he will wait calmly for the day of doom that will
dawn upon the people who would assail them (vv. 3–16).
Ch. iii. 17–19. Crops and flocks may fail, but he will rejoice in the
God of his salvation.

UNITY AND DATE

It is almost universally agreed that the book is not a literary unit but
a compilation. The theory that chapter iii is the genuine work of
Habakkuk has won little support. It is quite different in thought,
language and structure, being a psalm with musical directions, indicating that it once formed part of a collection of psalms designed
for temple worship. It was probably transferred to the book of
Habakkuk because it bore the title, 'A Prayer of Habakkuk the
Prophet', just as the Septuagint ascribes Psalms cxlvi–cxlviii to
the prophets Haggai and Zechariah. Such ascriptions have little

evidential value, since such compositions were often assigned to prominent characters on the strength of some real or fancied appropriateness. The scroll of the 'Habakkuk Commentary', one of the Dead Sea scrolls discovered in 1947, deals only with the first two chapters of the book. The omission of the third chapter supports the view that it is a later insertion. It is difficult to determine its date but it is probably of post-exilic origin.

The question of the unity and date of the first two chapters is intimately bound up with the interpretation of the text. The precise interpretation is difficult mainly for two reasons. First, it is not clear whether the protest in ch. i. 1–4, refers to the sins of Judah or the oppression of a foreign power; and second, in ch. i. 5–11, the Chaldeans are represented as the agents of Yahweh, summoned by Him to execute judgement upon the wicked oppressors mentioned in the previous section, whereas in chs. i. 12–ii. 20 they appear to be identified with the oppressors who are doomed to be destroyed for their sins.

Various solutions of the problem have been advanced by scholars, but none is satisfactory. Some accept the whole of the two chapters as the work of Habakkuk who wrote about 600 BC. Others maintain that the two chapters, with the exception of certain additions, are the work of two prophets—one who, about 605 BC, wrote ch. i. 1–11, protesting against the sins of the ruling classes in Judah, and predicting the coming of the Chaldeans at Yahweh's command to execute judgement upon her; and the other, who, towards the close of the Exile, wrote chs. i. 12–ii. 20 predicting the punishment of the Chaldeans.

Some omit ch. i. 5–11 on the ground that it is a fragment of an older prophecy, composed by another prophet and dating from about 610 BC. But the elimination of this section would increase the difficulty since we should have no idea as to the identity of the oppressors mentioned in chs. i. 12–ii. 20.

Budde maintains that the oppressors are the Assyrians, not the Babylonians, and that the latter are Yahweh's agents for punishing the former. The prophet protests against their tyranny in chs. i. 1–4, 12–17, while in ch. ii. 1–4 Yahweh replies that the wicked shall perish but that the righteous by their faithfulness shall survive. The sequel to ch. ii. 1–4 is ch. i. 5–11 which Budde accordingly places immediately after ch. ii. 4. He assigns the prophecy to about 615 BC.[1]

[1] K. Budde, *Zeitschrift der deutschen morgenlandischen Gesellschaft*, 1930, pp. 139–47.

Against this theory it may be urged that the Assyrians were not in a position to oppress Judah in the reign of Josiah, as by that time they had lost the supremacy in western Asia, and Josiah had succeeded in establishing his independence. Moreover the Babylonians did not move from west to east as it is implied in ch. i. 9.

Duhm assigns the entire book to the time of Alexander the Great on the following grounds. The text is corrupt; 'Chaldeans' (i. 6) should read 'Kittim' (properly 'Cypriotes' but also 'Greeks') and the word 'wine' (ii. 5) should read 'Greek'. The picture portrayed fits the reign of Alexander the Great following the battle of Issus in 332 BC. He regards the psalm in ch. iii as an integral part of the book.[1] The theory, however, can be rejected for the following reasons. (1) The corruption of the text cannot be proved; (2) the history of the reign of Alexander the Great is not faithfully portrayed; (3) the language reflects the age of Jeremiah.

One more theory may be mentioned. Humbert argues that Habakkuk was a cultic prophet, and that he composed the book as a liturgy for a service of intercession in the Temple at Jerusalem in 602 or 601 BC.[2] This theory, however, need not be taken seriously.

Doubts have been cast upon the authenticity of two of the woes, namely the third (ii. 12–14) and the fifth (ii. 18–20). The former contains quotations from Jeremiah li. 58 and Isaiah xi. 9, while the latter breathes the spirit of Deutero-Isaiah. Both of them probably belong to the post-exilic period.

PERMANENT INFLUENCE

The book gives us slight information concerning the moral and social conditions of Judah about the close of the seventh century BC. Assuming that the oppressors of Judah were the ruling classes, we conclude that they were indifferent to the moral demands of their religion. Robbery, strife and faction were rampant throughout the land, the Law was paralysed and men could not obtain justice in the public courts. Evil was enthroned and Yahweh appeared to be silent in the presence of the suffering of the righteous.

Habakkuk contributes little to Hebrew religious thought. He was not the first to proclaim that Yahweh was the Creator of the Universe and the Lord of History, that He was a righteous God, who punished

[1] B. Duhm, *Das Buch Habakuk*, 1906.
[2] P. Humbert, *Problèmes du livre d'Habacuc*, 1946.

men and nations for ignoring the claims of the moral law, and that
He raised up an unrighteous nation to punish other nations for their
sins. He is, nevertheless, important, because he raises the problem
of human suffering which has engaged the attention of serious-
minded men down to the present day. The problem could not have
been raised unless the prophetic conception of the omnipotence and
righteousness of Yahweh had been accepted. Granted such teaching
as to the character of Yahweh, the problem was bound, sooner or
later, to arise and to call for a solution. According to the popular
belief, Yahweh rewarded the righteous and punished the wicked;
but this comfortable belief was not in harmony with the facts of
human experience. Habakkuk expressed the doubts of the serious-
minded men of his day who were perplexed by the suffering of the
righteous. 'Thou that art of purer eyes than to behold evil, and that
canst not look on perverseness, wherefore lookest thou upon them
that deal treacherously, and holdest thy peace when the wicked
swalloweth up the man that is more righteous than he; and makest
men as the fishes of the sea, as the creeping things, that have no
ruler over them?' (i. 13, 14). Meditating in solitude on the problem,
he received the revelation from Yahweh that the powers of the
impious man shall fail, 'but the just shall live by his faith' (ii. 4).
The meaning of the words is obscure; it is uncertain whether the
prophet means that the righteous man will literally escape destruction through his steadfastness or that he will save his soul even
though he may suffer death. The thought was taken up by Paul in
his doctrine of justification by faith (Rom. i. 17; Gal. iii. 11), by the
writer of Hebrews in his exhortation to patience (Heb. x. 38) and
by Luther in his assertion of Christian freedom. In each case the
thought was given a deeper meaning, 'faith' being used not in the
sense of steadfastness but in that of trust in God's redeeming grace
through Christ.

STYLE

Though the book is short and only a portion of it can with confidence
be ascribed to Habakkuk, that portion is sufficient to enable us to
form some idea of the prophet's style. Habakkuk is endowed with
imagination, the observant eye and the power of graphic description.
His style is clear, vigorous and vivid, frequent use being made of apt
figures of speech, such as simile (i. 8, 11, 14), metaphor (i. 10, 12),

personification (ii. 11), and the rhetorical question (i. 2, 17, ii. 13). He shows his keen interest in Nature from which he draws much of his imagery. He knows all about the swiftness of the leopard, the ravenous wolves prowling in the evening and the eagle hastening to its prey (i. 8). He has watched the fisherman catching the fish in a net, and has studied the ways of 'the creeping things, that have no ruler over them' (i. 14–17). He has been impressed by the sand of the desert (i. 9) and the rush of the wind (i. 11); the bird's nest set on high has not escaped his attention (ii. 9). He believes that the conqueror would be punished for destroying the forests of Lebanon, slaughtering the wild beasts and devastating the land (ii. 17). If ch. iii is from his pen, we have, according to Driver, 'a lyric ode, which, for sublimity of poetic conception and splendour of diction, ranks with the finest which Hebrew poetry has produced.'[1]

[1] S. R. Driver, *An Introduction to the Literature of the Old Testament*, 9th ed., 1913, p. 339.

CHAPTER XIII

Jeremiah

INTRODUCTION

Thanks to the labours of an unknown compiler, we know more of Jeremiah's career than of that of any other prophet of the Old Testament. The book of Jeremiah, however, is not without its difficulties. The fact that it is a compilation and not a literary unit, presents us with the problem of the sources from which the material was derived and of their authorship. The various sections of the book are not arranged in chronological order: the incidents relating to Zedekiah, for example, instead of appearing at the end, as they chronologically should, occur in different parts of the book. The dates of a considerable number of prophecies, which are probably genuine, are doubtful, while in some chapters we find detached utterances which break the sequence of thought, but which cannot now be placed in their proper contexts. Like all the prophets, he has suffered from much post-exilic editing, so that the determination of what is genuine is often extremely difficult, frequently turning on intricate questions of metre; and often the most divergent views concerning his meaning have been put forward. Finally there is the question of the relationship between the Hebrew and Greek texts of the book.

LIFE AND CHARACTER OF JEREMIAH

Jeremiah was born in the Benjamite village of Anathoth, some four miles north-east of Jerusalem. It is clear that the countryside made a deep impression upon his mind, for his prophetic utterances reveal a love of Nature greater even than that of Amos and Hosea. He was endowed with keen powers of observation. During his sojourn in the country he noted the almond-tree awakening from its winter sleep (i. 11), the tree spreading out its roots by the river (xvii. 8), the snow of Lebanon and the cold streams flowing down the hillside (xviii. 14), the jungle of the Jordan valley (xii. 5), the dreary wastes (ii. 31, xxii. 6), and the hot wind blowing 'from the bare heights in the wilderness' (iv. 11). He knew all about the homing instinct of the migratory birds (viii. 7), the nesting habits of the partridge (xvii. 11), the swift dromedary 'traversing her ways' (ii. 23), the danger from wild beasts (iv. 7, v. 6), and the sufferings of wild asses in a drought (xiv. 6). Anathoth, however, was not a remote village. It was only a few miles from Jerusalem, where he lived for many years and became familiar with the lives of the city dwellers. He watched the metal worker refining silver (vi. 29), the hypocritical worshippers making the Temple a den of robbers (vii. 11), men, women and children preparing cakes to the Queen of Heaven (vii. 18), and the potter moulding the clay (xviii. 3, 4). It was natural that when he came to write he should make use of such observations to give point and vividness to his messages.

His father, Hilkiah, belonged to a priestly family, and was probably a descendant of the unfortunate priest Abiathar whom Solomon deposed in favour of Zadok and banished to Anathoth where he owned some property (1 Kgs. ii. 26). It is, therefore, reasonable to suppose that he was born into the party which was opposed to the priestly house of Zadok at Jerusalem. From his father he would become acquainted with Israel's past and perhaps with the teaching of his predecessors in the prophetic office, especially Hosea, whose teaching exercised such a profound influence upon him.

His call came at an unusually early age. In answer to Yahweh's 'word' he declared, 'I am too young' (Moffatt's translation). Probably this meant no more than that he was younger than most prophets were at their call. Considering that he was not married and that early marriages were the rule among Orientals, he was probably under twenty years of age when the call came to him in the thirteenth year of Josiah's reign. But he was not unprepared for his call. Those who believe most unreservedly in the divine character of the call, would admit that the acceptance implied a mind ready to receive, while those who deny all divine influence would regard the call as entirely the projection of his own unconscious mind. Because of the greatness of the task to which he was summoned he hesitated to undertake it, although he felt that Yahweh had called him even before his birth to the prophetic office. But Yahweh reiterated His command, and touched his mouth as a sign that He had put His words into His servant's mouth and appointed him a prophet to the nations (i. 5)[1], 'to pluck up and to break down, and to destroy and to overthrow; to build and to plant' (i. 10).

Soon after his call he learnt from his vision of a blossoming almond-tree that Yahweh was awake to perform His word, and from that of a boiling cauldron that He was about to use a foe from the north to punish His people (i. 11–16). In a number of prophecies he described in words of terror the successive stages in the advance of the foe: it seemed to him that the end not only of Jerusalem, but also of the whole world, was at hand (iv. 5–8, 13–17, 19–26, 29–31, v. 15–17, vi. 1–7, 22–26, viii. 14–17, x. 19–22).

These northern invaders are generally identified with the Scythians, who, according to Herodotus, broke into the Assyrian Empire (c. 628–626 BC).[2] But the danger passed. As often happened, fertile Philistia and the road to Egypt proved more attractive to the northern invaders and they turned that way. What eventually happened to them we do not know: they were probably bought off by the Egyptian king and finally settled down in some place more fertile than the country round Jerusalem. Jeremiah was left with un-fulfilled prophecy, and with the reputation of being an excitable alarmist of whom no notice need be taken.

Nothing is definitely known concerning the public ministry of Jeremiah from the time when he predicted the coming of a foe from the north to the death of Josiah at Megiddo (609 BC). It would appear that he welcomed Josiah's reformation which followed the

---

[1] Some scholars hold that Jeremiah could not have been appointed 'a prophet unto the nations' (i. 5). Stade proposed to alter 'the nations' to 'my nation' and Duhm struck out the words as a late gloss. There is, however, no need to suppose that the original text has been tampered with. Jeremiah was appointed to speak the word of Yahweh who was a God of righteousness, and righteousness knows nothing of national frontiers.

[2] The identification of the 'foe from the north' with the Scythians is not accepted by all critics. Wilke ('Das Skythen-problem im Jeremia Buch' in *Alttest mentliche Studien fur Kittel*, 1913, pp. 222–54) identifies him with the Chaldeans who threatened Palestine in the days of Nebuchadrezzar. Welch (*Jeremiah, His Time and His Work*, 1st ed., 1928, reprinted 1951, pp. 120–125, who is followed by Elmslie (*How Came Our Faith*, 1948, p. 314) considers that Jeremiah used the term to signify, not a particular nation, but a terrible calamity which would come from the north. Torrey (*J.B.L.*, 56, 1937, pp. 208 ff.) identifies him with Alexander the Great and assigns Jer. i–x to the third century BC, while Hyatt (*J.B.L.*, 59, 1940, pp. 499–513) identifies him with the Chaldeans and Medes who destroyed Nineveh in 612 BC. Bentzen (*Introduction to the Old Testament*, vol. ii, 1948, p. 122), suggests that the foe the prophet meant is both a threatening political force from Mesopotamia and an 'actualization' of mysterious forces coming from the ends of the earth or the north.

discovery of the 'book of the Law' (substantially the present book of Deuteronomy) in 622 BC and went on a crusade in favour of its adoption. This seems to be the natural interpretation of ch. xi. 1–8, in which he pronounced a curse on all those who did not listen to the words of 'this covenant', and received a divine commission to proclaim them in the cities of Judah and the streets of Jerusalem. It would be natural for him, too, to welcome the humanitarian precepts of the covenant and the abolition of the local shrines which were centres of idolatrous worship and immoral practices. The hostility which he incurred at the hands of his own kinsmen would be best explained on the supposition that he supported a religious movement, which meant the abolition of the local shrine at Anathoth and the exaltation of the priestly house of Zadok at Jerusalem (xi. 18–23). Later, as we shall see, events were to force him to reconsider his judgement.[1] During this period he continued to believe in the genuineness of his revelations and evidently went on giving messages to a few close friends, among whom was Baruch.

After Josiah's death, Jehoahaz, though not the eldest son, was chosen to succeed him, but after three months he was dethroned by Pharaoh Necho and carried off to Egypt. He was replaced by his brother Eliakim whose name was changed to Jehoiakim (2 Kgs. xxiii. 31–34). With the accession of Jehoiakim (609–598 BC) Jeremiah now came out in public with the first utterance which we can fully date after the Scythian invasion. He told the people of Jerusalem not to weep for the dead Josiah but for the exiled Shallum (Jehoahaz), his son, who would never return (xxii. 10–12). It is likely that he was sympathetic towards Shallum because of his anti-Egyptian policy, which the prophet had always advocated. Next he attacked Jehoiakim

---

[1] The theory that Jeremiah welcomed Josiah's reforms is rejected by some scholars, chiefly for the following reasons: (1) The fact that no mention is made of the prophet in the historical accounts dealing with the discovery of the Book of the Law in the Temple and with Josiah's reforms, indicates that he was either unsympathetic or hostile towards the movement. (2) There is not a single genuine oracle of Jeremiah which can be adduced to support the theory. When in xi. 1–8, Jeremiah insists on the observance of 'this covenant' between Yahweh and Israel, the reference is not to the Deuteronomic Code but to the covenant given through Moses at Sinai. (3) Several passages indicate that he was opposed to the reforms. The Deuteronomists sought to centralize all sacrificial worship at Jerusalem, but he predicted the destruction of the Temple (vii. 1–15, xxvi. 1–6) and expressed his opposition to the need for sacrifices (vi. 20, vii. 21–4, xi. 15). (4) He accused certain scribes of falsifying Yahweh's Law, not by the interpretation they put upon it, but by their false pen. For a discussion of the subject see Skinner, *Prophecy and Religion*, 1922, reprinted 1951, pp. 89–107; and Welch, *Jeremiah, His Time and His Work*, 1928, reprinted 1951, pp. 76–96.

F

for employing forced labour in the erection of a spacious palace in Jerusalem. In the spirit of Amos he compared him with Ahab, and contrasted him with Josiah who enjoyed life but was scrupulously fair—a verdict on Josiah's personality which must be accepted as being the estimate of an impartial contemporary, but comes as a surprise to those who know Josiah only through the laudatory account in 2 Kings xxii–xxiii. 30.

To the beginning of Jehoiakim's reign belongs his great Temple address which has come down to us in two forms—a short summary in ch. xxvi. 1–6 and a longer summary in ch. vii. 1–15. In it he condemned the popular belief that the security of the nation depended upon the existence of the Temple, and predicted its destruction unless the people repented. In another address delivered about the same time he declared that Yahweh required not sacrifice but obedience to His moral demands. The priests and the prophets demanded his execution but he was saved by the intervention of certain elders, notably Ahikam, who recalled how in the reign of Hezekiah Micah had announced the destruction of Jerusalem and of the Temple yet no action had been taken against him (xxvi. 7–19).

In 605 BC Pharaoh Necho was defeated at Carchemish by Nebuchadrezzar who shortly afterwards succeeded his father, Nabopolassar, on the throne of Babylon. Jeremiah was convinced that Babylon was destined to conquer the world, and that she was the appointed agent through whom Yahweh would execute judgement upon all the nations and upon Judah. His predictions of disaster directed against Judah and Jerusalem roused the hostility of the people against himself. He proclaimed that they were under Yahweh's control just as the clay was under the control of the potter's hands (xviii. 1–17) and would be shattered like the earthen vessel which he had symbolically broken in the valley of Hinnom (xix. 1, 2, 10–13). He repeated his warnings in the Temple, and Pashhur, the overseer of the Temple, placed him for a night in the stocks (xix. 14–xx. 2). On his release he predicted that the inhabitants of Judah would be taken captives to Babylon, that Jerusalem should be despoiled of her treasures, and that Pashhur and his family and friends would die in exile (xx. 3–6).

Jeremiah now dictated the substance of his prophecies since the commencement of his ministry to Baruch, and directed him to read the roll in the Temple in the hope that the people might heed the warnings and repent. Word of this was brought to the princes, who summoned Baruch to bring his roll and read it to them. They decided to communicate its contents to the king, and gave Baruch the friendly advice that he and Jeremiah should go into hiding. As soon as they told the king, he ordered Jehudi to fetch the roll and read it aloud to him. As he listened, at the end of every three or four pages he cut them out and burnt them. Baruch reported the king's action to Jeremiah who dictated to him, 'all the words of the book which Jehoiakim king of Judah had burned in the fire: and there were added besides unto them many like words' (xxxvi). The precise contents of this roll cannot now be ascertained, but it was probably relatively short since it was apparently read three times in a single day.

It would appear that for several years he was compelled to live in seclusion, if not in hiding, and we may judge that it was during this period of his life that he wrote most, if not all, of his Confessions (xi. 18–23, xii. 1–6, xv. 10–21, xvii. 14–18, xviii. 18–23, xx. 7–12, 14–18). In these he revealed his fears, complained of the prosperity of the wicked, deplored his isolation and his rejection by the people, prayed for vengeance upon his persecutors, expressed his resentment against Yahweh for making him a prophet, and cursed the day that he was born. Yet throughout them there sound the notes of conviction, security and trust. 'But the Lord is with me as a mighty one and a terrible: therefore my persecutors shall stumble and they shall not prevail' (xx. 11). These 'Confessions' reveal Jeremiah in a way which enables us to know him better than any other prophet.

It was probably towards the close of the reign of Jehoiakim, when Babylonian forces, supported by Syrians, Moabites and Ammonites were overrunning the land (2 Kgs. xxiv. 2), that Jeremiah met the Rechabites who had sought refuge within the walls of the capital. He invited them to drink wine in one of the chambers of the Temple, but they refused on the ground that the founder of their sect, Jonadab, had forbidden them to drink wine, build houses or plant vineyards. The prophet contrasts the infidelity of the inhabitants of Judah to Yahweh with the fidelity of the Rechabites to the will of their ancestor (xxxv. 1–19).

The short reign of Jehoiachin —Koniah, as Jeremiah called him— produced two oracles, namely (1) ch. xxii. 24–30, in which the prophet announced that the unfortunate monarch would die in exile and that no descendant of his would ever be king, and (2) ch. xiii. 18, 19, in which he predicted the doom of the king and the queen-mother.[1] Actually, as the historical summary at the end of the book shows, Evil-merodach, as soon as he came to the throne, treated Jehoiachin not as a prisoner, but as a royal pensioner, who had his meals with the king all the rest of his life (lii. 31–34).

The reign of Zedekiah is much more conspicuous in the book. At its beginning Jeremiah in a vision saw two baskets, one containing good figs and the other bad, and learnt from Yahweh that the good figs represented the exiles in Babylon, whom He would restore to their native land and to prosperity, while the bad figs were those left in Palestine under Zedekiah and those in Egypt who would be destroyed (xxiv. 1–10).

About the same time he wrote a remarkable letter to the exiles in Babylon telling them to build, plant and marry as if they were in their own land, and to do their best for the city in which they were captives. The Babylonian rule was to last seventy years after which they would return (xxix. 10). The prophets who encouraged rebellion were false prophets (xxix. 8, 9) and would be roasted in the fire by Nebuchadrezzar (xxix. 22). One of these, Shemaiah, wrote to Zephaniah the Temple overseer, blaming him for not punishing Jeremiah as a madman. Zephaniah read the letter to Jeremiah, who wrote again to Babylon declaring that Yahweh would punish Shemaiah for his false teaching and that his descendants should not share in the restoration (xxix. 24–32).

The Kings of Edom, Moab, Ammon, Tyre and Zidon sent representatives to invite Zedekiah to join in a revolt against Babylon. Jeremiah performed the symbolic act of putting a yoke upon his neck as a sign of submission to Nebuchadrezzar, and sent a message to the five kings telling them to submit to the Babylonian rule. At the same time he sent a similar message to Zedekiah, and to the priests and all the people, in both cases denouncing the Babylonian prophets as false prophets (xxvii. 1–22). Another prophet, Hananiah, also performed a symbolic act: he broke the yoke from off Jeremiah's neck and predicted that within two years Yahweh would break the yoke of Nebuchadrezzar from off the neck of all the nations (xxviii. 1–11). Jeremiah received a word from Yahweh that He would replace the wooden yoke with one of iron and that Hananiah was a false prophet and would die within a year, as actually happened (xxviii. 12–17). The negotiations came to nothing.

[1] Some critics make this prophecy refer to Jehoiakim and his mother Zebidah (2 Kings xxiii. 36).

Zedekiah, in the hope of throwing off the Babylonian yoke, entered into negotiations with Egypt; but secretly he had a great respect for Jeremiah and sought his advice, only to be told that rebellion would simply mean the destruction of Jerusalem (xxi. 1–10). Nevertheless, the prophet promised the king a peaceful and an honourable death (xxxiv. 1–7). In spite of the prophet's warning rebellion was finally decided upon and in consequence Jerusalem was besieged. In the course of the siege an Egyptian force advanced to its relief and the investing army for a time retired. During the early days of the siege the king induced the inhabitants of Jerusalem to enter into a solemn covenant to release their Hebrew slaves, perhaps in order to win the co-operation of Yahweh and to provide additional defenders for the walls; but shortly afterwards, when the siege was temporarily raised, they broke their pledge and reclaimed them. This was just the kind of conduct which would rouse Jeremiah's indignation, and he proclaimed that as a punishment Nebuchadrezzar would return, slay those who had violated the agreement, take Zedekiah, his princes and Jerusalem, and make the cities of Judah a desolation (xxxiv. 8–22). In the face of imminent danger from the Babylonians, Zedekiah sent to ask for the prayers of Jeremiah, but the prophet declared that the Egyptian forces would retreat and that the Babylonians would return and burn Jerusalem (xxxvii. 1–10).

Two accounts of an arrest (or arrests) of the prophet are given; and it is far more probable that they are divergent traditions of one arrest than that there were two. The first account is in ch. xxxvii. 11–21, according to which Jeremiah proposed to visit his native village (probably in connection with a sale of property there), but was arrested at the city gate on a charge of deserting to the Babylonians, beaten and imprisoned in the house of Jonathan the scribe, from which he was rescued by Zedekiah who sought a 'word from Yahweh' from him, and received the answer that he would fall into the hands of Nebuchadrezzar. Nevertheless, Zedekiah did not allow him to be handed back to Jonathan, but committed him to the court of the guard where he was provided with food 'until all the bread in the city was spent'. This account implies that he was not released till after the fall of Jerusalem. According to the second account (xxxviii), his enemies declared that he was discouraging resistance by his prophecies of disaster, and thrust him into a muddy cistern from which he was rescued at Zedekiah's command by Ebed-melech, an

Ethiopian, and placed in the court of the guard. After telling the king at a private interview that if he surrendered, his life and the city would be spared, he remained under guard till the fall of the city. It is obvious that the striking points in the two accounts are identical. Of course, according to all modern standards Jeremiah was a collaborator and traitor: in ch. xxi. 9, he urged individual soldiers to escape and surrender (this is supported by ch. xxxviii, 2). We can only say that a Hebrew prophet, who believed that he had received direct messages from Yahweh, put them above all standards of duty to the king, the state and the Temple. But it has led the purely secularist historians of the present day to dismiss him as a Babylonian agent.

Towards the close of the siege of Jerusalem Zedekiah attempted to escape, but was captured in the plains of Jericho, blinded and carried in fetters to Babylon. A month later the city was destroyed and its inhabitants, with the exception of the poorest classes, were led into captivity. Gedaliah, a member of the old nobility of Judah, was made governor of the land. He set up his headquarters at Mizpah where he was joined by Jeremiah.

A double account persists regarding Jeremiah's decision to remain with Gedaliah. The first is in ch. xxxix in which, however, vv. 4–13 do not appear in the Septuagint and may be regarded as a later addition. We are left, therefore, merely with a statement that the Babylonian officials, whose names are given, rescued Jeremiah from prison and committed him to Gedaliah. The second account in ch. xl. 1–12, apart from putting into the mouth of the captain of the guard, words which express Jeremiah's own attitude but would have been unintelligible to a Babylonian, seems to be historically sound. From 2 Kings xxv. 22 we learn of Gedaliah's appointment as coming after a period during which Nebuzaradan, captain of the guard, was engaged in seizing and executing all who had taken part in the defence. Thus it seems most likely that Jeremiah was in the first instance marked out to be deported to Babylon (xl. 11), but, when Gedaliah took over, Jeremiah's record was discovered, and being such as would commend him to the Babylonian officers, he was allowed to choose whether he would go with the exiles or settle down with the peasants who were allowed to remain in the country under Gedaliah. He chose the second alternative. It was perhaps during his sojourn at Mizpah that he had his great vision of the New Covenant (see p. 193).

Everything, however, was destroyed by the murder of Gedaliah, who was too much of a gentleman to believe that anyone would try to deceive him, by one Ishmael, who slaughtered all the Jews and all the Babylonians who were with him as well as pilgrims from northern Israel (xl. 13–xli. 10). The surviving Jewish leaders sought to flee to Egypt but consulted Jeremiah, who forbade them and threatened them with all kinds of disasters if they went into Egypt (xlii); but they refused to take his counsel and carried him off against his will to Tahpanhes (xliii. 1–7). Two incidents concerning the prophet in Egypt are recorded. The first took place at Tahpanhes (Daphne), where he was bidden to take some large stones and hide them under the entry to Pharaoh's palace and to declare that Nebuchadrezzar would set his throne on them (xliii. 8–13). In the second account we are told that he encountered a body of women, who asserted their determination to return to the worship of the Queen of Heaven in fulfilment of a vow which they had made, because they had had no luck since they gave up that worship (xliv. 15–19). He declared that the fulfilment of the vow meant the end of the religion of Yahweh in Egypt (xliv. 24–28).

Skinner[1] regards the short chapter xlv which the editor of the book, as we now have it, regarded as the close of the roll, written by Baruch at Jeremiah's dictation in the fourth year of the reign of Jehoiakim, as really a farewell to Baruch when the prophet felt himself to be dying. It laments the failure of all for which he had striven and substantially tells him not to try to take his place, though Yahweh will spare his life. Jeremiah's death is nowhere recorded.

In estimating the character of Jeremiah we must first rid oursleves of the prevailing misconception concerning him. He has been commonly called the 'weeping prophet' and expressions of unrelieved gloom are even today termed 'jeremiads'. The title of the 'weeping prophet' has doubtless been ascribed to him because of the mistaken notion that he was the author of Lamentations. It is true that he was subject to moods of despondency and almost of despair, but he was far from being a complete pessimist. He saw Yahweh not only as a just God punishing iniquity, but also as a loving God eager to pardon the repentant sinner. He likened Him to a loving husband ready to take back the faithless wife, and to a loving father anxious that his children should love Him in return and never turn away from Him (iii. 1–5, 19, xxxi. 9). During the siege of Jerusalem he

[1] J. Skinner, *Prophecy and Religion*, 1st ed. 1922, reprinted 1951, pp. 346 ff.

exercised his right to purchase from his kinsman, Hanamel, a field of Anathoth, thereby proclaiming his belief that houses, fields and vineyards would again be bought in the land (xxxii. 6–15). He predicted that life would still go on in the territory of Judah, the environs of Jerusalem, the cities of Judah, of the hill country, the low country, and the Negeb, for Yahweh would restore their fortunes (xxxii. 42–44). Yahweh would bring the exiles home, Judah and Israel would be united under a ruler of the house of David, and the country would enjoy great prosperity (xxiii. 5, 6). With the restored people Yahweh would establish a new covenant which would be not a law inscribed on tables of stone or written in a book, but an illumination of the spirit and conscience of every man, from the least to the greatest (xxxi. 31–34).

Jeremiah was a naturally sensitive and timid man, but under the divine compulsion he conquered his fears, becoming 'a defenced city, and an iron pillar, and brasen walls' (i. 18; cf. xv. 20). His message was rejected by the people; he was hunted, arrested, imprisoned and reviled; his book was burnt and he himself was carried away into Egypt by force. But in spite of all the trials which he had to endure, he never lost his faith or his courage. He was a man who was destined to lead a lonely and isolated life. We may be reasonably certain that he was fond of children (cf. xxxi. 20), but he believed that it was Yahweh's will that he should remain unmarried (xvi. 1, 2). His life was to be lived out alone. The message which he was commissioned to deliver made him unpopular with all sections of the community—rulers, priests, prophets and the people generally. Though he predicted the destruction of the nation and counselled submission to the enemy, he was a patriot who loved his country and yet he met with nothing but hatred and derision. Hated and forsaken by men he found refuge in communion with God, though there were times when he felt that even Yahweh had deceived him, vowed that he would prophesy no more (xx. 9), and cursed the day that he was born (xx. 15). But the divine compulsion was upon him and he continued to prophesy.

He was thoroughly honest in his religion. He believed in the genuineness of his inspiration even when his predications appeared to be falsified. He held the view—quite sincerely—that during their wanderings in the wilderness the people of Israel had not offered sacrifices, for Yahweh had demanded not sacrifices but obedience to His moral demands (vii. 21–23). When the priests and prophets attacked him for predicting in the absence of repentance that the Temple would share the fate of Shiloh, he boldly declared, 'The Lord sent me to prophesy against this house and against this city all the words that ye have heard' (xxvi. 12). When four of the princes demanded his death for what they conceived to be his treachery, he continued to counsel submission to the Babylonians, because he was convinced that Nebuchadrezzar was the instrument of the divine purpose, and that it was Yahweh's will that he should besiege and destroy Jerusalem (xxxviii. 1–23).

Jeremiah's moral standards were high and they appeal to us even today. What strikes us most forcibly was his horror at injustice in high places and his anger against falsity. He denounced Jehoiakim for exacting forced labour from his subjects (xxii. 13–17), Zedekiah for allowing the people to recapture their slaves after entering into a solemn covenant to release them (xxxiv. 8–22), and the wealthy classes for laying up treasure at the expense of the orphan and the needy (v. 26–29). He exhorted kings and their subjects to practise justice and to abstain from wrong doing. 'Execute ye judgement and righteousness, and deliver the spoiled out of the hand of the oppressor; and do no wrong, do no violence to the stranger, the fatherless, nor the widow, neither shed innocent blood in this place' (xxii. 3). He longed to escape to a caravanserai for wayfarers, away from the sight of priests who polluted the Temple with their wickedness, of prophets with their immorality and lying visions, and of people who lied, cheated, deceived and passed from one crime to another (ix. 2–6, xiv. 14, xxiii. 9–40).

Jeremiah was not without his limitations. He took too pessimistic a view of the moral and spiritual condition of the people. He believed that from the day when they entered Canaan they had defiled the land and had made Yahweh's heritage an abomination (ii. 7). Everyone from the least to the greatest was given to covetousness, and everyone from the prophet to the priest dealt falsely (vi. 13). In the whole of Jerusalem it was impossible to find a single righteous man (v. 1). The leaders of the people were no better than the rank and file. 'The priests said not, Where is the Lord? and they that handle the law knew me not: the rulers also transgressed against me, and the prophets prophesied by Baal, and walked after things that do not profit' (ii. 8; cf. v. 30, vi. 13, xxiii. 11). The people were beyond redemption and it was futile to pray for them (vii. 16, xi. 14, xiv. 11, xv. 1). There was something unnatural about their disloyalty to

Yahweh. 'Can a maid forget her ornaments, or a bride her attire? Yet my people have forgotten me days without number' (ii. 32).

It is clear that not all the people were corrupt, as he supposed. He himself was part of the people whom he condemned, and was indebted to the heritage of Israel into which he had entered. There were his loyal secretary Baruch, the princes and the people who had saved him from death, the people who had protected him (xxxvi. 26) and those who had listened to his teaching, cherished his writings and preserved them.

Jeremiah had no idea of Yahweh as a God of love in the fullest sense. He never reached the stage when he found it possible to forgive his enemies. His utterances reveal hatred towards them and a desire for vengeance (xi. 20, xv. 15, xvii. 18, xviii. 23, xx. 12). In his attitude towards them he fell far below the ideal proclaimed in the Gospels, 'Love your enemies, and pray for them that persecute you; that ye may be sons of your Father which is in heaven' (Mt. v. 44).

CONTENTS

The book of Jeremiah falls into four main divisions:

(1) Chs. i–xxv. Poetical prophecies mainly relating to Judah, interspersed with autobiographical and biographical prose narratives, mainly the former.

(2) Chs. xxvi–xlv. Autobiographical and biographical prose narratives with a few poetical prophecies.

(3) Chs. xlvi–li. Prophecies concerning foreign nations.

(4) Ch. lii. A historical appendix taken practically verbatim from 2 Kings xxiv. 18–xxv. 21, 27–30 (verses 28–30 of the chapter are from an independent source).

These divisions may be summarized as follows:

Chapters i–xxv
Ch. i. The introductory title (vv. 1–3). Jeremiah is called to the prophetic office (vv. 4–10). Gazing upon an almond-tree and a boiling cauldron, fanned by a wind from the north, he learns the lesson that Yahweh is ever wakeful to fulfil His purpose and that calamity is about to come upon the nation from the north (vv. 11–16). He is promised divine strength for his task (vv. 17–19).
Ch. ii–iii. 5. Jeremiah reminds Israel of her desert wanderings when

she loved Yahweh. The people have forsaken Him, the source of all life, and have put their trust in idols, the worthless work of men's hands (ii. 1–13). Israel has incurred disaster by turning for help to Egypt and Assyria and to the impotent Baalim (ii. 14–28). The help of Egypt will be as futile as that of Assyria (ii. 29–37). She has been like a faithless wife whose promises of amendment are but as empty words (iii. 1–5).

Chapter ii. 14-17 is apparently a misplacement since it breaks the connection between vv. 13 and 18.

Ch. iii. 6–18. Jeremiah invites Israel, as less guilty than Judah, to repent and return to Yahweh that the people may be restored to their own land under worthy rulers. Jerusalem shall become the religious centre for all nations, and Israel and Judah shall return from exile and dwell together in their own land.

This passage interrupts the connection between vv. 5 and 19 and has apparently been inserted here from another context. The Messianic promise in vv. 17, 18 is regarded by many critics as a later insertion.

Ch. iii. 19–iv. 4. Yahweh expresses His desire to give Judah a son's portion in the best of lands, but she has left Him (iii. 19–20). When she sheds tears of penitence, Yahweh will invite her to return. She comes confessing that the Baalim have not profited her (iii. 21–25). Yahweh assures her that true penitence will be followed by the conversion of the heathen (iv. 1–2). The people are urged to make fresh efforts in their religious life: there must be a cleansing and dedication of the heart (iv. 3, 4).

Ch. iv. 5–31. Jeremiah urges the inhabitants of Judah to flee for safety to the walled cities, for the dread foe is approaching from the north to desolate the land. Horror, because of the magnitude of the calamity which threatens, shall overwhelm all classes. The inhabitants of Jerusalem are urged to repent before it is too late (vv. 5–18). The prophet grieves at the thought of the horrors of war and sees in a vision the desolation of Judah. In vain Zion will seek the favour of her lovers, for amid unutterable woes she shall fall before the murderous invader (vv. 19–31).

Verse 27 is unsuited to the context and is probably added by a later hand.

Ch. v. The inhabitants of Jerusalem are utterly corrupt, and Yahweh can do nothing else than deliver them as a prey to these hunters of men (vv. 1–9). Only a remnant of the people shall survive to taste the bitterness of slavery in a foreign land (vv. 10–19). The prophet dwells upon the moral cause of the coming disaster. Rich men acquire wealth at the expense of the needy and the orphan; the prophets tell lies, the priests rule at their direction and the people love to have it so (vv. 20–31).

Verses 18, 19 are generally considered to be an editorial addition.

Ch. vi. The Benjamites are urged to flee from Jerusalem for the city is doomed (vv. 1–8). Calamity shall fall upon all alike, for all seek gain, and prophets and priests are deceitful, treating the wounds of the people lightly, and saying 'Peace', when there is no peace (vv. 9–15). His favour cannot be purchased with far-fetched offerings and many sacrifices (vv. 16–21). The prophet again describes the advance of the merciless foe from the north and bids them lament (vv. 22–26). Yahweh has commissioned him to test and purify the people, but he has failed in his task and Yahweh has rejected them (vv. 27–30).

Ch. vii–viii. 3. Jeremiah warns the people that the possession of the Temple will not save them. Yahweh demands social justice, moral conduct and sincerity of worship. They break the commandments, and then persuade themselves that their presence in the Temple will be sufficient to absolve them from their crimes. Yahweh will not permit His Temple to become a robber's cave, but will destroy it as He destroyed the sanctuary at Shiloh, and will banish Judah from His sight as He banished Ephraim (vii. 1–15). The prophet is forbidden to intercede for the people who are worshipping the Queen of Heaven and other gods (vii. 16–20). Yahweh did not demand burnt offerings or sacrifices in the wilderness. He asked for moral obedience not sacrifice (vii. 21–28). The people of Jerusalem are called upon to lament for the destruction which is about to come upon Judah. Tophet shall become the scene of the great judgement and shall be renamed the Valley of Slaughter. The bones of the dead shall be dragged from their graves and left to moulder beneath the sun, moon and stars which they worshipped. The Jew who survives shall prefer death to life (vii. 29–viii. 3).

Ch. viii. 4–ix. 1. By their persistent refusal to return to Yahweh the people put themselves below the level of the migratory birds which know the time of their return in spring. They claim to be wise on the ground that they know Yahweh's law, but they delude themselves for the scribes have deliberately falsified it (viii. 4–12). They shall perish like a fruitless and withered tree. The sound of the approach of the foes from the north can already be heard, and no charm can avert their serpent-like attack (viii. 13–17). The prophet is overwhelmed with sadness. The time for deliverance has gone by and there is no way of saving the people. He cannot lament enough for their sufferings (viii. 18–ix. 1).

Ch. viii. 10–12, which breaks the connection between vv. 9 and 13, has been repeated here from ch. vi. 12–15. Ch. viii. 10b–12 is omitted in the Septuagint.

Ch. ix. 2–26. Jeremiah longs to escape to a caravanserai, away from the treachery and deceit of the people (vv. 2–9). He laments over the devastated land and the ruined cities of Judah (vv. 10–11). The wise men cannot explain the reason for the calamity; it is because the people have forsaken His law and worshipped the Baalim (vv. 12–16). He bids the professional mourners lament, for Death the reaper has come (vv. 17–22). The knowledge of Yahweh is the source of true glory (vv. 23, 24). Judah cannot rely for salvation on the rite of circumcision which she shares with other nations; she lacks the inward circumcision of the heart as much as they do (vv. 25, 26).

Verse 9 is repeated from ch. v. 9, 29. The prosaic wording and the vagueness or absence of metre of vv. 12–16 suggest that they are an editorial addition. Verses 23, 24, and 25, 26, form two detached utterances which have no relation to the context.

Ch. x. 1–16. False gods, which are made by workmen and are powerless for good or evil, are contrasted with Yahweh, the Creator of the world and the Controller of Nature.

This passage interrupts the connection between chs. ix. 22 and x. 17. It clearly resembles 2 Isaiah in thought and style. Verse 11 is in Aramaic. It was either a marginal note or was designed to provide the exiles with a ready answer to give in reply to the claims of heathen idolaters.

Ch. x. 17–25. The people of Jerusalem are told to prepare to be cast forth into exile. Already the news comes from the north that the foe is advancing to lay waste Judah (vv. 17–22). Identifying himself with the community the prophet appeals to Yahweh for mercy, and prays that His wrath may fall upon the heathen nations (vv. 23–25).

The genuineness of v. 25 is doubtful, for it is not in harmony with the prophet's teaching that Yahweh uses the nations as His instruments to punish Judah.

Ch. xi–xii. 6. Jeremiah is commanded to proclaim the law among the people, and to remind them of the penalty of disobedience as shown by past history (xi. 1–8). Like their forefathers they have violated the covenants by their idolatry. The prophet is forbidden to intercede for them (xi. 9–14). Because of their vile deeds they have no business in the Temple; vows and sacrifices cannot avert their doom (xi. 15–17). The prophet learns that the men of Anathoth were plotting against his life. He is assured that Yahweh will destroy them (xi. 18–23). He raises the problem of the prosperity of the wicked and is warned that he has worse trials to face in the future (xii. 1–6).

Ch. xi. 7, 8 is omitted in the Septuagint, except the words, 'but they did them not'. The passage may have been inserted here from the parallel passage, ch. vii. 23, 24. Ch. xi. 13a is repeated from ch. ii. 28b. Ch. xi. 17 is a later insertion. Ch. xii. 4 has little point in this context except for its close. For 'He shall not see our latter end', the Septuagint reads, 'God will not see our ways'.

Ch. xii. 7–17. Yahweh laments over the desolation of the land by neighbouring foes (vv. 7–13). Her foes shall be driven into exile; but they shall be restored to their own land if they learn to worship Him (vv. 14–17).

Ch. xiii. By means of the acted parable of the linen waistcloth Jeremiah warns the inhabitants of Judah and Jerusalem that their pride will be humbled by exile because of their disobedience and idolatry (vv. 1–11). By means of the parable of the wine jars he warns them that Yahweh will throw them into confusion in the coming disaster (vv. 12–14). He bids them acknowledge Yahweh before it is too late (vv. 15–17). He warns the king (probably Jehoiachin) and the queen-mother of their approaching humiliation (vv. 18, 19). The foe from the north draws near to Jerusalem, and the people will have to endure the harsh rule of those whom they trained as allies. If they seek the cause of the disaster they will find it in the multitude of their sins: it is impossible to change them since evil has become second nature with them (vv. 20–27).

Ch. xiv–xv. 9. The prophet described the suffering caused by a drought (xiv. 1–6). He confesses the people's sins and pleads with Yahweh to deliver them (xiv. 7–9). Yahweh rejects his petition and bids him cease from interceding for them. He will not accept their fasting and offering (xiv. 10–12). The prophet pleads that they have been misled by promises of peace and prosperity from the false prophets. In reply Yahweh declares they and those who allowed themselves to be deceived shall be destroyed (xiv. 13–16). The prophet is bidden to lament over the horrors that are coming upon Judah (xiv. 17, 18). The people confess their sins, beseech Yahweh not to break His covenant with them, and acknowledge His supremacy over Nature (xiv. 19–22). Yahweh declares that even such pleaders as Moses and Samuel could not turn Him from His purpose or undo the evil which Manasseh wrought for Judah. Pestilence, war, famine and captivity shall claim them (xv. 1–4). No one shall pity Jerusalem or lament over her. She has forsaken Yahweh who is weary of relenting in His purpose to punish her. Destruction shall come upon her suddenly and unexpectedly and the inhabitants shall be dispersed as chaff (xv. 5–9).

Some of the material in this section is genuine, but there are passages which show the influence of 2 Isaiah.

Ch. xv. 10–21. The prophet laments that he was ever born to quarrel with all men. He appeals for vengeance on his enemies and protests his faithfulness. He cannot understand why he is called upon to suffer endless pain. Yahweh disappoints him like a dried-up watercourse (vv. 10–18). Yahweh declares that if he overcomes his human weaknesses, He will restore him to His service (vv. 19–21).

Verses 13, 14 interrupt the dialogue between Yahweh and the prophet and are probably an insertion from ch. xvii. 3, 4.

Ch. xvi–xvii. 18. Jeremiah is forbidden to marry and raise a family (xvi. 1–9). The crime of the people is that they have forsaken Yahweh who will fling them into a land where they will have to serve foreign gods who will show them no favour (xvi. 10–13). But He purposes ultimately to restore them to their own land (xvi. 14, 15). The people shall be hunted down and receive double punishment for desecrating the land with their detestable idols and abominable rites (xvi. 16–18). Nations from distant lands will abandon their gods and turn to Yahweh (xvi. 19–21). Judah's sin is so deeply engrained that it is impossible to pass it over. Her cherished possessions and high places shall be laid waste, and she shall serve her foes in a foreign land (xvii. 1–4). He who relies on human aid shall lead a stunted life like some desert scrub, but he who trusts in Yahweh shall be like a tree planted by the waters, vigorous and abundant in foliage (xvii. 5–8). Yahweh sees everything in the human heart and rewards accordingly. No one but a fool relies on ill-gotten riches which leave him before his life is over. Yahweh is the true glory and hope of His people. Disgrace and oblivion shall be the fate of all who forsake Him, the source of life and joy (xvii. 9–13). Jeremiah appeals for deliverance from evil thoughts towards Yahweh, roused in him by his enemies, who taunt him with the fact that his predicted doom has not been fulfilled. He prays that evil may fall on his enemies not on him (xvii. 14–18).

Ch. xvi. 14, 15 interrupts the connection between vv. 10–13 and vv. 16–18. The verses are repeated in ch. xxiii. 7, 8, where they are more suitably placed. In the Septuagint they are placed inappropriately after ch. xxiii. 40. Ch. xvii. 1–4 is omitted in the Septuagint, but the passage is doubtless genuine.

Ch. xvii. 19–27. The people are exhorted to observe the Sabbath but they refuse to listen (vv. 19–23). If they will observe it, then they and their rulers shall be permanently secure, and offerings shall be brought to the Temple from all the surrounding parts of the country. If they do not Jerusalem shall be destroyed (vv. 24–27).

Many critics consider that this passage belongs to the post-exilic period when the Sabbath had assumed an important place among the Jews (cf. Neh. xiii. 15–22).

Ch. xviii. Under divine direction Jeremiah observes how the potter, when his work is marred, fashions the clay into another vessel. So Yahweh deals with His people. For nations and individuals He has a purpose. He does not utterly cast away the rebellious; for such there is hope in repentance. The prophet appeals to the people to repent but they refuse. Their conduct is unnatural, contrary to the course of Nature. Yahweh shall scatter them as 'with an east wind' (vv. 1–17). The leaders of the people conspire to circulate slanders against him. He protests against this return of evil for good and prays for vengeance on them (vv. 18–23).

Some critics think that vv. 21–23 are not genuine because the bitter prayer for vengeance is unworthy of Jeremiah. He was, however, a man of his own age and capable of strong emotions.

Ch. xix. 1–13. At Yahweh's command, Jeremiah, accompanied by leading persons, goes to the valley of Hinnon and there proclaims the impending destruction of the inhabitants of Jerusalem because of their idolatrous worship and their sacrifice of children by fire. A new name, 'The Valley of Slaughter', shall be given to the valley to denote the terrible carnage which shall take place there (vv. 1–9). As a symbol of this destruction he breaks an earthen jar, and declares that for want of room the dead shall be buried in the valley of Topheth, and the houses, the roofs of which have been defiled by idolatry, shall become unclean like Topheth (vv. 10–13).

Verses 3–9 are probably an editorial addition since (1) the message which the prophet is to give in the valley of Hinnon is given here before he goes there, (2) the subject matter of the passage is drawn to a large extent from other portions of the book, especially the last part of ch. vii, (3) the style is different from that employed elsewhere. Verses 5, 6 and 11b are insertions from ch. vii, 32, 32a and 32b respectively.

Chs. xix. 14–xx. 6. The prophet repeats his warning in the Temple with the result that Pashhur, the chief officer, places him in the stocks. On his release he predicts that the inhabitants of Judah will be taken captives to Babylon, that Jerusalem will be despoiled of her treasures, and that Pashhur, his family and friends will die in exile. Ch. xx. 7–18. The prophet complains that Yahweh has beguiled him into the work of a prophet in the fulfilment of which he is subjected to ridicule. Yet he cannot refrain from speaking; the word is as a fire in his bones. Many slander him, perils thicken, and trusted friends fail and seek to betray him (vv. 7–10). But Yahweh is with him and his persecutors shall not prevail. He prays to Yahweh for vengeance upon them and praises Him for deliverance (vv. 11–13). He curses the day of his birth (vv. 14–18).

Verse 12 is virtually identical with ch. xi. 20.

Ch. xxi. Jeremiah, replying to a message of inquiry addressed to him by Zedekiah, regarding the result of the siege of Jerusalem, declares that Yahweh will fight against the city. The king and those who survive pestilence, sword and famine will be delivered into the hands of Nebuchadrezzar who will show them no mercy (vv. 1–7). Those who submit will escape with bare life, and the people are bidden to choose between life and death (vv. 8–10). The king is warned to make the administration of justice his chief concern, lest Yahweh's anger be kindled against him (vv. 11, 12). The inhabitants of Jerusalem will be punished (vv. 13, 14).

Verses 11, 12 are based on chs. xxii. 23 and iv. 4 and are a misplaced fragment. Verses 13, 14 are obscure. The compiler evidently meant them to refer to Jerusalem, but the city is not in a valley, nor on a rock in a plain, nor would the foe come down to attack her. Possibly the original reference was to some other city.

Ch. xxii–xxiii. 8. Jeremiah is sent to the palace to bid the king and his subjects practise justice and abstain from wrong-doing, otherwise the palace shall be laid in ruins (xxii. 1–5). Though in the eyes of Yahweh Jerusalem is like the well-wooded regions of Gilead and Lebanon, she shall be made a wilderness and other nations shall learn the reason for her desolation, namely, idolatry (xxii. 6–9). He bids them lament for Shallum (Jehoahaz) who shall die in exile

(xxii. 10-12). He denounces Jehoiakim for exacting forced labour from his subjects in the building of his palace, and contrasts his oppressive rule with the just rule of Josiah. Jehoiakim shall die unwept and be interred without honour (xxii. 13-19). The prophet calls upon Jerusalem to lament for the loss of lovers (probably allies). She who thought herself secure shall endure great suffering (xxii. 20-23). Coniah (Jehoiachin) and his mother shall be exiled to Babylon and shall die there. None of Jehoiachin's seed shall rule in Judah (xxii. 24-30). Yahweh denounces the unworthy rulers of Judah and promises to restore His people to their own land and set over them faithful rulers (xxiii. 1-4). Under a righteous king of David's line, Israel and Judah shall be united and enjoy uninterrupted peace and prosperity. The restoration shall eclipse the memory of the deliverance from Egypt (xxiii. 5-8).

It is probable that only vv. 6, 7 of ch. xxii. 1-9 are genuine. Ch. xxiii. 5, 6 may confidently be attributed to Jeremiah in spite of the fact that it is often assigned to a later writer. The characteristics of the ideal king and of his rule are in accord with his views. The prediction is not of a world conqueror, but rather of a just and righteous king of the Davidic dynasty. The name, 'The Lord is our Righteousness', can be interpreted as a play on the name of Zedekiah, which means, 'Yahweh is my righteousness'. Verses 7, 8 of the same chapter are also found in ch. xvi. 14, 15. The Septuagint inserts them inappropriately after v. 40. They are probably of post-exilic origin.

Ch. xxiii. 9-40. Jeremiah is distressed by the general wickedness in which both priests and prophets share. The prophets of Samaria prophesied by Baal, while those of Jerusalem shock Yahweh still more by their immorality, lying and encouragement of evil-doers. They inspire baseless hopes which are without divine warrant and prophesy peace and prosperity, rather than doom. Yahweh's anger shall burst upon them like a storm (vv. 9-20). They have not been commissioned or inspired by Yahweh, otherwise they would have turned the people from their evil ways. Yahweh is omnipresent and they cannot hide from Him (vv. 21-24). He knows their false predictions which they claim to have received in dreams. The prophet who has a dream should tell it, but not as the true word of Yahweh. Such a dream is mere straw, having nothing in common with wheat, the word of Yahweh, which has irresistible power (vv. 25-29). Yahweh is against the prophets, who steal their messages from the true prophets and claim that they are from Him, and lead the people astray with their delusive dreams and claims to divine authority (vv. 30–32). When men tauntingly ask, 'What is the burden of the Lord?' they shall be told that they themselves are a 'burden' which Yahweh will no longer endure. If they persist in using the expression 'the burden of the Lord', which they have perverted, they shall be banished for ever from Jerusalem and from His presence (vv. 33–40).

The greater part of this passage reads like a genuine utterance of the prophet but it doubtless contains editorial additions, though critics are not agreed as to the number of these additions. A part of v. 15 is identical with words in ch. ix. 15. Here it may have been originally a marginal note by a copyist. Verses 19, 20 recur with slight variations in ch. xxx. 23, 24, and are probably introduced here from that passage. The greater part of v. 37 is omitted in the Septuagint; it is the same as v. 35 with the exception of the substitution of 'prophet' for 'neighbour'.

Ch. xxiv. Jeremiah sees two baskets of figs, one containing good figs and the other bad (vv. 1–3). Yahweh tells him that the good figs represent the Jewish exiles in Babylon who shall be brought back, and the bad figs the leaders and the people left in Judah under Zedekiah, and those who have found refuge in Egypt who shall be destroyed (vv. 4–10).

Ch. xxv. In the fourth year of Jehoiakim Jeremiah reminds the people that they have not listened to his call to repentance (vv. 1–7). As a result Yahweh shall bring the Babylonians against Judah and the surrounding nations to destroy them, and the supremacy of Babylon shall last seventy years. At the end of that period Babylon shall be made desolate (vv. 8–14). Yahweh's fury shall fall upon all the kingdoms of the world (vv. 15–29). Rulers as well as subjects shall experience the horrors of this world-wide judgement (vv. 30–38).

Most critics consider that this chapter has received a number of later additions. The text of vv. 1–14 in the Septuagint is much shorter than the Hebrew, on which the English is based. The Septuagint probably represents the original form of these verses, or it may have been even shorter. In the Septuagint chs. xlvi–li follow immediately after v. 13a; v. 14 is omitted and 13b is used as a title of the foreign prophecies.

Chapters xxvi–xlv

Ch. xxvi. Jeremiah warns the people that unless they repent the Temple shall suffer the same fate as the sanctuary at Shiloh (vv. 1–6). The priests and prophets demand his death for prophesying against the Temple and the city (vv. 7–9). The case is tried by the royal officials, who recognize the right of a prophet to utter his message and accordingly acquit him (vv. 10–16). Certain elders support the decision by quoting the case of Micah, who prophesied in similar terms in the reign of Hezekiah who took no action against him (vv. 17–19). The prophet Uriah delivered a similar message but was slain by Jehoiakim (vv. 20–24).

Ch. xxvii. Jeremiah, wearing a yoke (a symbol of submission) warns the kings of Edom, Moab, Ammon, Tyre and Zidon, who have invited Zedekiah to join them in a plot against Babylon, that Yahweh has given their lands to Nebuchadrezzar. Nations that refuse to submit to him shall be destroyed (vv. 1–11). He repeats the warning to Zedekiah, and urges the priests and the people not to be deceived by the false prophets who promise the speedy return of the Temple vessels. The vessels still remaining in the Temple shall be removed to Babylon (vv. 12–22).

Verses 1, 7 are omitted in the Septuagint. The Septuagint, too, has a shorter text in vv. 16–22: there is no promise of the restoration of the sacred vessels.

Ch. xxviii. The prophet Hananiah announces that the yoke of Babylon shall be broken, and that the exiles and the Temple vessels shall be restored within two years. Jeremiah wishes that it might be true, but points out that true prophets have never flattered with promises of good fortune. Hananiah breaks Jeremiah's yoke and reaffirms the prophecy (vv. 1–11). Jeremiah replies that the yoke of Babylon shall become more burdensome and that Hananiah shall die within the year. Hananiah dies as predicted (vv. 12–17).

Ch. xxix. Jeremiah sends a letter to the exiles in Babylon advising them to settle down there and to pay no heed to false prophets who promise a speedy return (vv. 1–9). Not till after seventy years shall they be restored to their own land (vv. 10–14). On Zedekiah and his people left in Jerusalem Yahweh shall send sword, pestilence and famine, and shall drive them into captivity to be objects of scorn among the nations (vv. 15–19). Two lying prophets in Babylon shall be slain for their immorality and for their false claim to speak in Yahweh's name (vv. 20–23). Shemaiah, a false prophet, has written to Zephaniah, the overseer of the Temple, blaming him for not punishing Jeremiah as a madman. Zephaniah shows the letter to Jeremiah, who condemns Shemaiah's conduct and declares that neither he nor any of his descendants shall share in the restoration (vv. 24–32).

Some critics regard vv. 10, 11 as an editorial addition. Verses 16–20 are out of place here since v. 15 is naturally continued by vv. 21–23. They are not in the Septuagint but the omission seems to be an error of a scribe.

Ch. xxx. In view of the restoration Jeremiah is bidden to write down all his prophecies (vv. 1–3). Panic and terror are coming upon the world, but in the great day of judgement Israel shall be delivered from her conquerors and shall serve Yahweh under a Davidic ruler. Other nations shall be destroyed, but Israel shall be preserved after bearing just punishment (vv. 4–11). Her oppressors shall feel the pains of conquest and captivity while she shall be restored, Jerusalem shall be rebuilt, and the people shall live under a native ruler who shall enjoy the privilege of direct access to Yahweh (vv. 12–22). Yahweh shall be fully avenged on the wicked. The purpose of the divine judgement will be understood in the end (vv. 23–24).

In this chapter only vv. 5–7, 12–15 can be attributed to Jeremiah with any degree of probability. Verses 10, 11 recur with slight variations in ch. xlvi. 27, 28, but they are not found in the Septuagint. They show the influence of 2 Isaiah. Verses 23, 24 are almost identical with ch. xxiii. 19, 20. The editor has evidently inserted them here to complete the picture of the 'great day'.

Ch. xxxi. Jeremiah predicts the restoration of the Northern Israelites. The territory of Ephraim shall again be cultivated and the people shall worship in the Temple at Jerusalem. The exiles shall return in penitence, the way being made easy and attractive for their weary feet, for Yahweh's love for them is like that of a father for his child (vv. 1–10). The nations shall know that their restoration is the work of Yahweh alone. Leaving their sorrows behind they shall return to enjoy peace and plenty (vv. 11–14). The prophet pictures Rachel weeping at Ramah for her children, the Northern Israelites, but she can refrain from weeping, for they shall yet show penitence and be restored (vv. 15–22). Judah shall also be brought back, and the hearts now hungering shall be satisfied with peace and plenty (vv. 23–26). Children shall no longer suffer for the sins of their fathers, but every individual shall bear the consequences of his own sin (vv. 27–30). Yahweh shall make a New Covenant with His people. His laws shall be written in the heart and all men shall know Him (vv. 31–34). Jerusalem shall be extended beyond her former limits and shall be holy to Yahweh for ever (35–40).

Verses 7–14 in thought and expression closely resemble 2 Isaiah and are probably of post-exilic origin. Some critics have rejected vv. 31–34 as non-Jeremianic, but they are in harmony with the prophet's teaching and there is no sufficient reason for doubting their genuineness.

Ch. xxxii. During the siege of Jerusalem, when Jeremiah is under arrest, he purchases a field in Anathoth from his kinsman Hanamel and entrusts the deed to Baruch (vv. 1–15). He prays to Yahweh expressing his doubts as to the issue of the siege, but is told that nothing is too difficult for 'the God of all flesh' (vv. 16–27). Yahweh declares that the city shall be completely destroyed by the Babylonians because of the persistent idolatry of the inhabitants (vv. 28–35). Nevertheless the exiles shall be brought back to Palestine, where they shall live in security and Yahweh shall be their God. Fields, now desolate, shall be bought with all the formalities of law (vv. 36–44).

Verses 1–5 are probably an editorial insertion to explain why Jeremiah is in prison. Doubts have been cast upon the genuineness of vv. 17–23, because the long and elaborate introduction leading up to the prayer, which consists of two verses only (vv. 24, 25) is unlike Jeremiah and bears a close resemblance to Nehemiah ix. 5–38. Of vv. 26–44 only vv. 26, 27 and possibly vv. 42–44 have any claim to being original. Verses 34, 35 are almost identical with ch. vii. 30, 31.

Ch. xxxiii. Yahweh promises to reveal His secret purposes to Jeremiah (vv. 1–3). In spite of the dire condition of Jerusalem, Yahweh will restore it to its former state and establish its prosperity (vv. 4–10). Joy shall return to the desolate land and normal life shall be resumed (vv. 11–13). Under a righteous ruler of the Davidic line and the Levitical priesthood both Israel and Judah shall be united and dwell in security. The royal and priestly succession shall be permanently established (vv. 14–18). The taunt that Yahweh has rejected Israel and Judah and that they are no longer a nation shall be disproved. As surely as Yahweh created day and night and fixed the frame of heaven and earth, so surely will He keep His covenant with David and deliver His people (vv. 19–26).

Verses 1–13 probably contain a considerable number of editorial additions. Verses 14–26 are omitted in the Septuagint. They repeat ch. xxiii. 5, 6 and then make a long commentary on it. They probably originated in the post-exilic period when there was need to encourage the Jewish people in the continuation of the state under a Davidic kingship and Levitical priesthood.

Ch. xxxiv. During the siege of Jerusalem Jeremiah tells Zedekiah that the city shall be destroyed and that he shall die a captive in

Babylon (vv. 1–7). Zedekiah and the people solemnly agree to observe a neglected law and set free their Hebrew slaves. At first they carry out their obligations, but later cancel the agreement and force their former slaves into the old state of bondage (vv. 8–11). Jeremiah denounces this breach of faith, and declares that the people shall die by the sword, the king and his princes shall be taken captive, Jerusalem destroyed and Judah left desolate and uninhabited (vv. 12–22).

Ch. xxxv. Jeremiah invites the Rechabites to drink wine in one of the chambers of the Temple, but they refuse, observing the prohibition laid down by their founder, Jonadab (vv. 1–11). The prophet contrasts their obedience to the rules of their order with the disobedience of the inhabitants of Judah to the commands of Yahweh. Evil shall come upon the rebellious people, but the Rechabites shall never want descendants to serve Yahweh (vv. 12–19).

Ch. xxxvi. In the fourth year of Jehoiakim, Jeremiah dictates his prophecies to Baruch and tells him to read them publicly in the Temple on a fast day. Baruch does as he is commanded (vv. 1–8). In the ninth month of the following year he reads the roll publicly in the chamber of Gemariah. Miccaiah reports the contents to the princes who summon Baruch and command him to read the roll again. They advise him and Jeremiah to go into hiding and then report the matter to the king. He sends Jehudi to fetch the roll and asks him to read it to him. As fast as it is read he cuts off the different sections of the roll and burns them. He gives orders that Jeremiah and Baruch shall be seized but they elude capture (vv. 9–26). The prophet again dictates his prophecies to Baruch with many additions (vv. 27–32).

Ch. xxxvii. At the time when the siege of Jerusalem by the Babylonians is temporarily raised by the approach of an Egyptian army, Zedekiah sends to Jeremiah to ask him for his prayers. Jeremiah replies that the Egyptians will retire, and that the Babylonians will advance, besiege the city, capture it and destroy it by fire (vv. 1–10). Jeremiah, on attempting to leave the city on business, is arrested as a deserter and imprisoned by the princes in the house of Jonathan the scribe (vv. 11–15). The king sends for him secretly to inquire if there is any message from Yahweh. The prophet predicts his capture by the king of Babylon, protests his innocence, and asks not to be sent back to his prison. The king commits him to the court of the guard and provides him with food (vv. 16–21).

Ch. xxxviii. Four of the princes denounce Jeremiah to the king, and demand his death on the ground that his predictions weaken the courage of the soldiers and of the people. Zedekiah hands over his prisoner to them and they cast him into a muddy cistern (vv. 1–6). He is rescued by Ebed-melech, an Ethiopian, at the king's command and placed in the court of the guard (vv. 7–13). Zedekiah again consults the prophet who advises him to save himself and the city by surrender. The king urges him to keep the true nature of the interview secret (vv. 14–28).

Verse 2 is almost identical with ch. xxi. 9 and is probably a later insertion.

Ch. xxxix. After a siege of eighteen months by Nebuchadrezzar Jerusalem is captured. Zedekiah tries to escape, but is captured, blinded and carried in fetters to Babylon. The city is destroyed and the people, except the poor, who are given fields and vineyards to cultivate, are carried captive to Babylon (xxxix. 1–10). Jeremiah is released and entrusted to the care of Gedaliah (xxxix. 11–14). While Jeremiah is still in the court of the guard, he promises Ebed-melech that his life shall be spared because he trusted in Yahweh (xxxix. 15–18).

Ch. xxxix. 1, 2, 4–10 is a shortened form of ch. lii. 4–16, which is virtually equivalent to 2 Kings xxv. 1–12. Verses 1, 2 interrupt the connection between chs. xxxviii. 28 and xxxix. 3. Verses 4–13 are omitted in the Septuagint, either because most of the material is contained in ch. lii or simply by accident. Verses 15–18, though probably genuine, are misplaced.

Ch. xl. 1–6. Jeremiah, one of the band of captives to be deported to Babylon, is released and allowed complete liberty to choose where he will go. He decides to join Gedaliah at Mizpah.

Verses 2, 3 are probably a later insertion. It is unlikely that Nebuzaradan would declare that the fall of Jerusalem was due to the people's sins.

Ch. xl. 7–xli. Gedaliah at Mizpah is joined by the scattered Jewish forces. He urges them to serve the Babylonians faithfully and to settle down to civilized life. Their example is followed by many of the Jews from the surrounding countries (xl. 7–12). Johanan warns Gedaliah that the king of Ammon has sent Ishmael to kill him, but he refuses to believe the charge (xl. 13–16). Ishmael murders him and all the Jews and Babylonians who are with him, together with a number of pilgrims from Shechem, Shiloh and Samaria. He sets out for the country of Ammon, taking with him the surviving Jews. Johanan rescues the captives and takes them to the vicinity of Bethlehem with the intention of finding a refuge in Egypt (xli. 1–18).

Ch. xlii–xliii. 7. The leaders of the people beg Jeremiah to seek Yahweh's will and promise to obey it (xlii. 1–6). The prophet declares that flight to Egypt is not the will of Yahweh. If they remain in the land Yahweh will protect them, but if they go to Egypt they will perish there (xlii. 7–22). They refuse to believe that he is speaking in Yahweh's name, and suggest that his message has been inspired by Baruch. The captains, therefore, take all the people, including Jeremiah, to Tahpanhes in Egypt (xliii. 1–7).

Some critics consider that ch. xlii. 15–18 is a later insertion. Verse 14 connects well with v. 19.

Ch. xliii. 8–13. Jeremiah buries great stones at the entrance to Pharaoh's house in Tahpanhes, and proclaims that Nebuchadrezzar will conquer Egypt and set his throne upon them. He will burn her temples and carry away her gods.

Ch. xliv. Jeremiah rebukes the fugitives in Egypt for relapsing into idolatry. Yahweh shall destroy the remnant in Egypt with the exception of a few fugitives who shall return (vv. 1–14). The people refuse to abandon the worship of the Queen of Heaven, alleging that in the past so long as they worshipped her they had prospered, whereas since they had ceased to worship her they had experienced nothing but disaster (vv. 15–19). Jeremiah warns them that their land is desolate, and they are suffering evil because Yahweh can no longer stand their idolatrous worship (vv. 20–23). Jeremiah repeats his warning and predicts that the Egyptians shall fall before their enemies (vv. 24–30).

Doubts have been cast upon the genuineness of vv. 20–23 since they reproduce the thoughts contained in vv. 2–14. Verses 11–14 are repeated with slight variations from ch. xlii. 15–18. Verses 29–30 are thought by some critics to be an interpolation after the event.

Ch. xlv. Baruch, on writing the roll in the fourth year of Jehoiakim, complains that only sorrow and pain are his lot and that he can find no rest. Jeremiah bids him seek no great thing for himself, and promises him that in the midst of disaster his life shall be preserved.

Chapters xlvi–li

Ch. xlvi. Jeremiah summons the Egyptian army to prepare for battle and describes its defeat by the Euphrates (a reference to the defeat of Pharaoh Necho at Carchemish by Nebuchadrezzar in 605 BC). Yahweh has avenged Himself on the Egyptian army by inflicting a bloody defeat upon it, for which there is no cure (vv. 1–12). The Egyptians are summoned to prepare to withstand an attack from the north and their utter overthrow is described (a reference to the invasion of Egypt by Nebuchadrezzar, either immediately after the battle of Carchemish or at a later time). In the end Egypt shall be reinhabited (vv. 13–26), Israel shall return and dwell secure in Yahweh's favour while other nations shall be blotted out (vv. 27, 28).

Verses 27, 28 are found with slight variations in ch. xxx. 10, 11, but they are omitted in the Septuagint. They show the influence of 2 Isaiah.

Ch. xlvii. Philistia shall be destroyed by a foe from the north. Fathers shall flee in panic forgetting their children, and the cities shall be spoiled and empty.

Ch. xlviii. The cities of Moab shall be overthrown. Chemosh, her god, and his priests and princes shall go into captivity (vv. 1–10). Hitherto Moab has been undisturbed, like wine the flavour of which has endured unaltered; but she shall be driven forth and shall be ashamed of Chemosh in whom she has trusted (vv. 11–19). Destruction shall come upon her many cities. As she mocked Israel so shall she become a derision: her people shall take refuge in the rocks (vv. 20–28). Her pride shall be brought low, worship shall cease, and the land shall be filled with mourning (vv. 29–39). The enemy shall swoop upon Moab like an eagle and none shall escape death or exile, but in the end she shall be restored (vv. 40–47).

Verses 45–47 are missing in the Septuagint and are probably a later insertion here.

Ch. xlix. 1–6. Milcom, the god of the Ammonites, has seized the territory of Gad. As a penalty their capital, Rabbah, shall be laid waste and Israel shall recover her rights. The Ammonites shall be driven forth by their foe, but afterwards they shall be restored.

Verse 6 is omitted in the Septuagint.

Ch. xlix. 7–22. The people of Dedan are advised to flee from the coming calamity, for Yahweh shall utterly destroy Edom but shall preserve the orphans and widows. She shall surely drink the wine of destruction (vv. 7–12). Bozrah and the other cities shall be laid waste. The nations are summoned to fight against her; she shall be humiliated, derided, overthrown and left desolate like Sodom and

Gomorrah. The foe, like a lion, shall drive her away and her mighty men shall be as women (vv. 13–22).

Verses 7, 9, 10a, 14–16 are almost identical with Obadiah 8, 5, 6, 1–4 respectively. Verses 19–21 recur with variations in ch. l. 44–46, where they refer to Babylon.

Ch. xlix. 23–27. Hamath and Arpad shall be terror-stricken. Damascus shall be seized with panic and turn to flee. Her warriors shall fall and Ben-hadad's palaces shall be burnt.

Verse 27 is taken from the refrain in Amos i. 4, 10, 12, 14, ii. 5.

Ch. xlix. 28–33. Yahweh summons the foe (here identified with the Babylonians) to attack Kedar (an Arab nomadic tribe) and promises that they shall capture the nomads' tents and camels. The inhabitants of Hazor (probably a collective term denoting villages in which Arabs lived) are advised to flee afar off to a nation secure from invasion; the foe is summoned to attack the defenceless people who shall be spoiled and scattered, and their villages laid waste.

Verses 31, 32 are similar to Ezekiel xxxviii. 10, 11 and probably belong to the post-exilic period.

Ch. xlix. 34–39. Yahweh shall break the military strength of Edom and scatter the people among the nations. He shall pursue them with His anger, destroy them and reign supreme in Elam; but they shall ultimately be restored.

Ch. l–li. 58. The overthrow of Babylon by a nation from the north (i.e. Media) is foretold. Israel and Judah shall return to Palestine in penitence (l. 1–7). They are bidden to flee from Babylon, for Yahweh shall bring a resistless foe from the north against her, and she shall be spoiled because she rejoiced in spoiling Israel (l. 8–13). The foe is urged to attack; the city is stormed and she is treated as she treated others; the foreign residents flee to escape the sword (l. 14–16). Babylon shall be punished even as Assyria has been, and Israel shall be restored to her own land (l. 17–20). The foe is summoned to destroy Babylon, and news of Yahweh's vengeance for the destruction of the Temple is brought to Jerusalem (l. 21–28). The foe is again summoned to recompense her according to her work (l. 29–32). Israel and Judah are both oppressed and held fast captive, but their redeemer is strong. He will take their part and daunt the Babylonians that the world may live at peace (l. 33, 34). The war against Babylon and her destruction and desolation are now described in fierce invective (l. 35–40). The king of Babylon hears of the approach of the pitiless foe from the north and is panic-stricken. At the noise of Babylon's fall the earth trembles and the noise resounds all through the nations (l. 41–46). Yahweh is stirring up destroyers against Babylon who shall winnow her and leave her bare. But His people are not forsaken; they are bidden to flee from Babylon to escape the vengeance on her guilt (li. 1–6). Babylon with her brilliance and luxury has been an evil influence among the nations but now she is destroyed (li. 7–10). Yahweh is stirring up the king of the Medes (i.e. Cyrus) to execute His vengeance upon Babylon for the destruction of His Temple. A swarm of invaders will fill her and shout in triumph over her (li. 11–14). Yahweh's power is contrasted with the powerlessness of idols (li. 15–19). Babylon has been Yahweh's agent in destroying other nations, now she shall be repaid in the sight of Israel for her own evil-doing. The nations are summoned to attack Babylon where soldiers have lost their strength and are as weak as women. The city is stormed and set on fire (li. 20–33). Like a dragon Nebuchadrezzar has devoured Israel, but Yahweh shall plead their cause and take vengeance upon Babylon. She shall become 'heaps, a dwelling place for jackals, an astonishment, and an hissing without inhabitant'. Then the heaven and the earth and all in them shall sing for joy over the fall of Babylon (li. 34–49). The exiles who escape death should hasten their return to Jerusalem, for Babylon's broad walls shall be razed to the ground and her high gates burned with fire (li. 50–58).

There are wide differences of opinion among critics on the question of the authenticity of the prophecies against foreign nations. Some have denied all these prophecies to Jeremiah. Volz regards them as the work of an anonymous prophet writing soon after the death of Nebuchadrezzar in 562 BC.[1] Others, while recognizing that l–li. 58, which predicts the imminent fall of Babylon, is of exilic origin, have discovered a Jeremianic nucleus in chs. xlvi–xlix. Bardtke holds that all these prophecies were written by Jeremiah early in his career and that he collected them himself.[2]

Ch. li. 59–64. When Seraiah accompanied Zedekiah to Babylon, Jeremiah gave him a scroll, containing a prophecy of doom, against

[1] P. Volz, *Jeremia*, K.A.T., 2nd ed., 1928, 378–443.
[2] H. Bardke, *Jeremia der Fremdvölkerprophet*, Z.A.W., 1935, pp. 209–39; 1936, pp. 246–62.

Babylon, and bade him read it aloud there, and afterwards sink it in the Euphrates as a symbol of Babylon's approaching fall.

The genuineness of this passage is denied by many critics on the ground that there is no proof that Zedekiah ever visited Babylon. It is quite possible, however, that he did visit the city to clear himself of the suspicion of complicity in the plotted rebellion.

Chapter lii
Ch. lii. This chapter gives a summary of Zedekiah's reign (vv. 1–3), and an account of the siege and capture of Jerusalem (vv. 4–27), the three deportations to Babylon (vv. 28–30) and the release of Jehoiachin from prison (vv. 31–34). Verses 1–27, 31–34 are taken practically verbatim from 2 Kings xxiv. 18–xxv. 21, 27–30, while vv. 28–30 are from an independent source.

AUTHORSHIP AND DATE

Tradition ascribes the whole of the book of Jeremiah to the prophet whose name it bears. But it is now almost universally recognized that the book is not a literary unit but a compilation derived from three main sources, commonly designated A, B and C.

First there were separate collections of poetic utterances, A, written or dictated by Jeremiah. The sections of the book of Jeremiah derived from this source are: i. 15–iii. 5, iii. 19–vi. 30, viii. 4–x. 25, xi. 15–xii. 17, xiii. 15–27, xiv. 1–10, xiv. 17–xvii. 18, xviii. 13–23, xx. 7–18, xxi. 11–14, xxii. 6–xxiii. 40, xxv. 30–38, xxx. 4–xxxi. 22, xlvi. 1–li. 58.

Second there were biographical prose narratives, B, about Jeremiah, written probably by Baruch who was the prophet's friend and secretary and rendered him devoted service for many years (cf. xxxii. 12–16, xxxvi. 1–32, xliii. 3, 6, xlv. 1–5). The sections in the book derived from this source are: xix. 1–xx, 6, xxi. 1–10, xxvi, xxix, xxx. 1–3, xxxiii, xxxiv, xxxvi–xlv, li. 59–64, lii.

Third there were autobiographical prose narratives, C, describing the inner experiences of the prophet. The sections in the book derived from this source are: i. 4–14, iii. 6–18, vii. 1–viii. 3, xi. 1–14, xiii. 1–14, xiv. 11–16, xvii. 19–xviii. 12, xxii. 1–5, xxiv, xxv. 1–29, xxvii, xxviii, xxxi. 23–40 (probable), xxxii, xxxv. The style of these narratives, especially the speeches, closely resembles that of the book of Deuteronomy. They are probably to be assigned to

Jeremiah himself, though a few of them belong to a later period than that of the prophet.[1]

Two other theories may be mentioned concerning the authorship of the present book of Jeremiah. Torrey affirms that Jeremiah i–x is a pseudepigraphic work belonging to the third century BC.[2] According to May it is the work of a biographer, who lived at the very earliest during the first half of the fifth century BC and wrote under the influence of the redactor of the book of Deuteronomy, Deutero-Isaiah and other Old Testament prophets.[3] His biography consists of sayings and recollections of Jeremiah and other material ascribed to him, together with speeches or prophecies, entirely or largely of his own invention.

The date of composition of the present book of Jeremiah cannot be accurately determined. Since, however, additions and alterations were apparently made to the original material contained in the three main sources down to the close of the fifth century BC, it is reasonable to suppose that the present book was compiled in the early part of the fourth century BC.[4]

THE HEBREW AND GREEK TEXTS

The book of Jeremiah has been transmitted to us in two editions, the Hebrew and the Greek, which differ considerably from each other. In the first place the arrangement is different. In the Greek text the prophecies against foreign nations (xlvi–li) follow immediately after ch. xxv. 13a (v. 14 being omitted). Further, the order of the prophecies within the section is different. The order in the Hebrew text is Egypt, Philistia, Moab, Ammon, Edom, Damascus, Kedar, Elam and Babylon, and that in the Greek, Elam, Egypt, Babylon, Philistia, Edom, Ammon, Kedar, Damascus and Moab.

---

[1] There is no unanimity of opinion regarding the authorship of the autobiographical prose narratives. Some consider that the whole or many of them are the work of the Deuteronomic school of writers; Mowinckel (*Zur Komposition des Buches Jeremia*, 1914) believes that they were originally spoken of Jeremiah in the third person, but were changed to the first person at a later stage. Pfeiffer (*Introduction to the Old Testament*, 1948, p. 505) holds that Baruch prepared an edition of the book of Jeremiah, combining the prophet's book with his own, and revising or rewording entirely many of his master's speeches in his own Deuteronomic style.

[2] C. C. Torrey, *The Background of Jeremiah*, i–x, J.B.L., 1937, pp. 193–216.

[3] H. G. May, *Towards an Objective Approach to the Book of Jeremiah: the Biographer*, J.B.L., lxi, 1942, pp. 139–155.

[4] For late additions to the book see 'Contents'.

In the second place the Greek text is shorter than the Hebrew by 2,700 words or one-eighth of the whole, though it has 100 words not found in the Hebrew. The omissions consist of words, clauses and sections, the chief of these being: viii. 10b–12, x. 6–8, 10, xi. 7, 8, xvii. 1–4, xxix. 16–20, xxxiii. 14–26, xxxix. 4–13, lii. 28–30. The variations between the Hebrew and the Greek versions of the book show that in about the third century BC the text was not fixed. The obvious conclusion is that the Greek represents the older and purer text, but of this we are not certain.

PERMANENT INFLUENCE

The book provides a certain amount of information concerning the moral and religious conditions which prevailed in Judah during the period extending from the prophet's call to the destruction of Jerusalem. Rulers, prophets, priests and the people generally were corrupt (vi. 28–30). The rulers oppressed the poor and the helpless and denied them justice, 'For among my people are found wicked men: they watch, as fowlers lie in wait; they set a trap, they catch men. As a cage is full of birds, so are their houses full of deceit: therefore they are become great, and waxen rich. They are waxen fat, they shine: yea, they overpass in deeds of wickedness: they plead not the cause, the cause of the fatherless, that they should prosper; and the right of the needy do they not judge' (v. 26–28; cf. xxii. 3). Two cases of glaring injustice are cited, namely, the exaction of forced labour from his subjects by Jehoiakim (xxii. 13–19) and the liberation of the Hebrew slaves in accordance with a solemn agreement and their recapture shortly afterwards in violation of that agreement (xxxiv. 8–22). But wickedness was not confined to the rulers of the land. All from the least to the greatest were given to covetousness (vi. 13); all stole, murdered, committed adultery and swore falsely, believing that the possession of the Temple would give them security and save them from the consequences of their crimes (vii. 3–11). The prophet summed up the moral condition of the nation thus: 'Oh that I had in the wilderness a lodging place of wayfaring men; that I might leave my people, and go from them! for they be all adulterers, an assembly of treacherous men. And they bend their tongue as it were their bow for falsehood; and they are grown strong in the land, but not for truth: for they proceed from evil to evil, and they know not me, saith the Lord' (ix. 2, 3).

As regards religion the people worshipped the Canaanite Baalim in the high places and under green trees, and indulged in the super-stitious rites and immoral practices associated with them (ii. 20, iii. 6, ix. 14, xi. 13, 17, xvii. 1-4). Gods were as numerous as the cities of Judah (ii. 28). They bowed down to images of wood and stone (ii. 27, iii. 9, viii. 19) and worshipped the Queen of Heaven (vii. 18, xliv. 15-19) and the heavenly bodies (viii. 1, 2, xix. 13) and offered human sacrifices (vii. 31, xxxii. 35). Religion had no connec-tion with morality. The prophet declared that frankincense from Sheba and the sweet cane from a far country, burnt offerings and sacrifices would not help them in the day of disaster, for they had not listened to His words and had rejected His law (vi. 19, 20).

Jeremiah had much in common with his predecessors, Amos, Hosea, Micah and Isaiah. Like them he held that Yahweh was the Creator of the Universe and the Lord of history, controlling the destinies of nations and using them as His instruments in the fulfil-ment of His purpose (v. 22, x. 7, xxvii. 5). Yahweh had chosen Israel from the beginning. He had planted her 'a noble vine, wholly a right seed' (ii. 21). She was His beloved (xi. 15, xii. 7), His heritage (xii. 7, 9) and His flock (xxiii. 1-4). It was Yahweh who had com-missioned Nebuchadrezzar to rule over Judah and the surrounding nations (xxvii. 6). Like them he held that Yahweh was a righteous God who required from His worshippers obedience to His moral demands (vi. 16-21, vii. 21-28, xi. 15-17). Like Amos he was a monotheist, though he did not actually proclaim his belief in the existence of only one God. Yahweh controlled the destiny of other nations besides Judah, even though they did not recognize Him. He described other gods as 'vanity' (ii. 5, x. 3, 15), 'no gods' (ii. 11), and as 'broken cisterns that can hold no water' (ii. 13). He was, however, so far as we know, the first to proclaim that religion was essentially a personal relationship between God and man. Before his time the religious unit was the nation rather than the individual. It was the nation that Yahweh had called out of Egypt and with whom He had made a covenant in Egypt. The individual had access to Him by virtue of his membership of the community. To cut off a man from his people was to cut him off from his God (cf. 1 Sam. xxvi. 19). It would, however, be an exaggeration to say that before Jeremiah there was among the Israelites no individual experience of God or sense of responsibility to Him. At their call Jeremiah's predecessors in the prophetic ministry passed through an intense religious experience and recognized their responsibility for the exercise of their ministry.

As the result of his own bitter experience Jeremiah learnt that he could enter into communion with Yahweh, not because he was a member of the community, but because Yahweh cared for him as an individual. His relationship with Him was essentially personal rather than national.

He promoted the ideal of personal religion in various ways. He taught that true worship was not dependent upon the existence of the Temple (vii. 1-15) and its sacrifices (vi. 20, vii. 21-28, xiv. 12), or the ark (iii. 16), or upon residence in Palestine (xxxix. 1-14). Yahweh was everywhere and could be approached in Babylon no less than in Jerusalem. So in a letter to the exiles in Babylon he wrote, 'And ye shall call upon me, and ye shall go and pray unto me, and I will hearken unto you. And ye shall seek me, and find me, when ye shall search for me with all your heart' (xxix. 12, 13).

The ideal of personal religion was promoted still further by his doctrine of the New Covenant. With the reign of Jehoiakim all the old evils returned, and Jeremiah came to realize that Josiah's reforms had not produced that change of heart among the people or led to that deeper knowledge of Yahweh for which his soul yearned. Hence he proclaimed that the day would come when Yahweh would make a New Covenant with His people, the terms of which would not be inscribed in stone but in the hearts of men. Then all men, from the least to the greatest, would know Yahweh without the instruction of the priest or the oracle of the prophets, and their sins would be blotted out by His mercy. 'But this is the covenant that I will make with the house of Israel after those days, saith the Lord; I will put my law in their inward parts, and in their heart will I write it; and I will be their God, and they shall be my people; and they shall teach no more every man his neighbour, and every man his brother saying, Know the Lord: for they shall all know me, from the least of them unto the greatest of them, saith the Lord: for I will forgive their iniquity, and their sin will I remember no more' (xxxi. 33, 34). There was, however, an important limitation to the operation of this New Covenant: it was a covenant for Israel and not for all mankind. The prophet had no idea of a universal religion.

Jeremiah looked forward to the day when all the material symbols of the presence of Yahweh would be swept away. There would be no need for Temple or ark, for Yahweh's presence would be with men

G

wherever they might be; no need for sacrifices (the divinely appointed means by which the covenant between Yahweh and His people was renewed and sins were forgiven), for Yahweh would no longer remember their past sins but would forgive them; no need for legal codes for Yahweh's law would be written on the hearts of men.

This idea of personal religion exercised a profound influence both upon Judaism and Christianity. 'Without it the characteristic features of later Judaism would have been impossible. It struck the keynote of the teaching of Jesus about the Fatherhood of God and His care for each of His children. It underlay the evangelical message of the Apostles and of the early Church. It was the fundamental assumption of the great call of the Reformation for repentance and a personal approach to God. Without it there could be no genuine doctrine of a future life, and it is that which has inspired the mysticism inherent in all really efficient Christianity. In a very true and profound sense Jeremiah was the father of all the saints.'[1]

Since the essence of religion was personal communion with Yahweh it followed naturally that every man was responsible for his own sins. Hence Jeremiah proclaimed that the sins of the fathers, no matter what the Decalogue might say (Exod. xx. 5), were not visited upon the children. 'In those days they shall say no more, The fathers have eaten sour grapes, and the children's teeth are set on edge. But every one shall die for his own iniquity' (xxxi. 29, 30).

Jeremiah accepted Isaiah's doctrine of the Remnant. At first he found it among the exiles deported to Babylon in 598 BC. They were the 'good figs' of his vision, while those who were left behind were the 'bad figs', so bad that they could not be eaten (xxiv. 1–10). Uprooted from their native land and deprived of their Temple, they would discover in their new surroundings the religion of the spirit. 'For I know the thoughts that I think toward you, saith the Lord, thoughts of peace and not of evil, to give you hope in your latter end. And ye shall call upon me, and ye shall go and pray unto me, and I will hearken unto you. And ye shall seek me, and find me, when ye shall search for me with all your heart' (xxix. 11–13).

After the fall of Jerusalem he chose to settle down with the peasants who were allowed to remain in the country under Gedaliah rather than to be carried captive to Babylon. Clearly at this time he saw in the common people in agricultural Palestine the Remnant

[1] T. H. Robinson, *Prophecy and the Prophets in Ancient Israel*, 1st ed. 1923, reprinted 1950, p. 140.

from whom the new Israel could be built up. We see here the ancient equivalent of romanticism, the belief that the countyman is in the position where rectitude of life and religious simplicity are natural. Jeremiah may ultimately have hoped to find the Remnant among the exiles, but we do not know. All seemed lost, and probably he had faith that Yahweh would find it somewhere and sometime, but he had no conception where or when.

Jeremiah was opposed to the prevailing belief in the inviolability of Jerusalem and its Temple—a belief for which Isaiah was responsible. Jeremiah found in Israel's history evidence to the contrary. Yahweh had allowed His first sanctuary at Shiloh to be destroyed, and if the priests of the Temple at Jerusalem were wicked like those at Shiloh, He would treat it similarly (vii. 1–15, xxvi. 1–6). The prophet also warned Zedekiah that unless he submitted to Nebuchadrezzar Jerusalem would be destroyed (xxxviii. 14–18).

'The Confessions' of Jeremiah mark the beginning of a new type of poetry which culminated in the Psalms. The poetry is devotional and even mystical in character and expresses all the varied emotions of the human heart—hopes, fears, doubts, joys and sorrows. He has been called the creator of the Psalms because, through the conflicts in his own soul, he created the devotional language which the Psalmists employed in their approach to God.

Jeremiah seems to have been the first to raise the problem of the undeserved suffering of the innocent and the prosperity of the wicked. He suffered intensely but could see no reason for his undeserved punishment. 'Why is my pain perpetual, and my wound incurable, which refuseth to be healed?' (xv. 18). It was obvious to him that the theory that Yahweh rewarded the good and punished the wicked was falsified by the facts of human experience, so he asked the question, 'Wherefore doth the way of the wicked prosper?' But he could give no answer, though he realized that if he purified his heart Yahweh would restore him to His service, make him His spokesman and strengthen him, so that he would be invulnerable to all attacks (xv. 19–21). He thus discovered the truth that it is only as a man purifies his heart that he sees God. The problem of human suffering became Israel's greatest religious problem, but no adequate solution has been found to it, either by Jewish or Christian thinkers.

What then had Jeremiah left us as his work in creating the Jewish and ultimately the Christian outlook? He passed on the idea of religion as being essentially personal communion with God. He created the idea of the New Covenant based on the conscience of the individual and not on any legal code. He made known the truth that every man is responsible to God for his own sins. In taking over Isaiah's idea of the Remnant he made it more spiritual. He destroyed the popular idea that Jerusalem and the Temple were inviolable. He created a new type of literature which came to full expression in the Psalms. Finally he raised the problem of the mystery of human suffering, and left behind him the knowledge that it was possible for a great prophet to be a great sufferer. In him Hebrew prophecy reached its greatest height, so that when a later Jew spoke of 'The Prophet' he meant not Isaiah but Jeremiah.

STYLE

It is difficult to form a true estimate of Jeremiah's literary style since his writings have come down to us in fragmentary form and have suffered from editorial revisions and expansions. If we take into consideration the portions of the present book of Jeremiah which can reasonably be assigned to the prophet, we must conclude that he was a writer of no mean order. He wrote prose and poetry, and it is often pointed out that there is a difference of literary quality between the two kinds of writing. It is true that the prose portions are often dull, monotonous, repetitious and uninspiring; but these faults may be due, in part at any rate, to the fact that they have been rewritten or expanded. These portions, however, have in many instances a peculiar rhythm which raises them to the level of what might be called poetical prose. In many of the poetical passages he rises to heights of lyric power which have seldom been equalled in the whole range of literature.

In his style he has not the vigour of Amos, nor the sublimity of Isaiah, nor yet the dramatic power of his contemporary Nahum. It shows the influence of the writings of the earlier prophets, notably Hosea, and of the author of Deuteronomy. Like Hosea he spoke the language of the heart rather than that of the head. Sensitive and tender-hearted, he lamented again and again over the sins and misery of his own people, or expressed Yahweh's love for them and His eagerness to pardon them if only they would repent. He revealed his own isolation and loneliness, expressed his anxieties, doubts, fears, sorrows and joys, and found comfort in the thought of the nearness of Yahweh's presence. Regarding himself as a teacher inspired by Yahweh, he was more concerned with his message than with the manner of its presentation, and so wrote naturally and simply with little attempt at elaboration, though he often achieved great beauty of thought and expression. Like Hosea, too, he was familiar with the country from which he drew much of his imagery (see pp. 95, 96).

More than any of the other prophets he excelled in the description or suggestion of terror. We read of the terror of evil and disaster coming from the north (iv. 7, 13, v. 15–17, vi. 24–26, viii. 15–17), and the terror of darkness when the way is lost on the 'twilight hills' (xiii. 16). Death is represented as the Reaper who climbs into the window, cuts down children and young men in the streets and lets their bodies fall like grain-stalks behind the harvester (ix. 17–22).

Deeply moving are his descriptions of desolate silent places where no man dwells. Yahweh led the Israelites 'through a land of deserts and of pits, through a land of drought and of the shadow of death, through a land that none passed through, and where no man dwelt' (ii. 6). In a vision the prophet 'beheld the earth, and, lo, it was waste and void; and the heavens, and they had no light. I beheld the mountains and, lo, they trembled, and all the hills moved to and fro. I beheld, and lo, there was no man, and all the birds of the heavens were fled' (iv. 23). Yahweh would 'cause to cease from the cities of Judah, and from the streets of Jerusalem, the voice of mirth and the voice of gladness, the voice of the bridegroom, and the voice of the bride: for the land shall become a waste' (vii. 34).

The sound of lamentation is heard throughout the verses. He calls upon the nation to mourn and wail (iv. 8, vi. 26, vii. 29), listens to the lament of mountains and pastures (ix. 10) and writes a dirge for the women of Jerusalem to sing (ix. 17–22). He hears Rachel at Ramath lamenting over her banished children (xxxi. 15), wishes that his eyes were a fountain of tears that he might weep day and night for the slain of Judah (ix. 1), and curses the day he was born, for life had brought him nothing but labour and sorrow (xx. 14–18). We have, however, already shown (pp. 167, 168) that in spite of the prevailing gloom of his writings they are occasionally lit up with gleams of light.

For the sake of emphasis and to secure dramatic effect he makes frequent use of the literary device of repetition. Sometimes he repeats words. 'Lo, I will bring a nation upon you from afar, O house of Israel, saith the Lord: it is a mighty nation, it is an ancient nation, a nation whose language thou knowest not, neither understandest what they say' (v. 15). At other times he repeats favourite phrases (sometimes with slight variations) like 'to pluck up and to break down, and to destroy and to overthrow, to build and to plant' (i, 10, xviii. 7, 9, xxiv. 6) and 'to make a full end' (iv. 27, v. 10, 18, xxx. 11), or favourite sentences (sometimes with slight variations) like, 'Therefore pray not thou for this people, neither lift up cry nor prayer for them, neither make intercession to me: for I will not hear thee' (vii. 16, xi. 14).

His favourite metre is the 'Quinah' or 'Dirge' metre, consisting of a line of three beats followed by one of two, which is admirably adapted to his theme and spirit. The translation of ch. ii. 32 by G. A. Smith is a good example of this metre.

> Can a maiden forget her adorning?
> Or her girdle the bride?
> Yet me have my people forgotten,
> Days without number.

CHAPTER XIV

Ezekiel

AUTHORSHIP, PLACE AND DATE OF COMPOSITION

Until recently the authorship of the book of Ezekiel was regarded as the best attested of the major books of the Old Testament. The traditional view is that it is the work of one man who was deported to Babylon in 598 BC. Five years later he was called to the prophetic ministry and proceeded to pronounce judgement upon Jerusalem and the surrounding nations, and to predict the restoration of both Israel and Judah and their eventual reunion under a single ruler of the Davidic line. Finally, he drew up a plan for the organization of the restored community. The book was published shortly after the prophet's last prophecy (571 BC). 'The dates of the several prophecies,' wrote Driver, 'are in many cases stated with precision. No critical question arises in connection with the authorship of the book, the whole from beginning to end bearing unmistakably the stamp of a single mind.'[1]

From about 1924 onwards the traditional view has been vigorously challenged by many critics and the most conflicting theories have been put forward. According to Hölscher, Ezekiel was primarily a poet and not a prose writer. He ascribes to him only the finest poetical portions of the book, amounting to 170 verses and a few short prose passages. The rest, which constitutes the larger portion and is written in prose, is the work of an editor who flourished in the fifth century BC.[2] Torrey maintains that the whole book is a pseudepigraph, written originally about 230 BC, purporting to have been written in the thirteenth year of the reign of Manasseh and addressed to the Palestinian circle, but that it was revised by an editor who

---

[1] S. R. Driver, *An Introduction to the Literature of the Old Testament*, 9th ed., 1913, p. 279.

[2] G. Hölscher, *Heskiel, der Dichter und das Buch*, 1924.

transferred the sphere of the prophet's activity to the period of the Exile.[1] Smith holds that Ezekiel was a native of the Northern Kingdom, who was deported in 734 BC, began his prophetic career in Exile, returned home in 691 BC and continued his ministry in the homeland.[2] Herntrich alleges that Ezekiel was active in Jerusalem shortly before 586 BC and that he took the book to Babylon where it was remodelled about 573 BC by an exilic editor, who transferred the prophet's activity to the exilic community and added much secondary material, including the whole of chs. xl–xlviii.[3] Bertholet thinks that Ezekiel exercised a ministry in Jerusalem to which he was called in the vision of the Book-roll (ii. 3–iii. 9) in 593 BC, and that after the fall of the city he moved to Babylon where in 585 BC he received a second call to prophesy to the exiles (i. 4–ii. 2).[4] Berry makes the real Ezekiel prophesy in or near Jerusalem between 597 and 586 BC and supplies him with two later editors, one who added promises for the chosen people and threats against the foreign nations, and a second in the third century BC, who revised the whole with the addition of all the passages which locate the prophet among the exiles, and chs. xl–xlviii.[5] Irwin locates Ezekiel in Jerusalem until 586 BC and then in Babylon, but allows him only certain poetical passages, a fifth of the whole book, the rest being added by numerous editors who cannot be distinguished or dated.[6] Messel makes Ezekiel write in Jerusalem after the return of the exiles. He ascribes to him the body of chs. i–xxiv and xl–xlviii, while xxv–xxxii are attributed to an editor.[7] Browne holds that Ezekiel was a priest in Jerusalem in the fourth century BC, that he was deported to Hycrania with other Jews in 344 or 343 BC, and that it was from this captivity that most of the dates were reckoned. The prophet used the exile of Jehoiachin to deceive the authorities.[8] It is interesting to note that Cooke accepts the traditional view that Ezekiel's work was confined to Babylon, but admits that additions were made to it by an editor.[9]

[1] C. C. Torrey, *Pseudo-Ezekiel and the Original Prophecy*, 1930.
[2] J. Smith, *The Book of the Prophet Ezekiel*, 1931.
[3] V. Herntrich, *Ezechielprobleme*, 1932.
[4] A. Bertholet, *Hesekiel* (H.A.T. 1, 13, 1936).
[5] G. R. Berry, *The Composition of the Book of Ezekiel* (J.B.L., lviii, 1939, pp. 163–75).
[6] W. A. Irwin, *The Problem of Ezekiel*, 1943.
[7] N. Messel, *Ezechielfragen*, 1945.
[8] L. E. Browne, *Ezekiel and Alexander*, 1952.
[9] G. A. Cooke, *The Book of Ezekiel*, 1936.

PROBLEMS IN THE BOOK

The above theories are the result of attempts of critics to find a satisfactory solution of the problems which confront them in their study of the book. First, there is the problem of the trance in which, we are told, the hand of Yahweh was laid upon the prophet and he saw visions. Some cannot believe that certain materials in the book, especially the elaborate details of the Temple and its organization in chs. xl–xlviii, could possibly have been revealed in visions. The upholders of this view have a wrong conception of the psychology of the prophetic trance. In modern language we should call the trance a product of self-hypnosis, as distinct from the mass hypnosis of which we often read in historical books. How precisely this self-hypnosis was produced we do not know and it does not matter. But these critics hold that such a trance can give the counterpart of every kind of sensory experience in ordinary life but cannot give the purely intellectual matter embodied in chs. xl–xlviii. The reply to this theory must be taken from the nearest experiences which the ordinary man gets, namely, from dreams. Dreams are normally incoherent but definitely of a sensory character. In the half-awake moments which follow the dream, while these sensory experiences are still in consciousness, the dreamer rationalizes them, makes them coherent, and supplies what is in line with his ordinary modes of thought. So, if the prophet in his trance imagined that a set of measurements was being given to him, on waking he would supply measurements which seemed appropriate, without afterwards distinguishing what was supplied by the vision and what by the working of the mind while still under the influence of the vision.

Second, there is the problem of the prophet's residence. Some find it impossible to believe that the prophet, while living in Babylon, would have addressed many of his prophecies to the people in Jerusalem. But the fact that many of his prophecies were directed against Jerusalem is no evidence that they were delivered in that city. We find no difficulty in believing that they were addressed to the exiles in Babylon. Surely they would be disposed to listen to him, for their thoughts would naturally turn to Jerusalem and the Temple, especially if they hoped that one day they would be allowed to return. Moreover, there is evidence of communication between the exiles and the people in the homeland, so that it is quite possible that the prophet's words would eventually be reported in Jerusalem.

Third, there is the problem of the prophet's claim to have been carried by the Spirit from Babylon to Jerusalem, to have seen what was going on there, and then to have been carried back. There is, of course, nothing to surprise us in the prophet's impression of such a transfer: if his mind was concentrated on what was happening in Jerusalem, it was quite natural for him to imagine himself carried away there. But how, it is asked, could his information be correct. The answer is perfectly simple. What he sees in visions is what he saw in Jerusalem before he was deported; and there is no reason to suppose that any change had taken place. Further, it is not impossible, that information was occasionally carried to him just as in ch. xxxiii. 21, where we are told that 'one that had escaped out of Jerusalem came unto me, saying, The city is smitten'. Why should we have the words 'come unto me' instead of 'come unto us'? It looks as if the prophet had his secret service and was regarded as a leader of those who recognized Jehoiachin and not Zedekiah as still the lawful king. Nebuchadrezzar for his own reasons held this view, and he was a far more sensible man than are modern dictators; a party which without realizing it was supporting his own policy was not to be interfered with.

Fourth, there is the problem that arises from the fact that the book contains both poetry and prose. Some, unable to believe that the poetry, which often possesses considerable literary merit, could have been written by the same person who wrote the prose which is frequently dull, repetitious and obscure, assume that the book is the work of two authors, a prophet who wrote mostly in poetry, and a priest who wrote in prose. But prophets often wrote both poetry and prose. The absurdity of the theory in Ezekiel's case is that it makes the prophecies against Tyre and Egypt the core of the work; and as both prophecies were contradicted by events, it seems absurd to suppose that they should have been preserved in their existing form, unless the prophet had obtained such a big reputation for something else that his successors did not venture to amend them. Alterations would have been perfectly easy.

Fifth, there is the problem of what is called the 'dual personality' of the prophet, in which some find it impossible to believe. In the early part of the book he is the prophet in communion with Yahweh, while in the latter part he is the priest preoccupied with the Temple and its ritual. Such a combination of elements, it is alleged, could not exist in the same personality. But these apparently diverse elements do not necessarily imply plurality of authorship. There is, it is true, a great difference between his early method of composition in 593–587 BC and his later method in 586–571 BC, but in both he is the priest, the advocate of the exiled leaders and the Jewish nationalist. Between the two periods he changed from the critic and the denouncer to the constructive leader; but his personality remained unchanged. He began by recognizing his responsibility; he ended by discharging that responsibility in a successful form. His minute description of Yahweh's living chariot in the first chapter of the book displays the same mentality as his minute description of the measurements of the Temple in the later chapters. Moreover, complex personalities are not unknown. The apostle Paul, for example, was a mystic, a missionary, a pastor, an organizer, a theologian, and a controversialist, all in one.

Sixth, there is the problem of the recurring phrase 'house of Israel', which, according to Smith, appears to refer to the Northern Kingdom and to have no reference to Judah. The phrase cannot be used to prove that Ezekiel was a northern Israelite. Battersby-Harford, after a careful investigation of the eighty-three occurrences of the phrase in the book, has demonstrated that it is often used for the inhabitants of Judah and Jerusalem.[1]

Seventh, there is the problem of the definite dates given in the book. There are fourteen of these dates which are found in chs. i. 1, 2, viii. 1, xx. 1, xxiv. 1, xxvi. 1, xxix. 1, xxix. 17, xxx. 20, xxxi. 1, xxxii. 1, xxxii. 17, xxxiii. 21, xl. 1. They are almost all in chronological order and range from the fifth year of Jehoiachin's captivity (593 BC) to the twenty-seventh year (571 BC). Some reject these dates as purely fictitious, the work of an editor. It is true that difficulties have arisen regarding some of the dates, but they do not warrant the assumption that all the dates are unreliable. The date at the beginning of the book has never been satisfactorily explained. It is given as 'the thirtieth year', but there is no indication of the point from which the reckoning is made. Elsewhere, as in ch. i. 2, Ezekiel dates his prophecies from the captivity of Jehoiachin. Thirty years previous to this would take us back to the time of Josiah's reformation. The date has also been interpreted as the age of the prophet at his call, or the thirtieth year after the foundation of the New-Babylonian empire. It has also been suggested that 'thirtieth' is a scribal error

[1] J. Battersby-Harford, *Studies in the Book of Ezekiel*, 1935, pp. 31 and 93–101.

for 'thirteenth', and that the date should be reckoned from the captivity of Jehoiachin as in the other cases. With the exception of Torrey it has not been regarded by critics as an important clue to the true or fictitious chronology of the book.

The chief difficulties are concerned with the dates attached to the predictions against Tyre (xxvi–xxviii. 19) and Egypt (xxix–xxxii), and the scheme for the organization of the restored community (xl–xlviii). Ezekiel predicted the imminent capture and destruction of Tyre and the conquest of Egypt by the Babylonians. According to Josephus Nebuchadrezzar besieged Tyre for thirteen years (585–572 BC) but failed to capture it. The prophet admitted that his prediction had not been fulfilled and foretold that Egypt would be given to Nebuchadrezzar as compensation for his failure against Tyre. It is supposed that Nebuchadrezzar invaded Egypt in 568 BC but there is no definite proof of this. So far as we know, therefore, the prophet's predictions against both Tyre and Egypt were not fulfilled. It does not follow, however, that the dates are fictitious. The recording of these prophecies as they stand is only intelligible if they are genuine, so easy would it have been to alter them at a later date, to make it appear that those against Egypt referred to its conquest by Cambyses and those against Tyre to Alexander's successful siege of that city.

No date other than that alleged in the book fits the plan for the organization of the restored community in chs. xl–xlviii. There is no mention of Babylon, or of Persia, from which we may infer that at the time when the plan was drawn up Babylon was still the dominant power, and that Persia had not emerged from obscurity. The book is entirely unlike Deutero-Isaiah which was composed towards the close of the Exile. In ch. xlvii. 1–12 the prophet sees a river issuing from the Temple and flowing eastwards until it finally falls into the Dead Sea, making its waters sweet and fresh. The river makes the desert through which it passes wonderfully fertile, and every month the trees on its banks provide food for the hungry and leaves for healing. This combination of the severely practical and the miraculous distinguishes the prophet from Haggai and Zechariah, who had to deal with the immediate practical task of building the Temple. Might not Zechariah have had Ezekiel in mind when he wrote, 'And I lifted up mine eyes, and saw, and behold a man with a measuring line in his hand. Then said I, Whither goest thou? And he said unto me, To measure Jerusalem, to see what is the breadth thereof, and what is the length thereof. And, behold, the angel that talked with me went forth, and another angel went out to meet him, and said unto him, Run, speak to this young man, saying, Jerusalem shall be inhabited as villages without walls, by reason of the multitude of men and cattle therein. For I, saith the Lord, will be unto her a wall of fire round about, and I will be the glory in the midst of her' (Zech. ii. 1–5). Ezekiel's measurements are set aside. If the period of Zerubbabel does not suit Ezekiel's plan, far less does that of Nehemiah or that of Ezra.

We may notice the views of the critic Finegan in connection with the dates in the book of Ezekiel. He works from clay tablets found on the site of Babylon which give dates ranging from the tenth to the thirty-fifth year of Nebuchadrezzar (595–570 BC), during which period Jehoiachin is treated as the legitimate king of Judah. He claims that these tablets make Ezekiel's dates both intelligible and historical. It is noteworthy that Finegan is the only critic working from contemporary records.

We conclude that the dated passages, with the probable exception of some editorial additions and alterations, are genuine and that the dates are substantially correct.

Eighth and last, there is the problem of the undated passages some or all of which have been denied to Ezekiel by certain critics for one reason or another. Of these passages the most important are chs. xxxviii and xxxix in which there is a long prophecy against Gog 'of the land of Magog'. It contains apocalyptic elements which, it is alleged, Ezekiel, with his fondness for historical facts, would not have introduced into his work. But apocalyptic elements are characteristic features of other parts of the book, especially in the prophecies of the restoration. Moreover, the passage contains the prophet's fundamental teaching that all nations would be brought to recognize Yahweh through His mighty acts. There are no adequate reasons for denying the genuineness of the majority of these undated passages.

Much research work still remains to be done on this complicated book. We believe that the traditional view is nearer the truth than the modern theories. We shall assume, therefore, in our study of the book, that with the exception of a few secondary elements, which now cannot be exactly determined, it is the work of the prophet Ezekiel, who exercised his ministry in Babylon before and after the fall of Jerusalem in 587 BC.

LIFE AND CHARACTER OF EZEKIEL

Our knowledge of Ezekiel is derived entirely from his writings. He was a contemporary of Jeremiah and was the son of Buzi, a member of the priestly family of Zadok. His familiarity with the Temple and its imposing ritual suggests that he had at one time exercised the priestly functions. He was among those who with Jehoiachin were deported to Babylon in 598 BC. With a group of his fellow country-men he found himself quartered at Tel-abib by the river Chebar, probably a large canal south-east of Babylon. He was married either before or after his arrival in Babylon, for we are told that in the ninth year of Jehoiachin's captivity his wife died (xxiv. 15–18). He occupied his own house (iii. 24, viii. 1, xii. 1–7) and was evidently reckoned a leader among the exiles, for the elders of Israel are repre-sented as coming to listen to his words (viii. 1, xiv. 1, xx. 1). It was in the fifth year of Jehoiachin's captivity (593 BC) that he received his call to the prophetic ministry (i–iii. 27). After his inaugural vision he made his way to the colony of his fellow exiles at Tel-abib, where, after a period of seven days during which he sat 'astonied', he began his work as a prophet. His ministry lasted at least twenty-two years, the latest dated prophecy in the book being 571 BC (xxix. 17–20). His first duty was to denounce the folly and wickedness of the survivors in Jerusalem and to predict the fall of the city; but his words of warning fell on deaf ears. He was obliged to refrain from speaking in public, and to confine himself to addressing those who came to him to inquire what message Yahweh had sent through him, until the fall of the city proved the truth of his predictions, and gave him an influence which had hitherto been denied to him.

His thoughts now turned to the task of reconstruction. He pre-dicted the complete destruction of Israel's rivals and foes—Ammon, Moab, Edom, Philistia, Tyre, Zidon and Egypt (xxv–xxxii)—and encouraged the exiles with the promise of restoration to their native land, the reunion of the two kingdoms, Israel and Judah, under a single ruler of the house of David, a new Temple with an elaborate ritual and a reformed priesthood, the redistribution of the land among the tribes, and the abiding presence of Yahweh in Jerusalem (xxxiii–xlviii). Apparently his work was now finished except for one short prophecy (xxix. 17–20). Of his later life we know nothing. There is nothing in his book to show that he outlived Nebucha-drezzar who died in 562 BC, or that he had the happiness of seeing

Jehoiachin released from prison in the reign of Evil-merodach (562–560 BC).

In Ezekiel the prophetic consciousness was very strong. Like Isaiah and Jeremiah he was absolutely convinced that Yahweh had called him to the prophetic office, and had charged him with a message of denunciation and doom for the rebellious house of Israel. If he failed in the task entrusted to him, he would be held guilty of the blood of those men whom he had not warned. In this faith he lived and worked, proclaiming his message with a passionate intensity and with great moral courage. He opposed those who refused to listen to his predictions with a stubbornness equal to their own; even when his wife, the desire of his eyes, died, he restrained his tears and resumed his teaching (xxiv. 15–18). There was, however, something about him that was harsh and forbidding; he seems to have had little sympathy for those who were weaker than himself. On two occasions he was dismayed at the thought of the destruction of Jerusalem and prayed that the remnant might be spared (ix. 8, xi. 13), but we feel that he was never deeply moved at the thought of human suffering. The people had sinned and must pay the penalty. 'And as for me also, mine eye shall not spare, neither will I have pity, but I will bring their way upon their head' (ix. 10). At times we can detect the note of fierce exultation in the fearful spectacle of destruction which he so graphically described (e.g. vi, xxiv, xxv–xxxii). He could not conceive of Yahweh forgiving His people through motives of compassion and love, as is the case with Hosea. The whole motive behind Yahweh's restoration of the exiles to their own land was that His honour might be vindicated in the sight of the heathen. 'I do not this for your sake, O house of Israel, but for mine holy name, which ye have profaned among the nations, whither ye went' (xxxvi. 22).

Ezekiel was a mystic who was subject to trances in which he had visionary experiences. As he was among the captives by the river Chebar, he saw visions of God (i. 1). After the inaugural vision the spirit lifted him up and took him away, setting him down among his fellow exiles at Tel-abib (iii. 12–15). As he sat in the midst of a company of elders, a strange luminous figure took him by the hair and brought him to Jerusalem where he saw the idolatries practised in the Temple. After seeing Yahweh leave the desecrated sanctuary, the spirit lifted him up and brought him 'in the vision' to Chaldea (xi. 22–25). In another vision Yahweh carried him off and set him down in a valley full of dry bones (xxxvii. 1–14). Finally, Yahweh brought him in a vision to the land of Israel, and set him down upon a very high mountain upon which he saw Jerusalem with its Temple (xl. 1, 2).

We have already expressed the opinion that he was a combination of the priest and the prophet. His priestly instincts are seen in his reverence for holy things and in his horror of profaning them, in his preoccupation with the Temple, and with its ritual and priesthood, and in his emphasis upon the necessity of obedience to the Law. But by his overwhelming sense of the transcendence of Yahweh, his prophetic consciousness, and his spiritual intensity he belongs to the goodly fellowship of the prophets. He was, in fact, by nature a priest who, under divine compulsion, become a prophet.

CONTENTS

The book may be divided into four sections.

(1) Chs. i–xxiv. Prophecies concerning Judah and Jerusalem during the period 593–587 BC.

(2) Chs. xxv–xxxii. Prophecies against foreign nations.

(3) Chs. xxxiii–xxxix. Mainly prophecies of the restoration of Jerusalem.

(4) Chs. xl–xlviii. An ideal sketch of the restored community.

These sections may be summarized as follows:

Chapters i–xxiv
Chs. i–iii. Introduction with date (i. 1–3). Ezekiel sees in a vision the Deity enthroned on a kind of platform, supported by four living creatures (cherubim) which enclose a four-wheeled chariot. The prophet falls prostrate upon his face and hears a voice (i. 4–28). Yahweh commissions him to proclaim His message to the rebellious house of Israel and bids him not to fear (ii. 1–7). The prophet is commanded to eat a roll, inscribed with lamentations, symbols of the message which he is to deliver (ii. 8–iii. 3). He is warned that the people are stubborn and defiant, but is assured that he will be made as unyielding as adamant and harder than flint. He is bidden to announce himself to the exiles by using the prophetic formula, 'Thus saith the Lord' (iii. 4–11). The Spirit lifts him up and he hears the

sound of the departing chariot. The prophet joins his fellow exiles
at Tel-abib, where for seven days he remains dumb with amazement
(iii. 12–15). At the end of the seven days he is reminded of the
responsibility placed upon him. He is a 'watchman' appointed to
warn men of the consequences of sin. If he fails to deliver Yahweh's
message he shall bear the consequences of his neglect (iii. 16–21).
He sees again the same vision as in ch. i and is ordered to remain
silent and stay in his house (iii. 22–27).

Chs. iv–vii. Unable to proclaim his message publicly he resorts to
symbolic action. He portrays symbolically the siege of Jerusalem by
drawing on a brick a plan of a besieged city (iv. 1–3). He lies down
for two periods, once on his left side for 390 days (190 days according to the Septuagint) and once on his right side for 40 days, to
indicate the time during which the two kingdoms, Israel and Judah
respectively, will be in exile (iv. 4–8). To indicate the horrors of the
famine consequent upon the siege and the uncleanness of the Exile,
he rations his food and drink and eats food prepared in a disgusting
way (iv. 9–17). To symbolize the fate of the inhabitants of Jerusalem
he cuts off his hair and beard, burning a third, smiting a third with
the sword, and scattering a third to the wind (v. 1–4). In plain
language he now predicts the destruction of Jerusalem (v. 5–17). He
pronounces judgement upon the mountains of Israel because the
high places upon them are seats of idolatrous worship. The high
places shall be destroyed and the idolatrous worshippers slain (vi.
1–7). A remnant shall be carried into exile where they will repent
and acknowledge Yahweh (vi. 8–10). Desolation shall reign from
the wilderness in the south to Diblah in the far north (vi. 11–14).
The time has come for the punishment of the land of Israel (Judah).
Yahweh will show no mercy to His idolatrous people and will teach
them that He can strike (vii. 1–9). Buyers and sellers shall be involved in a common ruin. None will have the courage to fight; so the
inhabitants of the city and of the country districts shall perish. The
few who escape to the hills shall mourn over their sins. Signs of
mourning shall be seen everywhere (vii. 10–18). Their gold and silver
shall not save them. Yahweh shall allow foreigners to profane the
Temple. The prophet shall be deprived of vision, the priest of instruction, and the 'ancients' of counsel. The authorities shall be dismayed and the common people troubled; and in their common calamity they shall recognize that Yahweh punishes iniquity (vii. 19–27).

Chs. viii–xi. In the sixth month of the sixth year of his exile Ezekiel is transported in a vision to the Temple of Jerusalem (viii. 1–4). Here he sees an image of jealousy (viii. 5, 6), seventy elders practising idolatrous rites in a dark chamber (viii. 7–13), women weeping for Tammuz (viii. 14, 15) and about twenty-five men worshipping the sun (viii. 16–18). Yahweh, standing at the threshold of the Temple after alighting from His throne borne by the cherubim, orders a scribe to set a mark on the foreheads of all those who deplore the abominations, and six executioners to destroy the rest. The prophet is appalled at the slaughter but Yahweh refuses to show mercy (ix. 1–11). The scribe is ordered to cast coals of fire, taken from the chariot of the cherubim, upon Jerusalem (x. 1–7). Then Yahweh departs from the sanctuary in the chariot, which is again described (x. 8–22). Ezekiel sees twenty-five men who give wicked counsel in Jerusalem and feel quite secure within its walls. He warns them that their confidence is misplaced and predicts their exile and death. Even as he speaks one of them, Pelatiah, falls dead. He prays that the remnant of Israel may be spared (xi. 1–13). Yahweh declares that those who have remained have boasted that they and not the exiles are the inheritors of the land. The exiles shall be brought back and shall establish the true religion of Yahweh. They shall purge the land of idolatry and He shall give them, instead of a callous heart, a soft impressionable heart on which His laws shall be easily impressed. The idolaters shall reap the reward of their sins (xi. 14–22). Yahweh now leaves the city, and Ezekiel awakes from his trance and narrates his vision to the exiles (xi. 23–25).

Chs. xii–xix. As the exiles refuse to listen to Ezekiel, he is ordered to enact in their sight a dumb show. In the daytime he collects his belongings, and in the dead of night carries them through a hole previously made in the wall of his house. Next morning he tells them that his action symbolizes the approaching exile of Zedekiah and the survivors of the siege of Jerusalem (xii. 1–16). Then he eats and drinks anxiously and fearfully to bring home to them the terrible privations of the inhabitants of Jerusalem (xii. 17–20). He warns those who say that the prophecies are never fulfilled or that they refer to the distant future, that the word of Yahweh shall be performed without delay (xii. 21–28). He condemns the false prophets whom he likens to foxes burrowing among ruins. Instead of stepping into the breach to save Jerusalem they are at home among its ruins. They claim to speak in the name of Yahweh but are not His messengers at all (xiii. 1–7). They shall be excluded from the community when the exiles return. Because they say that all is well when all is not well, they shall be destroyed (xiii. 8–16). The prophet denounces the women who tie amulets to the wrists of those who consult them, and mantle their heads in veils with the object of gaining control over them. Yahweh shall rescue the people from their sway and put an end to their vain visions and incantations (xiii. 17–23). When certain elders come to the prophet seeking an oracle, Yahweh reveals to him that they are idolaters at heart and that they, together with any prophet who gives them an answer, shall be destroyed unless they repent. Both the idolatrous inquirer and the prophet are equally sinful and shall receive the reward of their sins (xiv. 1–11). When Yahweh sends His four fatal judgements—famine, wild beasts, sword and pestilence—against Jerusalem, the most godly men like Noah, Daniel and Job, shall deliver no one but themselves. When the survivors reach Babylon, the exiles will see by their conduct that Yahweh was justified in destroying the city (xiv. 12–23). Ezekiel likens Jerusalem to a vine the wood of which is too poor to serve any useful purpose. As the wood of the vine is flung into the fire for fuel, so shall the people of Jerusalem be consumed in the flames (xv. 1–8). Jerusalem is likened to an exposed child whom Yahweh found in the desert, brought home, prepared to be His bride and married. In the full bloom of her womanhood she played the harlot with her neighbours (xvi. 1–34). She shall be put to death as an adulteress by her lovers (xvi. 35–43), for her sinfulness has surpassed that of her sisters, Sodom and Samaria (xvi. 44–52), who shall be restored before her (xvi. 53–58). After Jerusalem has borne her punishment, He shall renew an everlasting covenant with her and her two sisters shall become her daughters. This shall be done not because of her faithfulness in keeping the covenant, but of Yahweh's free grace (xvi. 59–63). Yahweh bids Ezekiel put forth a parable before Israel. (The parable is set forth in ch. xvii. 1–10 and its interpretation in vv. 11–21). A great eagle (Nebuchadrezzar) swooped down upon a stately cedar of Lebanon (Judah), plucked off the top of it (the aristocracy) and the topmost twig of all (Jehoiachin) and carried them to the land of traffic (Babylon). The eagle also took some seed of the land (Zedekiah) and planted it in Judah, intending it to become a spreading vine of low size (i.e. intending that Judah should become a prosperous kingdom but dependent upon Babylon). The vine, however, turned for nurture to another great eagle (a reference to Zedekiah's revolt from Babylon and his appeal to Egypt). The first eagle shall pluck it up by the roots and it shall wither away (i.e. Judah shall be destroyed, Zedekiah captured and taken into captivity, many slain and the rest scattered (xvii. 1–21)). Yahweh shall plant a tender cedar twig on a high mountain. It shall grow into a noble tree and birds shall shelter in it (a reference to the restoration of the Davidic kingdom (xvii. 22–24)). The people complain that they are suffering for their father's sins. Ezekiel declares that all persons belong to Yahweh and each is immediately related to Him as an individual. No one dies save for his own sins (xviii. 1–4). Every man is rewarded according to his works: the righteous man lives because of his goodness and the unrighteousness man dies because of his wickedness. The son does not bear the iniquity of the father, nor does the father bear the iniquity of the son (xviii. 5–20). The wicked man, who repents of his wickedness, lives and his past sins are not brought against him. The righteous man who turns from his righteousness dies and his former righteousness does not count (xviii. 21–29). Ezekiel appeals to the people to repent for Yahweh has no pleasure in the death of the wicked (xviii. 30–32). The prophet laments over the princes of Judah. Judah is likened to a lioness that reared two whelps, one of which (Jehoahaz) was taken to Egypt and the other (Jehoiachin) to Babylon (xix. 1–9). Judah is also likened to a vine rich in branches (i.e. Davidic kings) one of which grew into a royal sceptre, soaring into the clouds (Zedekiah). But the vine was uprooted, the east wind withered its fruit and its great branch was broken off. It is now planted in the wilderness (i.e. the nation is now in exile in Babylon). It has no great branch, no royal sceptre (xix. 10–14).

Chs. xx–xxiv. In the fifth month of the seventh year of the exile certain elders came to consult Ezekiel (xx. 1–4). He recounts Israel's wickedness in the past—in Egypt (xx. 5–9), in the wilderness (xx. 10–26) and in Canaan (xx. 27–29). While the idolatry of the people continues Yahweh will not be consulted by them (xx. 30–32). Yahweh shall bring them into the wilderness and separate the rebels who shall be left there. But the good shall be restored to their own land, and with penitent hearts they will offer on Mount Zion acceptable worship. Yahweh's purpose shall be achieved and His power and character recognized (xx. 33–44). Yahweh shall kindle a fire in the forest of the south, that shall burn every tree and scorch every face from the south to the north. Ezekiel's hearers object to his speaking in parables (xx. 45–49). He now repeats his announcement in plain language. Yahweh shall draw the sword against Jerusalem and the land of Israel, and shall slay righteous and wicked alike (xxi. 1–7). Yahweh has put a glittering sword into the hand of the slayer (Nebuchadrezzar) for the slaughter of the people and the princes. The prophet pictures the sword darting hither and thither until the dead are heaped at every gate (xxi. 8–17). Nebuchadrezzar is represented as reaching a point in his westward march where two roads diverge, one leading to Rabbah, the capital of Ammon, and the other to Jerusalem. He seeks to ascertain the will of the gods by shaking two arrows in a quiver, one marked Rabbah and the other Jerusalem, by consulting the teraphim, and by inspecting the liver of an animal. The lot falls for him to advance against Jerusalem. The city shall be captured, the king (Zedekiah) deprived of his crown, and his kingdom laid in ruins until a worthy successor shall arise to whom it will be given (xxi. 18–27). The Ammonites also shall be destroyed and shall be forgotten (xxi. 28–32). Ezekiel denounces the sins of Jerusalem—bloodshed, idolatry, the dishonouring of parents, the oppression of the poor, contempt for what is sacred, the desecration of the Sabbaths, perjury, lasciviousness, bribery, usury, extortion and forgetfulness of Yahweh. Yahweh shall scatter them among the nations (xxii. 1–16). Yahweh will smelt the ore (Israel) in the furnace (Jerusalem) and obtain nothing but dross (xxii. 17–22). The corruption extends to all classes—the princes, the priests, the prophets and the common people. They shall all be consumed by the divine wrath (xxii. 23–31). Ezekiel depicts the past history of Samaria and Jerusalem by means of the allegory of the two sisters. Yahweh in Egypt married two sisters, Oholah (Samaria) and Oholibah (Jerusalem) who were harlots (xxiii. 1–4). Oholah played the harlot with the Assyrians, defiling herself by adopting their idolatrous practices. Yahweh punished her by handing her over to the Assyrians who executed judgement upon her (xxiii. 5–10). Oholibah became worse, playing the harlot first with the Assyrians and then with the Babylonians (xxiii. 11–21). With a great army the Babylonians shall come against her, strip her naked, and compel her to drink the cup of bitterness to the dregs (xxiii. 22–35). The two sisters shall be brought to judgement and suffer the penalty due to adulteresses (xxiii. 36–49). In the tenth month of the ninth year Ezekiel predicts the destruction of the city by means of the allegory of the rusty cauldron. The city is compared to a rusty cauldron filled with pieces of flesh (the inhabitants), including choice pieces (the leaders). Beneath the cauldron is a fire, symbolic of the siege. After the boiling the pieces are removed (the Exile). As the cauldron cannot be cleansed of its rust (the foulness of the people), it is placed on the fire and consumed (xxiv. 1–14). It is revealed to the prophet that his wife is to die, but he is forbidden to exhibit the customary signs of mourning. So they are not to mourn for the destruction of Jerusalem and especially of the Temple, but to grieve in silence (xxiv. 15–24). On the day when a fugitive arrives with news of the fall of Jerusalem, the prophet's enforced silence shall come to an end (xxiv. 25–27).

Chapters xxv–xxxii

Ch. xxv. 1–17. Ammon, for exulting over the fall of Judah, shall be destroyed by the 'children of the east' (nomads of the Arabian desert) and shall cease to be a nation (vv. 1–7). A similar fate for substantially the same reason shall befall Moab (vv. 8–11). Edom, for taking vengeance on Judah, shall be desolate and Israel shall be Yahweh's instrument of punishment (vv. 12–14). Philistia for seeking to destroy Israel in spiteful vengeance, shall suffer heavy vengeance from Yahweh (vv. 15–17).

Ch. xxvi–xxviii. In the eleventh year of his exile Ezekiel proclaims the imminent destruction of Tyre. Nebuchadrezzar shall raze it to the ground and reduce it to a bare rock (xxvi. 1–14). The city that traded with the whole world shall become desolate to the dismay of all seafaring nations (xxvi. 15–xxvii. 36). The king, who claims to be a god, shall be slain by an attacking army. A dirge is sung over the fall of Tyre impersonated by her king (xxviii. 1–19). Yahweh shall slay the people of Zidon by pestilence and the sword, to glorify His name and to teach them by the manifestation of His power that He is the only true God. The enemies of Israel shall trouble her no more. When He has inflicted punishment upon all her enemies, He shall restore His people to their native land where they shall dwell in safety (xxviii. 20–26).

Ch. xxix–xxxii. In the tenth month of the tenth year of the Exile Ezekiel denounces Egypt. Pharaoh is likened to a crocodile, claiming to be the creator of the Nile in which he lives. The crocodile with all the fish that stick to its scales shall be dragged out to perish upon the open field. Egypt has always been to Israel like a broken reed that pierces the hand that leans upon it (xxix. 1–7). The land shall become a desolation and the inhabitants shall be scattered among the nations. After forty years the exiles shall be brought back and they shall establish a new kingdom, but one so weak that it will never again hold sway over the nations or tempt Israel to look to her for help (xxix. 8–16). In the first month of the twenty-seventh year of his exile Ezekiel announces that Nebuchadrezzar, who has failed to capture Tyre, will conquer Egypt, as compensation for his un-rewarded service to Yahweh (xxix. 17–21). The day of the Lord, marking Egypt's doom, is at hand. Her army, her people, her idols and her cities shall all suffer alike (xxx. 1–19). In the first month of the eleventh year of his exile Ezekiel predicts that Nebuchadrezzar, who has already broken one arm of Pharaoh (probably an allusion to the failure of the Egyptian army to relieve Jerusalem), shall break the other arm and shall scatter the Egyptians among the nations (xxx. 20–26). In the third month of the eleventh year of his exile Ezekiel predicts the downfall of Egypt in his allegory of the cedar tree. Pharaoh is likened to a cedar of surpassing height and beauty, fed by deep waters and giving shelter to birds and beasts (xxxi. 1–9). The most ruthless of the nations (i.e. the Babylonians) shall cut it down; all the nations shall forsake its shadow in dismay, and all the living creatures that once found shelter in it shall rest upon the fallen trunk. Its fall will serve as a warning to others not to pride them-selves on their stature and height, for all trees (i.e. all nations) must come at last to the underworld (xxxi. 10–14). The deep waters and Lebanon will mourn for it and all the trees will droop. All the trees (i.e. other dead nations) of the underworld will be comforted to find this mighty cedar sharing their fate. Thus this incomparable tree (i.e. Pharaoh and all his host) shall go down to the underworld, where it will lie dishonoured among men whom the sword has slain (xxxi. 15–18).

In the twelfth month of the twelfth year Ezekiel is bidden to raise a dirge over Pharaoh, king of Egypt. He is compared to a sea-monster which Yahweh will catch in a net and cast upon dry land. In the day of doom darkness shall cover Egypt, and nations shall be appalled at Pharaoh's downfall and shall fear for themselves. The king of Babylon shall lay waste the land and slay both man and beast (xxxii. 1–16). In the twelfth month of the twelfth year Ezekiel is again bidden to utter a dirge over Pharaoh and his multitude. He describes their descent into the underworld and the ironical wel-come which they will receive from the various peoples, who once spread terror on the earth but who now repose in the recesses of the underworld. He and all his multitude shall be among those slain by the sword (xxxii. 17–32).

Chapters xxxiii–xxxix

The responsibility of the prophetic office is impressed upon Ezekiel. He will be held responsible for warning the wicked to give up their evil ways (xxxiii. 1–9). The people are despondent and feel that they are paying the penalty of the sins of the past. The prophet declares that Yahweh desires not the destruction but the conversion of the wicked. The righteous man who commits iniquity shall die, and his former righteousness shall not save him from punishment. The wicked man who repents and does what is lawful and right shall live, and his past sins shall not be remembered against him. Yahweh is just in condemning the righteous man when he sins, and in pardoning the wicked man when he repents. It is, therefore, futile to say that he does not act fairly (xxxiii, 10–20).

In the tenth month of the twelfth year of his exile Ezekiel hears of the fall of Jerusalem and breaks his long silence. The people left in Palestine regard themselves as the children of Abraham and the true heirs of the land. But they shall not possess it because of their sins. They shall die by sword, wild beasts and pestilence, and the land shall be made a desolation (xxxiii. 21–29). The exiles talk about Ezekiel and come to hear his oracles but do not obey them. Yet when the hour comes they will realize that there has been a prophet among them (xxxiii. 30–33).

Ezekiel denounces the shepherds of Israel (i.e. the leaders of Israel). They have neglected their duties so that the sheep (i.e. the people) have been devoured or scattered abroad. Yahweh will take the place of these evil shepherds. He will gather the dispersed sheep (i.e. the exiles) and bring them back to their own pasture land (xxxiv. 1–16). Among the flock there have been strong sheep (i.e. the rich), which have not only eaten the best of the pasture and drunk the clearest water, but have also trampled and fouled what has been left. Yahweh will save the weak sheep and will judge between 'cattle and cattle' (xxxiv. 17–22). Yahweh will appoint a single ruler of the Davidic line to be their earthly shepherd (i.e. instead of a divided kingdom there will be a united kingdom under one ruler). Yahweh will make a covenant of peace with His people; they shall enjoy prosperity and security and none shall make them afraid. They shall learn that they are his people (xxxiv. 23–31).

Ezekiel predicts that Edom will become a perpetual desolation (xxxv) while the mountains of Israel will be cultivated and become more fertile, prosperous and populous than ever before (xxxvi. 1–15).

Israel's dispersion caused Yahweh's power to be doubted and His holy name sullied among the heathen. He will restore her to her own land, not for her own sake but for the sake of His holy name. He will purify the people and give them a new spirit. The land will be blessed with fertility, and the people shall loathe themselves because of their past sins (xxxvi. 16–32). The desolate land shall again be tilled and become like the garden of Eden, the ruined cities shall be rebuilt, and the men shall be as numerous as the flocks of sheep brought to Jerusalem for sacrifice on feast days (xxxvi. 33–38).

Ezekiel sees in a vision a valley full of dry bones. As he gazes at them Yahweh bids him prophesy over them. Accordingly he prophesies. There is a sound of rattling and the bones become bodies clothed with flesh, but they lack life. Once again he prophesies, and the bodies become living men forming 'an exceeding great army'. He now gives the meaning of the vision. The bones represent the exiled people of Israel who are as good as dead and in their graves. Yahweh will bring them forth from the grave and restore them to their own land (xxxvii. 1–14). Ezekiel is bidden to take two sticks and to join them together. The union of the two sticks symbolizes the union of Israel and Judah under a king of the Davidic line. They shall be a cleansed and obedient people and their descendants shall dwell forever in the land. Yahweh will make a covenant of peace with them, and will show the heathen that they are his chosen people by establishing his sanctuary permanently among them (xxxvii. 15–28).

At the end of the age Yahweh will summon Gog with his mighty army to invade the mountains of Israel (xxxviii. 1–9). Gog boasts of his intention to attack a people living in security without walls, bars or gates; the merchants of Sheba and Dedah and the traders of Tarshish hope to win rich spoil (xxxviii. 10–16). But he and his hordes shall be destroyed by sword, pestilence and earthquake, and Yahweh's greatness and holiness shall be made known among the nations (xxxviii. 17–23). So great will be the destruction that the people of Israel will find weapons for use as fuel for seven years (xxxix. 1–10). To cleanse the land from defilement they will spend seven months in burying the dead (xxxix. 11–16). Birds and beasts will feast on the dead bodies of princes and warriors (xxxix. 17–20). Israel will never again doubt the power of Yahweh, and the heathen will understand that she was exiled because of the iniquity of the people (xxxix. 21–24).

The exiles shall be restored to their own land. They will forget the shame of the past and dwell in security for ever, because Yahweh has put His spirit within them (xxxix. 25–29).

Chapters xl–xlviii
Ch. xl. 1–4. On New Year's Day in the twenty-fifth year of his exile Ezekiel is brought in a vision to Jerusalem where he sees a new Temple. He is accompanied by a supernatural guide prepared to take the measurements of the building. He is bidden to tell the people all that he is shown.

A description is now given of the Temple (xl. 5–xliv. 3), its officers and festivals (xliv. 4–xlvi. 24), and the Holy Land with its life-giving river flowing from the Temple (xlvii. 1–12), its boundaries and tribal divisions (xlvii. 13–xlviii. 35).

The Temple (xl. 5–xliv. 3). (a) The outer court with its gateways and chambers (xl. 5–27); (b) the inner court with its gateways and chambers (xl. 28–47); (c) the Temple and its surroundings—the vestibule (xl. 48, 49), the nave and the most holy place (xli. 1–4), the side buildings (xli. 5–11), the building behind the Temple (xli. 12), the general measurements of the Temple (xli. 13–15a), the interior decoration of the Temple (xli. 15b–26); (d) buildings north and south of the Temple for the use of the priests (xlii. 1–14); (e) measurements of the Temple area (xlii. 15–20); (f) Yahweh's return to the Temple (xliii. 1–12); (g) the altar—its dimensions and consecration (xliii. 13–27); (h) the east gate of the outer court by which Yahweh entered to remain permanently closed, but the prince to be allowed to eat within it (xliv. 1–3).

The Officers and Festivals (xliv. 4–xlvi. 24). (a) No foreigner to be admitted to the Temple (xliv. 4–9); (b) menial offices to be discharged by the Levites who had officiated at the high places (xliv. 10–14); (c) priestly function to be confined to the sons of Zadok (xliv. 15, 16); (d) regulations on the dress, habits, duties and revenues of the priests (xliv. 17–31); (e) a consecrated area to be reserved for the Temple, the priests, the Levites, the city and the prince (xlv. 1–8); (f) duties of the prince (xlv. 9); (g) correct weights and measures (xlv. 10–12); (h) dues to be paid to the prince to enable him to provide for the services of the Temple (xlv. 13–17); (i) a day of atonement to ensure the ceremonial purity of the sanctuary to be held twice yearly (xlv. 18–20); (j) the Feast of the Passover and the Feast of Tabernacles to be held on the fourteenth day of the first month and the fifteenth day of the seventh month respectively, each to last a week (xlv. 21–

25); (k) regulations for the prince and the people at the sacrifices on
the Sabbath and new moon days (xlvi. 1–12); (l) the daily burnt
offering (xlvi. 13–15); (m) the prince to be free to give part of his
estate to his sons as a permanent possession, but any gift made to a
courtier to revert to the prince at the year of release; the prince not
to be free to seize any of the land of the common people (xlvi. 16–18);
(n) the chambers reserved for the cooking of the sacrificial offerings
(xlvi. 19–24). The Holy Land (xlvii–xlviii. 35). (a) A river flows from
the Temple eastwards to the Dead Sea. It turns the desert through
which it passes into a paradise and the Dead Sea into a fresh-water
lake, abounding in fish. Only the salt swamps and the marshes in the
neighbourhood of the sea remain unaffected (xlvii. 1–12); (b) the
boundaries of the land (xlvii. 13–20); (c) resident aliens to share in
the allotment of the land (xlvii. 21–23); (d) location of the tribes—
seven tribes to the north of the Temple (xlviii. 1–7) and five to the
south (xlviii. 23–29), with a sacred portion between Judah in the
north and Benjamin in the south for the sanctuary, priests, Levites,
city and prince (xlviii. 8–22); (e) city to have twelve gates named
after the tribes and to bear the name, 'Yahweh is there' (xlviii. 30–35).

PERMANENT INFLUENCE

The book of Ezekiel embodies a noble conception of the Deity. The
prophet, overwhelmed by the thought of the majesty, power and
holiness of Yahweh, stressed His transcendence rather than His love.
His majesty is well brought out in the description of the wonderful
chariot which the prophet saw in the first recorded vision. The four-
winged and four-faced creatures (cherubim), which enclosed the
four-wheeled chariot, faced all ways and possessed the intelligence
of a man, the majesty of a lion, the strength of an ox, and the swiftness of an eagle. In the midst of the creatures a fire gleamed and
flashed out lightning. Above their heads was a platform on which the
semblance of a fiery human form sat enthroned. Round the throne
was a bright halo like a rainbow. The creatures and the wheels
moved harmoniously together, as they were animated by the spirit
of the enthroned Deity and directed by eyes that saw everywhere
and everything. Before the terror and beauty of the vision the prophet
fell upon his face (i).

As regards the power of Yahweh He is depicted as the Lord of
history, the supreme Controller of men and nations. All souls be-

longed to Him (xviii. 4) and He would judge every man according to his ways (xviii. 30, xxxiii. 20). It was He who would destroy Jerusalem (ix), the surrounding nations (xxv–xxxii) and the hordes of Gog (xxxviii–xxxix. 20). Both Israel and the nations would learn to recognize His power. Again and again we come across the words, 'And they (or ye) shall know that I am the Lord' (e.g. vi. 10, xxx. 26). His presence was not confined to the Temple or to Palestine. The people went into exile believing that they were leaving their God behind them, only to find by experience that He was with them in Babylon. Over against the majesty and power of Yahweh the prophet set the wickedness of man. In Yahweh's presence he himself was only a 'son of man' (ii. 1, 3, 6, iii. 1).

Great stress is laid upon the holiness of Yahweh. The prophet's message before the fall of Jerusalem was one of judgement. The sin of Israel was so great that her destruction was inevitable. She was corrupt from her birth, being the offspring of an Amorite father and a Hittite mother (xvi. 3, 45). Throughout her history she had persistently been unfaithful to Yahweh, worshipping Him at the local sanctuaries with the cruel and immoral rites of the Canaanite cults (vi. 3, 4, xx. 27–29), shedding blood (vii. 23, ix. 9), sacrificing children to Molech (xvi. 20, 21, xx. 26, 31, xxiii. 37), showing lack of reverence for holy things (xxii. 8, 26), profaning the Sabbaths (xxii. 8, 26, xxiii. 38), defiling the Temple (xxiii. 38, 39), and seeking alliances with foreign powers and adopting the worship of their gods (xvi. 26, 28, 29, xxiii. 8–10, 11–21). Again and again Yahweh had refrained from punishing her lest His holy name should be profaned in the sight of the nations who might regard her destruction as a sign of His weakness. With the destruction of Jerusalem Ezekiel became a prophet of hope. Yahweh would not allow His holy name to be profaned among the nations. He would restore the exiles both of the Northern and Southern Kingdoms to their native land, and there would be one kingdom under a Davidic prince (xxxvii. 19–25). He would restore Israel not for her sake, but in order to vindicate His holy name throughout the world (xxxvi. 22, 32). In the new Temple of the restored community everything possible was done to preserve His holiness. The Temple was surrounded by a thick wall (xl. 5). The 'most holy place' was protected by an inner and an outer court (xl. 17, 28). No layman could offer sacrifice at the altar (xlvi. 3, 9); the prince had the privilege of providing the material for the sacrifices (xliv. 17, 22–25) but could not enter the inner court (xliv. 3, xlvi. 2, 8, 10–12). Foreigners were to be rigidly excluded from the sacred precincts (xliv. 9). The priestly functions were to be restricted to the descendants of Zadok, that is, to the family which had controlled the Temple worship since the reign of Solomon (xliv. 15; cf. 1 Kgs. ii. 27, 35), while the menial duties were to be performed by the Levites (xliv. 10–14). Priests were to wear holy vestments (xliv. 17, 18) which were to be removed in the outer court lest the contagion of holiness should pass to the people (xlii. 14, xliv. 19). Round the Temple were to be the domains of the priests, Levites and prince, and the city (xlv. 1–8, xlviii. 8–22), and to the south and north of these the territories of the twelve tribes (xlviii. 1–7, 23–29).

By proclaiming his conception of an omnipotent, omniscient, omnipresent and holy God, Ezekiel played an important part in the development of the doctrine of monotheism which was soon to become explicit in the writings of Deutero-Isaiah.

With Ezekiel the individual came into greater prominence. The exiles were saying that they were suffering for the sins of their fathers, quoting the proverb, 'The fathers have eaten sour grapes and the children's teeth are set on edge' (xviii. 2; cf. Jer. xxxi. 29). Like Jeremiah he rejected the proverb and asserted that every man was responsible for his own sins (xviii. 3, 4; cf. Jer. xxxi. 30). The son would not bear the iniquity of the father nor would the father bear the iniquity of the son (xviii. 20). The wicked man, who continued in his wickedness, would die and the righteous man, who continued in his righteousness, would live. If, however, a man repented of his wickedness he would live and none of his transgressions would be remembered against him, for Yahweh had no pleasure in the death of the wicked but desired that he should turn from his wicked ways and live. If, on the other hand, a righteous man committed iniquity, he would die and none of the righteous deeds that he had done would save him (xviii. 21–24). This meant that by a single act a man could break completely with the past; a good man could sin and a bad man repent, and his past, whether good or bad, would not count. By proclaiming the freedom and responsibility of the individual Ezekiel helped not only to strengthen men's faith in the absolute justice of God, but also to make them realize that religion is essentially a personal relationship between man and his Maker.

Stress is laid in the book upon ritual and the Law. Ezekiel believed that religion would find expression in ritual forms and in the observance of the Law. In the restored community there was to be a new

Temple similar to the old one, with a modified sacrificial system and a reformed priesthood. There the people would worship Yahweh in accordance with 'law of the house' (xliii. 12). To the prophet, however, religion meant more than the worship of Yahweh in accordance with a prescribed ritual. Like his predecessors in the prophetic ministry, he taught that Yahweh was a righteous God who required from His worshippers obedience to His moral demands. Throughout the whole course of their history His people had spurned His laws (xx. 23). Among the moral offences which He condemned were adultery (xviii. 6, 11, 15, xxii. 11, xxiii. 37), murder (xviii. 10, xxii. 6, 9, 12, 27, xxiii. 37), robbery (xviii. 7, 12, 16, xxii. 29, xxxiii. 15), and the oppression of the poor and the helpless (xviii. 7, 12, 16, 18, xxii. 7, 29). The prophet made no distinction between moral and ritual offences. It was equally wrong to commit murder or to eat forbidden food. He tells us that from his youth he himself had strictly observed the food laws, 'Then said I, Ah Lord God! behold, my soul hath not been polluted: for from my youth up even till now have I not eaten of that which dieth of itself, or is torn of beasts; neither came there abominable flesh into my mouth' (iv. 14). Yahweh would restore His people to their own land, cleanse them from all filthiness and give them a new heart and a new spirit, and make them live by His laws (xxxvi. 25–27; cf. xi. 19, 20). They were to come into His sanctuary with clean hands and a pure heart and there worship Him in accordance with the prescribed ritual. Because of his transcendal conception of God, his dogma of individual retribution and his enthusiasm for ritual and the Law, Ezekiel is sometimes called the 'father' of post-exilic Judaism.

Ezekiel's ideal undoubtedly shows a decline from the spirituality of the earlier prophets, but it should be remembered that the average Israelite could not conceive of religion as something essentially spiritual, and that if the religion of Yahweh was to survive it had to be expressed in concrete forms which the mass of the people could understand. Without Ezekiel with his insistence upon external forms in religion and upon the strict observance of the Law, Israel might have succumbed to the heathen onslaughts in the second century BC.

The book contains elements of a type of literature which, because of its claim to reveal the hidden things of the future, is called Apocalyptic. Its essential features are symbolism, the catastrophic intervention of Yahweh in History, the destruction of the hostile heathen powers, and the establishment of a universal kingdom of peace and righteousness, with its centre at Jerusalem, Yahweh as its supreme ruler, and a Davidic king as His viceroy. In the description of his visions Ezekiel uses strange symbolism. He believes that Yahweh will raise the dead nation to life, gather the scattered exiles, restore them to their native land, and give them peace, prosperity and security under a ruler of the Davidic line. 'And I will set up one shepherd over them, and he shall feed them, even my servant David; he shall feed them, and he shall be their shepherd. . . . And I will make them and the places round about my hill a blessing; and I will cause the shower to come down in its season; there shall be showers of blessing. And the tree of the field shall yield its fruit, and the earth shall yield her increase, and they shall be secure in their land' (xxxiv. 23–27; cf. xxxvi. 34, 35). But the heathen nations will be destroyed (xxxviii–xxxix. 22). The description of the new Jerusalem and the life-giving river flowing out from the Temple, bringing life and fruitfulness to the desert, and whose leaves were for the healing of the nations (xlvii. 1–12) influenced later writers, especially the authors of 'Daniel' and 'The Revelation'.

From the critical point of view the book is of great importance. Chapters xl–xlvii stand mid-way between the Deuteronomic Code and the Priestly Code. This is especially seen in the laws referring to the priests and the Levites. In the Deuteronomic Code no distinction is made between them; any member of the tribe of Levi could exercise the priestly functions (xviii. 6–8). The phrase frequently used was 'the priests the Levites' (e.g. xviii. 1). In the book of Ezekiel the Levites, who had taken part in the idolatrous worship at the high places, were to be deprived of their rights and condemned to perform the menial duties of the sanctuary, while the priestly functions were to be exercised by the sons of Zadok who had remained faithful to Yahweh (xliv. 15, 16). In the Priestly Code the priestly functions were to be exercised by all the sons of Aaron and the Levites were to be their assistants, performing subordinate duties (Num. iii. 5–10, xviii. 1–7). The natural inference is that the Priestly Code is later than chs. xl–xlviii of the book of Ezekiel and is partly based upon them.

STYLE

Ezekiel cannot be reckoned among the great stylists in Hebrew literature. He wrote both prose and poetry, mostly the former, but in neither medium did he produce anything possessing outstanding literary merit. His poetry is superior to his prose. The former at its best is simple, clear and vivid, and is at times infused with intense passion, while the latter, though it occasionally rises into eloquence, is for the most part dull, repetitious and often obscure. A careful study of his work reveals several serious faults. He uses many peculiar words, while certain stereotyped phrases such as 'son of man' (e.g. ii. 1, 3, iii. 1, 3, 4), 'mountains of Israel' (e.g. vi. 2, 3, xxxiv. 13, 14), 'to pour out my fury upon' (e.g. vii. 8, xx. 8, 13, 21) and 'to disperse among the nations' (e.g. xii. 15, xx. 23) occur with monotonous frequency. He is fond of artificial forms of composition, especially symbol and allegory, which are often over-elaborated (xvi, xxiii, xxxvii. 1–14). He undoubtedly has the imagination of a poet, as may be seen from his graphic descriptions of the fate of the princes of Judah (xix. 1–9), the downfall of Tyre (xxvii. 3b–9a, 25b–36), and the valley full of dry bones (xxxvii. 1–14). He failed, however, to curb the exuberance of his fancy. His work abounds in imagery, but it is often of a strange and fantastic kind, and is sometimes distasteful, at least to western minds (e.g. xvi, xxiii).

CHAPTER XV

Isaiah xl–lv

AUTHORSHIP AND DATE

Chapters xl–lv of the book of Isaiah are generally called the Second Isaiah or Deutero-Isaiah. It is now almost universally recognized that they are not the work of Isaiah, who lived in the latter part of the eighth century BC, but that of a later prophet. The evidence on which this theory is based is as follows:

(1) In chs. i–xxxix the prophet's name and his acts are frequently mentioned, whereas in chs. xl–lv no name is mentioned and no account of the author's acts is given.

(2) The historical background of chs. i–xxxix is the latter part of the eighth century BC when the two kingdoms, Judah and Israel, are still in existence (Israel fell in 722 BC) and when the dominant power is Assyria. That of chs. xl–lv is the exilic period. The two kingdoms have disappeared (Judah fell in 587 BC) and the dominant power is Babylon (xlvii). The Jews are in exile in Babylon (xlii. 24, 25, xlvii. 5, 6), Jerusalem and the cities of Judah are in ruins but are going to be rebuilt (xliv. 26, 28, xlv. 13, xlix. 14–21, li. 3, lii. 2, 9). Babylon will be overthrown (xliii. 14, xlvi. 1, 2, xlvii. 1–5, xlviii. 14). The Jews will return to their homeland (xl. 9–11, xlvi. 13, xlviii. 20, li. 11). Cyrus is twice mentioned (xliv. 28, xlv. 1) and is clearly referred to in other passages (xli. 2, 25, xlv. 13, xlvi. 11, xlviii. 15).

One must allow that it is possible for a prophet, inspired by God, to predict events long before they happen. Isaiah, for example, predicted the coming of the Assyrians and Jeremiah the rise of the Chaldeans, but such predictions are always closely related to contemporary events, and even then precise details are not given. It is extremely unlikely and without precedent in Hebrew prophecy that Isaiah, living in the latter part of the eighth century BC, should have predicted in detail events that were going to take place about 150 years later.

H

(3) The theological conceptions of the two sections are different. In the genuine Isaianic passages of chs. i–xxxix monotheism is implicit, whereas in chs. xl–lv it is explicit and absolute. Greater stress is laid upon the infinite power of Yahweh. He is the Creator of the Universe, the Author of Life, the Ruler of History and the Redeemer of Israel. Greater stress is also laid upon the powerlessness of idols and of those who worship them. The doctrine of the Remnant, which is one of the most characteristic doctrines of chs. i–xxxix, occupies a very subordinate place in chs. xl–lv.

(4) The style of the genuine Isaianic passages in chs. i–xxxix is different from that of chs. xl–lv. Isaiah's style is forceful and compact while that of chs. xl–lv is eloquent, profuse, repetitious and often lyrical. There are also marked differences in phraseology between the two sections. Many words and phrases are frequently employed in the genuine Isaianic passages of chs. i–xxxix, which appear seldom or not at all in chs. xl–lv, and new words and phrases appear instead.

The evidence points emphatically to the conclusions that chs. xl–lv were composed by an unknown prophet towards the close of the Exile (c. 548–538 BC). Torrey denies the exilic origin of all the chapters, assigns chs. xl–lxvi, together with chs. xxxiv, xxxv, to about 400 BC and claims that the references to Cyrus, Babylon and the Chaldeans are interpolations in the text. This view has won little support.[1]

UNITY

Opinions differ regarding the unity of chs. xl–lv. It is usual to divide them into two parts, namely, chs. xl–xlviii dealing mainly with Israel's approaching deliverance, the mission of Cyrus and the prediction of Babylon's downfall, and chs. xlix–lv in which the chief topics are the restoration of Israel, and the prediction of her future glory. It has been suggested that chs. xlix–lv were written after the return to Palestine, but since the release of the exiles is still represented as being in the future (li. 11, lii. 11, 12, lv. 12, 13) it is more likely that they were written before the Return. According to a tradition preserved in the book of Ezra (vi. 1, 2), the edict for the rebuilding of the Temple was issued at Ecbatana the Median capital, implying that it was issued some time after the fall of Babylon. The

[1] C. C. Torrey, *The Second Isaiah*, 1928.

chapters, therefore, could have been written in the interval between the fall of the city and the issuing of the edict at Ecbatana.

Many critics do not agree with this two-fold division of the chapters. They hold that they consist of a large number of small units, many of them not more than a verse or two in length, composed by a single author, and arranged without any strict logical order. Gressmann finds forty-nine such units, Mowinckel forty-one (excluding the 'Servant Songs') and Volz forty, excluding the 'Servant Songs'. Others again reject the 'small unit' theory, arguing that the chapters have been arranged according to a definite literary pattern, and that the number of separate units is probably less than ten.

Controversy has raged over the authorship of the 'Servant Songs' (xlii. 1–4, xlix. 1–6, l. 4–9, lii. 13–liii. 12). It has been suggested that (1) they come from the hand of the author of the rest of Deutero-Isaiah; (2) they are the work of another prophet who wrote in the early years of the Exile, and that they were taken over by the author of Deutero-Isaiah and incorporated by him in his work; and (3) they were written in the post-exilic period by a later writer, and that they were inserted by an editor at suitable places in Deutero-Isaiah.

CONTENTS

Chapters xl–lv may be divided into two parts.

(1) Chs. xl–xlviii. Israel's approaching deliverance, the mission of Cyrus, the fall of Babylon, the inculcation of monotheism and the denunciation of idolatry.

(2) Chs. xlix–lv. The restoration of Israel and her future glory.

The two parts may be summarized as follows:

Chapters xl–xlviii
Ch. xl. Yahweh bids the prophet and others proclaim to Jerusalem that her bond-service is over and her guilt pardoned (vv. 1, 2). A voice is heard commanding that a way be made across the desert for Yahweh (vv. 3–5). Another voice proclaims that man and his power are transitory but that the word of the God of Israel shall endure for ever (vv. 6–8). Zion's heralds are commanded to announce to the cities of Judah the triumphal approach of Yahweh with his ransomed people (vv. 9–11). He is the all-mighty and the all-wise Creator (vv. 12–14); before him all the nations are as nothing (vv. 15–17). He

cannot be represented by the work of men's hands (vv. 18–20). He rules Nature and History and marshals the hosts of heaven (vv. 21–26). He is a God of tireless energy, who renews the strength of all those who wait upon Him (vv. 27–31).

Verses 6–8 break the connection between vv. 5 and 9 and should probably come immediately after v. 11.

Ch. xli. The nations are summoned into the presence of Yahweh, who tells them that He has raised up Cyrus from the east (vv. 1–4). In their alarm the nations make new idols to reassure themselves against the advance of the conqueror (vv. 5–7). Israel, the chosen people of Yahweh, has nothing to fear; she shall crush and scatter her foes, and water and vegetation shall be miraculously provided for her in the desert (vv. 8–20). Yahweh challenges the idols to prove their divinity by giving any instance of their power to predict or any proof of life and activity; but they cannot (vv. 21–24). He has raised up Cyrus and announced it beforehand, but none of the heathen gods had foreseen the event (vv. 25–29).

Some critics remove vv. 6 and 7 to a position immediately after ch. xl. 19 and delete v. 5 as an attempt to connect these verses with vv. 1–4.

Ch. xlii. The first Servant Song (vv. 1–4; see p. 232). Yahweh has called His servant to bring the nations into a covenant with Himself and to release them from spiritual bondage (vv. 5–9). The whole earth is summoned to praise Yahweh who is about to attack His enemies: He will lay waste their lands, but will bring the exiles home and overwhelm the idolaters with shame (vv. 10–17). He rebukes Israel for failing to see His hand in her misfortunes and to profit by the chastisement (vv. 18–25).

Ch. xliii. Yahweh assures Israel that He will redeem her, compensating her conqueror (Cyrus) with the gift of Egypt, Ethiopia and Seba. He will gather the scattered members of Israel and bring them home (vv. 1–7). Israel can bear witness to the fact that He has given proof of His divinity by predicting this great deliverance (vv. 8–13). He will destroy Babylon and deliver Israel. The glory of her deliverance will be more wonderful than the Exodus from Egypt (vv. 14–21). Israel has been indifferent to Him, burdening Him not with lavish offerings but with her sins, yet He will forgive her freely. Jacob and the prophets sinned against Him and desecrated His sanctuary; therefore He gave Jacob to the ban and made Israel a by-word (vv. 22–28).

Ch. xliv. 1–23. Yahweh promises Israel that He will pour out His spirit upon her and cause her to prosper, and that foreigners will attach themselves as proselytes to her (vv. 1–5). He is the only true God and predicted the future truly, as they can testify (vv. 6–8); but other gods are but images of wood and metal (vv. 9–20). He entreats Israel to return to Him and calls on heaven and earth to celebrate her redemption (vv. 21–23).

Many critics regard the passage (vv. 9–20) as an interpolation, on the ground that (1) it breaks the connection between vv. 6–8 and 21; (2) its language and style are unlike anything else in the prophecy; (3) its cold didactic aim and prosaic love of detail are foreign to the genius of the author of Deutero-Isaiah. These reasons, though cogent, are not decisive.

Ch. xliv. 24–xlv. 25. Yahweh, the Redeemer of Israel and the Creator of all things, has decreed the restoration of Jerusalem, the Temple, and the cities of Judah through His servant Cyrus, whom He has called not for his own sake, but Israel's. He will gird Him with strength, that men throughout the world may recognize that He is the one true God (xliv. 24–xlv. 8). The prophet rebukes those who refuse to believe that He will work through a foreigner; they are like clay that would instruct the potter. Yahweh has commissioned Cyrus to rebuild Jerusalem and set the exiles free (xlv. 9–13). Captives from Africa shall pass before Israel (or Cyrus) as tributaries and slaves, and acknowledge Him as the only saving Deity (xlv. 14–17). He has sworn that all mankind shall worship Him (xlv. 18–25).

Ch. xlvi. The prophet, sure of the coming downfall of Babylon, pictures its gods, Bel and Nebo, being carried into safety before the approaching conqueror. But Yahweh has carried His people from their birth and will carry them to the end (vv. 1–4). A god, made of precious metal, is powerless to move from its pedestal (vv. 5–7). The apostate Jews are bidden to remember the former predictions of Yahweh which have been fulfilled, thus proving His power to carry out His purpose. He is the only true God and is bringing Cyrus to execute His plan. Yahweh announces to the opponents of His purpose the speedy deliverance of Israel (vv. 8–13).

Ch. xlvii. The chapter is a taunt-song on the approaching fall of Babylon. The city is personified as a voluptuous and tenderly-nurtured lady who shall be degraded to the status of the meanest slave (vv. 1–4). She shall no more be called 'The lady of kingdoms', but shall go into captivity because she showed no mercy to the people of Yahweh (vv. 5–7). She thinks herself immune from disaster but sudden destruction shall come upon her in spite of her sorceries and enchantments (vv. 8–12). Her astrologers, with their monthly calendars of lucky and unlucky days, shall not save her or themselves from the flames. Her merchants shall scatter and she shall be left to her fate (vv. 13–15).

There is so much dispute about the metre of this song that critics are inclined to think that the text of the poem has not been preserved in its regular form.

Ch. xlviii. Yahweh rebukes the people for their inveterate obstinacy, apostasy and persistent idolatry. He predicted in advance the events that have taken place that Israel might not be able to attribute them to the false gods. He has refined Israel in the furnace of affliction and will now save her for the sake of His own honour (vv. 1–11). Yahweh announces the conquest of Babylon by Cyrus (vv. 12–16). If only Israel had obeyed Him she would have enjoyed perpetual peace and prosperity beyond measure (vv. 17–19). The exiles are exhorted to depart from Babylon to proclaim to the ends of the earth that Yahweh has redeemed His people, repeating the wonders of the Exodus (vv. 20–22).

Verse 22 is taken from ch. lvii. 21 where it seems to be in its proper place. It is added here by an editor, probably to mark the end of a section.

Chapters xlix–lv

Ch. xlix. 1–13. The second Servant Song (xlix. 1–6; see p. 233), Yahweh promises Israel, now scorned and oppressed, that He will restore her to her native land, leading her, like a shepherd, along a way miraculously prepared for her over mountain and plain (vv. 7–12). Let heaven and earth rejoice that He has comforted His people (v. 13).

Chs. xlix. 14–l. 3. Zion laments that Yahweh has forsaken her, but He affirms His love for her and promises a large increase in her population (xlix. 14–21). At a sign from Yahweh the nations shall bring back the exiles to Zion, and kings and queens shall tend them and do abject homage to them (xlix. 22, 23). Yahweh shall fight their battles and their oppressors shall destroy themselves by civil war (xlix. 24–26). Yahweh has not divorced His bride, Israel. He has banished her because of her iniquities but He will redeem her. The Exodus and the crossing of Jordan prove that He has the power to do this (l. 1–3).

Ch. l. 4–11. The third Servant Song (vv. 4–9; see p. 233). The pious

Jews are exhorted to listen to the voice of the Servant and to trust in Yahweh. Those who kindle the flames of persecution and strife shall become the victims of their own fire (vv. 10, 11).

Ch. li. 1–16. Yahweh bids His people consider their origin. Abraham was one but He blessed him with many descendants. He shall console Zion and make her waste places as fruitful as Eden (vv. 1–3). Instruction in the true religion shall go forth to all nations. Though heaven and earth should pass away and men perish like gnats His salvation shall be eternal. The oppressors of His people shall vanish like moth-eaten garments (vv. 4–8). Yahweh is entreated to manifest His power as He did at Creation and at the Exodus. The exiles shall return with singing to Zion (vv. 9–11). Yahweh reproaches Israel for her fear of her oppressors and for her forgetfulness of Him who made heaven and earth. Soon the exiles shall be set free, for Yahweh is their God (vv. 12–16).

Verse 11 is almost identical with ch. xxxv. 10, whence it must have been transferred by a scribe.

Ch. li. 17–lii. 12. The prophet pictures Jerusalem as a woman who has been compelled to drink the cup of Yahweh's wrath, which has left her staggering. But she is assured that the cup shall be taken from her and given to her enemies (li. 17–23). Zion is exhorted to put on her garments of beauty for pagans and profane men shall never again enter her (lii. 1, 2). She shall be freed without any payment, and in the day of deliverance shall learn what His name means (lii. 3–6). The prophet, in imagination, sees the messengers hastening over the hills of Judah with tidings of Israel's deliverance, and hears the watchmen on the walls of Zion joyfully announcing the approach of Yahweh to reign over His people (lii. 7, 8). He calls upon the waste places of Jerusalem to break forth into singing and summons the exiles to leave Babylon (lii. 9–12).

Ch. lii. 3–6 is written in prose and differs in style from that of the context. Many critics regard the passage as a later insertion.

Ch. lii. 13–liii. The Fourth Servant Song (see p. 233).

Ch. liv. Zion, addressed as a woman separated from her husband, is comforted with the assurance that her children shall become more numerous than ever before. Her shame has been forgotten for Yahweh has called her to Him. His kindness and covenant of favour and friendship shall be more enduring than the mountains (vv. 1–10). Jerusalem shall be built in great magnificence; her citizens shall all be disciples of Yahweh; she shall enjoy perfect peace and shall have no need to fear oppression or terror. No weapon forged against her shall prosper and no false accusation brought against her shall meet with success (vv. 11–17).

Ch. lv. The prophet, addressing those who are absorbed in business in Babylon, appeals to them to take advantage of the spiritual nourishment freely provided and permanently satisfying. Yahweh will make an everlasting covenant with them, transferring to them the mercies which He promised faithfully to David. As David by his conquests had been a witness to Yahweh's power, so Israel by her restoration shall be a witness to His power, thereby bringing many a nation, hitherto unknown to her, to a knowledge of Himself (vv. 1–5). Yahweh appeals to the people to seek Him while He is near and while they may obtain pardon through repentance. His thoughts transcend those of men as much as the heavens are higher than the earth. As the rain and snow make the earth fruitful, so shall His word go forth and accomplish His purpose. He shall lead forth the joyful exiles from Babylon; the desert route shall be transformed and be a memorial to His praise (vv. 6–13).

THE SERVANT SONGS

There are four passages in Deutero-Isaiah which are known as the 'Servant Songs' because in them we find a striking conception of the Servant of Yahweh. There is no agreement as to the precise delimitation of these songs but they are usually given as chs. xlii. 1–4, xlix. 1–6, l. 4–9, lii. 13–liii. 12.

Contents

The passages may be paraphrased thus:

Ch. xlii. 1–4. Yahweh bids the nations consider His Servant, whom He has chosen and endowed with His spirit that he may carry the true religion to the nations. He shall make no clamour, not crushing a broken reed or quenching a dimly-burning wick. He shall set forth true religion faithfully. He shall not fail nor be discouraged until he has established the true religion in the earth; and the far lands shall wait with eager expectation for His coming.

In v. 1 the Septuagint reads 'Jacob my servant' and 'Israel my chosen', thus showing that ancient readers identified the Servant with the nation. Some scholars include vv. 5–9 in the Song while others regard them as a separate Servant Song.

Ch. xlix. 1–6. The Servant, speaking to the nations, tells them that Yahweh called him from his birth, made him His servant, gave him a penetrating message, and kept him in instant readiness. He affirms that his past labours have been fruitless, but that he is content to leave his reward to the justice of Yahweh. Yahweh replies that the task of restoring the survivors of Israel is too slight a service for him, and He will therefore make him a light to the Gentiles that His salvation may reach to the end of the earth.

Some scholars include vv. 7–9 in the Servant Song while others treat vv. 7–13 as a separate Song.

Ch. l. 4–9. The Servant declares that Yahweh has given him a trained tongue that he may rightly answer the ungodly. Every morning He instructs him and he has never disobeyed Him or shrunk from the tasks imposed upon him. He has submitted without complaint to ill-treatment and personal indignity. Through Yahweh's help he has not been overwhelmed; he is determined to be true to His message, confident that he will never be put to shame. Yahweh will vindicate him in the end and his adversaries shall perish like a moth-eaten garment.

Some scholars include vv. 10–11 in the Song.

Chs. lii. 13–liii. 12. Yahweh announces that His Servant shall prosper and be exalted. Even as many as were appalled at his pitiable sight—he was so disfigured that he scarcely seemed human—so shall many nations and kings stand in silent awe in his presence, for in his exaltation they shall see an event the like of which has never been known (lii. 13–15). The heathen nations (or the Jews) affirm that it was an incredible report that reached them. Only those to whom the divine purpose had been revealed could have believed it. The Servant grew up before them like a sapling, like a shoot springing from the dry soil. He had no beauty to attract their eyes and no charm to make them choose him. He was despised and shunned by men, a man of pain, who knew what sickness was, so that men turned from him with shuddering and paid him no regard (liii. 1–3). But now they recognize that when they thought that he was smitten by the hand of God, it was their griefs and sorrows that he bore. It was their sins that crushed him; it was for their welfare that he suffered chastisement. The blows that fell upon him have brought them healing. They had wandered as sheep without a shepherd, but on him Yahweh had laid the sins of them all (liii. 4–6). He was harshly treated though he humbled himself and never complained; he was dumb as a sheep led to the slaughter and as a ewe before the shearers. He was put to death unjustly and none heeded how he fell; he was cut off from the land of the living and struck down for their rebelliousness. They laid him in a felon's grave and buried him with criminals, although he had done no violence and had not uttered one false word (liii. 7–9). Yet it pleased Yahweh to crush him with sickness. When he shall make an offering for sin, he shall have many children and enjoy long life, and the purpose of Yahweh shall prosper in his hand. When he sees the result of all that he has endured, he shall see light and be satisfied with his knowledge. He shall make many righteous and bear their iniquities. Therefore he shall win victory and succeed triumphantly, because he shed his life-blood and let himself be numbered among the rebellious, when all the time he was bearing the sins of the world and interceding for rebellious men (liii. 10–12).

The words 'his visage was so marred more than any man, and his form more than the sons of men' (v. 14) are bracketed in the Revised Version. It is probable that they should follow ch. liii. 2. In vv. 10–12 the idea of a resurrection from the dead seems to be necessarily implied. Verses 10, 11 are obscure and there is reason to suspect that the text is corrupt.

INTERPRETATION

From the days of Deutero-Isaiah down to the present day the question has been asked, 'Who is the Suffering Servant?' In pre-Christian times there were differences of opinion among the Jews regarding his identification. Some identified him with the nation, some with the pious minority of the nation, and others with the Messiah, though they did not picture him as represented in ch. liii since the idea of a suffering Messiah was foreign to them. In time, however, the view gradually prevailed that the Suffering Servant was the nation; and this view still prevails among them.

Turning to the Christian Church, we find that from the very beginning ch. liii was interpreted as a prophecy of Christ (Acts viii. 26–39; 1 Cor. xv. 3; 1 Pet. ii. 21–25). There seems no reason to doubt that Christ identified Himself with the Suffering Servant of Yahweh as portrayed in the passages, Mk. x. 45; Lk. xxii. 37, xxiv. 45–47. Until the end of the eighteenth century this view was almost universally accepted; but today it has few supporters, because, with the advent of the critical approach to the Old Testament, it was recognized that Isaiah xl–lv was not the work of the prophet Isaiah who lived in the eighth century BC, but of the exilic prophet in Babylon, and that it was improbable that an eighth-century prophet could have given a detailed account of a character who was not to appear for several centuries. The problem of the identification of the Servant has produced endless discussion but none of the theories put forward has won much support. These theories may be divided into two groups, namely, those in which he is represented as the embodiment of a group, and those in which he is regarded as an individual.

In the first group the original theory was probably that which identified him with the nation. It arose from the fact that Israel is spoken of as Yahweh's servant in contexts quite outside the Servant passages (xli. 8–10, xlii. 18–25, xliv. 1, 2, 21, xlv. 4, xlviii. 20). But the Servant of Yahweh does not, like the servant Israel, suffer for his own sins but for the sins of others, and his patience under suffering (liii. 7) is in marked contrast to the resentment of the servant Israel (xl. 27, xlix. 14, l. 1–3). So obvious was this, that critics began to declare that the Servant of Yahweh represented a righteous remnant of Israel, who bore the transgressions of the rest and restored them to Yahweh. But though it could be metaphorically said that Israel died at the Exile and rose again at the Restoration, it could not be said that the faithful remnant had so died and risen again. Moreover, suffering came to all the exiles; it was not a case of the minority suffering for the rest.

Another theory is based upon the concept of corporate personality, according to which Hebrew thought could pass easily and naturally from the individual to the community. In the light of this conception the Servant can be both the prophet himself and the nation.[1] It is, however, hard to believe that the prophet is thinking of himself in the Servant Songs, especially in the fourth. Moreover, the conception of the character of the Servant in the Songs is different from that of Israel in the main prophecy. Rowley accepts the theory of corporate personality but in a slightly different form. He thinks that the individual portrayed in the Servant Songs, especially in the fourth, is a 'future figure' who, in fulfilling his mission in bringing all men to acknowledge the true religion, will be Israel's representative.[2]

[1] H. W. Robinson, *The Cross of the Servant*, 1926, p. 59; cf. the same writer's *The Old Testament: Its Making and Meaning*, 1937, p. 111.
[2] H. H. Rowley, *The Servant of the Lord*, 1952, p. 54.

We now turn to theories in which he is regarded as an individual. Jehoiachin has actually been put forward on the strength of his imprisonment followed by his release and recognition as a royal personage. It is sufficient to say that he could never have done what the Suffering Servant is said to have done or have been the least likely to do it. A halting attempt has been made to put forward Jeremiah, presumably at least to obtain a respectable character; but the end of his career puts him out of the question. Another person who has been put forward is Moses, on the ground that he was murdered by his own countrymen who were so ashamed of their action that they suppressed the story. This theory can be rejected at once, since there is no evidence to prove that Moses suffered martyrdom. More recently the prophet himself has been proposed, but it is difficult to accept the view, since we should have to suppose that he wrote an account of his own death and resurrection. Some critics try to get over the difficulty by supposing that the fourth Song belongs to a much later age. The Servant has also been identified with the Messianic king of the line of David. This theory seems quite improbable since the Servant is not thought of as a king but as a sufferer. It has been suggested that the sufferings of the Servant are related to the ritual sufferings or penances which the Davidic king had to undergo at the New Year Festival. 'The fact is that we are here dealing with a ritual humiliation of the Davidic king which in principle is not unlike that suffered by the Babylonian king in the analogous New Year Festival.'[1] This theory rests on little more than conjecture.

A mythological interpretation has been given to the Servant Songs. It has been maintained that ch. liii is to be interpreted in terms of the Tammuz cult, and that it is based on one of the ritual songs of the dying and rising god. But against this view it may be argued that Tammuz was a nature god and that his death had no atoning significance. Moreover, it is very unlikely that the author of the Songs would have used a ritual song of a god for his purpose, since he was absolutely convinced that Yahweh was the only true God and that idols were nothing but useless pieces of wood and metal.

We arrive, therefore, at the conclusion that the Servant cannot be identified with any group or any historical individual contemporary

---

[1] A. R. Johnson, 'The Role of the King in the Jerusalem Cultus', in *The Labyrinth*, edited by S. H. Hooke, 1935, p. 100.

with the author or of an earlier age, or with any mythological figure. All we can say is that in Christ we find the perfect expression of the conception of the Suffering Servant.

PERMANENT INFLUENCE

In Deutero-Isaiah we find the noblest conception of the Deity to be found in the whole range of prophecy. To encourage the exiles in Babylon, who had lost faith in the power of their God to protect and deliver them, the author proclaims the inconceivable greatness of Yahweh. He has 'made the earth, and created man upon it' (xlv. 12). He has 'measured the waters in the hollow of his hand, and meted out heaven with the span, and comprehended the dust of the earth in a measure, and weighed the mountains in scales, and the hills in a balance' (xl. 12). He gives breath to the people on the earth 'and spirit to them that walk therein' (xlii. 5). Compared with Him man and nations are nothing. He 'sitteth upon the circle of the earth, and the inhabitants thereof are as grasshoppers' (xl. 22). 'The nations are as a drop of a bucket, and are counted as the small dust of the balance' (xl. 15). Men and nations are under His control. 'Behold I have created the smith that bloweth the fire of coals, and bringeth forth a weapon for his work; and I have created the waster to destroy. No weapon that is formed against thee shall prosper; and every tongue that shall rise against thee in judgement thou shalt condemn' (liv. 16, 17). He brings princes to nothing and makes the judges of the earth as vanity (xl. 23). He has called Cyrus, the king of Persia, to execute His purpose. The king shall build His city and let His exiles go free 'not for price nor reward, saith the Lord of hosts' (xlv. 13). He is 'a just God and a saviour' (xlv. 21), and there is none other who can save (xliii. 11). He is the redeemer of Israel (xli. 14, xliii. 1, xliv. 6) and offers His salvation to all nations (xlv. 22, 23, li. 4–6). He is a God of love. When He delivers His people He will comfort them (xl. 1, xlix. 13, li. 3, 12, 19) and lead them gently, as a shepherd caring for his flock (xl. 11, xlix. 9–13), and pardon their sins (xliii. 25).

In Deutero-Isaiah the two great doctrines, namely monotheism and universalism, are proclaimed. Monotheism is implicit in the teaching of the pre-exilic prophets from the days of Amos, but here it is fully and explicitly stated. Yahweh is the one and only God. 'Thus saith the Lord, the king of Israel, and his redeemer the Lord of hosts: I am the first, and I am the last; and beside me there is no

God' (xliv. 6; cf. xlv. 5, 6, 14, 21, 22). The reality of idols is denied (xl. 19, 20, xli. 7, xlvi. 5–7) and scorn is poured upon the man who makes an idol of one part of a tree and worships it, and uses another part to kindle a fire to cook his food and to warm himself (xliv. 9–20). The doctrine of monotheism, so clearly stated in Deutero-Isaiah, is of supreme importance for it is the fundamental doctrine of Judaism, Christianity and Islam.

If Yahweh is the one and only God, it naturally follows that He must be the God of all men. Hence the author proclaims the doctrine of universalism. The election of Israel is not merely a privilege but also a service. Yahweh has chosen her that she may carry the true religion to the nations. 'I the Lord have called thee in righteousness, and will hold thine hand, and will keep thee, and give thee for a covenant of the people, for a light of the Gentiles; to open the blind eyes, to bring out the prisoners from the dungeon, and them that sit in darkness out of the prison house' (xlii. 6, 7). Yahweh has sworn that unto Him 'every knee shall bow and every tongue shall swear' (xlv. 23). Israel's mission to the nations is to be fulfilled, not so much by active propaganda as by bearing witness to the truth of Yahweh's divinity, and by proving that He has the power to restore His people in accordance with His predictions, and that there is no God beside Him (xliii. 10–12, xliv. 8).

Deutero-Isaiah contains the conception of the Servant of Yahweh whose mission it is to convert the nations through his own endurance and undeserved suffering. In this conception the Old Testament makes its chief contribution to the problem of human suffering. The conception of redemption through suffering does not solve the problem, but it does in some measure lighten the burden of the mystery by opening our eyes to the truth that voluntary suffering, resulting from the wrong-doing of those whom the sufferer loves, can lead to repentance, when punishment has no effect. The conception has exercised a profound influence on the Christian faith. Our Lord identified Himself with the Suffering Servant (Mk. viii. 31, x. 45) and Christians have found in Him the complete fulfilment of the prophecy.

Finally, in dark days Deutero-Isaiah, with its message of hope and encouragement, and its promise of deliverance and of the glorious future that awaits the people of God, has been a source of comfort and inspiration to both Jews and Christians throughout the ages.

STYLE

The author of chs. xl–lv is not only a prophet but also a poet of the first rank. The chapters are written almost entirely in poetic form, and contain but few ideas which are repeated again and again, with the result that at times the writing tends to become somewhat monotonous.

The style of the writing is eloquent, profuse and flowing and for the most part easy to understand. At times it rises to the level of the sublime (xl. 12–31, lii. 7–12, liv. 11–14). The author has a remarkable lyrical gift. The contemplation of the Creation or of Israel's redemption rouses within him the desire to break forth into songs of praise (xlii. 10–13, xliv. 23, xlv. 8, xlix. 13). So lost is he in wonder at the thought of the power, the wisdom and the love of Yahweh, that he calls not only the redeemed of Israel, but also upon inanimate nature to sing His praise and glorify His name. At the thought of the sufferings of his exiled brethren he is moved with compassion, and produces some of the tenderest passages to be found in the whole of Scripture (xliii. 1–4, xliv. 21–22, xlix. 14–16, liv. 5–8). So great is his faith in Yahweh, that he never doubts that He will carry out His purpose for Israel. If the present is dark, the future for him is bright with hope. He looks forward to the time when the blind shall see and the deaf hear, when the faint shall receive power, and when 'the crooked shall be made straight and the rough places plain, and the glory of the Lord shall be revealed' (xl. 5).

Another feature of the style is its dramatic quality. Some of the episodes described, such as the council in heaven (xl. 1–11), the downfall of the gods of Babylon (xlvi. 1–13) and the triumphal return of Yahweh to Zion (lii. 7–12) are intensely dramatic.

Turning to the specific features of the style, we find that great use is made of figures of speech. The author personifies cities (xlvii. 5, lii. 1), the points of the compass (xliii. 6) and Nature (xliv. 23, xlix. 13, lv. 12). Throughout the various chapters of the book are scattered numerous similes (xl. 11, 22, liii. 2) and metaphors (xl. 6, xli. 15, xlix. 6). Effective use is made of the rhetorical question (xl. 18, xlviii. 14, lv. 2) and climax (xl. 28–31, lii. 7). The reader's interest is stimulated and maintained by the frequent use of the imperative (xl. 1, xlv. 21, lv. 1), contrast (xl. 15, 22, xli. 14, 15, xlii. 15, lv. 13), and repetition (xl. 1, xli. 27, xliii. 11, 25, xlviii. 11, 15, li. 9, 12, 17, lii. 1, 11).

Note

Reasons for the attachment of chs. xl–lv to the book of Isaiah.

First we have to explain why the name of their real author does not appear. That is easy. Their contents were treasonable; it was unsafe for the author to disclose his identity. Second, we have to explain how the chapters came to be attached to the book of Isaiah. Here we have to face a problem which meets us in connection with practically all the prophetic books, but which has never been explained and probably never will be. Many prophetic utterances were preserved of which the names of the authors were unknown. They were inserted in the writings of known prophets and in course of time came to be treated as part of these writings. In the case of the Minor Prophets more were attached to some than to others; and it is suspected that those prophets to whom more were attached were at one time the last of the then known writers. In any case, the amount which was attached to any prophet bore relation to the length of his genuine work. So large an addition as chs. xl–lv, was too much to add to any of the Minor Prophets; hence it was attached to the first of the Major Prophets (the same is also true of chs. lvi–lxvi). But why the work of unknown writers could not have been preserved separately as such, is a problem of the mentality of the Jewish priesthood, which it is impossible for us with our entirely different outlook to explain.

CHAPTER XVI

Haggai

LIFE AND CHARACTER OF HAGGAI

Nothing is known of Haggai save what we learn from his own brief prophecies and from the allusions to his work in Ezra v. 1 and vi. 14. The period of his activity extended from the beginning of September to the latter part of December, 520 BC. According to a late tradition, he was born in Babylon and was among those who went with Zerubbabel to Jerusalem where he died. Some, however, infer from ch. ii. 3 that he was carried into captivity by Nebuchadrezzar, that he was one of the surviving exiles in Babylon who had seen the first Temple, and that as an old man he returned to Jerusalem. Whether he was born in Babylon or Palestine is not certain, but it is highly probable that he had lived in Babylon, for we infer from ch. ii. 12–14 that he belonged to the circle of priests who during the Exile were engrossed in the study of the Law. There is nothing to prove that the priests were active in Palestine at the time when he delivered his prophecies.

Haggai was a man of unconquerable faith and iron resolution, with a burning zeal for the restoration of the Temple as the centre of the national life, and with the power to rouse men to action. Having succeeded in inducing the leaders, Zerubbabel and Joshua, and the 'remnant of the people' to undertake the work of restoration, he encouraged them with promises that the latter glory of the house would be greater than the former (ii. 9) and that Yahweh would bless them (ii. 19). He was also an ardent nationalist, who proclaimed that Yahweh would destroy the heathen nations and invest Zerubbabel with divine authority (ii. 20–23).

AUTHORSHIP AND DATE

There is no need to doubt the genuineness of the four addresses, though it is unlikely that Haggai is the compiler of the book, since he is consistently referred to in the third person. Moreover, the addresses have the impression of being mere outlines: had the prophet compiled the book he would surely not have been satisfied with such brief summaries. The book is probably the work of a contemporary who has shortened the full addresses given on the stated occasion. There are, however, some who contend that it must be ascribed to Haggai himself, on the assumption that the third person 'He' is used instead of the first person 'I' in order to create a stronger impression of objectivity. It has also been suggested that it is an extract from a historical work on the Temple which would naturally embody the prophecies of Haggai. In any case the prophecies were delivered between September and December in the year 520 BC.

CONTENTS

The book consists of four dated prophecies, all connected with the restoration of the Temple.

(1) Ch. i. 1–15. Exhortation to rebuild the Temple and its effects.

(2) Ch. ii. 1–9. Prophecies of the future glory of the Temple.

(3) Ch. ii. 10–19. Priestly instruction on the contaminating influence of the unclean and the promise of a new era of prosperity.

(4) Ch. ii. 20–23. Prediction of the downfall of the heathen nations and the promise of the Messianic kingship to Zerubbabel.

These four parts may be summarized thus:

Chapter i. 1–15
Ch. i. 1–6. On the first day of the sixth month in the second year of Darius (September 1, 520 BC) Haggai rebukes the people, through their leaders, Zerubbabel, the governor of Judah, and Joshua, the High Priest, for dwelling in their own panelled houses while the Temple lies in ruins. It is no excuse to say that the time has not arrived for them to undertake the work of restoration. Their crops are poor, men are insufficiently fed and clothed, and their wages quickly disappear in providing the merest necessities of life.
Ch. i. 7–15. The prophet urges them to go up to the hill country, procure wood, and build the Temple, in order that Yahweh may take pleasure in it and see Himself honoured. They have expected

great harvests but have had poor ones, and what they have brought
home Yahweh has spoiled. Their calamities are due to the fact that
Yahweh's house still lies in ruins, while everyone takes pleasure in
building and adorning his own house. Hence He has sent a drought
upon the land. On the twenty-fourth day of the same month the
people, encouraged by the prophet's exhortation, begin to work 'in
the house of the Lord of Hosts'.

Chapter ii. 1–9
On the twenty-first day of the seventh month (October 21, 520 BC)
the prophet addresses words of encouragement to those who remember the magnificence of Solomon's Temple, and compare the New
Temple now in course of erection unfavourably with it. He exhorts
them to be strong for Yahweh's spirit is ever present with them. Soon
there will be political convulsions, accompanied by earthquakes, and
the costly treasures of the nations will be brought to adorn the
Temple. The wealth of the world belongs to Yahweh. The future
glory of the sanctuary shall be greater than that of Solomon's
Temple.

Chapter ii. 10–19
Ch. ii. 10–14. On the twenty-fourth day of the ninth month (December 24, 520 BC) the prophet, by eliciting from the priest the information that while a holy thing only makes holy that which it directly
touches, a person, unclean by contact with an unclean object, can
render everything he touches unclean, teaches the people that so
long as the Temple remains unbuilt, they are unclean and their
offerings are unacceptable.
Ch. ii. 15–19. Before a stone was laid upon a stone in Yahweh's
Temple the return from the fields and vineyards had not fulfilled
their expectations. It was because Yahweh had sent the blasting east
wind, mildew and hail to destroy the work of their hands. Now from
the day on which the foundation of Yahweh's Temple has been laid,
even though they may see no sign of the future harvest, Yahweh will
bless them.

Chapter ii. 20–23
On the same day as the preceding exhortation the prophet assures
Zerubbabel that Yahweh will overthrow the heathen nations and
make him 'as a signet', that is, invest him with His authority.

PERMANENT INFLUENCE

Historically the book of Haggai is of great importance for the light it sheds upon the political, economic and religious conditions of the age. We gather that in 520 BC, when Haggai delivered his message, the Jews who had returned from Babylon were under the leadership of the Persian governor, Zerubbabel, who belonged to the house of David, and Joshua, the High Priest (i. 1). It would appear that in the general uprising which followed the death of Cambyses (522 BC), Zerubbabel dreamt of achieving national independence and of the speedy approach of the Messianic Age (ii. 20–23). The people were passing through a time of great hardship. Drought and a succession of poor harvests had brought in their train poverty and starvation (i. 6, 9–11, ii. 15–17). The prices of commodities were so high that the little money they earned vanished quickly as if through holes in a bag (i. 6). A few prospered and built panelled houses for themselves (i. 4), but the people generally were impoverished. So hard was the struggle for existence, that they tended to become wholly immersed in material things to the exclusion of the spiritual. The Temple lay in ruins before their eyes; and in their poverty and bitter disillusionment they concluded that the time had not yet come to undertake the work of restoration (i. 4–6, 9–11). We infer from the absence of any reference to idolatry, gross immorality and social injustice, which had been denounced by the earlier prophets, that these evils had largely disappeared.

Haggai is inferior in originality and spirituality to most of his predecessors in the prophetic ministry. He has nothing new to add to man's conception of the character of God, and has nothing to say about the moral demands of religion, or the national sins and the need of repentance. He is a man of one idea—the restoration of the Temple. Unlike some of the earlier prophets he laid stress upon the externals of religion; to him the Temple and its ritual were essential elements in religion. He declared that the calamities which had fallen upon them were a sign of Yahweh's displeasure, because they had all taken pleasure in building and adorning their own houses but had allowed the Temple to remain a desolate ruin (i. 9–11). During the exile the people had been compelled to worship without a sanctuary, but they had not yet grasped the idea that God did not dwell in temples made with hands. Still to him and to his contemporary Zechariah belongs the credit of stimulating the people to rebuild the

Temple, which played such a vital part in the preservation of their national identity and their religious faith. By insisting upon its restoration he helped to pave the way for the work of Ezra and Nehemiah and must, therefore, be reckoned among the founders of modern Judaism. His dream of the Messianic Age was never realized, but he passed on that dream undimmed to future ages.

STYLE

On the assumption that the book, which is written in prose, consists of shortened versions of Haggai's prophecies, it is obviously impossible to form a true estimate of the prophet as a literary artist, since we have not got his prophecies in the exact form in which they were first delivered. As they have come down to us, they possess no great literary merit. They contain no flights of the imagination, no graphic descriptions and no vivid imagery. The style is simple and unadorned and not without a certain force, though it lacks the intense fervour which we generally associate with the works of the earlier prophets.

CHAPTER XVII

Zechariah i–viii

INTRODUCTION

The book of Zechariah falls into two parts, namely, chs. i–viii and chs. ix–xiv. It is almost universally agreed by modern critics that the second part is not by the same author as the first. The reasons for distinguishing the two parts are as follows:

(1) In chs. i–viii, there are visions and they are all related in the first person, but the headings (i. 1, 7, vii. 1) are in the third person. In chs. ix–xiv there are no visions and the first person is used only in one passage (xi. 4, 5).

(2) In chs. i–viii the prophecies are exactly dated (i. 1, 7, vii. 1) and are said to be the work of Zechariah (i. 1, 7, vii. 1, 8); but in chs. ix–xiv, there are no dates and no ascriptions of authorship, apart from the indefinite title in chs. ix. 1 and xii. 1, namely, 'The burden of the word of the Lord'.

(3) The style of chs. i–viii is markedly different from that of chs. ix–xiv.

(4) The historical situation of chs. i–viii is different from that of chs. ix–xiv. The allusions in chs. i–viii fit exactly the years to which they are assigned, namely, from the second to the fourth year of Darius I. The leaders of the restored community are Zerubbabel (iv. 6, 10) and Joshua (iii. 1, 8), and their chief concern is the rebuilding of the Temple (iv. 9, vi. 15). The people are promised speedy deliverance from their present distress and peace and security in the immediate future (i. 16, 17; ii. 9–11, iii. 10, viii. 1–15). In chs. ix–xiv there is not a single allusion to this period. The leaders of the community are unnamed 'shepherds' (xi. 4–17) and no interest is shown in the restoration of the Temple. War and siege are imminent (ix. 4–6, 8, 13–15, x. 3–7, xi. 1–3, xii. 1–9, xiii. 7–9, xiv. 12–19), and only when Jerusalem has been captured and plundered by the heathen nations will salvation come to Judah (xiv. 5b–11).

(5) The conception of the Messiah and of the Messianic Age in chs. i–viii is different from that in chs. ix–xiv. In chs. i–viii the Messiah is Zerubbabel who will build the Temple and rule with Joshua, the High Priest, by his side (vi. 12, 13). In chs. ix–xiv the Messiah is a different figure. He enters Jerusalem in triumph, not as a military conqueror, but as the Prince of peace. He abolishes the weapons of war and maintains peace among the nations: his dominion extends to the ends of the earth (ix. 9, 10). The Jerusalem of the future, depicted in chs. i–viii, is different from that depicted in chs. ix–xiv. In chs. i–viii it is an ordinary city spreading beyond its walls 'by reason of the multitude of men and cattle therein' (ii. 4), with old men and women sitting in the sun (viii. 4), boys and girls playing in the street (viii. 5) and Jews and foreigners worshipping together (viii. 20–23). In chs. ix–xiv, it is a creation of the prophet's imagination. It is free from extremes of heat and cold, and enjoys one long continuous day without alternating light and darkness. Running streams flowing out from the city irrigate and fertilize the whole land (xiv. 6–8).

LIFE AND CHARACTER OF ZECHARIAH

Zechariah was the son of Berechiah and the grandson of Iddo the prophet (i. 1). In Ezra v. i and vi. 14 he is called the 'son of Iddo', but as 'son' is used elsewhere for 'grandson' (e.g. Gen. xxix. 5) no stress need be laid upon the discrepancy. According to Nehemiah xii. 4 an Iddo was among the priests and Levites who returned from Babylon to Jerusalem with Zerubbabel and Joshua. He is generally identified with the Iddo of the book of Zechariah. Nehemiah tells us that in the High Priesthood of Joiakim, the son of Joshua, the head of the house of Iddo was Zechariah (Neh. xii. 16). If this is our prophet, as there is some reason to believe, he was both prophet and priest. He prophesied in Jerusalem in the years 520–518 BC and co-operated with Haggai in urging the people to rebuild the Temple (i. 16, iv. 9, vi. 12; cf. Ezra v. 1, 2, vi. 14).

Zechariah, like his contemporary Haggai, was a man of unconquerable faith and hope, to whom the future was full of blessings. The people whom he addressed had lost heart, and had come to believe that their plight was desperate and that nothing short of a miracle could save them. But to the prophet nothing was impossible provided Yahweh was on their side: if the glorious future which he predicted for them was marvellous in their eyes, Yahweh would nevertheless bring it to pass. 'If it be marvellous in the eyes of the remnant of this people in those days, should it also be marvellous in mine eyes? saith the Lord of Hosts' (viii. 6). Such was his faith in Yahweh, that he was confident that the Temple would be rebuilt (i. 16, iv. 9, vi. 12), that the exiles would return (viii. 7, 8) and that an age of unbounded prosperity and peace would dawn for the nation (viii. 11–13). So he exhorted the people to be strong and to have no fear (viii. 9, 13, 15).

A passionate believer in righteousness of life as an essential element in religion, he hated injustice and oppression by those who professed to be followers of Yahweh, and sympathized with the poor and the defenceless (vii. 8–10, viii. 16, 17). He was also essentially a practical man. He dealt with such practical problems as the rebuilding of the Temple (i. 16, iv. 9, vi. 12), the position of the priests and the scribes in the new sanctuary (iii. 1–7) and the abolition of crime in the land (v. 1–4). As we have already indicated (see p. 247), his ideal city was a real city, not a figment of the imagination.

CONTENTS

These chapters may be divided into three sections:

(1) Ch. i. 1–6. An exhortation to repentance, dated November, 520 BC.

(2) Chs. i. 7–vi. 15. Eight visions and their interpretations, followed by an appendix dealing with the crowning of Joshua (clearly in the text not Joshua but Zerubbabel) and dated February, 519 BC.

(3) Chs. vii, viii. An answer to an inquiry concerning the observance of the fasts, followed by promises of future bliss for Zion, and dated December, 518 BC.

These sections may be summarized thus:

Chapter i. 1–6
Title (v. 1). Zechariah exhorts the people to return to Yahweh. Their fathers had refused to listen to the warnings of the prophets and Yahweh's judgements had overtaken them. Their fathers and the prophets had died but not the words of Yahweh. They should take a lesson from their example (vv. 2–6).

Chapters i. 7–vi. 15

Ch. i. 7–17. The prophet sees in a vision four horsemen who report to the interpreting angel that all is quiet in the earth. He is assured that Yahweh has never ceased to love and cherish the inhabitants of Jerusalem and Judah, and that He is sore displeased with the nations, for they have inflicted upon them more punishment than He desired. His anger is now turned to compassion. The Temple shall be rebuilt and Jerusalem restored. The land shall again overflow with prosperity and Jerusalem shall be the special object of His favour.

Ch. i. 18–21. The prophet sees in a vision four horns and four smiths. The four horns symbolize the hostile powers which have scattered Judah, and the four smiths the supernatural forces which Yahweh will use to overthrow the enemies of His people.

Ch. ii. 1–5. The prophet sees in a vision a man with a measuring line going forth to measure the city with a view to rebuilding it on the old lines, but the latter is informed through the interpreting angel, that his attempts to mark the boundaries of Jerusalem will be in vain, for the city will spread far beyond the limits of her old walls. She will need no walls, for Yahweh shall be her defence and glory.

Ch. ii. 6–9. The prophet calls upon the Jews still in exile to return to Jerusalem. Yahweh is about to execute judgement upon the nations that have plundered them, for he who touches them touches His most precious treasure. The nations shall be plundered by their victims, so shall they know that Yahweh has sent him to proclaim His glory.

Ch. ii. 10–13. The prophet calls upon Zion to rejoice, for Yahweh is about to take up His abode in Jerusalem, and many nations shall join themselves to Him and become His people. Yahweh shall take possession of Judah within the sacred land and shall once more delight in Jerusalem. Let all mankind be silent for He has roused Himself in His holy habitation.

Ch. iii. The prophet sees in a vision the High Priest, Joshua, and the Satan, standing for trial before Yahweh and dressed in foul garments, symbolizing the sins of the people. He is accused by the Satan but is acquitted: his foul garments are taken from him, and he is clothed in rich apparel and assured that the guilt of the past has been removed. Furthermore, he is told that if he faithfully discharges his duties, he shall be given complete control over the Temple and the privilege of free access to Yahweh. He and the rest of the priesthood shall be a guarantee of the approach of the Branch (i.e. Zerubbabel). A jewel with seven facets shall be in the royal crown (or 'in the coping stone of the Temple') and upon one of these Yahweh shall engrave the name of His chosen servant. When the Messianic Age dawns all men shall enjoy security and peace.

Ch. iv. The prophet sees in a vision a seven-branched golden lampstand with seven lamps, fed by seven pipes from a reservoir of oil standing above them, and two olive trees standing beside it, one on each side, which supplies oil to reservoir (vv. 1–6a). The seven lamps represent the all-seeing eyes of Yahweh who watches over His people, and the two olive trees Zerubbabel and Joshua, the temporal and spiritual representatives of Yahweh, who stand before Him and derive their power from Him (vv. 10b–14). Zerubbabel shall accomplish the work which he has undertaken, not by his own strength but by the spirit of Yahweh. Zerubbabel shall put on the coping stone of the Temple and the assembled multitude shall praise the beauty of the completed structure. Just as his hands laid the foundation of his Temple, so his hands shall complete it. Those who sneered at the small beginnings of the Temple shall rejoice when they see the finished structure (vv. 6b–10a).

Ch. v. 1–4. The prophet sees in a vision a scroll, inscribed with curses, flying through the air. It enters the house of every thief and every perjurer in the land and destroys it.

Ch. v. 5–11. The prophet sees in a vision a barrel with a leaden cover in which a woman, the personification of wickedness, is seated. Two winged women carry it through the air and deposit it in Babylon, the proper home of all that is evil.

Ch. vi. 1–8. The prophet sees in a vision four chariots with horses of different colour emerge from between two mountains of bronze. They represent the four winds of heaven and come forth with their commission from the presence of Yahweh. They go forth to different parts of the earth to execute Yahweh's vengeance upon any power which may threaten Israel. Those which go to the north country will satisfy His anger by pouring it upon that country (Babylon).

Ch. vi. 9–15. The prophet is ordered to take some of the gold and silver, brought by a deputation from the Jewish exiles in Babylon, and to make a crown and place it on the head of Zerubbabel whom he is to proclaim as the 'Branch'. Zerubbabel shall complete the Temple and then rule as king, with Joshua the High Priest by his side. Both shall hold council together in perfect harmony.

In v. 11 read 'crown' instead of 'crowns' and 'Zerubbabel the son of

Shealtiel' instead of 'Joshua the son of Jehozadak'. The crown was intended originally for Zerubbabel who, Zechariah expected, would become
the Messianic king. When in the course of time the supreme authority
was vested not in a descendant of David's line, but in the High Priest,
the text was altered in accordance with the history. The work was done
so clumsily that quite varying accounts appear in different chapters. In
ch. iii. 9 Joshua is the subject for the honouring. In ch. iv, Zerubbabel is
the more important, but both he and Joshua are apparently to be crowned.
In ch. vi. 11 a crown is set on the head of Joshua, but in ch. vi. 12, 13a
the reference is clearly to Zerubbabel. Verse 13b in the Septuagint reads
'and shall be priest at his right hand'.

Chapters vii, viii

Ch. vii. A deputation of Jews from Bethel appears in Jerusalem
and raises the question of the continuance of the fasts of the exile.
The prophet declares that their fasting, like their eating and drinking, had no reference to Yahweh. Through the earlier prophets
Yahweh had demanded not fasting, but justice, kindness and compassion in their social relations. Neglect of these moral demands had
been responsible for all the miseries of the past. Yahweh in His
wrath had scattered the people among strange nations and made
their pleasant land a desolation.

Ch. viii. Yahweh will return and dwell within Jerusalem which
shall be called, 'the faithful city', and the mountain of Yahweh, 'the
holy mountain'. Men and women shall live to a ripe and contented
old age, and its streets shall swarm with happy children. These predictions may seem impossible of fulfilment to the people, but with
Yahweh nothing is impossible. He shall rescue His people from the
east and the west and bring them back to Jerusalem (vv. 1–8). The
people are exhorted to be courageous and hopeful, for the land shall
again be blessed with fertility and all the misfortunes of the past shall
be turned into blessings, provided they obey the moral demands of
Yahweh (vv. 9–17). The fasts shall become joyous festivals, and
peoples and citizens of great cities shall come to worship Yahweh and
to join themselves to Israel (vv. 18–23).

PERMANENT INFLUENCE

The book of Zechariah throws a welcome light upon the condition
of the Jews in Palestine shortly after the Return. We gather that
they had become discouraged and fearful (viii. 9, 13, 15). The crops

were so poor that they yielded little or no return for the labours of either man or beast; the fierce struggle for existence caused internal dissensions, so that there was no peace 'to him that went out or came in because of the adversary' (viii. 10). The administration of justice was apparently corrupt and the people were insincere in word and deed (viii. 16, 17). Jerusalem was but a shadow of her former self and there were few children and old people to be seen in her streets (viii. 4, 5). It would appear that not only Zechariah but also the people generally, dreamt of independence under Zerubbabel, a descendant of David (v. 12; cf. iv. 7–9). The spread of this hope among the people may have led to the removal of Zerubbabel from his office of governor by the Persian authorities, for he suddenly disappears from history. Altogether the people were so wretched that the bright future which Zechariah depicted for them seemed nothing but an impossible dream (viii. 6).

Zechariah is important because at a time when prophecy is exhausted he stresses the teaching of the earlier prophets. To him Yahweh is an omnipotent and merciful God. He is supreme in both His heavenly dominions and in the earth. Before the heavenly tribunal Joshua is acquitted of the charge brought against him by the Satan and given full authority over the Temple, while the establishment of the cleansed priesthood in Jerusalem is a guarantee of the advent of the Branch (the Messianic king) and the approach of the age of blessedness (iii. 1–10). The eyes of Yahweh 'run to and fro through the whole earth' (iv. 10b) and He has the power to overthrow the enemies of His people (i. 18–21, vi. 1–8). On His return to Jerusalem many nations shall join themselves to Him (ii. 11) and entreat His favour (viii. 20–22). In His dealings with His people He is ready to be merciful; if only they will repent and turn to Him He will turn to them (i. 3). He watches over them and sends His angel to encourage them (iv–vi. 8). He is jealous for Jerusalem (i. 14, viii. 2) and shall dwell in the midst of her (viii. 3) and watch over her. 'For I, saith the Lord, will be unto her a wall of fire round about, and I will be the glory in the midst of her' (ii. 5).

Yahweh is not only an omnipotent and a merciful God, but also a righteous God who demands righteousness of life from those who would worship Him. Though Zechariah is anxious that the Temple should be rebuilt, he does not consider that it is essential to true worship or that the people have incurred the wrath of Yahweh by their failure to rebuild it. Far more than the Temple and its ritual is righteousness of life, without which the Temple and its ritual are a mockery. Like the earlier prophets he hates sin with his whole soul. In the opening prophecy he exhorts the people to repent of their sins, and reminds them of the fate which had overtaken their forefathers who had disregarded the warnings of the 'former prophets' (i. 1–6). His hatred of sin is clearly shown in the vision of the High Priest, Joshua, standing before Yahweh clad in filthy garments, symbolizing the iniquities of the people (iii. 1–10), in that of the Flying Roll, symbolizing the elimination of sinners from the community (v. 1–4) and in that of the Woman in the Ephah, who is the personification of wickedness (v. 5–11). He insists upon the moral demands of Yahweh as taught by the 'former prophets'. Men are to be just and merciful, to defend the widow and the orphan, the stranger and the poor, to plot no evil against one another (vii. 7–10, viii. 16, 17) and to love truth and peace (viii. 19). It was because the people in times past had refused to listen to the 'words which the Lord of hosts had sent by his spirit by the hand of the former prophets' that he had scattered them among all the nations and that the land was desolate (vii. 11–14). Zerubbabel is reminded that he will accomplish his work not by dependence upon human power, but by dependence upon the spirit of Yahweh (iv. 6). Jerusalem is to be called the 'City of Truth' (viii. 3), while her only walls are to be Yahweh Himself (ii. 5).

Zechariah makes a slight contribution to the doctrine of angels. In the writings of the pre-exilic prophets angels are rarely mentioned, for the prophets were so deeply conscious of holding direct communication with Yahweh that they felt no need of an intermediary. In exilic and post-exilic times there was a great development in the doctrine of angels. Ethical monotheism became firmly established, and as a consequence there arose an increased sense of the divine transcendence. It was felt that Yahweh was so far removed from men that intermediaries were necessary as channels of communication. Angels appear in the book of Ezekiel, though not under that name: they are regularly called 'men' but they are clearly superhuman. They are also prominent in the book of Zechariah (i–viii), where they are called not only 'men' but also 'messengers' or 'angels'. The prophet converses with Yahweh through an intermediary angel and the visions are interpreted in like manner (i. 9, 13, 14, ii. 3, iv. 1, 4, v. 5, 10, vi. 4, 5). In this book different orders of angels are mentioned for the first time (ii. 3, 4, iii. 1–6).

Among the angels mentioned is one who is called the 'Satan' or the 'Adversary'. The word is not a proper name but a title, expressing the function which the angel exercises. This figure appears three times in the Old Testament. In this book he accuses the High Priest, Joshua, before the heavenly court of Yahweh, though the charge is not actually stated. In the book of Job i. 9–11, ii. 1–5, he is one of the 'sons of God', and appears in the heavenly court as the public prosecutor who challenges Job's claim to righteousness. In 1 Chronicles xxi. 1 the title has become a proper name. Here the Satan and not Yahweh, as in 2 Samuel xxiv. 1, induces David to commit the sin of numbering the people. The conception is post-exilic and is doubtless influenced by oriental thought. He has not yet developed into the Devil, the arch-enemy of mankind, of whom we read in the New Testament.

Finally by his dreams of the coming of the Messiah (vi. 12, 13) and of the Messianic Age (ii. 4–12, viii. 3–8, 12, 13, 15), and by his use of symbolism (i. 7–vi. 8) Zechariah shows that Prophecy is beginning to merge into Apocalyptic.

STYLE

Apart from the narratives of the visions, the style of the chapters is simple, direct and pure. The narratives of the visions show that the author possessed a vivid imagination and the gift of graphic description, but their style lacks the simplicity, directness and purity of the rest of the book being artificial and involved. According to G. A. Smith, the involved and misty subjects of the visions 'naturally forced upon the description of them a laboriousness of art, to which there was no provocation in directly exhorting the people to a pure life, or in straightforward predictions of the Messianic era'.[1] Throughout the chapters the literary device of parallelism is common and frequent use is made of the formulas, 'Thus saith the Lord' (e.g. i. 3, ii. 8, vi. 12), and 'The word of the Lord came unto . . .' (e.g. i. 7, vii. 8, viii. 1).

[1] G. A. Smith, *The Book of the Twelve Prophets*, 1898, p. 262.

CHAPTER XVIII

Isaiah lvi–lxvi

AUTHORSHIP AND DATE

Chapters lvi–lxvi of the book of Isaiah were collectively called Trito-Isaiah by Duhm, on the assumption that they were not the work of the author of chs. xl–lv but of a later prophet of the post-exilic period. In several respects they resemble chs. xl–lv: like the latter they look forward to the return of all the Jewish exiles to their native land, to the rebuilding of Jerusalem, to the submission of the nations to her, and to her future prosperity and glory. The differences, however, are so serious that it is difficult to believe that they come from the same writer and from the same period as chs. xl–lv. The most important of these differences are the following:

(1) The historical background is different. There is no mention of Cyrus or Babylon. Though many of the Jews are represented as being in exile, some of them have returned to Palestine (lvi. 8). At times the people addressed seem to be living not on the alluvial plains of Babylon, but in the rocky mountainous country of Palestine (lvii. 5–7). They are subject to native rulers (lvi. 10–12) and to native tribunals (lix. 4). The Temple has been rebuilt (lvi. 5–7, lx. 7, lxii. 9, lxv. 11, lxvi. 6); the walls of Jerusalem are still in ruins (lviii. 12, lx. 10); many of the cities of Judah are desolate (lxi. 4); and much of the land is waste (lxii. 4).

(2) The moral and religious conditions are different. The native rulers are greedy, slothful and self-indulgent: they are represented as blind watchmen, dumb dogs, that instead of barking, lie dreaming in the sleep they love, and as shepherds, insatiable in their greed and without understanding except for their own gain (lvi. 10–12). Murder and falsehood are rife (lix. 3); the administration of justice is corrupt (lix. 4); and men devise schemes which are false to others and useless to themselves (lix. 5, 6). Of the people generally we read, 'Their feet run to evil, and they make haste to shed innocent blood; their thoughts are thoughts of iniquity; desolation and destruction are

in their paths. The way of peace they know not; and there is no judge-ment in their goings: they have made them crooked paths; whosoever goeth therein doth not know peace (lix. 8). A section of the community is guilty of idolatrous practices (lvii. 3–13, lxv. 1–7, 11, 12, lxvi. 1–4, 17). The idolaters seem to be in the majority and persecute those who are faithful to Yahweh (lxvi. 5). Even those who remain faithful and are punctilious in the discharge of their religious duties, forget their religious obligations and oppress their labourers (lviii. 1–4). The sins of the people have cut them off from Yahweh so that He will not hear them (lix. 1, 2).

(3) Stress is laid upon the Temple and its sacrificial system (lvi. 7, lx. 7, lxii. 8, 9, lxvi. 20, 21), and upon the observance of the Sabbath (lvi. 2, 4, 6, lviii. 13, 14).

(4) The style for the most part is inferior.

The evidence which we have produced, points to the conclusion that chs. lvi–lxvi are of post-exilic origin. The fact that they are a miscellaneous collection of oracles makes it difficult to believe that they are the product of a single author, as some critics suggest. It is more likely that they come from more than one hand, though several may be the work of a single author. The fact that the Temple is standing and the walls of Jerusalem are in ruins indicates that the chapters were written after the completion of the Temple in 516 BC and before the restoration of the city walls in 445 BC. The moral and spiritual corruption, the emphasis laid upon the Temple and its ritual and upon the observance of the Sabbath, reflect the conditions existing at Jerusalem shortly before Nehemiah's arrival there in 445 BC. The general consensus of opinion is that the chapters are the work of disciples of Deutero-Isaiah who sought to perpetuate his teaching and to develop his ideas, and that they are to be assigned to the period 516–445 BC. Some critics maintain that they belong not only to different authors, but also to different periods. Among the periods which have been suggested are 700–400 BC, 600–400 BC, and 450–350 BC. Oesterley and Robinson assign chs. lix, lxiii. 7–lxiv. 12 and lxiv. 17–34 to the latter part of the fourth century BC.

CONTENTS

Chapters lvi–lxvi. A series of prophecies dealing mainly with the faults of the restored community and the glory of the New Jerusalem.
The prophecies may be summarized as follows:

Chapters lvi. 1–8

Eunuchs and foreigners are assured that they will be allowed to participate in the Temple worship provided they observe the Sabbath and keep the covenant, for Yahweh's house shall be a sanctuary in which all nations shall offer prayer, for not only the Jews of the Dispersion, but aliens as well shall find a place there.

Chapters lvi. 9–*lvii.* 21

Chs. lvi. 9–lvii. 2. The prophet denounces the worthless rulers of the nation and commands the wild beasts (i.e. the heathen nations) to come and devour the flock. The rulers neglect their duty. Instead of being on the alert they are asleep and useless; instead of caring for the people, they seek their own advantage and spend their lives in drunken idleness. The righteous are allowed to perish: only in the grave can they find rest.

Ch. lvii. 3–13. The prophet denounces the idolaters in the community who deride the faithful, practise immoral rites at the high places, sacrifice their children, and send representatives to the shrines of distant gods. But their gods shall bring them neither help nor gain. The wind shall carry them away; but those who put their trust in Yahweh shall inherit the land.

Ch. lvii. 14–21. Yahweh, the High and Lofty One, who sits enthroned for ever, dwells with the crushed and lowly and shall restore their fortunes. He will not punish His people for ever, for men's spirits would break under the strain. Because of their covetousness He smote them and hid Himself from them; but He has watched their ways, and shall heal them and grant them rest and comfort. He shall cause praise and thanksgiving to spring forth, and create peace (or prosperity) for those still in exile and for those who have already returned. For the wicked there is no peace.

Verse 21 is almost identical with ch. xlviii. 22.

Chapter lviii

The prophet is commanded to expose the sins of his fellow countrymen. Daily they turn to Yahweh, question the priests as to the correct ritual, and delight in daily worship. To their complaint that Yahweh disregards their fasts, the prophet declares that their fasting is a hollow pretence. On their fast-days they pursue their business, oppress their labourers and become fretful and quarrelsome. Such fasting will never bear their prayers on high. True fasting consists

I

in abstaining from oppressing the weak and in making provision for the destitute. When they fulfil the requirement of true religion, Yahweh will be their guide and renew their strength. They shall flourish like a watered garden and their sons shall rebuild the ancient ruins. If they observe the Sabbath, they shall ride over the mountains of Palestine and enjoy the inheritance of their ancestors.

Verses 13, 14 are rejected by some critics as a late insertion but without cogent reasons.

Chapter lix

Ch. lix. 1–8. The prophet reminds the people that their troubles are due not to the impotence of Yahweh, but to their sins which have come between them and Him. They are guilty of murder, lying, dishonesty, acts of violence and perversion of justice in the law-courts. They devise schemes which are fatal to those who acquiesce in them and to those who oppose them. They follow the path of desolation and destruction and care not for what leads to peace.

Ch. lix. 9–15a. Identifying himself with the people, the prophet confesses their sins. They have looked for salvation but their hopes have been disappointed. They grope like blind men along a wall and stumble in broad daylight. Their sins testify against them and are ever in their thoughts. There is no possibility of justice and righteousness, for truth is never to be seen and moral sense departs from the city.

Ch. lix. 15b–21. Since there is no human champion to intervene, Yahweh shall arm Himself to undertake the work of salvation and requite Jews and foreigners alike according to their deeds. His judgement shall bring Him world-wide glory, for His vengeance shall be swift like a pent-up stream driven by a blast of wind. To Zion He shall come as a redeemer to remove rebellion from Jacob. His spirit, which rests upon them, and His words, which He has put into their mouths, shall never depart from them.

Verse 21, on account of its want of connection with what precedes and its change of person and number, is considered by some critics to be a late insertion.

Chapter lx

Ch. lx. 1–9. The prophet depicts the future splendour of Zion. The light of Yahweh shall shine upon her and attract the nations to her. The scattered exiles shall return and the wealth of the nations shall flow into her by land and sea.

Ch. lx. 10–14. The city shall be rebuilt by her former enemies, and her gates shall be open day and night to allow the nations to bring in their treasures. The glorious cedars of Lebanon shall be brought to beautify the Temple, and the descendants of the people, who have oppressed them, shall come as suppliants and recognize Zion as the dwelling place of the Holy One of Israel.

Ch. lx. 15–22. Instead of being forsaken and hated Zion shall become a proud city, a joy to all ages. From the nations and their kings she shall receive new strength, and shall recognize that Yahweh is her redeemer. Gold and silver shall take the place of brass and iron; Peace shall be her governor and Justice her ruler; violence and destruction shall cease; her ramparts shall be called Protection and her gates Renown. She shall no longer depend upon the sun and moon for light, for Yahweh shall be her everlasting light. All her inhabitants shall be righteous and possess the land for ever; they shall increase in number until they become a strong nation. Yahweh shall hasten the accomplishment of this in His own good time.

Chapter lxi

Ch. lxi. 1–4. The prophet announces that Yahweh has appointed him to bring good news to the distressed, to proclaim freedom to the captives, a year of favour to those who love Yahweh, and a day of vengeance on His foes, and to comfort all those who mourn, transforming their sorrow into joy. They shall be trees of righteousness planted by Yahweh in His honour; they shall rebuild the ancient ruins which have lain waste for ages.

Ch. lxi. 5–11. The prophet declares that foreigners shall serve them as labourers and call them 'Yahweh's priests' or 'ministers of our God'. They shall enjoy the wealth of nations and deck themselves out in their splendour. Just as they suffered shame in double measure, so shall they have a double portion in their own land and lasting joy. Yahweh shall make a lasting covenant with them. Their offspring shall be famous among the nations, and all who see them shall acknowledge that they are the race that Yahweh blesses. Yahweh shall cause righteousness and praise to spring forth before all nations.

Verse 10 interrupts the connection between vv. 9 and 11 and is probably a misplaced fragment.

Chapter lxii

Ch. lxii. 1–5. The prophet declares his determination to work on behalf of Zion until her righteousness shall be manifest to all nations. Yahweh shall confer upon her a new name, the symbol of a new character and a new relationship to Himself. Instead of being forsaken and desolate, she shall be reunited to her husband and children and again become His delight. Her God shall rejoice over her as a bridegroom over a bride.

Ch. lxii. 6-9. Upon the walls of Jerusalem, the prophet in imagination sees sentinels, whose function is to remind Yahweh of His promises and to give Him no rest until He makes the city renowned on earth. Strangers shall no longer rob the people of the fruits of their labours.

Ch. lxii. 10-12. The prophet bids the inhabitants prepare the way for the returning exiles, for Zion's salvation draws near. They shall be called 'the holy people', 'the redeemed of Yahweh', and the city 'sought out, a city not forsaken'.

Chapter lxiii. 1-6

The prophet in imagination sees Yahweh approaching from the direction of Edom where He has overthrown single-handed the oppressors of His people. He has trampled them in His wrath, and smashed them in His fury, spilling their blood upon the earth.

Chapters lxiii. 7-lxiv

Ch. lxiii. 7-14. The prophet celebrates Yahweh's goodness to His people in the past, when He proved Himself their saviour and brought them safely through all dangers. But they rebelled against Him and pained His holy spirit, so that He was compelled to fight against them, until calamity directed their thoughts afresh to their glorious past and caused them to long again for divine help.

Ch. lxiii. 15-19. The prophet beseeches Yahweh to have compassion upon them, for He, not Abraham or Israel (i.e. Jacob) is their Father and Redeemer. He reproaches Him for making them stray from His ways, so that their hearts are hardened until they become godless. They have become like those who have never known Yahweh as their God.

Ch. lxiv. 1-7. The prophet longs that Yahweh may make Himself known to His foes by terrible acts, surpassing all that men have ever known. Yahweh, who is the only God and who works for those who wait for Him in the way of righteousness, is wrath with His people. They have become like men who are unclean and their sins hurry them away to destruction. No one calls upon His name or rouses himself to take hold of Him, for He has hidden His face from them and left them to their guilt.

Ch. lxiv. 8–12. The prophet prays that Yahweh, who is their Father, will cease to be angry with them. The holy cities are a wilderness, Jerusalem is a desolation, and their holy and beautiful Temple, where their fathers worshipped, is burned with fire. The prophet prays that Yahweh will restrain His anger and afflict them no more.

Chapter lxv

Ch. lxv. 1–7. The prophet declares that Yahweh has ever been ready to renew intercourse with His people, but they have not approached Him or called upon His name. Instead, they have provoked Him with their abominable superstitions and their claim to the acquisition of 'taboo holiness'. He will not be silent, until He has punished their sin and those of their fathers who defied Him with their sacrifices at the high places.

Ch. lxv. 8–12. Just as a man preserves a cluster of grapes with only a few sound grapes in it for the wine juice which they will produce later, so Yahweh will not utterly destroy His people. Those who are faithful to Him shall possess the land and shall pasture their cattle from Sharon (the maritime plain from Joppa to Carmel) to the valley of Achor (near Jericho). But those who forget His Temple and spread a meal for the gods Fortune and Destiny, are destined to destruction, because they were deaf to all His appeals and chose what He abhorred.

Ch. lxv. 13–16. Yahweh's servants shall be well-nurtured and re-joice; but the idolaters shall go hungry and thirsty and cry for sorrow of heart, moaning in misery; and nothing shall be left of them but their names which shall be used as a form of imprecation. Yahweh's servants shall be called by a new name, so that he who prays for a blessing on himself shall invoke the God of truth, and he who takes an oath shall swear by the God of truth.

Ch. lxv. 17–25. Yahweh shall create a new earth and the troubles of the past shall be forgotten. He shall rejoice in Jerusalem and in her people, and the sound of mourning shall no more be heard in her. There shall be no more untimely deaths, for life shall be prolonged; men shall long enjoy the fruits of their labours; they shall not labour in vain or rear children for sudden destruction, for they are a race blessed of Yahweh. Their prayers shall be anticipated and answered even while they are being uttered. Peace shall reign in the animal world, and none shall hurt or destroy on Yahweh's sacred mountain.

Verse 25 is quoted from Isaiah xi. 6–9, partly abbreviated and partly expanded. The words, 'and dust shall be the serpent's meat' is rejected by some critics as a gloss.

Chapter lxvi

Ch. lxvi. 1–4. Addressing those Jews who refuse to accept the true religion and propose to build a rival temple, the prophet reminds them that Yahweh's habitation is the universe and that no earthly Temple is adequate to His Majesty. A temple and a resting place He has already made for Himself; but the only worship that is acceptable to Him is that which proceeds from a humble and crushed spirit. As for those who combine legitimate rites with heathen rites, Yahweh shall bring upon them what they fear.

Ch. lxvi. 5–18a. The believing Jews, whose hopes have been ridiculed by their adversaries, are comforted with the assurance that their mockers shall be put to shame. Yahweh shall come forth from His Temple to punish His enemies, and there shall be a large addition to Zion's population. The prophet bids Jerusalem rejoice, for Yahweh shall extend peace (prosperity) to her, like a river and the wealth of the nations shall flow into her. Yahweh's favour shall be manifested to His servants, but His enemies shall feel His wrath. With fire and sword He shall enter into judgement with all mankind, and many shall be slain. Those who consecrate and cleanse themselves for the worship not of the Temple, but of the groves, shall perish, together with their heathen rites.

Ch. lxvi. 18b–22. Yahweh shall assemble all nations before Jerusalem and shall manifest His glory to them. The survivors of the judgement shall be sent as missionaries to distant nations, and they shall bring back to Jerusalem all the Jewish exiles, some of whom shall be chosen as Levitical priests. The nation shall be as enduring as the new heavens and the new earth which Yahweh shall make.

Ch. lxvi. 23, 24. Month by month and week by week men shall come to Jerusalem to worship, and shall go outside the city to gloat over the corpses of the apostates.

It is agreed by most critics that these two verses are a late addition.

PERMANENT INFLUENCE

These chapters are important for the light they shed upon the conditions existing in Judah in the period 516–445 BC, which is one of the most obscure periods in Jewish history. The number of Jewish exiles in Babylon who took advantage of the permission of Cyrus to return to their homeland must have been comparatively small, for they are encouraged with the hope of a large increase in the population by the return of other exiles from all parts of the world (lx. 4, 8, 9, 22, lxvi. 7–9, 22), and by the adherence of foreigners to the community (lvi. 3–8). From the chapters we gain the impression of an impoverished and decadent community. Apart from the rebuilding of the Temple, little progress seems to have been made in the work of restoring the ruined cities of Judah and in bringing back the desolate lands into cultivation. We read of incompetent leaders (lvi. 9–12), lawlessness (lix. 3), oppression (lviii. 3–7), the corruption of the law-courts (lix. 4), gross idolatry and vice (lvii. 3–13, lxv. 1–7, 11, 12, lxvi. 1–4, 17), and formalism in religion (lviii. 1–4).

As regards religious ideas these chapters show little originality. Their authors were strongly influenced by Deutero-Isaiah to whom they were indebted for the doctrines of monotheism and universalism, and for their views concerning the restoration of the Jewish exiles to their own country, the rebuilding of Jerusalem, the conversion of the heathen and the glorious future in store for her. In their views on the Temple and its sacrificial system they were influenced by Ezekiel rather than by Deutero-Isaiah.

Stress is laid upon the Temple and its sacrificial system. The second Temple would be adorned with the choicest timber from Lebanon (lx. 13) and the pastoral tribes of Northern Arabia—Kedar and Nebaioth—would provide sacrifices for it (lx. 7). Foreigners would no longer plunder the corn and the wine of Yahweh's people, 'but they that have garnered it shall eat it, and praise the Lord; and they that have gathered it shall drink it in the courts of my sanctuary' (lxii. 8, 9). The remote nations would bring the Jews dwelling among them to Jerusalem as their due offerings to Yahweh, just as 'the children of Israel bring their offerings in a clean vessel into the house of the Lord' (lxvi. 20). The Temple would be called a 'house of prayer for all peoples' (lvi. 7). Though the importance of the Temple and its sacrificial system were emphasized, the people were reminded that the only worship that was acceptable to Yahweh was that which proceeded from a crushed and lowly spirit (lvii. 15, lxi. 1, 2).

A new emphasis was laid upon the observance of the Sabbath. The Sabbath had been observed as a day of rest from very early times (Exod. xxxiv. 21); but in Babylon, with neither Temple nor sacrifice, the exiles had learnt to value it as a day when they could meet for worship and prayer. To the authors of Trito-Isaiah the Sabbath seemed to be more important than it had ever been before. A blessing was pronounced upon the man who kept the Sabbath (lvi. 2). Eunuchs and foreigners were to be allowed to participate in the Temple worship provided they observed the Sabbath and kept the Covenant (lvi. 3–8). If the people delighted in the Sabbath and refrained from doing any business on that day, they would ride over the mountains of Palestine and enjoy the inheritance of their ancestors (lviii. 13, 14).

It is noteworthy that the Servant of Yahweh does not appear as a distinct figure as he does in Isaiah xl–lv. Some critics, however, regard ch. lxi. 1–3 as a Servant Song, but there are important differences. The speaker is the prophet, not the Servant of Yahweh. He has the task of proclaiming the 'day of vengeance of our God' (lxi. 2), whereas the Servant of Yahweh works by self-sacrifice and has no thought of vengeance.

These chapters contain apocalyptic elements. The day of salvation was about to dawn for His people, when Yahweh would intervene in person to take vengeance upon His enemies and come to Zion as a redeemer to remove transgression from Jacob (li. 15b–21). While the rest of the nations would be enshrouded in darkness, Zion would be illuminated by the light of the divine presence and the nations would be attracted to her (lx. 1–3). Her sons would return from distant lands and the treasures of the nations would flow into her. Across the desert would come caravans laden with gold and frankincense from Ephah and Sheba (in Southern Arabia), and flocks from Kedar and Nebaioth (in Northern Arabia) for the sacrifices of the glorified Temple. From the West ships would bring her exiled sons with their treasures of gold and silver (lx. 4–9). Foreigners would build her walls and kings would be her servants. Her gates would be open continually that men might bring the wealth of nations into her, and the Temple would be adorned with the choice wood of Lebanon. Her former oppressors would pay homage to her and call her 'The city of the Lord, The Zion the Holy One of Israel'. She would draw strength from the nations and recognize Yahweh as her redeemer (lx. 10–16). Peace would be her governor and Justice her ruler. Violence and ruin would no more be found in her midst: her walls would be called Salvation and her gates Praise. Yahweh would be her everlasting light and the days of her mourning would be ended. The people would all be righteous and possess the land for ever (lx. 17–22). Peace would reign in the animal world and none would hurt or destroy on Yahweh's sacred mountain (lxv. 25). In some passages all Israel would participate in the coming salvation (lvii. 14–19, lix. 21, lx–lxii), and in others only the faithful members of the community, after the wicked, rebellious and apostate members had been punished (lvii. 20, 21, lix. 15–20, lxv. 1–15, lxvi. 5, 6, 15–17, 23, 24).

STYLE

The style of these chapters closely resembles that of Deutero-Isaiah, but it is not uniform throughout, that of some passages being much inferior to that of others. This unevenness of style is probably due to the fact that the chapters are the work of several authors who attempted to write in the spirit and manner of the author of Deutero-Isaiah but were not always successful. There are certain passages, such as chs. lvii. 15–21, lviii. 6–14, lx. 1–20, lxi. 1–3, lxv. 17–25 and lxvi. 1, 2. which are characterized by beauty of thought and expression and are worthy to compare with the finest passages in Isaiah xl–lv. Chapter lxi. 1–3 will always be a favourite passage with Christians because our Lord read it (excluding the words, 'and the day of vengeance of our God') in the synagogue at the beginning of His ministry (Lk. iv. 18). It was under the influence of ch. lx. 19, 20, that the author of 'The Revelation' wrote the words, 'And the city hath no need of the sun, neither of the moon, to shine upon it: for the glory of God did lighten it, and the lamp thereof is the Lamb' (xxi. 23).

CHAPTER XIX

Obadiah

LIFE AND CHARACTER OF OBADIAH

Of the prophet Obadiah nothing is known except what may be inferred from the book which bears his name: we cannot be sure even of the age in which he lived. The name, Obadiah, which means 'Servant of the Lord', is common among the Hebrews, but all attempts to identify this prophet with any of the other persons so named and mentioned in the Old Testament—and there are thirteen of them—have failed. As we shall show later (see p. 268), the book which bears his name and is ascribed to him in the superscription (v. 1) is probably not a literary unit but a compilation. In vv. 1–14, 15b, which most critics agree are from his pen, he is revealed as one whose conception of Yahweh was that of a righteous but merciless God, and as an ardent patriot who kept alive the memory of the wrongs done to his people by Edom, and longed to see her hurled from her proud position and trampled in the dust. 'Though thou mount on high as the eagle, and though thy nest be set among the stars, I will bring thee down from thence, saith the Lord' (v. 4).

CONTENTS

The book falls into two clearly defined sections:

(1) Vv. 1–14, 15b. Denunciation of Edom and causes of her downfall.

(2) Vv. 15a, 16–21. Judgement upon all the nations, including Edom, and the exaltation of Zion.

These two sections may be summarized as follows:

Vv. 1–14, 15b
Vv. 1–9. The prophet hears a report of divine origin that a messenger

has gone forth to stir up the nations against Edom. Yahweh declares that though she trusts in the security of her mountain fortress and vaunts herself among her neighbours, He shall pull her down. If thieves came to her by night, they would take no more than they required and grape-gatherers would leave some gleanings; but her destruction shall be complete. Her former allies, whose plots she had not the wit to see, shall rifle her treasures and drive her to the borders of her own land. Her wise men and her warriors shall be wiped out.

Vv. 10–14, 15b. The calamity shall come upon Edom as a punishment for her outrageous and merciless violence to her brother Jacob (i.e. Judah) on the day when she stood aloof, while strangers carried off his wealth, and foreigners entered his gates and cast lots for Jerusalem. She gloated over her brother's agony on his day of disaster, looted the goods of Yahweh's people, and cut off the escaping fugitives and handed them over to the enemy. Now her deeds shall recoil upon her own head.

Vv. 15a, 16–21

The day of Yahweh is approaching with doom for all the nations. Just as the inhabitants of Jerusalem have drunk the cup of His fury, so shall all nations drink the cup of His fury and shall be annihilated. Those of His people who escape shall dwell in safety on Mount Zion which shall become a true sanctuary, and they shall regain their former territory. Judah and Israel shall unite and utterly destroy Edom just as a flame devours dry stubble. They shall possess the Negeb, the Shephelah, and the fields of Ephraim and Samaria; and Benjamin shall possess Gilead. Exiles from Halah shall possess Phoenicia as far as Zarephath and the exiles deported from Jerusalem, who are in Sepharad, shall possess the cities of the Negeb. Saviours shall come to Mount Zion to ensure the safety of the Jews gathered there, and the reign of Yahweh shall begin.

UNITY AND DATE

The unity and date of the book are much disputed and no certainty is possible on the subject. Rudolf holds that the whole book, with the exception of vv. 19–21, is the work of a single author who wrote at the beginning of the Exile. Rowley thinks that there is nothing in it that could not come from the mouth of a prophet of the exilic

period, living still in Palestine. The theory that the book is a unity
has won little support.

Many critics consider that the book, although it is the shortest in
the Old Testament, is a compilation containing material drawn from
different periods. It is alleged that vv. 1–14, 15b refer to the expulsion of the Edomites from their land under pressure of invasion by
their former allies in retaliation for their hostile attitude towards
Judah at the time of the fall of Jerusalem, when they sided with the
Babylonians and seized the opportunity to capture the southern
part of Judah (cf. Lam. iv. 21, 22; Ezek. xxv. 12–14, xxxv; Ps.
cxxxvii. 7). It is not known when that invasion began, but we learn
that at the time when the book of Malachi was composed (c. 460 BC),
the Edomites had suffered a severe defeat at the hands of invaders
(Mal. i. 2–5). Though these invaders are not named, it is possible
that they were the Nabatean Arabs, who, according to Diodorus
Siculus, were by 312 BC in possession of Edom and its capital Petra.
If the identification is correct, these verses can be assigned to about
the middle of the fifth century BC. The reference to the conduct of
the Edomites at the time of the fall of Jerusalem (vv. 10–14, 15b)
can be accounted for by the fact that the memory of it would be kept
alive by the inhabitants of Judah and passed on from one generation
to another. Verses 15a, 16–21 are entirely different from the preceding verses. Here the prophecy predicts the coming of the day of
Yahweh, the judgement not only of Edom but of all nations, the
return of the exiles of both Israel and Judah, the recovery of their
lost territory and the establishment of the kingdom of Yahweh in
Zion. The change in outlook suggests that these verses are the work
of a different author (or different authors). The date of their composition cannot be determined with precision but they are probably
later than vv. 1–14, 15b. Pfeiffer assigns vv. 16–18 to about 400 BC
and vv. 19–21 to the first half of the fourth century BC (v. 15b is the
title of the second part of the book).

The book raises the question of its relationship to the book of
Jeremiah. There is a close resemblance between the prophecy
against Edom in Obadiah 1–9 and that on the same subject in
Jeremiah xlix. 7–22 (Ob. 1–4=Jer. xlix. 14–16; Ob. 5, 6=Jer. xlix.
9, 10a; Ob. 8=Jer. xlix. 7). The resemblance between the two
books has been explained by the assumption that both prophets
were indebted to an earlier oracle against Edom, uttered in the eighth
century BC in the time of Joram, or Ahaz, kings of Judah (2 Kgs.

viii. 20–22, xvi. 6 margin). This assumption, however, is not necessary, if, as is likely, Jeremiah xlix. 7–22 in its present form is later than Jeremiah himself. It is probable that the passage is original in Obadiah 1–9 and that it was utilized in Jeremiah xlix.

PERMANENT INFLUENCE

On the supposition that the early portion of the book (vv. 1–14, 15b) is the work of Obadiah, we conclude that his influence has been harmful, for he has helped to foster the spirit of a narrow nationalism among the Jewish people. His work is pervaded by a spirit of hatred and revenge, and is far removed from the teaching of Jesus who said, 'But I say unto you, Love your enemies, and pray for them that persecute you; that ye may be sons of your Father which is in heaven: for he maketh his sun to rise on the evil and the good, and sendeth rain on the just and the unjust' (Mt. v. 44, 45).

CHAPTER XX

Malachi

AUTHORSHIP AND DATE

Of the personal history of the author of the book nothing is known. The name, which means 'my messenger', occurs nowhere else in the Old Testament, and it is doubtful if it is a proper name at all. The Septuagint has in ch. i. 1, the words, 'Oracle the word of Yahweh unto Israel by the hand of his messenger', and the Targum has, 'by the hand of Malachi (or "my messenger") whose name is called Ezra the scribe'. The tradition that it was the work of Ezra continued to prevail among the Jews and was accepted by Jerome and other Christian scholars, but had Ezra been the author, it is unlikely that his authorship would have been concealed. It has been suggested that the book originally had no author's name attached to it, and that an editor borrowed the title from ch. iii. 1, 'Behold, I send my messenger, and he shall prepare the way before me'. In any case it must have been regarded as the proper title of the book before the whole collection of the 'Minor Prophets' could receive the title of the 'Twelve'.

The book clearly belongs to the post-exilic period.

The grounds for this view are as follows:

(1) The land is ruled by a 'pekah' or governor (i. 8; c.f. Hag. i. 1; Neh v. 14), indicating the time subsequent to the destruction of Jerusalem in 587 BC.

(2) The second Temple is in existence and public services are being held in it (i. 10, iii. 1, 10). The book, therefore, must be later than 516 BC when the Temple was completed and dedicated.

(3) The author of the book condemns mixed marriages, the laxity of the priesthood, and the refusal of the laity to pay their tithes and other offerings to the sanctuary. These evils were prominent in Judah when Nehemiah arrived in Jerusalem (445 BC) and against

which he took strong measures (cf. Mal. ii. 10–16 and Neh. xiii. 23–27; Mal. i. 6–ii. 9 and Neh. xiii. 29; Mal. iii. 8–10 and Neh. xiii. 10–13). The author apparently knows nothing of Nehemiah's reforms.

(4) It is unlikely that the book was written during Nehemiah's governorship, because in ch. i. 8 the people are represented as offering gifts to the governor, whereas Nehemiah tells us that he refused to accept any (Neh. v. 15, 18).

(5) In the book no distinction is made between priests and Levites (ii. 4–9, iii. 3). The priests are the 'sons of Levi' as in Deuteronomy, while in the Priestly Code the priesthood is confined to the 'sons of Aaron'. The book, therefore, was probably written before the promulgation of the Priestly Code. It is true that there is one point which might suggest that the book is later than the promulgation of the Priestly Code. Chapter iii. 10, which deals with the question of the payment of tithes, agrees with the latter (Num. xviii. 21–23) as against Deuteronomy (Deut. xiv. 22–29). Since, however, a new code contains both old and new material, it is possible that this agreement is due to the fact that the practice touching the payment of tithes is much older than the promulgation of the Priestly Code.

We conclude that the book was written between 516 BC and 397 BC probably shortly before the time of Nehemiah, about 460 BC.

CONTENTS

The book may be divided into seven parts:

(1) Ch. i. 1–5. Yahweh's love for Israel.

(2) Ch. i. 6–ii. 9. Denunciation of the priests.

(3) Ch. ii. 10–16. Violation of the covenant of marriage.

(4) Ch. ii. 17–iii. 5. The coming judgement.

(5) Ch. iii. 6–12. Temple offerings and the divine blessing.

(6) Ch. iii. 13–iv. 3. The final triumph of righteousness.

(7) Ch. iv. 4–6. Concluding appeal and promise.

These parts may be summarized as follows:

Chapter i. 1–5
Title (i. 1). To those who doubt the love of Yahweh for Israel the prophet points to the condition of Edom, Judah's enemy, as proof

of that love. Edom and Israel, sprung from twin brothers, might have been expected to share equally in Yahweh's favour, but the recent desolation of Edom shows that He loves Israel and hates Edom. He will frustrate all Edom's attempts to recover her lost territory, and His people shall recognize that He is great far beyond the borders of Israel (vv. 2–5).

Chapters i. 6–ii. 9

Ch. i. 6–14. The prophet denounces the priests, because they do not render to Yahweh the honour and reverence due to a father from his son or to a master from his servant. They have brought His service into contempt by offering upon His altar blemished and imperfect animals which they would not dare to offer to their governor. It would be better to close the Temple than to kindle useless fires upon His altar, for He will not accept their sacrifices. While the Gentiles are honouring His name by offering to Him a pure sacrifice, they are dishonouring it, treating His worship with disrespect and contempt and regarding the service of the sanctuary as merely a wearisome routine. They bring the proceeds of their robbery as if Yahweh will accept their offering. Yahweh is not the petty god of an insignificant Kingdom, but a great King who is feared among the Gentiles. Ch. ii. 1–9. Unless the priests alter their ways, Yahweh will send His curse upon them and openly disgrace them. He has sent this solemn warning because of His ancient covenant with the tribe of Levi. According to that sacred contract, He agreed to give them life and peace on condition that they gave Him reverence. Their ancestors gave sound oral instruction in matters of religion and faithfully discharged their duties, and in so doing saved many from committing acts of sin. The priests should be educated teachers, for to them the people turn for instruction since they are recognized as Yahweh's spokesmen. But they have forsaken the high ideals of their ancestors. They have caused many to commit evil by giving them false direction and destroyed the covenant of Levi. For all their sins Yahweh has made them contemptible and base before all the people.

Chapter ii. 10–16

The prophet declares that the Jewish people are the children of one Father, but by marrying foreign wives they have dealt treacherously with one another, breaking the bonds of brotherhood and profaning the covenant which Yahweh made with their fathers. They have polluted the holiness of Yahweh's sanctuary by marrying foreign wives. They drench His altar with the tears of the divorced wives, so that the gifts offered upon it are no longer acceptable to Him. He does not accept their offerings, because He was a witness to their marriages in youth to the wives with whom they have broken faith. Not one of them has any moral sense. When wives have borne children, they have fulfilled Yahweh's purpose and their own, and men have no right to divorce them afterwards because they have grown old. Yahweh hates divorce and cruelty to a wife.

Chapters ii. 17–iii. 5

To those who complain that the wicked enjoy Yahweh's favour and prosper and who question His justice, the prophet declares that Yahweh is on His way, preceded by a messenger, and shall suddenly come to His Temple, first to purge the corrupt priesthood, and afterwards to rid the land of all evil-doers—sorcerers, adulterers, perjurers, those who defraud labourers, widows and orphans, and those who wrong the foreigner.

Chapter iii. 6–12

Yahweh's love for them has not changed; it is they who have changed. They are the sons of Jacob, cheaters still. Ever since the days of their fathers they have failed to keep Yahweh's laws. If they return to Him in penitence He will grant them forgiveness. They have robbed Him by withholding the tithes and offerings which are His due. Their dishonesty has brought a curse upon them. If they pay all their tithes into the Temple treasury, the curse shall be removed and showers of blessing shall make the ground fruitful. All nations shall call them happy for they shall dwell in a 'delightsome land'.

Chapters iii. 13–iv. 3

The people murmur that it is vain to serve Yahweh since no distinction is made between the evil and the good. But the faithful few take courage from mutual counsel, refusing to be moved from faith by the arguments of the sceptics. The prophet comforts them with the assurance that Yahweh has the names of those who fear Him recorded in His book of remembrance, and that the day is coming when He shall guard and preserve them as His own special treasure, sparing them 'as a man spareth his own son that serveth him'. Then shall they distinguish clearly between the righteous and the wicked.

In that day the wicked shall be consumed like stubble in an oven, while upon the righteous the sun shall arise with healing in his rays. They shall gambol like calves freed from the stall and shall tread down the wicked like ashes beneath their feet.

Chapter iv. 4–6

The prophet exhorts the people to obey the law of Moses, and promises them that Yahweh shall send Elijah to restore harmony in the ruined homes before the day of the Lord comes upon them with its curse.

UNITY

The only portion upon which serious doubts as to its genuineness have been cast is ch. iv. 4–6. Many critics hold that the book originally ended at ch. iv. 3, and that vv. 4–6 were added by an editor in the belief that the Law took the place of Prophecy which died out with Malachi, and that the 'Messenger', mentioned in ch. iii. 1, was Elijah, who, according to 2 Kings ii. 11, 'was carried up into heaven in a chariot of fire'.

PERMANENT INFLUENCE

The book of Malachi is a source of valuable information upon the moral and religious conditions of the Jewish community during the period extending from the completion and dedication of the second Temple in 516 BC to about the middle of the fifth century BC. It was a time not only of despair, but of moral and spiritual decline. The priests had become lax and degenerate, despising the Temple and its service and neglecting their sacrificial duties (i. 6–ii. 9). The people generally withheld the payment of tithes and other offerings from the sanctuary (iii. 8). Men divorced the wives of their youth and married foreign women, who were a menace to the very existence of the nation and the purity of the faith (ii. 10–16). Sorcery, adultery, perjury and oppression were prevalent (iii. 5). Confronted by the spectacle of suffering and injustice many people began to doubt the popular views. They questioned the love of Yahweh for Israel (i. 2), and murmured that the wicked prospered and escaped punishment (ii. 17, iii. 15). It was vain to serve Yahweh and walk in penitent garb before Him since there was nothing to be gained by it. Seeing no trace of the moral government of the world, they doubted if He really was a God of Justice (ii. 17, iii. 14, 15). There were, however, a few people who feared Him and 'thought upon His name' (iii. 16).

By stressing the importance of the Temple with its ritual and priesthood, Malachi (or better, the unknown writer of the book) helped to pave the way for the work of Nehemiah and Ezra, and thus may be regarded as one of the founders of post-exilic Judaism. Sacrificial victims should be without blemish. He sternly rebuked the unworthy priests for offering blemished and inferior animals upon the altars—animals which they would not dare to offer as tribute to the governor—and in finding Yahweh's service wearisome. It were better to close the Temple than to profane it by offering a polluted worship. He contrasted their contempt for Yahweh and His Temple with the reverence paid to His name among the Gentiles, whose devoted but ignorant worship was more acceptable to Him than their hypocritical worship (i. 6–ii. 9). The prophet also rebuked the people generally who were no better than the priests. They had brought blemished and inferior animals for sacrifice (i. 14) and had robbed Yahweh by failing to pay into the Temple treasury their tithes and offerings which were His due (iii. 8). Finally, he exhorted them to keep the law of Moses 'with the statutes and judgements' (iv. 4).

Though Malachi stressed the importance of the Temple with its ritual and priesthood, he was not a mere formalist. In certain aspects of his teaching he was in the true succession of the great pre-exilic prophets. Like them he proclaimed the omnipotence and absolute righteousness of Yahweh, His love for Israel, and His demand for right conduct from His worshippers, and predicted the coming of the day when the wicked would be punished and the righteous exalted. Yahweh was a great King whose name was feared among the Gentiles (i. 14). The disaster, which had overtaken their hated foe, the Edomites, would convince His people that His sway extended far beyond the borders of Palestine (i. 5). Unless the priests rendered to Him the honour that was His due, His curse would fall upon them (ii. 1, 2). His love for His people had never ceased (i. 2–5). The day was approaching when Yahweh would suddenly come to His Temple, purge the priesthood and punish all evil-doers. 'And I will come near to you to judgement; and I will be a swift witness against the sorcerers, and against the adulterers, and against false swearers; and against those that oppress the hireling in his wages, the widow and the fatherless, and that turn aside the stranger from his right, and fear not me, saith the Lord of Hosts' (iii. 5). On the day of judgement the wicked would be destroyed like stubble in an oven, but upon the righteous the sun would arise with healing in his wings, and joy inexpressible would fill their hearts (iv. 1–3).

The book is also important because it sounds the note of universalism. Though the prophet limited the Fatherhood of God to the Jews, he affirmed that when the heathen offered to their gods a worship that was infused with the right spirit, Yahweh, the only true God, accepted it as offered to Himself. 'For from the rising of the sun even unto the going down of the same my name is great among the Gentiles; and in every place incense is offered unto my name, and a pure offering: for my name is great among the Gentiles, saith the Lord of hosts' (i. 11). This conception that all genuine worship is offered to Yahweh, whether the worshippers realize it or not, is found nowhere else in the Old Testament. It is almost incredible that the conception should have been grasped by any Jew, however broad-minded.

Finally the book is important for its teaching on divorce. The prophet denounced those who divorced their rightful wives, with whom they had entered into a solemn marriage contract in the presence of Yahweh and with whom they had lived since the days of their youth in the closest relations, in order to marry foreign wives. He was utterly opposed to divorce for the following reasons: (1) It was an offence against the love and faithfulness, which, as children of one Father, they owed to one another. (2) It was cruelty towards the wives who had been bound by ties of affection to their husbands from the days of their youth. (3) When wives had borne children, they had fulfilled Yahweh's purpose and their own, and men had no right to discard them afterwards because they had grown old. (4) Divorce and cruelty to wives were hateful to Yahweh. In his attitude to divorce the prophet anticipated the teaching of Christ (Mk. x. 5–12).

STYLE

As literature the book has little to commend it. The author is engaged in argument so that there is little room for inspired eloquence. The style is for the most part prosaic with occasional bursts of poetry (i. 11, iii. 1–8, 10–12, 16, 17, iv. 2). Its most prominent feature is the discussion of a subject by means of questions and anwer. This method of exposition was well known in Athens through the labours of Zeno (*c*. 489–420 BC) who employed it against the Pythagorean geometry, and of Socrates (470–399 BC) who applied it to questions of ethics and aesthetics. Later the method became common in the Rabbinic schools.

CHAPTER XXI

Joel

___

LIFE AND CHARACTER OF JOEL

Of Joel we have no direct information except that he was the son of
Pethuel (i. 1). From his keen interest in Judah and Jerusalem (ii. 1,
15, 23, 27, 32, iii. 1, 2, 6, 8, 16, 17–21) we conclude that he was a
native of the Southern Kingdom. His familiarity with the Temple
(i. 14, ii. 17), the priests (i. 9, 13) and the daily sacrifices (i. 9, 13,
ii. 14) suggests that he was a resident in Jerusalem. He seems to have
held the priesthood in high esteem, but whether he himself was a
priest is unknown. He was evidently a cultured man, well-versed in
the earlier writings of his country, which influenced his style and
from which he took numerous quotations.

CONTENTS

The book may be divided into three parts:

(1) Ch. i.–ii 17. A description of the sufferings of Judah under a
    devastating plague of locusts, followed by an appeal of the
    prophet to both priests and people to repent.

(2) Ch. ii. 18–27. Yahweh's promise of deliverance following re-
    pentance, and His assurance of renewed fertility for the land
    and material blessings for the people.

(3) Ch. ii. 28–iii. 21. The outpouring of Yahweh's spirit and the
    advent of the day of judgement.

These three parts may be summarized as follows:

Chapters i–ii. 17

Ch. i. 1–12. Title (i. 1). A terrible plague has fallen upon the land—
a plague the like of which has never been experienced before. The
story of the unprecedented disaster will be handed down from
generation to generation. Locusts have devoured the crops and the

foliage and laid bare the land (vv. 2–4). The wine-bibbers are summoned to lament over the devastated vineyards. Like a well-organized army the locusts have invaded the land, ruined the vines and barked the fig trees, so that the branches gleam white (vv. 5–7). The land is bidden to mourn like a young wife mourning for her husband. No corn, wine or oil can be obtained for the daily sacrifices in the Temple. The priests, who minister at Yahweh's altar, lament; the farmer is downcast and the vine-dresser waits, for the harvest of the field is ruined and joy fades from the hearts of men (vv. 8–12). Ch. i. 13–20. The prophet bids the priests proclaim a fast and summon a solemn assembly of all the people, in order that they may appeal to Yahweh for pardon and help, for the terrible devastation is a sign that the dreaded day of Yahweh is approaching. The people cry to Yahweh for mercy.

Ch. ii. 1–11. The prophet bids the priests sound the alarm in Mount Zion in order that the people may know that the day of Yahweh is near. The mountains are darkened by a vast horde of locusts the like of which has never been seen before. The country before them seems fair as the garden of Eden, but behind them it resembles a fire-swept wilderness. The locusts resemble horses in appearance and in the speed of their advance. The noise of their wings is like the rumble of chariot-wheels or the crackling of flames in the stubble. At their approach the people are stricken with fear. They advance in perfect order, storming the walls of the city and entering the houses. At their approach the earth quakes, the heavens tremble, sun and moon are darkened and the stars cease to shine. They are Yahweh's mighty host before which He thunders, for they herald the dreaded day which none may endure.

Ch. ii. 12–17. The prophet bids the people repent with all their hearts, for Yahweh is ready to forgive and bless. It is not too late for Him to relent and leave a blessing behind Him. Once again the prophet bids the priests arrange a fast, summon a solemn assembly of all the men, women and children, and plead with Yahweh to spare His people, lest the surrounding nations should taunt them with the powerlessness of their God.

Chapter ii. 18–27
Ch. ii. 18–27. Yahweh, through the prophet, promises to restore the fertility of the land and to destroy the locusts, driving them into the desert, the Dead Sea and the Mediterranean. He bids the land, the

beasts of the field, and the inhabitants of Jerusalem rejoice over the restoration of the fertility of the land. Fields, vineyards and olive gardens shall yield abundant harvests, and the damage done by the locusts shall be repaired. The people shall praise Yahweh for His wondrous bounty and the assurance of His presence with them, and for His continual care. Never again shall they be humiliated by the nations.

Chapters ii. 28–iii. 21

Ch. ii. 28–32. Yahweh shall pour out His spirit upon all Jews without distinction of sex, age or social position, and they shall all have ecstatic visions and prophesy. When the day of Yahweh draws near, extraordinary signs shall appear in heaven and earth. The earth shall be filled with the bloodshed of war and smoke shall ascend from burning cities; the sun shall be turned into darkness and the moon into blood. But all the worshippers of Yahweh shall be saved: they shall be found in Mount Zion and Jerusalem.

Ch. iii. 1–8. When Yahweh restores the fortunes of Judah and Jerusalem, He shall gather all the nations in the valley of Jehoshaphat to execute judgement upon them, because they have divided His land among colonists and scattered His people, selling them into slavery for small sums which they have used for the gratification of their lusts. More especially shall He punish the Phoenicians and Philistines, who have robbed Judah of her treasure and sold her children to the Greeks as slaves. Yahweh shall gather again His people from exile and deliver the oppressors into their hands. The Jews shall sell them into slavery to the men of Sheba, a remote nation (a trading people in South-Western Arabia).

Ch. iii. 9–17. The nations are summoned to arm themselves and to appear in the valley of Jehoshaphat where Yahweh shall execute judgement upon them. They shall be cut down like ripe corn and crushed like grapes in the wine-press. Multitudes await their fate in the valley of decision, for the day of Yahweh is near. The sun and moon shall be darkened and the stars shall cease to shine. Yahweh's voice shall be heard from Zion like the roar of a lion springing upon its prey, and heaven and earth shall quake before Him. But to His people He shall be a refuge and a stronghold. They shall be convinced that He is their God dwelling in Mount Zion, and that never again shall Jerusalem be defiled by the foot of strangers.

Ch. iii. 18–21. Judah shall become astonishingly fertile and attractive. Water shall be abundant, and from the Temple shall issue a stream which shall flow through the valley of Shittim. Egypt and Edom shall become a desolation, but Judah shall be inhabited from generation to generation and Yahweh shall dwell for ever in Zion.

UNITY AND DATE

The unity and date of the book have been much discussed. The older critics generally recognized the book as the work of a single author, who delivered his message in the ninth century BC during the minority of Jehoash (837–800 BC) or in the seventh century BC immediately before or after the death of Josiah (609 BC). Most of the recent critics, while accepting the theory of unity of authorship for the book, have rejected that of its pre-exilic origin, assigning it to the post-exilic period for the following reasons.

(1) The Northern Kingdom is not mentioned. Where the name 'Israel' occurs, the context shows that the word is synonymous with Judah (ii. 27, iii. 2, 16). This points to a time after the Exile.

(2) The destruction of Jerusalem by Nebuchadrezzar (587 BC) and the Exile are implied, for the people of Judah have been scattered among the nations and the land has been divided among strangers (iii. 1, 12, 17).

(3) The second Temple is in existence. There are several references to meal and drink offerings (i. 9, 13, ii. 14, 17), and a solemn assembly is summoned to 'the house of the Lord your God' (i. 14). The phrase 'my holy mountain' (ii. 1, iii. 17) also suggests the Temple.

(4) The importance attached to the daily meal and drink offerings in the Temple points to the post-exilic period. They are regarded as essential to assuage the divine wrath. Joel does not protest against sacrifice as the pre-exilic prophets do (cf. Amos v. 21–25; Is. i. 11–15; Mic. vi. 6–8; Jer. vii. 21–23).

(5) There is no reference to the Syrians, Assyrians and Babylonians who figure so prominently in the pre-exilic prophetic books.

(6) The reference to the sale of Jewish slaves to the Ionian Greeks (iii. 6) suggests a late rather than an early date.

(7) The people are called upon to repent of their sins in general terms (ii. 12, 13). There is no mention of specific sins, such as idolatry, social injustice, and gross immorality, which are sternly denounced by the pre-exilic prophets.

(8) The reference to city wall (ii. 9) carries us down below the time of Nehemiah (445 BC).

None of the above considerations is decisive, but cumulatively they afford convincing evidence for a post-exilic date. The book may be assigned to about 350 BC.

Of late years there has been a tendency to regard the book, not as a literary unit, but as a compilation. The upholders of this theory argue that the book consists of two parts, namely, (1) a narrative part (i. 2–ii. 27, excepting i. 15, ii. 1, 2, 10, 11) and (2) an apocalyptic part (ii. 28–iii. 21, i. 15, ii. 1, 2, 10, 11). The two parts differ so widely from each other that it is felt that they must be of independent origin. The first part is said to be the work of Joel and the second that of a later writer. The discovery of resemblances between the second part and the apocalyptic writings of the last two centuries BC have led some critics to fix the date of the former in the second century. The arguments of these critics, however, are not convincing. The two parts of the book seem to have been written about the same time, and there is no compelling reason for attributing the two parts to different authors.

PERMANENT INFLUENCE

The book of Joel tells us little concerning the state of the country during the period in which it was written. The only definite piece of information which it supplies is that swarms of insects, accompanied by drought and heat, had devastated the land, causing a famine of such a magnitude that the sacrifices in the Temple could not be maintained. We may infer also that the monarchy had ceased to exist, that the administration of Judah and Jerusalem was in the hands of the priests and elders of the community, that the Temple and its worship occupied a central position in the life of the people, and that the social evils which the earlier prophets had denounced had already disappeared. Such inferences, however, are of doubtful historical value, for arguments based upon silence are generally precarious.

The prophet was not a creative thinker, being content to reiterate the thoughts of the earlier prophets. In his religious thinking he could not rid himself of his narrow nationalism, failing to grasp the conception of the universality of the love of God. His hopes of a glorious future were confined to his own nation; for the heathen nations nothing but annihilation awaited them. He declared that Yahweh would pour out His spirit upon 'all flesh', but the expression 'all flesh' was limited to the Jews only, as is shown by the words 'and your sons and your daughters shall prophesy, your old men shall dream dreams, and your young men shall see visions' (ii. 28). He represented Yahweh as being a God who was 'gracious and full of compassion, slow to anger, and plenteous in mercy' (ii. 13); but apparently His love and mercy did not extend to all mankind. He had no vision of Jerusalem as the centre of worship for all nations, or as the place from which the true religion would spread to other lands and peoples. He doubtless expressed the popular view of his day, but nobler views concerning the character of God and His dealings with mankind are to be found in some of the prophetic writings (e.g. Is. ii. 2–4, xxv. 6–8, xlv. 22; Joh. iii–iv). His teaching falls immeasureably below the level of that found in the New Testament with its doctrines of the Fatherhood of God and the Brotherhood of man.

Finally, the book shows that the prophet's mind was dominated by the thought of the day of Yahweh. Its approach would be heralded by an outbreak of prophesying among His people, and by strange warnings in the heavens and on the earth (ii. 28–31). The nations that had oppressed Israel were summoned to gather for battle in the valley of Jehoshaphat where they would be overthrown by the might of Yahweh. 'Let the nations bestir themselves, and come up to the valley of Jehoshaphat: for there will I sit to judge all nations round about. Put ye in the sickle, for the harvest is ripe: come, tread ye; for the winepress is full, the vats overflow; for their wickedness is great' (iii. 12–13). In contrast to the fate of the nations, Yahweh would save His people, make their land amazingly fertile, cleanse and sanctify Jerusalem, and take up His permanent abode in Zion (iii. 21). Joel 'marks the great transition from the earlier ethical prophets, who addressed themselves to the living problems of their day, to the new type of prophet, who lived largely in the future, and dreamed of some great, miraculous, divine interposition to right the evils of the world, and to institute that righteous social order which the earlier prophets had sought to develop through the appeal to the consciences of their countrymen'.[1]

---

[1] C. F. Kent, *The Growth and Contents of the Old Testament*, 1926, p. 127.

STYLE

Though Joel must be reckoned one of the lesser prophets he has
considerable distinction as a poet. He possesses imagination, powers
of keen observation and the gift of graphic description. His style is
superior to that of Haggai or Malachi, who also wrote in the post-
exilic period but some time before him. It is characterized by fresh-
ness, smoothness and fine imagery. His book contains numerous
reminiscences in thought and expression of the earlier prophetic
writings, especially those of Amos, Zephaniah, Nahum, Obadiah
and Ezekiel. Some of the passages in his work possess a lyrical
quality which entitles them to be ranked among the best in Hebrew
poetic literature.

CHAPTER XXII

Jonah

AUTHORSHIP AND DATE

Of the author of the book nothing is known. The book purports to record an episode in the life of the prophet Jonah, the 'son of Amittai' who, according to 2 Kings xiv. 25, lived in the reign of Jeroboam II (786–746 BC) and predicted the restoration of Israel to its ancient boundaries. The traditional view that it is the work of the prophet has been abandoned, for not only is there no hint in the contents that he is the author of it, but also there is overwhelming evidence to prove that it is of post-exilic origin. The main arguments for a post-exilic date are as follows:

(1) In ch. iii. 3, Nineveh is mentioned as a city of the distant past. As Nineveh fell and was practically destroyed in 612 BC, the book must be later than that date.

(2) There is no reference to the name of the Assyrian King, suggesting a considerable interval between Assyrian times and the composition of the book.

(3) Aramaisms and late Hebrew words and expressions frequently occur, implying a post-exilic date, probably not earlier than the fourth century BC.

(4) The author quotes from the book of Joel, which belongs to about the middle of the fourth century BC (cf. Jonah iii. 9 and Joel ii. 14; Jonah iv. 2 and Joel ii. 13).

(5) A missionary consciousness did not appear in Israel until after the rise of the universalistic school in the late post-exilic period. It is, therefore, extremely unlikely that Jonah ever went on a mission to Nineveh.

Considering all the circumstances, we conclude that a date for the book in the second half of the fourth century BC would not be far wide of the truth.

CONTENTS

The story falls into three parts:

(1) Ch. i. Jonah's flight from the presence of Yahweh which ends in his being swallowed by a great fish.

(2) Ch. ii. Jonah's prayer for deliverance and his ejection, uninjured upon land.

(3) Chs. iii. iv. Jonah's preaching to the Ninevites, their sudden conversion and Yahweh's rebuke to the prophet.

The three parts may be summarized as follows:

Chapter i
Jonah is commanded by Yahweh to go to Nineveh to proclaim its doom because of the wickedness of its inhabitants, but fearing that Yahweh may spare them if they repent, he boards a ship bound for Tarshish, hoping to escape from the divine presence. But Yahweh raises a storm which threatens to break the vessel. Jonah sleeps through the storm which his own sin has raised, while the terror-stricken sailors struggle to keep the vessel afloat and pray to their gods. Finding their prayers of no avail the latter decide that someone on board must have incurred the wrath of the gods. They cast lots and the lot falls upon Jonah who, with his consent, is cast into the sea, whereupon the sea 'ceased from her raging'. Jonah is swallowed by a great fish, specially created by Yahweh for that purpose, and is in its belly for three days and three nights.

Chapter ii
Jonah prays for deliverance and the fish casts him forth uninjured upon dry land.

Chapters iii, iv
Again Jonah is commanded to go to Nineveh. This time he obeys and proclaims his message of doom. The King and all the people believe his prediction and repent, whereupon Yahweh, moved with compassion, revokes the penalty. Jonah is angry because Israel's foes have been spared and wishes to die. He builds himself a booth outside the city to shield himself from the sun, and watches in the hope that the prediction may be fulfilled. A gourd quickly springs up beside him and shelters him from the heat of the sun and as quickly

dies, smitten by a worm. Exposed to a sultry east wind and to the full force of the sun's heat, he again prays for death. Yahweh uses the gourd to teach him the lesson that His love embraces all mankind. Jonah pities the gourd which had sheltered him for a day and for which he had not laboured. If such were his feelings for a short-lived plant, should not Yahweh have mercy upon Nineveh, 'wherein are more than six score thousand persons that cannot discern between their right hand and their left hand; and also much cattle'?

UNITY

The unity of the book has been questioned by several scholars. The psalm in ch. ii. 2–9, has almost certainly been inserted in the text, as it is not strictly appropriate to Jonah's situation. It is not a prayer for deliverance to come, as we should naturally expect in the case of Jonah, but a thanksgiving for an escape from drowning. The details refer to a man who has almost been drowned in the depths of the sea, with the weeds wrapped about his head, not to one imprisoned in the belly of a great fish. As a psalm of thanksgiving it would be more appropriate if it appeared after v. 10, which records the prophet's escape from the fish. Its omission would not break the continuity of the story, for then v. 2, which states that Jonah 'prayed unto the Lord his God out of the fish's belly' would be followed immediately by v. 10 which gives the answer to the prayer. 'And the Lord spake unto the fish, and it vomited out Jonah upon the dry land.' The date of the poem cannot be fixed with certainty, but as there are many points of contact between the psalm and the Psalter (Pss. v. 7, xviii. 6, xxxi. 2, xlii. 6, cxxi, cxlii 3, cxliii. 4), it probably belongs to the post-exilic period. Attempts have been made to prove that the book is a compilation of different stories from several different hands but without success.

INTERPRETATION

The traditional view that the book is a record of actual facts can no longer be maintained. Some supporters of this view have gone to the trouble of collecting doubtful stories of sailors who have been swallowed by sharks and afterwards vomited out alive. The chief argument for the traditional view is based not on doubtful stories, but on the fact that several incidents of the narrative are referred to by our Lord (Mt. xii. 39–41=Lk. xi. 29, 30, 32), indicating that He recognized the prophetic mission of Jonah and the truth of the prophet's imprisonment in the belly of the great fish. But it may be argued that Our Lord was using the story as an illustration without giving a single thought to the question of its historical character. Moreover, doubts have been cast upon the genuineness of Matthew xii. 40 in which he compares Jonah's imprisonment in the belly of the fish to His own burial. The verse is not found in the parallel version in Luke xi. 30 and is generally considered an interpolation.

The book contains a miraculous element which constitutes an insuperable obstacle to a belief in its historicity. Such marvels as the raising of the storm and its sudden cessation, the imprisonment of Jonah in the great fish and his ejection uninjured upon dry land, and the sudden growth and death of the gourd do not usually occur in real life. There are other circumstances, too, which put a severe strain upon our credulity. Nineveh is represented as being so large that it requires three days to cross, but as a matter of fact the walls of the city were less than eight miles in circumference. It is impossible to believe that all the inhabitants of the city were suddenly converted, or that the king of Nineveh would clothe himself in sackcloth and sit in ashes. Many details, which we should expect to find in a historical record, are lacking. There is, for example, no mention of the place where Jonah was cast out upon the land, or of his journey to Nineveh, or of the sins of which the city was guilty, or of the name of the Assyrian king, or of the prophet's return to his own land.

The book is interpreted by some scholars as an allegory. Jonah (the 'dove') represents Israel and Nineveh the heathen world. Yahweh has commissioned Israel to carry the knowledge of Himself to the heathen but she shrinks from executing the commission. The great fish signifies the Babylonian Empire which swallows up Israel in the Exile (cf. Jer. li. 34, 44). Just as Jonah is released from his imprisonment in the belly of the fish and ordered again to preach to the Ninevites, so Israel is released from captivity that she may carry out her mission to the heathen world. The gourd represents Zerubbabel, called by Zechariah the 'branch' or 'shoot' (Zech. iii. 8, iv. 12), who failed to fulfil the expectations of the people. This view, however, is open to serious objections. There is comparatively little evidence in the Old Testament that Israel was ever symbolized by a dove. The symbolism does not seem consistent throughout the story. The Babylonian empire is represented by a great fish and the heathen world by a historical city. It should be stated, however, that J. C. Ball contends that the cuneiform symbol for Nineveh and its tutelar goddess was a combination of a 'house' and a 'fish', and that Jonah's three days sojourn in Nineveh, 'the house of the fish', may be taken to represent a three days' abode in the belly of a fish.[1] The explanation of the plant as the symbol of Zerubbabel is forced. Finally the allegorical interpretation obscures the truth, which the story is intended to convey, that the love of God is not restricted to Israel but extends to all mankind.

The book, probably, is neither a record of actual facts nor an allegory, but a fictitious story or parable, like that of the Prodigal Son, intended to convey spiritual truth. It may be aptly described as 'truth embodied in fiction'. We find in it all the characteristics of a good short story. Though slight the plot is well-knit and is developed in three clearly defined scenes, namely, (1) the flight of Jonah which ends by his being swallowed by a fish and vomited on land; (2) his preaching to the Ninevites and their sudden conversion; (3) his meeting with Yahweh who rebukes him for his intolerance. From the moment Jonah appears, fleeing from the presence of Yahweh, our interest is roused and is sustained throughout the story, which ends abruptly, leaving us to wonder what happened to the Ninevites and to Jonah. Though the characters are lightly sketched, they are not dim shadowy figures but real individuals who can be easily distinguished. Even Yahweh is not a mere abstraction but a living personality, who speaks and acts like a human being. The book is the work of a born storyteller endowed with a fertile imagination, a sense of drama, a touch of kindly humour and the power of graphic description. As literature it is worthy to be classed among the great short stories of the world.

PERMANENT INFLUENCE

It is a tragedy that one of the greatest books of the Old Testament should have been disparaged and ridiculed through ignorance of its true nature and through the prominence given to the incident of the great fish. As a work of the imagination written with a definite object, it has a two-fold message. On the one hand it is an impassioned protest against the narrow exclusiveness of the current Judaism and the vindictive longing for the destruction of the heathen

[1] J. C. Ball, *Proceedings of the Society of Biblical Archaeology*, xx, 1898, pp. 9 ff.

K

nations, while on the other hand it is the declaration of a great truth that the love of God embraces the whole of mankind. To appreciate the greatness of the book, it is necessary to see it against the background of the age in which it was produced. In pre-exilic times, the belief that they were the chosen people of Yahweh had engendered in the Israelites a spirit of pride and a feeling of superiority over other nations. Forced into a state of vassalage by the Assyrians and carried into captivity by the Babylonians, they became embittered by their sufferings and humiliations and learned to hate their enemies. That hatred was fanned by some of the prophets who taught them to hope that retribution would eventually overtake all their foes. Though they were in the course of time allowed to return to their native land, they were not allowed their independence but remained under the domination of the Persians. In the days of Nehemiah (445 BC) and Ezra (397 BC) it was apparent that they were in danger of losing their national identity and their religious faith through intermarriage with the people of the land. Accordingly Nehemiah banned mixed marriages for the future (Neh. xiii. 23–31) while Ezra enforced the strict observance of the Law, which differentiated them from the Gentiles, and not only banned mixed marriages, but also compelled the dissolution of all marriages which had hitherto been contracted with 'women of the peoples of the land' (Ezra x. 2–6). This policy of 'separation' fostered still further the spirit of exclusiveness among the Israelites and increased their hostility towards the heathen world. These two features are prominent in some of the Psalms and assume their worst form in the book of Esther. Among the Israelites, however, there were a few like the author of the book of Ruth, who had a nobler conception of the character of God and a higher ideal of human relationships. To this small band of choice spirits belonged the writer of the book of Jonah, which, with its matchless proclamation of the all-embracing love of God and with its wide humanity, reaches the level of the New Testament. Cornill describes it as one of the 'deepest and grandest things ever written', while Peake characterizes the last chapter as 'the most marvellous monument of the religious genius of Israel'.

CHAPTER XXIII

Zechariah ix–xiv

DATE AND AUTHORSHIP

Of the date and authorship of these chapters nothing definite is known. It was once customary to assign them to the pre-exilic period, but to-day they are generally recognized as post-exilic in origin. Some critics maintain that they were written in the third century BC by a single author, basing their view on the following grounds: (1) the reference to the Greeks as a hostile world power (ix. 13) points to the Greek period; and (2) the mention of Egypt and Assyria (i.e. Syria, x. ii) denotes the two kingdoms of the Ptolemies and the Seleucids respectively, which, in the third century BC, engaged in a struggle for the possession of Palestine. Some critics agree that the chapters are a unity and therefore the work of a single author, but assign them to the Maccabaean period (*c.* 160 BC), on the ground that they are more applicable to the historical situation of that period than to the third century BC. It is alleged by a few critics that the chapters are not a unity but a compilation, consisting of two or more independent documents. Chapters ix–xi, xiii. 7–9 are assigned by some of these critics to the pre-exilic period. Oesterley and Robinson divide the chapters into seven sections and assign them to dates varying from 218 or 199 BC to after 134 BC.

CONTENTS

These chapters fall into two parts:

(1) Chs. ix–xi, xiii. 7–9. Yahweh's judgement upon Syria, Phoenicia and Philistia and His protection of Jerusalem; the triumphal
entry of the Messiah into Jerusalem, the return of the Jewish
exiles and their victory over the Greeks; the fall of the nations;
the denunciation of the people's leaders; the people's rejection
of the good shepherd and the substitution of a worthless shepherd.

(2) Chs. xii–xiii. 6, xiv. Deliverance of Jerusalem from the assaults of the heathen nations; the cleansing of Jerusalem from sin, idolatry and prophecy; the capture of Jerusalem by the heathen nations, its deliverance by Yahweh, and its elevation into the religious centre of the world.

These two parts may be summarized thus:

Chapters ix–xi, xiii. 7–9

Ch. ix. 1–8. The judgement of Yahweh is about to fall upon the cities of Syria, Phoenicia and Philistia. The place of the native population of Philistia shall be taken by a race of half-breeds, delighting in idolatrous sacrifices. In time they shall be cleansed from their idolatry and incorporated by Judah, so that the inhabitants of a city like Ekron shall be regarded as on a level with the inhabitants of Jerusalem. Yahweh Himself shall encamp as an army to protect Jerusalem and no oppressor shall march through the land any more, for He has seen the violence done to His people.

Ch. ix. 9, 10. The Messianic king shall enter Jerusalem in triumph, riding not upon a war-horse, the symbol of power, but upon an ass. He shall abolish the weapons of war from His kingdom and maintain peace among the nations. His dominion shall embrace the whole world.

Ch. ix. 11–17. Because of Yahweh's covenant with Israel, concluded solemnly with sacrificial blood, Yahweh shall release the Jews still in captivity: they must return to their homes where they will be safe. They shall receive double compensation for all their sufferings. Yahweh shall use them as His weapon against the Greeks. Zion shall be as the sword of a mighty man and Yahweh shall appear to help His people. They shall prevail and tread down the sons of Greece; they shall drink their blood like wine and shall be as full of it as altar-bowls, and as drenched with it as the sides of the altar. After the great deliverance He shall tend them as a flock because they are as jewels upon His head, and an age of great prosperity shall dawn. The young men and maidens shall be the sustaining elements of the nation.

Ch. x. 1, 2. The people are exhorted to pray to Yahweh for rain in the time of the spring-rain, for He makes the lightning flash and gives to everyone the winter rain and the grass of the field. Neither household-gods, nor diviners, nor interpreters of dreams are of any real help.

Ch. x. 3–12. Yahweh's anger is kindled against the shepherds of His people (i.e. foreign rulers) who shall be punished. He shall visit His flock, transform the poor, leaderless sheep into war-horses and give them leaders of their own. With Him on their side they shall trample their enemies into the mire. He shall strengthen Judah and save Israel (i.e. the ten northern tribes) and bring them back from Egypt and Assyria (i.e. Syria) to Gilead and Lebanon until there is no more room for them. Egypt and Assyria shall be humbled and the restored nation shall glory in Yahweh.

Ch. xi. 1–3. Fire shall destroy the glorious cedars of Lebanon and the oaks of the inaccessible forest of Bashan shall be felled. Shepherds shall deplore the ruin of their pastures and lions roar because the jungle of Jordan is destroyed. (This passage is perhaps a figurative description of the downfall of the foreign rulers).

Ch. xi. 4–14. The prophet is commissioned to enact the part of a good shepherd to the sheep which are doomed to slaughter. Their buyers kill them and go unpunished; their sellers have no pity upon them and have the effrontery to thank Yahweh for their ill-gotten gains. The prophet undertakes the task and as symbols of his office takes two staves, one called 'Graciousness', symbolizing his aim to promote the welfare of the people by entering into happy relations with the surrounding nations, and the other called 'Union', symbolizing his aim to promote unity among his own people. In a single month he removes three shepherds, but the people refuse to accept his guidance, and so, becoming impatient with them, he leaves them to their fate. He breaks the staff called 'Graciousness' to symbolize that Yahweh's favour towards them is at an end. He asks for his wages and is paid the sum of thirty pieces of silver, which he casts into the Temple treasury, thus indicating that it was to Yahweh Himself that they have paid such a small sum. Despairing of maintaining any longer the unity of the nation, he breaks the staff called 'Union'.

Ch. xi. 15–17, xiii. 7–9. The shepherd is now commanded to assume the role of a worthless shepherd who shall prey upon the flock, but who shall eventually be smitten with blindness and paralysed (xi. 15–17). Two-thirds of the flock shall perish, but the surviving third, purified by further trial, shall become the devoted people of Yahweh (xiii. 7–9).

Chapters xii–xiii. 6, *xiv*

Ch. xii. 1–9. The prophet predicts an attack upon Jerusalem by the

heathen nations, abetted by Judah. Yahweh shall smite them with a
sudden panic and the leaders of Judah, perceiving that He is fighting
for Jerusalem, shall turn against their allies, with the result that the
heathen nations shall be destroyed and Jerusalem shall again be a
prosperous city. Judah shall be saved first in order that the house of
David and the inhabitants of Jerusalem may have no occasion to
boast of their prowess. On that day Yahweh shall protect the inhabitants of Jerusalem; and the lame and feeble among them shall be
as valiant as David, and the descendants of David like the angel of
Yahweh in might.

Ch. xii. 10–14. In that day Yahweh shall pour upon His people a
spirit of grace and supplication, and they shall lament bitterly for
the men whom they have murdered. Every member of every family
in the land shall join in the lamentation.

Ch. xiii. 1–6. A fountain for purification from sin and uncleanness
shall be opened in Jerusalem, and all idolatry, uncleanness of spirit,
and false prophecy shall be abolished. Any man who claims to be a
prophet shall be put to death by his parents. Every prophet shall be
ashamed of his vision and will not wear a hairy mantle to deceive
the people, but will claim that he has been a peasant all his life, and
that the wounds on his hands were received in the house of friends.

Ch. xiv. 1–5a. The prophet predicts another attack upon Jerusalem
by the heathen nations. The city shall be captured and half the inhabitants taken into captivity. Yahweh shall appear to rescue the
remainder. He shall stand upon the Mount of Olives, which shall be
rent asunder beneath Him, and through the chasm the fugitives shall
escape.

Ch. xiv. 5b–11. Yahweh shall arrive with all his holy angels. There
shall be no interchange of light and darkness but one continuous day.
A perennial stream shall flow east and west bringing fertility to the
whole land. Yahweh shall be recognized as King over all the earth
and as the only true God. The mountains of Judah shall become a
fertile plain, but Jerusalem shall remain lofty and inhabited upon its
site. The city shall be perfectly secure and the curse of destruction
shall fall upon her no more.

Ch. xiv. 12–21. The people who attacked her shall be smitten with
the plague, and shall perish miserably as they stand upon their feet.
A great panic shall seize them, and in their bewilderment they shall
slay one another. Judah shall fight against Jerusalem and vast spoil
shall be gathered from the nations. Similarly the plague shall affect

the animals which they possess. The survivors of the nations shall go up to Jerusalem every year to worship Yahweh and to celebrate the Feast of Tabernacles. Drought shall be the punishment of any nation which neglects to make the pilgrimage. If the people of Egypt neglect to do this, they shall be smitten with the plague. Horses shall no longer be used for war but shall be consecrated to the service of Yahweh. The pots used for ordinary purposes shall be as large as the great altar-bowls, and every pot in Jerusalem shall be consecrated for use in the ritual. No trader shall ever again set foot in the house of Yahweh.

PERMANENT INFLUENCE

Assuming that these chapters belong to the third or second century BC, we conclude that they shed some light upon the political and religious conditions of Judah in the late post-exilic age. It would appear that the spirit of nationalism and intolerance was intensely strong among the Jews. They hated the heathen nations, and looked forward with eager expectation to their speedy destruction (ix. 1–8, 13–15, x. 3–7, 11, xi. 1–5, xiv. 1–5a, 12–15) and to the establishment of the Messianic kingdom with Jerusalem as its political and spiritual centre (ix. 9, 10, xiv. 5b–11, 16–21). Apparently idolatry was still practised in the land, and the earlier prophets with their message from Yahweh had given place to the professional prophets who traded upon the credulity of the foolish (xiii. 1–6). Ritual evidently played a prominent part in religious worship. The half-breeds of Philistia, who would be incorporated into Judah, would be forced by Yahweh to abstain from food prescribed by the Levitical laws. 'And I will take away his blood out of his mouth, and his abominations from between his teeth' (ix. 7). In the Messianic Age a fountain would be opened in Jerusalem for sin and uncleanness (xiii. 1); and survivors of the warring nations would not be allowed to worship in their own way but would have to go up to Jerusalem to keep the feast of Tabernacles (xiv. 16).

Yahweh is revealed as the Lord of Creation. He stretched out the heavens, founded the earth and formed the spirit of man within him (xii. 1). He made the lightning flash and sent the rain which brought fertility to the earth (x. 1). He was the universal ruler of mankind and the only true God. He could bring down the pride of Assyria and take away the sceptre from Egypt (x. 11). When the day of the

Lord came He would be king over all the earth and there would be 'one Lord and his name one' (xiv 9). But He was not a God of love and mercy, and of peace and truth. The old idea of Yahweh as the God of war had been revived. Yahweh would encamp round Jerusalem like an army and no oppressor would ever again march through the land (ix. 8). In the battle between the Jews and the Greeks, He would appear above the combatants in order to help His people. 'And the Lord shall be seen over them, and his arrow shall go forth as the lightning: and the Lord God shall blow the trumpet, and shall go with whirlwinds of the south' (ix. 14). When the nations captured Jerusalem, He would go forth 'and fight against those nations, as when He fought in the day of battle' (xiv. 3). He would deal ruthlessly with His enemies. The half-breeds, who were to take the place of the native populations of Philistia, would be compelled to give up their idolatrous practices and unite with Judah in the worship of Him. With His help the Jews would prevail against the Greeks and drink their blood like wine (ix. 15). All those who fought against Jerusalem would be smitten with the plague. 'Their flesh shall consume away while they stand upon their feet, and their eyes shall consume away in their sockets, and their tongue shall consume away in their mouth' (xiv. 1–12). The survivors of the warring nations would go up to Jerusalem to observe the Feast of Tabernacles under threat of famine and plague (xiv. 16–19).

These chapters show that at the time when they were written prophecy was practically dead and that its place had been taken by apocalyptic. It had fallen into such disrepute that the writer predicted that in the Messianic Age anyone who claimed to be a prophet would be put to death by his parents, and that every prophet would be ashamed of his visions, and disclaim his profession (xiii. 3–6). There is a strong apocalyptic element in the chapters (ix. 9–10, xiv).

It is interesting to note that several phrases and sentences, which are either household words or have been taken up into Christianity, are from Zechariah ix–xiv, such as, 'thirty pieces of silver' (xi. 13), 'and they shall look unto me whom they have pierced' (xii. 10), 'wounded in the house of my friends' (xiii. 6) and, 'at evening time there shall be light' (xiv. 7).

LIST OF ABBREVIATIONS

H.A.T.	Handbuch zum Alten Testament
H.T.R.	Harvard Theological Review
J.B.L.	Journal of Biblical Literature
R.H.P.R.	Revue d'Histoire et de Philosophie religieuses
Z.A.W.	Zeitschrift für die alttestamentliche Wissenschaft

APPENDICES

THE PRIESTHOOD

Its Development

According to the Priestly Code the priesthood was instituted by Moses at Sinai. We are told that for seven days he acted as priest in order that he might instal his brother Aaron and his sons in the priestly office (Exod. xxix. 35–37; Lev. viii). Aaron, a Levite, was therefore the first true priest and the ancestor of all subsequent priests. At the head of the priesthood was the High Priest, who was consecrated to his office by an elaborate ritual (Exod. xxix. 1–37; Lev. viii, ix) and wore distinctive vestments (Exod. xxviii). He alone had the right to enter the Most Holy Place but only once a year (Lev. xvi. 2). The inferior priests also wore a similar dress but inferior to that of the High Priest; they ministered in the Holy Place, but were not permitted to pass the veil into the Most Holy Place. The Levites, as distinct from the family of Aaron, were excluded from offering sacrifices (Num. xvi. 40), but acted as servants of the priests, performing subordinate duties in the Tabernacle (Num. iii. 6–9, viii. 19, xviii. 6). They were divided into three families, named after the three sons of Levi, Gershon, Kohath and Merari, to each of which particular duties in connection with the Tabernacle were assigned (Num. iii. 21–39). There is reason to believe that the hierarchical system, which existed in the post-exilic period and is described in the Priestly Code, was not handed down in its completeness from the time of Moses but was the result of a gradual growth. The priestly writers projected into the past the hierarchical system as it existed in their own age.

It is universally agreed that there was some kind of a priesthood from early times. We read that there were holy places marked by trees (Gen. xii. 6; Jud. ix. 37), pillars (Gen. xxviii. 18, 22) or wells (Gen. xiv. 7, xxi. 22, 23) which people visited 'to enquire of the Lord'. Such pillars suggest sanctuaries and priests. The presence of priests is recognized in Exodus xix. 24: before approaching Yahweh on Mount Sinai the priests were to consecrate themselves lest He should break out upon them.

At first the priesthood was not restricted to the tribe of Levi. Joshua, who was an Ephraimite, exercised the priestly functions in the Tabernacle (Exod. xxxiii. 11) and David, who was a Judaean, made his two sons priests (2 Sam. viii. 18). How the Levites came to secure the monopoly of the priestly office is unknown. There is evidence to prove that they were not originally a priestly caste but a warlike tribe. It may be inferred that the tribes of Simeon and Levi met with a crushing defeat at the hands of the Canaanites (Gen. xlix. 5–7), probably as a result of their treacherous raid on Shechem (Gen. xxxiv). It is likely that the Simeonites found their way into Judah while the Levites were scattered among the tribes. The disorganization of the tribe of Levi took place before the entry into Egypt. Moses, who was a Levite, exercised the priestly functions for seven days, so that there would be a tendency to make Levites priests because of their association with him. The suggestion has been made that they were the priests of the cult of Yahweh at Kadesh when Kadesh was a place of assembly for the Israelites during their sojourn in the wilderness. It would be natural, therefore, for them to be chosen to take charge of the sanctuaries in Canaan. The story of the establishment of the sanctuary at Dan shows clearly that in the time of the Judges it was considered a good thing to have a Levite as the custodian of a sanctuary rather than a member of another tribe. Micah consecrated one of his sons as priest to take charge of the graven image, ephod and household gods, but subsequently installed a Levite with the words, 'Now I know that the Lord will do me good, seeing that I have a Levite to my priest' (Jud. xvii. 1–13). Later the Danites stole not only the graven image, ephod and household gods but also the priest, whose heart was glad because it was better to be a priest of a tribe rather than of a single family (Jud. xviii. 18, 19).

Towards the end of the time of the Judges the central shrine was at Shiloh (Jud. xviii. 31), but whether Eli and his sons, who were its guardians (1 Kgs. ii. 27), belonged to the tribe of Levi we do not know. When the Philistines destroyed Shiloh and captured the Ark, the priests migrated to Nob, probably a little town to the north of Jerusalem. Because of the help given to David by Ahimelech, the priest and eighty-five of the priestly community were slain by Saul's orders; only Abiathar escaped and fled to David (1 Sam. xxi. 1, xxii. 6–22). At Jerusalem we find associated with him another priest, Zadok, whose descent is not known, though later he came to be regarded as a descendant of Eleazar, the son of Aaron (1 Chron. vi. 50–53). On the death of David Abiathar supported Adonijah, while Zadok supported Solomon, with the result that the sons of Zadok continued as priests down to the Exile. At Dan, in the far north, the sons of Moses were priests (Jud. xviii. 30). Jeroboam II (786–746 BC) set up calves of gold, one at Bethel and the other at Dan, 'and made priests among all the people, which were not the sons of Levi' (1 Kgs. xii. 31). It would appear that in the time of the two kingdoms the Levites were at the southern sanctuaries, the non-Levites at the northern sanctuaries, the sons of Zadok at Jerusalem and the sons of Moses at Dan.

According to the Deuteronomic Code all Levites were priests and could, therefore, exercise the priestly functions (Deut. xxviii. 6–8). Ezekiel proposed that in the restored community only the sons of Zadok should be priests (Ezek. xliv. 5), and that the Levites should perform the menial tasks of the Temple because of their alleged responsibility for the idolatrous worship at the high places (Ezek. xliv. 10–14). In the Priestly Code the priesthood was confined to the sons of Aaron (Num. xviii. 2–7; Lev. viii). Just why the priesthood in the post-exilic period should be referred to as Aaronic, especially when the Zadokites outnumbered the Aaronites by two to one, is unknown. It has been suggested that the Aaronites were priests at Bethel, and that they occupied Jerusalem when the Zadokites were carried into captivity. By the time the latter returned they found that the Aaronites were too strong to be ousted from their position.

In the post-exilic period the Temple singers and porters were at first distinguished from the Levites (Ezra ii. 40–32, vii. 24, x. 23, 24; Neh. vii. 1, x. 28), but in the fourth century BC they were included among them by the Chronicler (1 Chron. xv. 16, xxvi. 1–19). This shows that by that time the singers and porters had come to be reckoned as Levites. It is probable that the Nethinim, originally captives taken in war and given by David and the princes 'for the service of the Levites' (Ezra viii. 20), or non-Israelite slaves employed by Solomon in his building operations (Ezra ii. 55, 58; Neh. vii, 57, 60, xi. 3), had also come to be reckoned as Levites.

The number of priests who returned from exile was not large but they soon became the most influential party in the nation. The High Priest especially became a personage of great importance. The prophet Haggai addressed the people through Zerubbabel, the governor of Judah, and Joshua, the High Priest (Hag. i. 2, ii. 2), while the prophet Zechariah declared that Zerubbabel would rebuild the Temple and afterwards rule with Joshua at his right hand, and that both would hold council in perfect harmony (Zech. vi. 12, 13). In the course of time the High Priest came to be recognized as both the spiritual and temporal head of the community.

The High Priesthood reached the zenith of its power in the person of Simon II (225–200 BC) who was eulogized by Ben Sirach in Ecclesiasticus i. 5–11. On his death there seems to have been a weakening of the power of the High Priest, for in the reign of Antiochus IV (175–163 BC) two unscrupulous men, Jason and Menelaus, obtained the office, which was hereditary, by bribery. After the death of Judas Maccabaeus (160 BC) the leadership of the nation passed to his brother Jonathan. In 152 BC Alexander Balas, a rival claimant to the Seleucid monarchy, sought to flatter him by conferring upon him the High Priesthood, sending him at the same time a purple robe and a crown, and investing him with the title of 'King's Friend'. He was, however, not recognized as such by the people. On his death in 142 BC his brother Simon succeeded to the leadership of the nation and to the High Priesthood. At a public ceremony he was officially confirmed in the office, which now became hereditary in the Hasmonaean house. The last of the Hasmonaean rulers was Antigonus (40–37

BC) who was executed by Herod the Great. From the beginning of the second century BC to the fall of Jerusalem in AD 70 the office of High Priest was held by very few capable and worthy men.

Priestly Functions

The main functions of the priests were to take charge of the sanctuary and to minister at the altar (Num. xviii. 1–5), and to give the oracles (Deut. xxxiii. 10; cf. Hag. ii. 11, 12; Mal. ii. 7). To ascertain the divine will use was made of the ephod and the sacred lots, the Urim and Thummim. The oracles given by the priests were 'teachings' ('Toroth', plural of 'Torah'). The primary function of the priest was to teach. Hosea complained that the priests of his day had forgotten the 'Torah' of their God, with the result that the people were destroyed for lack of knowledge (Hos. iv. 5, 6), while Micah denounced them because they taught for pay (Mic. iii. 11). Sacrifice at first was not a necessary part of the priestly functions. Any layman could offer sacrifice without the presence of a priest. Saul (1 Sam. xiii. 9, 10), David (2 Sam. vi. 17), Solomon (1 Kgs. viii. 63) and Elijah (1 Kgs. xviii. 33) are all represented as offering sacrifices without any indication that the law was being infringed. There is no reason to doubt, however, that from the time when the local sanctuaries were abolished and sacrificial worship was centralized at one place in the reign of Josiah (640–609 BC) the priests, who knew better than anyone else how Yahweh should be approached, played an ever increasing part in the offering of every sacrifice. In the case of animal sacrifice in particular the most significant part of the ritual—the pouring, dashing or sprinkling of blood upon the altar—was reserved for the priests and might not be performed by laymen, who were allowed to take no part in the ritual beyond that of slaughtering the sacrificial victim (Lev. v. 1–10). From the time of Ezra onwards the priests became more and more sacrificing officials, leaving the 'teaching' part of their ministry to others. Priesthood and sacrifice in fact came to be looked upon as more or less correlative terms.

Priests and Prophets

It was formerly universally held that there was a deep antagonism between priests and prophets. The two classes, it was said, were diametrically opposed to each other on the question of sacrifice, the priests naturally supporting it and the prophets utterly condemning it. Amos (v. 21–25), Hosea (vi. 6), Isaiah (i. 11–15), Micah (vi. 6–8), and Jeremiah (vii. 21–23) condemned sacrifice in no uncertain terms. Today, however, there is not the same unanimity of opinion on the subject. Some scholars argue that the prophets favoured sacrifice but condemned its association with the corrupt ritual of the Canaanite cults, and others that they favoured it, provided that those who brought their offerings exercised justice and mercy in their dealings with their fellow men and did not trust to them for salvation. Moreover, according to Johnson, as we have already shown (see p. 68), the prophets, like the priests, were cult officials at the sanctuaries, and therefore both classes had much in common. It is now suggested by many scholars either that there was no hostility between priests and prophets, or that if there was, it was not as great as it was formerly supposed to be.

SACRIFICE

Its Development

The elaborate sacrificial system, which is described in the Priestly Code and attributed to Moses, was actually the culmination of a long process of development extending from immemorial antiquity down to the post-exilic period. The origin of sacrifice is lost in the mists of time but it need not concern us here. Evidence shows that among the Hebrews sacrifice constituted the most important part of worship from the earliest times. Two types of sacrifice may be distinguished. First there was the 'solemn meal' type of sacrifice called Zebah (lit. 'slaughter'), in which the blood was splashed upon the sacred stone, or poured out at its base and the flesh eaten by the worshipper. The object of the sacrifice was to restore the bond between the god and the individual. To this end both partook of the flesh of the same victim. Second there was the gift sacrifice called 'minhah' (lit. 'gift' or 'tribute'), the object of which was to express gratitude to the god for benefits received, to retain his favour and to appease his wrath. According to W. R. Smith (*Religion of the Semites*, 3rd ed., 1927), the 'common meal' type of sacrifice was earlier in date and correspondingly more primitive than the 'gift' type, which was a later development ensuing on agricultural life. Other authorities, including G. B. Gray (*Sacrifice in the Old Testament*, 1925), hold that the 'gift' type of sacrifice was at least equally primitive with the other. Certainly in the Old Testament the two types of sacrifice are found side by side.

After the settlement in Canaan the Hebrews adopted an agricultural way of life and this meant a change in the materials of sacrifice. The term 'minhah' now came to denote a vegetable offering as distinct from an animal offering. A division was thus made between animal and vegetable offerings—between offerings 'of the fruit of the land' and 'of the herd and of the flock'. There is evidence to show that human beings were sometimes offered for sacrifice (Jud. xi. 30–35; 2 Kgs. xvi. 3, xxiii. 10; Mic. vi. 7; Jer. vii. 31; Ezek. xx. 26). As late as the time of Manasseh (687–642 BC) children were 'passed through the fire to Molech' (2 Kgs. xxi. 6, xxiii. 10). The practice was forbidden in the Deuteronomic Code (Deut. xviii. 10).

From early times the custom prevailed of offering sacrifices at places where there had been a manifestation of the divine presence and power, such as in the deliverance from famine or plague, victory over an enemy, or even an abundant harvest. 'In every place where I record my name I will come unto thee and I will bless thee' (Exod. xx. 24). After the conquest of Canaan sacrifices were also offered at the high places (bamoth, sing. bamath) or local sanctuaries, which had formerly belonged to the Canaanites (1 Kgs. iii. 3). From the settlement in Canaan down to the close of the seventh century BC most of the sanctuaries were of this kind, and it is highly probable that every small community throughout the land had its local bamath. In the Josianic reformation these local sanctuaries were destroyed (2 Kgs. xxiii. 5–20) and worship was centralized at Jerusalem (Deut. xii. 13, 14). The reformation, however, was only partially successful, and the ideal of a single sanctuary was not realized until after the Exile.

Principal Sacrifices

In the fully developed sacrificial system of the post-exilic period the following are the principal sacrifices:

The burnt-offering (Heb. 'olah', lit. 'that which ascends'). This sacrifice was offered on public occasions (Exod. xxix. 42; Num. xxviii. 24) and by private individuals (Lev. xxii. 18; Num. xv. 3). The victim was a male and unblemished. The blood was dashed all round the sides of the altar and the whole of the flesh consumed by fire (Exod. xxix. 15–18; Lev. i. 1–17). The burnt offering was accompanied by both a meal offering and a drink offering. In the post-exilic period there was a daily morning and evening burnt-offering called 'Tamid' (Exod. xxix. 38–42; Num. xxviii. 3–8). This was a development of the morning burnt-offering and the evening meal-offering of the pre-exilic period (2 Kgs. xvi. 15). The object of the offering was to make expiation for sin (Lev. i. 4, xvi. 24) and to serve as a 'sweet savour' to Yahweh (Lev. i. 9).

The peace-offering (Heb. 'shelem', plural 'shelamim'). The only public peace-offerings prescribed were those for the consecration of priests (Exod. xxix) and for the celebration of the Festival of Pentecost (Lev. xxiii. 19). With these exceptions the peace-offering was a private and family sacrifice. The victim was either a male or a female. Normally it was without blemish but an exception was allowed in the case of free-will offerings. The blood was dashed all round the altar and the fat burnt thereon; but the rest of the carcase was eaten, the breast and right thigh by the priests and the remainder by the offerer and his friends. There were three kinds of peace-offerings, namely, thank-offerings, votive-offerings, and freewill offerings (Lev. iii. 1–16, vii. 11–21, 28–34, xxii, 23). Nothing is said about the object of the peace-offering except that it was an 'offering made by fire, of a sweet savour unto the Lord' (Lev. iii. 5).

The meal-offering (lit. 'gift' or 'tribute'). This was a cereal or vegetable offering, consisting of flour, oil and frankincense. A handful of the offering was burnt on the altar and the rest went to the priests. The meal-offering was regarded as the regular accompaniment of the burnt-offering and of the peace-offering, but it could be offered independently (Lev. ii. 1–16).

The wine-offering (Heb. 'nesek'). This accompanied the burnt-offering. The quantity varied according to the size of the burnt offering. The manner of offering is not defined (Exod. xxix. 40; Lev. xxiii. 13; Num. xv. 1–16, 24).

The guilt-offering (Heb. 'asham'). This was made in expiation for the misappropriation of the property of another (Lev. vi. 1–7) or of the sacred dues—'the holy things of the Lord' (Lev. v. 14–19). The offender had to restore the property or dues withheld and pay a compensatory fine (a fifth of its value). Part of the blood was dashed all round the sides of the altar and part poured out at its base. Specified portions of the victim were burnt and the flesh was given to the priest to be eaten in a holy place (Lev. vii. 1–7). The object of the guilt-offering was to make expiation for sin and to secure forgiveness (Lev. vi. 7).

The sin-offering (Heb. 'hattath'). This was made as part of the rite of consecration to a sacred office (Lev. viii. 14), after certain breaches of the law committed accidentally or through ignorance (Num. xv. 22–29), and after accidents, maladies or natural processes which led to ceremonial impurity (Lev. xii. 6, xiv. 19). Different kinds of animals were offered according to the rank of the offerer—High Priest, community, ruler, private individual or the poor. For the ordinary person part of the blood was smeared on the horns of the altar of burnt offering and the rest poured out at its base. The fat was burnt and the flesh given to the priests (Lev. iv. 22–31, vi. 26, 29). For the High Priest or the community, part of the blood was sprinkled seven times before the veil of the inner sanctuary and the rest poured out, part was smeared on the horns of the altar of incense, and the rest poured out at the base of the altar of burnt-offering. The fat and certain other portions were burnt on the altar, and the rest of the carcase was burnt outside the camp (Exod. xxix. 10–14; Lev. iv. 1–21). The primary purpose of the sin-offering was to make expiation for sin and to secure forgiveness (Lev. iv. 26, 35, v. 10, 13).

Sacrifice in the Post-Exilic Period

After the Exile increasing stress was laid upon the idea of sacrifice as a means of atonement and of reconciliation with Yahweh. This is clearly seen in the guilt-offering and sin-offering which had been first mentioned by Ezekiel, though not specifically as new institutions (Ezek. xl. 39, xlii. 13). The prominence given to the idea of atonement and reconciliation through sacrifice was the result of several factors. The disasters, which had befallen the nation, had caused men to lose confidence in the protection and goodwill of Yahweh, and convinced them of the need of making atonement for their sins. The teaching of Ezekiel and Deutero-Isaiah on the transcendental character of Yahweh had produced in them an exalted conception of the divine holiness and a deep consciousness of their own sinfulness. Their inability to fulfil all the demands of the Law had given them a sense of failure and unworthiness. The idea of atonement reached the climax of its expression in the Day of Atonement, which has been called 'the crown of the sacrificial worship of the Old Testament'. It was held annually on the tenth day of the seventh month. On that day all work ceased and expiation was made for the sins of the High Priest, the priesthood and all the people (Lev. xvi. 1-34, xxiii. 27-29; Num. xxix. 7-10).

APPENDIX C

THE MESSIANIC HOPE

By the phrase 'Messianic Hope' is meant the expectation entertained among the Israelites long before the eighth century BC, that the day was speedily approaching when Yahweh would intervene in the course of human history, triumph over the heathen, exalt His own people and inaugurate a new age of prosperity, righteousness and peace. To that new age is generally given the title of the 'Kingdom of God', though the phrase does not actually appear in the Old Testament. The basis of Israel's hope is to be found in the hope that springs eternal in the human breast, but more especially in the peculiar relationship existing between Yahweh and His people. It was commonly assumed that because He was their God and they were His people, He would favour them and confer benefits upon them. But the prophet Amos in the eighth century BC shattered that false assumption, declaring that the 'day of the Lord' would be for them a day of judgement—a day of 'darkness and not light' (v. 20). Disaster would fall upon them because they had refused to obey the moral demands of Yahweh, who was a righteous God, requiring righteousness of life from His worshippers. He was a living God, acting in History to the end that His people should bring forth the fruits of righteousness.

The Kingdom which Yahweh would establish is usually called 'Messianic', but the term is misleading for two reasons. In the first place the ideal king is never called the 'Messiah'. Actually the term in its technical sense is found in one passage only in the Old Testament in the Authorized Version, namely the book of Daniel ix. 25, 26 (Revised Version has 'the anointed one'). There is no evidence to show that in the Old Testament times the term 'the anointed one' was used as a synonym for the expected Davidic ruler. The term, however, is found in later Jewish literature. Nevertheless, it may be used for the sake of convenience in speaking of the expected Davidic ruler. In the second place the figure of the Messiah does not appear in all the pictures of the Kingdom of God. The Jewish prophets and apocalyptists had no difficulty in conceiving that kingdom without a Messiah. There is, for example, no mention of a Messiah in Amos (ix. 11, 12) and Zephaniah (ii. 8–20) or in the long eschatological prophecies in Isaiah xxiv–xxvii, or in the descriptions of the new age in Isaiah liv. 11–17, lx–lxii, lxv–lxvi. The same is also true of Jewish literature outside the Old Testament. No reference, for example, is made to the Messiah in 1 and 2 Enoch, 1 and 2 Maccabees, 1 Baruch and the Assumption of Moses. It follows that in both Jewish prophecy and apocalyptic a Messiah is not an essential element in the conception of the Kingdom. When he is absent, the Kingdom is always represented as under the direct rule of Yahweh. Thus the Kingdom is represented either as under the direct rule of Yahweh or of the Messiah as His representative.[1]

The figure of the ideal king was a development from the idea of the Hebrew King as 'the Lord's anointed', and especially from the idealized kingdom of David. In Old Testament usage Yahweh was the real king of Israel and the earthly king ruled as His viceregent. The latter was consecrated to his office by the rite of anointing with holy oil, which, it was believed, imparted to him a special endowment of the spirit (cf. 1 Sam. x. 1, 10, xvi. 12, 13), and rendered his person sacrosanct (cf. 1 Sam. xxiv. 6, 10, xxvi. 9–23; 2 Sam. i. 14–16). Moreover David was regarded as the true founder of the monarchy. His kingdom stretched from the borders of Egypt to the gates of Damascus, and under him reached the zenith of prosperity and influence. It soon passed away, but the memory of its splendour lived on and men dreamt of a second Davidic kingdom more glorious than the first.

Isaiah is perhaps the first canonical prophet to refer to the advent of an ideal king. In Isaiah ix. 2–7 it is stated that Yahweh had broken the yoke of the oppressor and that the soldier's blood-stained war-attire would be burnt. For a child had been born who would wear the royal dignity upon his shoulders, and bear the four-fold title of 'Wonderful Counsellor, God-like Hero, Father for ever, Prince of Peace'. He would sit upon the throne of David and rule over a wide domain in righteousness and peace. In Isaiah xi. 1–9, we are told that the Messianic king would spring from the stock of the almost ruined Davidic family and would be endowed with the spirit of wisdom and understanding, the spirit of counsel and might, and the spirit that knew and reverenced Yahweh. Righteousness and faithfulness would be the strength of his government. He would inaugurate an era of peace the blessings of which would extend to the animal world. From Isaiah xxxii. 1–8, we learn that in the Messianic age kings and princes would rule in righteousness, and that protection would be extended to all who needed it. Some critics maintain that Isaiah vii. 14–17 is also a Messianic passage but there is no mention in it of the advent of an ideal king.[2] Micah v. 2–4, predicts the coming of the Messianic king from Bethlehem, the birth-place of David; He would rule in the strength of Yahweh and the people would continue to dwell in security, for he would

[1] R. H. Charles, *Between the Old and New Testaments*, 1914, pp. 75 f.
[2] The genuineness of the Messianic passages in Isaiah has been disputed. Questions of authorship and date, however, do not call for discussion here, since we are concerned only with the relationship between the Messiah and the Kingdom of God.

be great 'unto the ends of the earth'.[1] Jeremiah predicted that in the
coming days Yahweh would raise up a righteous branch or stock belonging
to the Davidic line, who, as king, would rule over a united people—Israel
as well as Judah—and would execute justice and righteousness in the
land. He would bear the title of 'The Lord our righteousness' (xxiii. 5, 6;
cf. xxxiii. 14–16). According to Ezekiel Yahweh would reunite Israel and
Judah under a Davidic king who would rule over a cleansed and obedient
people. They would dwell for ever in the land, and Yahweh would make
a new covenant of peace with them, establish His sanctuary permanently
among them and be their God (xxxvii. 15–28). The Servant Songs in
Deutero-Isaiah (xlii. 1–4, xlix. 1–6, l. 4–9, lii. 13–liii. 12) are not Messianic
in the strict sense of the term. Apart from these Songs the Old Testament
knows nothing of a suffering Messiah.

After the death of Cambyses in 522 BC widespread revolts broke out in
the Persian Empire, and the Jews hoped that in the general upheaval they
would be able to regain their independence. The prophets, Haggai and
Zechariah, reposed the most extravagant hopes in Zerubbabel, the Persian
governor, who was the grandson of Jehoiachin and therefore of the Davidic
line. Haggai declared that Yahweh would destroy the heathen kingdoms
and make His servant Zerubbabel 'as a signet', that is, invest him with
divine authority (Hag. ii. 20–23; cf. Jer. xxii. 24). Zechariah saw in him the
'Branch' or 'Shoot' (iii. 8, vi. 12), predicted by Jeremiah (xxiii. 5, xxxiii.
15), and told of the arrival at Jerusalem of Jews from Babylon, bearing
gifts of silver and gold, which were to be made into a crown for Zerubbabel.
He would rule with Joshua the High Priest seated on his right hand (vi.
9–15). What happened to Zerubbabel we do not know, for he disappeared
from history. The high hopes were followed by bitter disappointment, but
the Messianic hope lived on. It is painted in glowing colours in Isaiah
lx–lxii, lxv–lxvi, Malachi iii and Joel iii, iv. In Zechariah ix. 9–11, the
Messianic king appears riding in triumph into Jerusalem not on a horse,
the symbol of war, but on an ass, the symbol of peace. His sway would
extend 'from sea to sea, and from the River (Euphrates) to the ends of
the earth'. The Messianic hope is also found in several Psalms of uncertain
date (e.g. ii. 7–12, lxii). Some scholars maintain that these Psalms had a
liturgical origin in connection with the New Year's Day celebrations of
Yahweh's enthronement as king. In Daniel vii. 13, 14, we read of 'one
like unto a son of man', who comes on the clouds of heaven, approaches
'the ancient of days' and is given 'dominion and glory, and a kingdom,
that all the peoples, nations, and languages should serve him'. If the
figure is a personification of Israel, as some critics suggest, the passage is
not Messianic. It is quite possible, however, that he is a supernatural being
and denotes the Messianic king. In the 'Testaments of the Twelve

[1] Some critics assign this passage to a later period.

Patriarchs' the Messiah belongs to the tribe of Levi and appears as a warrior who destroys the wicked. In 1 Enoch xxxvii–lxxi, he is called the 'Son of Man' and is a supernatural being, pre-existing from the beginning, possessing universal dominion and coming to judge angels and men.

It will be seen that the picture drawn of the Messianic king varies. Sometimes the thought is theocratic and God Himself is king, while at other times he is a human figure—a Davidic prince of the tribe of Judah, or a priest of the tribe of Levi; or a supernatural being—the Son of Man, coming on the clouds of heaven and the object of man's worship.

The Messianism of the prophets was a simple doctrine. The day was speedily approaching when evil would be eradicated from the world and righteousness established for ever. Social injustice would be eliminated from the life of mankind and human societies infused with justice and love. War would be abolished and peace would reign over the whole earth. 'They shall not hurt nor destroy in all my holy mountain: for the earth shall be full of the knowledge of the Lord, as the waters cover the sea' (Is. xi. 9). Some of the prophets mention the reign of an ideal king.

The 'Messianic hope' was both the glory and the ruin of Israel. On the one hand, it inspired some of the noblest passages in the Old Testament and was a source of comfort to the people in the dark periods of their history. On the other hand, the revival of the hope in the first century of the Christian era led ultimately to the destruction of Jerusalem by the Romans in AD 70 and to the extinction of the Jewish state.

APPENDIX D

THE CALENDAR

THE DAY

The day was the smallest division of time. The natural day, that is, the period of daylight, was reckoned from sunrise to sunset and was roughly divided into periods—morning, noonday or mid-day, and evening. Any shorter division of time was unknown in Old Testament times. The night was divided into three watches, namely, 'the beginning of the watches' (Lam. ii. 19), 'the middle watch' (Jud. vii. 19), and 'the morning watch' (Exod. xi. 4, xiv. 24; 1 Sam. xi. 11). In post-exilic times the civil day (i.e. the day used in common reckoning) was reckoned from six in the evening to six the next evening.

THE WEEK

The week consisted of seven days which were indicated by numbers, with the exception of the seventh which was called the Sabbath. In the late post-exilic period the sixth day of the week came to be known as the 'Preparation' (Mt. xxvii. 62; Mk. xv. 42; Lk. xxiii. 54; Jn. xix. 31).

THE YEAR

In early times among the Hebrews the year was probably lunar, consisting of twelve lunar months—a month being the period of time taken by the moon to make one complete circuit round the earth (c. $29\frac{1}{2}$ days). As, however, it was found that the months moved out of their proper seasons, the solar year—the period of time taken by the earth to complete one circuit round the sun (c. $365\frac{1}{4}$ days)—was adopted, while at the same time the lunar months were retained. The year became what is known as 'luni-solar' because the months were lunar and the year was solar. Now the twelve months of the lunar year consisted of 354 days, so that the lunar year was approximately $11\frac{1}{4}$ days shorter than the solar year. Some method of adjusting the lunar year to the solar year must have been devised, but what that method was we do not know. After the Exile the Metonic cycle of 19 years (devised by Meton, an Athenian astronomer, about 432 BC) was adopted, whereby an extra (intercalary) month was added to the 3rd, 6th, 8th, 11th, 14th, 17th, and 19th years. When an extra month was required, the month Adar was repeated.

The months of the year were given Canaanite names, four of which are recorded in the Old Testament, namely, Abib (Exod. xii. 2, xiii. 4; Deut. xvi. 1), Ziv (1 Kgs. vi. 37), Ethanim (1 Kgs. viii. 2) and Bul (1 Kgs. vi. 38). They were also differentiated by numbers. After the Exile they were given Babylonian names, which were transliterated in Hebrew, though they were frequently designated by their order only.

In pre-exilic times New Year's Day was celebrated in the Autumn on the first day of Tishri. After the Exile it was celebrated in the Spring on the first day of Nisan as well as in the Autumn. The first day of Tishri marked the beginning of the civil year and the first day of Nisan the beginning of the sacred year.

The following Table gives the Canaanite and Babylonian names of the months, their positions in the civil and sacred years, and the corresponding months of our calendar (these are only approximate).

Month of Civil Year	Canaanite Name	Month of Sacred Year	Babylonian Name	Corresponding Month of our Year
7	Abib	1	Nisan	March–April
8	Ziv	2	Iyyar	April–May
9		3	Sivan	May–June
10		4	Tammuz	June–July
11		5	Ab	July–August
12		6	Elul	August–September
1	Ethanim	7	Tishri	September–October
2	Bul	8	Marchesvan	October–November
3		9	Chislev	November–December
4		10	Tebeth	December–January
5		11	Shebat	January–February
6		12	Adar	February–March

THE ERA

The Hebrews had no era for the recording of dates. Events were dated by reference to some memorable event (Exod. xii. 40, 41; Am. i. 1) or, under the monarchy, to the regnal years of the sovereigns.

APPENDIX E

FEASTS AND FASTS

FEASTS

Feast of the New Moon

The feast was celebrated on the day of the new moon and announced by the sound of trumpets (Num. x. 10, xxviii. 11–15). It is frequently mentioned in the Old Testament but no reason is given for its celebration. It was a holy day and a day of rest (1 Sam. xx. 18; 2 Kgs. iv. 23; Am. viii. 4, 5).

Feast of the Sabbath

This was a weekly feast. On this day all work was forbidden and the daily morning and evening sacrifices were doubled. Sabbath breaking was punishable by death (Exod. xxxi. 13–17; Num. xv. 32–36). Its close connection with the New Moon suggests that it was originally a lunar festival (Am. viii. 5; Hos. ii. 11; Is. i. 13, lxvi. 23; Ezek. xlv. 17, xlvi. 3). Various reasons are given in the Old Testament for its observance. In Exodus xx. 11, xxxi. 17, the weekly rest is commanded in order to commemorate the completion of the work of creation. In Exodus xxiii. 12 it is enjoined on humanitarian grounds—that the beasts may rest and that slaves may be refreshed. In Deuteronomy v. 14, 15 it is to be observed in order to commemorate the deliverance from Egypt.

Feast of the Passover

The Passover was a feast of great antiquity going back to Israel's nomadic period. It fell on the fourteenth day of the first month of the sacred year —Nisan, and commemorated the deliverance from Egypt (Exod. xii. 1–29; Num. xxviii. 16; Deut. xvi. 1–8). An animal from the flock was sacrificed and the blood was sprinkled on the doorposts and lintels of the houses of the worshippers. It was a night celebration and took place between sunset and sunrise.

Feast of Unleavened Bread (or Cakes)

The feast was probably adopted from the Canaanites after the transition of Israel from a nomadic to an agricultural way of life. It began on the fifteenth day of Nisan and lasted seven days (Exod. xiii. 3–10; Lev. xxiii. 6–8; Num. xxviii. 17–25). Its principal feature was the exclusion of leaven from bread. It marked the beginning of the barley harvest. At first it probably had nothing to do with the Feast of the Passover, but later the two feasts were combined (Exod. xxiii. 15; Deut. xvi. 1–8).

Feast of Harvest

Like the Feast of Unleavened Bread this feast was probably borrowed from the Canaanites. It is called the Feast of Harvest in Exodus xxiii. 16, the Feast of Weeks in Exodus xxxiv. 22, and Deuteronomy xvi. 10; and the day of 'First Fruits' in Numbers xxviii. 26. At a later date it became known as the 'Feast of Pentecost (Greek 'pentēcostē'=fiftieth). It was celebrated fifty days after the beginning of the Passover season (Exod. xxiii. 16, xxxiv. 22; Num. xxviii. 26–31), and marked the completion of the wheat harvest a few weeks after the April barley harvest. It probably lasted one day. It was a day of holy convocation on which no servile work might be done. Two leavened loaves of wheaten flour were offered to Yahweh as first fruits accompanied by burnt offerings (Lev. xxiii. 15–21; Num. xxviii. 26–31; Deut. xvi. 10). Later Jewish writers associated the feast with the giving of the Law on Mount Sinai, which was supposed to have taken place fifty days after the Exodus.

Feast of Tabernacles

Like the Feast of Unleavened Bread and the Feast of Harvest, this feast was probably borrowed from the Canaanites. It probably derived its name from the huts or booths, made of the branches of trees, in which the people engaged in gathering the grapes, etc., lived. In Exodus xxiii. 16, xxxiv. 22 it is called the Feast of Ingathering and its date is fixed at the end of the year. According to Deuteronomy xvi. 13, it lasted seven days, but according to Leviticus xxiii. 34–36 and Numbers xxix. 12–39, it was to begin on the fifteenth day of Tishri and to last eight days. It marked the ingathering of the grapes, olives and fruits and was also regarded as commemorating the wanderings of the Israelites in the desert. It was an occasion for great joy and for the giving of presents.

Feast of Trumpets

This feast was celebrated on the first day of Tishri, the seventh month of the sacred year and the first month of the civil year. People were summoned to the holy convocation by the blowing of trumpets. No servile work was done, and a burnt offering in addition to the usual daily and monthly offerings was presented (Lev. xxiii. 24, 25; Num. xxix. 1–6).

Feast of Dedication

The feast was instituted by Judas Maccabaeus to commemorate the purification of the Temple on the 25th day of Chislev in 164 BC, after its desecration by pagan ceremonies (1 Macc. iv. 59). It was observed for eight days and was marked by joyous meals, extra illumination of houses, uplifting synagogue services, and the carrying of branches as at the Feast of Tabernacles.

Feast of Purim

The feast was celebrated on the fourteenth and fifteenth days of Adar and commemorated the defeat of Haman's plot for the destruction of the Jews (Est. iii. 7, ix. 26). It is also called Mordecai's Day (2 Macc. xv. 36).

Feast of Nicanor

The feast was instituted by Judas Maccabaeus to commemorate the victory over Nicanor, the general of the Syrian forces of Demetrius I, at Adasa in 160 BC. It was observed on the thirteenth day of Adar (1 Macc. vii. 49; 2 Macc. xv. 36).

Feast of Wood Offering

The feast fell on the fifteenth day of Abib (or Nisan) at which time people brought wood to the Temple for altar use (Neh. x. 34).

Feast of Sheep-Shearing

The feast belonged originally to nomadic times. It is mentioned only three times in the Old Testament (Gen. xxxviii. 12, 13; 1 Sam. xxv. 4–11; 2 Sam. xiii. 23, 24) but it must have been celebrated at regular intervals. It was a joyful occasion when much eating and drinking took place.

Sabbatical Year

Every seventh year the land was to lie fallow for the benefit of the poor and the beasts of the field (Exod. xxiii. 10, 11). Hebrew slaves were to be released and debts remitted (Exod. xxi. 2; Deut. xv. 1, 12; Deut. xxxiv. 8–16). In Leviticus xxv. 1–7 there is no mention of the poor. Every seventh year was to be 'a sabbath of solemn rest for the land'—a sabbath in honour of Yahweh. The natural produce of the land was to serve as food for the owner, his slaves and hired servants, any strangers staying with him, and his cattle and livestock.

Jubilee Year

At the expiration of the period of forty-nine years a year of Jubilee was to be observed. The word 'Jubilee' is derived from a Hebrew word meaning 'ram's horn' (that is, 'trumpet'). The year was so called because it was proclaimed by the blowing of trumpets in convocation on the Day of Atonement. In that year all land was to lie fallow, all Hebrew slaves were to be liberated, and all land sold or mortgaged was to be returned to its original owner. Houses in walled cities, sold and not redeemed within one year, became the permanent possession of the purchasers and did not return to their original owners at the Jubilee. The houses of the Levitical cities could be redeemed at any time and did not come under the Jubilee provisions. These, if sold and not redeemed, returned to the Levites at the Jubilee (Lev. xxv. 8–55).

FASTS

The Day of Atonement

The Day of Atonement was the most solemn of all Hebrew fasts. It fell on the tenth day of Tishri and was the only fast commanded by the Law (Lev. xvi. 29, xxiii. 27–32). In Leviticus xvi. 33 it is said that on the Day of Atonement the priest 'shall make atonement for the holy sanctuary, and he shall make atonement for the tent of meeting and for the altar; and he shall make atonement for the priests and for all the people of the assembly'. It was thus an annual complete atonement for all sin. It involved abstinence from all labour, the calling of a holy convocation, and the entry of the High Priest into the Holy of Holies—his only entry during the year. It was a time of prayer, confession and fasting.

Other Fasts

According to Zechariah vii. 3–5, viii. 19, four fasts were observed in the post-exilic period. They were held:

(1) On the ninth day of Tammuz, to commemorate the capture of Jerusalem by Nebuchadrezzar (2 Kgs. xxv. 3–5; Jer. xxxix. 2, lii. 6–8).

(2) On the tenth day of Ab, to commemorate the destruction of the city and the Temple (2 Kgs. xxv. 8; Jer. lii. 12).

(3) In the month Tishri (no day is mentioned), to commemorate the murder of Gedaliah (2 Kgs. xxv. 25; Jer. xl. 1).

(4) On the tenth day of Tebeth, to commemorate the beginning of the siege of Jerusalem (2 Kgs. xxv. 1; Jer. lii. 4).

APPENDIX F

WEIGHTS, MEASURES AND MONEY

WEIGHTS

Babylonian measures used before the Hebrew conquest of Palestine:

10 gerahs	=	1 beka
2 bekas	=	1 shekel
60 shekels	=	1 mina
60 minas	=	1 talent

The shekel was the unit of weight. There were two standards for the shekel, mina and talent, namely, the heavy and the light, the former being double the latter. The heavy gold shekel weighed about 16·37 grammes or ·577 oz. (avoirdupois) or 252 grains.

Phoenician measures widely used after the Hebrew conquest of Palestine:

10 gerahs	=	1 beka
2 bekas	=	1 shekel
50 shekels	=	1 mina
60 minas	=	1 talent

The shekel was the unit of weight. The heavy silver shekel weighed about 14·55 grammes or 224·5 grains, but recent discovery of weights show that its weight varied at different periods.

DRY MEASURES

1 cab	=	c. 3·55 pts.
6 cabs	=	1 seah (c. 2·66 gals.)
3 seahs	=	1 ephah (c. 7·98 gals.)
5 ephahs	=	1 lethech (c. 39·9 gals.)
10 ephahs	=	1 homer or cor (c. 79·8 gals.)

LIQUID MEASURES

1 log	=	c. ·88 pts.
12 logs	=	1 hin (10·56 pts.)
6 hins	=	1 bath = 1 ephah (7·98 gals.)

MEASURES OF LENGTH

1 fingerbreadth	=	*c.* ·733 in.
4 fingerbreadths	=	1 handbreadth (*c.* 2·93 in.)
3 handbreadths	=	1 span (*c.* 8·8 in.)
2 spans	=	1 cubit (*c.* 17·6 in.)
6 cubits	=	1 reed (*c.* 105·6 in.)

The length of the cubit varied at different periods. The common cubit was about 17·6 inches, and the so-called 'royal cubit' used in the building of Solomon's Temple (2 Chron. lii. 3) and mentioned in Ezekiel in his account of the Temple in the New Jerusalem (Ezek. xl. 5), was a cubit and a handbreadth, that is, about 20·63 inches.

In the Old Testament distances are not measured directly but are suggested by such expressions as 'three days' journey' (Gen. xxx. 36) and 'seven days' journey' (Gen. xxxi. 23).

MEASURES OF AREA

Areas were reckoned in terms of the amount of land which a team of oxen could plough in one day (1 Sam. xiv. 14; Is. v. 10).

MONEY

Among the Hebrews in pre-exilic times money values were reckoned by weight, not by coinage. Allusions to money are confusing because words like 'shekel' and 'talent' first referred to weights (Gen. xxiii. 16; 1 Chron. xxi. 25), but were later used to mean coins. It was not till after the Exile that coined money was circulated in Palestine. The first coin to be circulated was the Persian gold 'daric', issued by Darius I (522–486 BC) and weighing about 130 grains (1 Chron. xxix. 7). There was also a gold 'daric' weighing about 86·4 grains. During the Persian period Judah was allowed to have a silver coinage of its own. Coins of Alexander the Great, the Ptolemies, and the Seleucids also circulated in Palestine as did those of Tyre and Zidon. Simon Maccabaeus (142-134 BC) gained the right to issue a coinage, but it is uncertain whether the silver shekels and half-shekels should be assigned to him or to another Simon of the Jewish revolt of AD 66–70. The conquest of Palestine by Pompey led to the introduction of the Roman coinage.

APPENDIX G

CHRONOLOGICAL TABLES

TABLE I

THE DIVIDED MONARCHY 922–587 BC

ISRAEL		JUDAH	
	BC		BC
Jeroboam I	922–901	Rehoboam	922–915
Nadab	901–900	Abijam	915–913
Baasha	900–877	Asa	913–873
Elah	877–876	Jehoshaphat	873–849
Zimri	876	Jehoram	849–842
Omri	876–869	Ahaziah	842
Ahab	869–850	Athaliah	842–837
Ahaziah	850–849	Jehoash	837–800
Jehoram	849–842	Amaziah	800–783
Jehu	842–815	Azariah (Uzziah)	783–742
Jehoahaz	815–801	Jotham (regent)	750–742
Jehoash	801–786	Jotham (king)	742–735
Jeroboam II	786–746	Ahaz	735–715
Zechariah	746–745	Hezekiah	715–687
Shallum	745	Manasseh	687–642
Menahem	745–738	Amon	642–640
Pekahiah	738–737	Josiah	640–609
Pekah	737–732	Jehoahaz (Shallum)	609
Hoshea	732–724	Jehoiakim (Eliakim)	609–598
Fall of Samaria	722	Jehoiachin (Jeconiah)	598
		Zedekiah (Mattaniah)	598–587
		Fall of Jerusalem	587

TABLE II

ASSYRIAN KINGS 811–612 BC

	BC
Adad-nirari III	811–782
Shalmaneser IV	782–772
Ashur-dan III	772–754
Ashur-nirari V	754–745
Tiglath-pileser III	745–727
Shalmaneser V	727–722
Sargon	722–705
Sennacherib	705–681
Esarhaddon	681–669
Ashurbanipal (Sardanapalus)	669–626
Ashur-etil-ilani	626–621
Sin-shum-lishir	621
Sin-shum-ishkun	621–612
Fall of Nineveh	612

TABLE III

BABYLONIAN KINGS 625–539 BC

	BC
Nabopolassar	625–605
Nebuchadrezzar	605–562
Amel-Marduk (Evil-merodach)	562–560
Nergal-shar-usur (Neriglissar)	560–556
Labashi-Marduk	556
Nabu-naid (Nabonidus)	556–539
Fall of Babylon	539

TABLE IV

IMPORTANT KINGS AND EVENTS IN EGYPTIAN HISTORY

	BC
Shabaka	712–700
Taharka (Tirhakah)	689–664
Destruction of Thebes	663
Psammetichus I	663–609
Necho	609–593
Necho defeated at Carchemish	605
Psammetichus II	593–588
Apries (Hophra)	588–569

TABLE V

EVENTS IN JEWISH HISTORY 538–63 BC

	BC
Return of the Exiles	538
Building of the Second Temple	520–516
Dedication of Second Temple	516
Nehemiah's governorship	445–433
Return of Ezra	397
Samaritan Schism	335
Conquest of Palestine by Alexander	331
Palestine under the Ptolemies	312
Palestine passes to Seleucids	198
Profanation of Temple	167
Revolt under Judas Maccabaeus	167
Rededication of Temple	164
Death of Judas Maccabaeus	160
Jonathan	160–142
Simon	142–134
John Hyrcanus I	134–104
Aristobulus I	104–103
Alexander Jannaeus	103–76
Alexandra	76–67
Civil War between Hyrcanus II and Aristobulus II	67–63
Pompey conquers Jerusalem and Palestine becomes a Roman Province	63

TABLE VI

PERSIAN KINGS 539–331 BC

	BC
Cyrus (counting from conquest of Babylon)	539–530
Cambyses	530–522
Darius I	522–486
Xerxes I (Ahasuerus)	486–465
Artaxerxes I (Longimanus)	465–424
Xerxes II	424–423
Darius II	423–404
Artaxerxes II (Mnemon)	404–358
Artaxerxes III (Ochus)	358–338
Arses	338–336
Darius III (Codomannus)	336–331
Alexander conquers Persian Empire	331

TABLE VII

THE PTOLEMIES (EGYPT)

	BC
Ptolemy I (Soter)	323–283
Ptolemy II (Philadelphus)	285–246
Ptolemy III (Euergetes)	246–221
Ptolemy IV (Philopator)	221–203
Ptolemy V (Epiphanes)	203–181
Ptolemies continue until Egypt becomes a Roman province in	30

TABLE VIII

THE SELEUCIDS (SYRIA)

	BC
Seleucus I (Nicator)	312–280
Antiochus I (Soter)	280–261
Antiochus II	261–247
Seleucus II	247–226
Seleucus III	226–223
Antiochus III (the Great)	223–187
Seleucus IV	187–175
Antiochus IV (Epiphanes)	175–163
Antiochus V (Eupator)	163–162
Demetrius I	162–150
Alexander Balas, a usurper	150–145
Antiochus VI	145–142
Demetrius II	142–139
Antiochus VII (Sidetes)	139–129

L*

APPENDIX H

BIBLIOGRAPHY

The following bibliography makes no claim to be exhaustive. It is simply a small selection of relevant works from a great volume of literature, and is designed primarily as a guide to those who may wish to pursue the study of the subject further. Reference is made to a few foreign works, but the student, whose reading is restricted to English, has been chiefly kept in mind.

COMMENTARIES

A Commentary on the Bible, new edition with Supplement, edited by A. S. Peake and A. J. Grieve, 1936.

A New Commentary on Holy Scripture, edited by C. Gore, 1928.

Handbuch zum Alten Testament, edited by O. Eissfeldt, 1934+

Handkommentar zum Alten Testament, edited by W. Nowack, 1892–1933.

One Volume Dictionary of the Bible, edited by J. Hastings, 1909.

The Abingdon Bible Commentary, edited by F. C. Eiselen, E. Lewis and D. G. Downey, 1929.

The Cambridge Bible, edited by A. F. Kirkpatrick, 1877+

The Century Bible, edited by W. F. Adeney, 1901–22.

The International Critical Commentary, edited by S. R. Driver, A. Plummer and C. A. Briggs, 1895+

The Westminster Commentaries, edited by W. Lock and D. C. Simpson, 1899+

INTRODUCTIONS

Bentzen, A., *Introduction to the Old Testament*, vol. I, 1948; vol. III, 1949.

Bewer, J. A., *The Literature of the Old Testament in its Historical Development*, 2nd ed., 1933.

Cook, S. A., *An Introduction to the Bible*, 1945.

Dodd, C. H., *The Authority of the Bible*, 1946.

Driver, S. R., *An Introduction to the Literature of the Old Testament*, 9th ed., 1913.

Eissfeldt, O., *Enleitung in das Alte Testament*, 1934.

McFadyen, J. E., *Introduction to the Old Testament*, rev. ed., 1932.

Gray, G. B., *A Critical Approach to the Old Testament*, 9th ed., 1913.

Hahn, H. F., *Old Testament in Modern Research*, 1954.
Kent, C. F., *The Growth and Contents of the Old Testament*, 1926.
Manson, T. W. (Ed.), *A Companion to the Bible*, rev. ed., 1956.
Moore, G. F., *The Literature of the Old Testament*, rev. ed., 1948.
Oesterly, W. O. E., and Robinson, T. H., *An Introduction to the Books of the Old Testament*, 1934.
Peake, A. S., *The People and the Book*, 1925.
Pfeiffer, R. H., *Introduction to the Old Testament*, rev. ed., 1948.
Robinson, H. W., *The Old Testament: its Making and Meaning*, 1937.
Robinson, H. W. (Ed.), *Record and Revelation*, 1938.
Rowley, H. H., *The Growth of the Old Testament*, 1950.
Rowley, H. H. (Ed.), *The Old Testament and Modern Study*, 1951.
Sellin, E., *Einleitung in das Alte Testament*, 8th ed., 1950.

HEBREW RELIGION

Albright, W. F., *From the Stone Age to Christianity*, 2nd ed., 1946.
Cook, S. A., *The Religion of Ancient Palestine in the Light of Archaeology*, 1930.
Elmslie, W. A. L., *How Came our Faith*, 1948.
Gray, G. B., *Sacrifice in the Old Testament*, 1925.
Leslie, E. A., *Old Testament Religion in the Light of its Canaanite Background*, 1936.
Meek, T. J., *Hebrew Origins*, rev. ed., 1950.
Oesterley, W. O. E., and Robinson, T. H., *Hebrew Religion, its Origin and Development*, 2nd ed., 1937.
Richardson, A. (Ed.), *A Theological Word Book of the Bible*, 1950.
Robinson, H. W., *Inspiration and Revelation in the Old Testament*, 1946.
The Religious Ideas of the Old Testament, 1913.
Rowley, H. H., *The Rediscovery of the Old Testament*, 1946.
Schofield, J. N., *The Religious Background of the Bible*, 1944.
Snaith, N. H., *The Distinctive Ideas of the Old Testament*, 1944.

CHAPTER I

THE PROPHETIC LITERATURE

Birkeland, H., *Zum hebräischen Traditionswesen: die Komposition der prophetischen Bucher des Alten Testament*, 1938.
Mowinckel, S., *Prophecy and Tradition*, 1946.
Robinson, H. W. (Ed.), Article on Modern Criticism by O. Eissfeldt in *Record and Revelation*, 1938.

Robinson, T. H., *Prophecy and the Prophets in Ancient Israel*, rev. ed., 1950.

Rowley, H. H. (Ed.), Article on The Prophetic Literature by O. Eissfeldt in *The Old Testament and Modern Study*, 1951.

Ryle, H. E., *The Canon of the Old Testament*, 2nd ed., 1925.

Widengren, G., *Literary and Psychological Aspects of the Hebrew Prophets*, 1948.

CHAPTER II

THE HISTORICAL BACKGROUND

Albright, W. F., *From the Stone Age to Christianity*, 2nd ed., 1946; *The Biblical Record*, 1952.

Baynes, N. H., *Israel amongst the Nations*, 1927.

Bertholet, A., *Kulturgeschichte Israels*, 1920 (Eng. trans. by A. K. Dallas, *A History of Hebrew Civilization*, 1926.)

Bevan, E. R., *Jerusalem under the High Priests*, 1924.

Bury, J. B., etc. (Eds.), Relevant Articles in *The Cambridge Ancient History*, vols. I–X, 1923–34.

Gadd, C. J., *The Fall of Nineveh*, 1923.

Grollenberg, L. H., *Atlas of the Bible* (Trans. and edit. by J. M. H. Reid and H. H. Rowley, 1956).

Hall, H. B., *The Ancient History of the Near East*, 8th ed., 1932.

Lods, A., *Les Prophètes d'Israël et les Débuts du Judaisme*, 1935 (Eng. trans. by S. H. Hooke, *The Prophets and the Rise of Judaism*, 1937).

Oesterley, W. O. E., and Robinson, T. H., *A History of Israel*, 2 vols., 1932.

Robinson, H. W., *The History of Israel: Its Facts and Factors*, 1938.

Schofield, J. N., *The Historical Background of the Bible*, 1938.

Smith, G. A., *Historical Geography of the Holy Land*, 25th ed., 1931.

CHAPTER III

ARCHAEOLOGY AND THE PROPHETIC PERIOD

Albright, W. F., *From the Stone Age to Christianity*, 2nd ed., 1946; *Archaeology of Palestine*, 1949; *The Bible after twenty years of Archaeology*, 1932–1952; *Archaeology and the Religion of Israel*, 3rd ed., 1953.

Burrows, M., *What mean these Stones?* 1941. *The Dead Sea Scrolls*, 1956.

Caiger, S. L., *Bible and Spade*, rev. ed., 1951.

Cowley, A., *Aramaic Papyri of the Fifth Century*, 1923.

Driver, G. R., *The Hebrew Scrolls*, 1952.

Duncan, J. G., *Digging up Biblical History*, 2 vols., 1931.

Dupont-Sommer, A., *The Dead Sea Scrolls*, 1952.

Jack, J. W., *The Ras Shamra Tablets*, 1935.

Kenyon, Sir F., *The Bible and Archaeology*, 1940.

Kraeling, E. G., *The Brooklyn Museum Aramaic Papyri. New documents of the fifth century* BC *from the Jewish colony of Elephantine*, 1953.

Luckenbill, D. D., *Ancient Records of Assyria*, 2 vols., 1927.

Rowley, H. H., *The Dead Sea Scrolls and their Significance*, 1954.

Thompson, R. C., *The Prisms of Esarhaddon and Ashurpanibal*, 1931.

Torczyner, H., *The Lachish Letters*, 1937.

British Museum, *Guide to the Babylonian and Assyrian Antiquities*, 1922.

CHAPTER IV

THE PROPHETS

Charles, R. C., *Religious Development between the Old and the New Testaments*, 1914.

Johnson, A. R., *The Cultic Prophet in Ancient Israel*, 1944.

Micklem, N., *Prophecy and Eschatology*, 1926.

Peake, A. S., *The Roots of Hebrew Prophecy and Jewish Apocalyptic*, 1923.

Ringgren, H., *The Messiah in the Old Testament*, 1956.

Robinson, T. H., *Prophecy and the Prophets in Ancient Israel*, 2nd ed., 1953.

Rowley, H. H., *The Relevance of Apocalyptic*, 1944.

Scott, R. B. Y., *The Relevance of the Prophets*, 1944.

Smith, J. M. P., *The Prophets and their Times*, 2nd ed., rev. by W. A. Irwin, 1941.

Welch, A. C., *The Religion of Israel under the Kingdom*, 1912; *Prophet and Priest in Old Israel*, 1936.

CHAPTER V

THE FORMS AND CHARACTERISTICS OF HEBREW POETRY

Burney, C. F., *The Poetry of our Lord*, 1925.

Gray, G. B., *The Forms of Hebrew Poetry*, 1915.

Macdonald, D. B., *The Hebrew Literary Genius*, 1933.

Robinson, T. H., *The Poetry of the Old Testament*, 1947.

Sands, P. C., *Literary Genius of the Old Testament*, 1924.

CHAPTER VI

AMOS

Bleeker, L. H. K. (See under *Hosea*.)
Cripps, R. S., *The Book of Amos*.
Lippl, J., and Theis, J. (See under *Hosea*.)
Robinson, T. H. (See under *Hosea*.)
Weiser, A., *Die Prophetie des Amos*, 1923.

CHAPTER VII

HOSEA

Bleeker, L. H. K., *Die Kleine Profeten I*, 1932.
Brown, S. L., *The Book of Hosea* (West. Com.).
Lindblom, J., *Hosea literarisch undersucht*, 1927.
Lippl, J., and Theis, J., *Hosea–Micha*, 1937.
Robinson, T. H., *Hosea–Micha*, 1936.

CHAPTER VIII

MICAH

Bleeker, L. H. K. (See under *Joel*.)
Lindblom, J., *Micha literarisch undersucht*, 1929.
Lippl, J., and Theis, J. (See under *Hosea*.)
Robinson, T. H. (See under *Hosea*.)
Wade, G. W., *Micah, Obadiah, Joel, Jonah*, 1925 (West. Com.).

CHAPTERS IX, XV, XVIII

ISAIAH I–XXXIX, XL–LV, LVI–LXVI

Bewer, J. A., *The Book of Isaiah*, vols. III and IV, 1950.
Box, G. H., *The Book of Isaiah*, 1908.
Duhm, B., *Das Buch Jesaia*, 1914.
North, R. N., *Isaiah, 40–55*, 1952.
Peake, A. S., *The Servant of Yahweh and other Lectures*, 1931.
Robinson, H. W., *The Cross of the Servant*, a Study in Deutero-Isaiah, 1926.
Rowley, H. H., *The Servant of the Lord*, 1952.
Skinner, J., *The Book of the Prophet Isaiah*, Chapters I–XXXIX, 1917 (Cam. B.).

Smith, S., *Isaiah, Chapters XL–LV*, 1944.
Torrey, C. C., *The Second Isaiah*, 1928.
Volz, P., *Jesaia II*, 1932.
Wade, G. W., *The Book of the Prophet Isaiah*, 1911 (West. Com.).
Whitehouse, O. C., *Isaiah*, 2 vols., 1905–8 (Cent. B.).

CHAPTER X

ZEPHANIAH

Bewer, J. A., Zephaniah in *The Twelve Prophets*, vol. II, 1950.
Driver, S. R. (See under *Nahum*.)
Horst, F. (See under *Nahum*.)
Stonehouse, G. G. V., and Wade, G. W., *Zephaniah, Nahum and Habak-kuk*, 1929 (West. Com.).

CHAPTER XI

NAHUM

Bévenot, H., *Nahum and Habakkuk*, 1937.
Bewer, J. A., Nahum in *The Twelve Prophets*, vol. II, 1950.
Driver, S. R., *Nahum, Habakkuk, Zephaniah, Haggai, Zechariah, Malachi*, 1906 (Cent. B.).
Horst, F., *Nahum–Malachi*, 1938.
Stonehouse, G. G. V., and Wade, G. W. (See under Zephaniah.)

CHAPTER XII

HABAKKUK

Bévenot, H. (See under Nahum.)
Bewer, J. A., Habakkuk in *The Twelve Prophets*, vol. II, 1950.
Driver, S. R. (See under Nahum.)
Horst, F. (See under Nahum.)
Stonehouse, G. G. V., and Wade, G. W. (See under Nahum.)

CHAPTER XIII

JEREMIAH

Bewer, J. A., *The Book of Jeremiah*, vol. I, 1951; vol. II, 1952.
Binns, L. E., *The Book of the Prophet Jeremiah*, 1919 (West. Com.).
Condamin, A., *Le livre de Jeremie*, 3rd ed., 1936.
Cornill, C. H., *Das Buch Jeremia*, 1905.

Leslie, E. A., *Jeremiah—Chronologically arranged, translated and interpreted*, 1954.

Peake, A. S., *Jeremiah*, 1912 (Cent. B.).

Rudolf, W., *Jeremia*, 1947.

Skinner, J., *Prophecy and Religion*, 1922.

Smith, G. A., *Jeremiah*, 1924.

Volz, P., *Der Prophet Jeremia*, 1930.

Welch, A. C., *Jeremiah, His Time and His Work*, 1928.

CHAPTER XIV

EZEKIEL

Battersby-Harford, J., *Studies in the Book of Ezekiel*, 1935.

Bertholet, A., *Hezekiel*, 1936.

Bewer, J. A., *The Book of Ezekiel*, vols. I and II, 1954.

Browne, L. E., *Ezekiel and Alexander*, 1952.

Cooke, G. A., *Ezekiel*, 1936 (I.C.C.).

Finegan, J., *The Chronology of Ezekiel*, 1950.

Herntrich, V., *Ezechiel probleme*, 1932.

Hölscher, G., *Hesekiel: der Dichter und das Buch*, 1924.

Irwin, W. A., *The Problem of Ezekiel*, 1943.

Messel, N., *Ezechielfragen*, 1945.

Smith, J., *The Book of the Prophet Ezekiel*, 1931.

Torrey, C. C., *Pseudo-Ezekiel and the Original Prophecy*, 1934.

CHAPTER XV (XL–LV)

(See under Isaiah)

CHAPTER XVI

HAGGAI

Driver, S. R. (See under Nahum.)

Horst, F. (See under Nahum.)

Mitchell, H. G., *Haggai and Zechariah*, 1912 (I.C.C.).

CHAPTERS XVII, XXIII

ZECHARIAH (I–VIII, IX–XIV)

Driver, S. R. (See under Nahum.)

Horst, F. (See under Nahum.)

Mitchell, H. G. (See under Haggai.)

CHAPTER XVIII (LVI–LXVI)
(See under Isaiah)

CHAPTER XIX
OBADIAH

Bleeker, L. H. K., *De Kleine Profeten II*, 1934.
Lippl, J., and Theis, J. (See under Hosea.)
Robinson, T. H. (See under Hosea.)
Wade, G. W. (See under Micah.)

CHAPTER XX
MALACHI

Horst, F. (See under Nahum.)
Smith, J. M. P., *Malachi*, 1912 (I.C.C.).
Von Bulmerincq, A., *Der Prophet Maleachi*, vol. I, 1926; vol. II, 1932.

CHAPTER XXI
JOEL

Bleeker, L. H. K. (See under Obadiah.)
Lippl. J., and Theis, J. (See under Hosea.)
Robinson, T. H. (See under Hosea.)
Wade, G. W. (See under Micah.)

CHAPTER XXII
JONAH

Bleeker, L. H. K. (See under Obadiah.)
Lippl. J., and Theis, J. (See under Hosea.)
Robinson, T. H. (See under Hosea.)
Wade, G. W. (See under Micah.)

CHAPTER XXIII
(See under Zechariah)

Index

b AUTHORS

GEORGE ALLEN & UNWIN LTD
London: 40 Museum Street, WC1

Auckland: 24 Wyndham Street
Bombay: 15 Graham Road, Ballard Estate, Bombay 1
Calcutta: 17 Chittaranjan Avenue, Calcutta 13
Cape Town: 109 Long Street
Karachi: Metherson's Estate, Wood Street, Karachi 2
New Delhi: 13-14 Ajmeri Gate Extension, New Delhi 1
São Paulo: Avenida 9 de Julho 1138-Ap. 51
Sydney, N.S.W.: Bradbury House, 55 York Street
Toronto: 91 Wellington Street West

NEW TESTAMENT LITERATURE

T. HENSHAW

This book gives, with admirable clarity, in a form suitable for those who have not had a theological training, the views of scholars on the authorship, date, and purpose of each of the books of the New Testament. It describes the situation in which it was written, its specific outlook, and its permanent religious value, and includes introductory chapters on the characteristics of the Jewish community and the Romano-Greek civilization into which primitive Christianity was launched.

It is not intended for specialist theological students, but for others to whom biblical study is one of several main subjects. Such are training college students seeking a qualification as teachers of the subject in schools, students in universities which have instituted courses in biblical knowledge in their pass B.A. schemes, and sixth forms in schools which are making such knowledge one of their main subjects of study.

'Lucid and orderly . . . it is thoroughly trustworthy in the information which it gives, and general students using it would find it a reliable guide. For a trustworthy readable account of the New Testament literature it cannot be bettered.' *Yorkshire Observer*

Second impression. Demy 8vo. 30s. *net*

CHRISTOLOGY AND MYTH IN THE NEW TESTAMENT

GERAINT VAUGHAN JONES

In this book the author inquires into the extent and origin of the 'mythological' language and ideas underlying the Christology of the New Testament. He begins with an examination of the 'demythologizing' principle advocated by Professor Bultmann and proceeds to inquire into its implications for Christology. He considers that the 'mythical' Christology of the New Testament writers should be understood poetically and metaphorically rather than as consisting of objective statements about Jesus and his place in creation.

The final section of the book is a defence of the retention of 'mythical' concepts and language as psychologically and theologically necessary expressions of a religious faith which cannot be adequately expressed in merely propositional form. We consider this book to be an important contribution not only to current theological discussion but also to the understanding of New Testament thought both against its historical background and when approached from the standpoint of 'modern' man.

Demy 8vo. 21s. *net*

THE LIVELY ORACLES

ERNEST MARSHALL HOWSE

In vivid, comprehensive fashion the author tells the most important story in the history of literature: the origins, and gradual accumulation through more than a thousand years, of the Manuscripts which constitute the Old Testament. He deals with the various books not in the order in which they were later arranged in canons of scripture but as the strata were laid down through centuries of turmoil and woe. The process reveals the background from which each book emerged as the passing Empires: Egypt, Assyria, Babylon, Persia and Greece, extended their power around the strategic land of Palestine. So 'Lamentations' is seen as a dirge at the fall of Jerusalem, 'Nahum' as a V-Day celebration at the fall of Nineveh, and Daniel as a summons to courage in the days of the Maccabees; so Isaiah, Jeremiah, Ezekiel and their company speak their word to their own day and to all time.

The book grew out of three series of sermons. Hence the chapters are in clear, understandable, colourful phrasing, and the general reader will find here a permanent ready reference on the books of the Old Testament, a helpful source of fresh material for illustration or historical allusion, and a most absorbing book.

'May be warmly recommended as an interesting and stimulating introduction to the Old Testament.' *Times Literary Supplement*

Demy 8vo. 20s. net

THE MESSIANIC IDEA IN ISRAEL

JOSEPH KLAUSNER

Dr Klausner's superb and scholarly history traces the consciousness of the Messiah among the Jewish people through their long and colourful history. He gives an exhaustive analysis and interpretation of the prophetic Messianic hope from the time of Moses to the completion of the Mishnah (i.e., AD 200). The whole vista of Biblical history, personalities and theology is unfolded in this stimulating work.

'The book is immensely learned and admirably translated. . . . The familiarity of Klausner with the Jewish writings from the Bible to the Talmud is phenomenal. Klausner's books in English are informative, original, and well constructed.'

ROBERT F. PFEIFFER in *Religion in Life*

Demy 8vo. 30s. net

GEORGE ALLEN & UNWIN LTD